MOLDED
IN THE
IMAGE OF
CHANGING
WOMAN

MOLDED IN THE IMAGE OF CHANGING WOMAN

NAVAJO VIEWS ON THE HUMAN BODY AND PERSONHOOD

Maureen Trudelle Schwarz

THE UNIVERSITY OF ARIZONA PRESS

TUCSON

The University of Arizona Press
Copyright © 1997
The Arizona Board of Regents
All rights reserved
∞ This book is printed on acid-free, archival-quality paper.
Manufactured in the United States of America

02 01   6 5 4 3 2

Library of Congress Cataloging-in-Publication Data

Schwarz, Maureen Trudelle
   Molded in the image of changing woman: Navajo views on the
human body and personhood / Maureen Trudelle Schwarz.
      p. cm.
   Includes bibliographical references (p.) and index.
   ISBN 0-8165-1602-2 (cloth: acid-free paper).—
   ISBN 0-8165-1627-8 (pbk.: acid-free paper)
   1. Navajo philosophy.   2. Navajo Indians—Psychology.   3. Self
(Philosophy)—Southwest, New.   4. Body, Human—Social aspects—
Southwest, New.   5. Body, Human—Symbolic aspects—Southwest,
New. I. Title.
E99.N5S36 1997   96-45816
128'089'972—dc21   CIP

British Library Cataloguing-in-Publication Data
A catalogue record for this book is available from the British Library.

Part of chapter 2 of this book appeared in a different form in "The Explanatory and
Predictive Power of History: Coping with the 'Mystery Illness,' 1993," in *Ethnohistory*
42(3): 375–401, copyright © 1995 by the American Society for Ethnohistory and
published by Duke University Press. Parts of chapters 1 and 5 of this book appeared
in a different form in "Unraveling the Anchoring Cord: Navajo Relocation, 1974–
1996," in *American Anthropologist* 99(1), copyright © 1997 by the American Anthropological Association, and are reproduced here courtesy of the association. Parts of the
introduction, chapter 1, and chapter 4 appeared in a different form in "Snakes in the
Ladies Room: Navajo Views on Personhood and Effect," in *American Ethnologist* 24(3),
copyright © 1997 by the American Anthropological Association, and are reproduced
here courtesy of the American Ethnological Society.

Publication of this book is made possible in part by the proceeds of a permanent
endowment created with the assistance of a Challenge Grant from the National
Endowment for the Humanities, a federal agency.

CHILDREN OF CHANGING WOMAN

—Wesley Thomas (Navajo)

Children, we are of Earth Woman
Children, we are of Mountain Woman
Children, we are of White Shell Woman
Children, we are of Changing Woman
From them we emerged
We are them
We are children of Changing Woman
Our mother, Asdzą́ą́ Nádleehé
Giver of life, of Navajo life

CONTENTS

POEMS

ILLUSTRATIONS

ACKNOWLEDGMENTS

The research upon which this book is based was made possible by the generous support of many individuals and institutions. So many people assisted with the project that it is hard to know where to begin my thanks. First and foremost, I wish to thank the Navajo people with whom I consulted and collaborated: *ahéhee'* to each of you. Your kindness and patience are immeasurable. You have given the ultimate gift—knowledge.

While I was a student at the University of Washington, I was mentored by several outstanding scholars, each of whom offered invaluable guidance on researching and writing. I wish to thank those who served on my supervisory committee at various times during the tenure of this project: Miriam Kahn (University of Washington), Tsianina Lomawaima (University of Arizona), Charlotte Frisbie (Southern Illinois University at Edwardsville), Gary Witherspoon (University of Washington), James Nason (University of Washington), David Spain (University of Washington), and Christopher Waterman (University of Washington). Each of them offered insight and support.

I thank Christine Szuter, acquiring editor for the social sciences at the University of Arizona Press, for her interest in this project. Thanks also to the anonymous reviewers who read and commented on this work for the press and to Jane Kepp, who carefully copy-edited the manuscript. In combination, their insightful comments contributed to the overall organization and clarity of presentation.

I wish to single out three of my Navajo colleagues for special thanks: Sadie Billie and Harry Walters of Tsaile, Arizona, and Wesley Thomas of Mariano Lake, New Mexico. Sadie took profound interest in my research, introduced me to the extended Tso-Billie family, tied my daughter, Ragen's, hair during her Kinaaldá, and looked out for the welfare of my family and me. Special thanks to Mrs. Billie and her husband for allowing a photograph of their daughter, Reytavia Billie, to appear as figure 9 in this book. Harry Walters acted as a sounding board, patiently discussing and clarifying the ideas presented in this work, and he read and commented on chapter drafts and drew figures 1 and 7, the latter of which was later redrawn by my husband, Greg Schwarz. Throughout this project, Wesley Thomas has been a colleague in the true sense of the word. He painstakingly translated interview tapes from Navajo into English, conducted the interview with Elizabeth

Yazzie, searched out obscure references, commented on drafts, and spent count-less hours discussing ideas. As a special gift, he wrote the poem that appears on the dedication page.

In addition to these three people, and those whose voices are foregrounded in this work, I wish to thank the many Navajo men and women and their families who assisted with my daughter's Kinaaldá or offered warmth, friendship, and hospi-tality during my visits to the Navajo reservation—or both. They include Nakai and Rosie Tso of White Valley, Arizona; Alice Kedelty of Navajo, New Mexico; Elizabeth Yazzie of Mariano Lake, New Mexico; Morjorie Begay of White Valley, Arizona; Katherine Thomas of Mariano Lake, New Mexico; Jonah and Dorothy Nez of Luka-chukai, Arizona; Oscar and Opal Tso of White Valley, Arizona, and their children; Tony Kaye of Coyote Canyon, New Mexico; Raymond Billie of Wheatfields, Ari-zona, and his and Sadie's children, Karletts, Reytavia, and Doug; Benson and Virginia Tso of Kayenta, Arizona, and their children, Benjamin, Altoveda, and Rhondale; Virgil and Verna Billie; Robert and Evelyn Tso of Wheatfields, Arizona, and their children, Tammy, Leland, and Tanya; Raymond and Pauline Pete of Fort Defiance, Arizona, and their children, Shauna, Jason, Laquita, and Racheline; Chester Kedelty of Tsaile, Arizona; Anita Benally of Del Muerto, Arizona; Thomas and Pauline Tso of Page, Arizona, and their children; Nellie Witherspoon of Eaton-ville, Washington; Leona Begay of White Valley, Arizona; Melissa Hardin of Na-vajo, New Mexico; David Harrison of Wheatfields, Arizona; Dorothy Edison of Tsaile, Arizona; Elsie Draper of Del Muerto, Arizona; Karl Dalton of Ganado, Ari-zona; Kathryn Arviso of Durango, Colorado; and Kathryn Ash Milby of New York City, New York. I also thank Rebecca Houze of Chicago, Illinois, for her assistance with my daughter's Kinaaldá. And I thank Pauline Escudero Shafer of Seattle, Washington, for the poem she composed especially for this book.

I am grateful to the following organizations and individuals for much-needed financial support: the Costume Society of America for a Stella Blum Research Grant (1990–91); the Whatcom County Museum for a Jacobs Research Fund Grant (1992); the Arizona Humanities Council for a Study Grant (1992); the Na-tional Science Foundation for a Summer Fieldwork Training Grant (1992); the Uni-versity of Washington for funds from a Royalty Research Grant (1993), an award from the Institute for Ethnic Studies in the United States (1993), a W. W. Stout Fellowship (1994), and an award from the Graduate School Research Fund (1995); and Mrs. Gaee Ellis of Great Falls, Montana.

Last, but certainly not least, I wish to thank my loving family—Greg, Ragen, and Ryan Schwarz—who participated in my field research, searched out library sources, created computer-generated graphics, photographed, and inserted illus-trations. Most importantly, they patiently put up with an often distracted and sometimes "crabby" wife and mother. Their generosity has been boundless—with-out their help there would be no book. *Ahéhee' shiyázhí* to each of you.

INTRODUCTION

A wealth of theoretical approaches has been developed for the study of cultural constructions of the human body, self, personhood, and effect in Melanesian, Southeast Asian, and African societies. In this book, I apply similar approaches to the analysis of Navajo constructs. The theoretical insights gained by researchers elsewhere are employed to move beyond the core of descriptive work available on the Navajo.[1] In accordance with the decentering, or disfranchisement from primacy, of Western science, and specifically of biomedical constructions of the body, I take a strongly constructionist stance. The cultural constructionist approach accepts the body, the self, and the person as culturally shaped, constrained, and invented.

The focus on bodily representations of social meanings has opened up studies of the effects that substances and events can have on the health, development, and well-being of people. Findings based on such analyses have resulted in new sensitivities to cross-cultural variations in constructions of the body or the self and of bodily experience, insights that have inspired a shift from focus on the body or self to focus on the "person." With these theoretical understandings in mind, I investigated Navajo theories of human conception with particular emphasis on the differing roles parental substances such as semen and female "fluids" play in the construction of the child, and I looked for shared substances and qualities among members of the community of life in the Navajo world.

The Navajo are the largest native nation in the contiguous United States. They number close to 220,000 people, most of whom occupy a 25,000-square-mile reservation that spans parts of Arizona, New Mexico, and Utah. On the basis of linguistic and archeological clues, Euro-American scholars have pieced together a story of Navajo origins, cultural adaptation, and development.

The Navajo belong to the Athapaskan language family, one of the largest linguistic groups in North America. They were among the Southern Athapaskan groups who, at the time of European contact, were located in Dinétah, the area the Navajo consider their ancestral homeland in what is now northeastern Arizona and northwestern New Mexico.[2] Their subsistence system was based on hunting and gathering, supplemented by some agriculture (Brugge 1983:489–501). Extended families centered on matrilocal residence and a strong clan system lived in widely dispersed settlements across a vast region. Navajo people endured many hardships at the hands of Spanish and Euro-American conquerors, and all facets of Navajo life—economic, political, and religious—have been altered in the face of four centuries of incursions into the area (Roessel 1983:506–23).

A herding economy based on sheep and goats developed after livestock were first introduced into the region by Spanish settlers. The Navajo population and its area of settlement expanded as new crops, animals, and technological innovations continued to be added to the subsistence base during the Spanish and American periods. After a lengthy period of war in the mid-1800s, nearly nine thousand Navajo were rounded up and forced to walk three hundred miles to Hwéeldi, or Fort Sumner, New Mexico, where they were incarcerated by the United States army from 1863 to 1868. A treaty signed on June 1, 1868, established a reservation on a portion of their homeland to which the Navajo were allowed to return. The terms of the treaty required the Navajo to refrain from any further military actions against Euro-Americans and to send their children to American schools.

Gradually, the Navajo economy and population recovered. Trading posts began to flourish on the reservation in the late 1800s, and a barter economy developed wherein male lambs and items of Navajo manufacture were traded for coffee, flour, lard, canned goods, and other food staples. The first biomedical physicians began servicing portions of the Navajo reservation during the closing decades of the nineteenth century (Adair, Deuschle, and Barnett 1988:10). The Euro-American legal system was introduced when the Navajo Court of Indian Offenses was established on the reservation in 1892. It operated until 1959, when it was replaced by the Courts of the Navajo Nation, a system developed within the Navajo Nation but framed on Euro-American legal principles (Yazzie 1994). To accommodate the growing Navajo population, tracts of land were annexed to the original reservation numerous times between 1878 and 1934. In addition, separate tracts of land were subsequently secured for the Alamo (1946), Canoncito (1949), and Ramah (1956) Navajo.

In direct response to economic hardships caused by droughts, the overgrazing of Navajo land, and fluctuations in livestock and wool prices, a shift toward increased dependence on wage labor, commercial herding, and production of woven goods and silverwork for the off-reservation market took place in the early twentieth century. To cope with the burgeoning of resource-extraction–based industries on tribal land, a federally designed centralized government—the Navajo Tribal Council—was installed on the reservation in the 1920s. Over the years, Navajo leaders have adapted and molded this system into an effective means by which to control and dispense much-needed goods and services (Iverson 1981). Since federally mandated stock reductions diminished family herds in the 1930s, dependence on wage labor, both on and off the reservation, has steadily increased. The devastation created by stock reduction also led to increased acceptance of non-Navajo religious beliefs and practices such as those of Catholicism, Protestantism, Mormonism, and the Native American Church (Aberle 1982 [1966]). Following record Navajo participation in the military service and employment in war related industries during World War II, Navajo access to and usage of government-run health care and educational facilities rapidly increased (Emerson 1983; Adair, Deuschle, and Barnett 1988: 15–45).

Despite these changes, Navajo language and culture have proven to be exceptionally resilient over time. The Navajo Nation has been a leader in bilingual education and in the development of educational curricula centered on native values (Emerson 1983: 659–71). Language retention is high, relative to other Native American groups, and Navajo tenets of philosophy are taught at all grade levels and in courses at Navajo Community College (NCC)—the first tribally operated college in the country. Newspapers and television and radio stations focused on issues of concern to Navajo people publish and broadcast in Navajo or English on a daily or weekly basis. In 1982, the Navajo Peacemaker Court was established. Based on Navajo principles of common law and the role of the *naat'áanii*, a traditional civil leader, rather than on Euro-American legal principles, this modern legal system offers Navajo a viable alternative to the adversarial system of justice embodied in the Courts of the Navajo Nation (Yazzie 1994).

Today, unemployment rates far exceed national norms. The majority of Navajo who are employed work in the fields of health care, education, or government service. In addition, agribusinesses on irrigated lands and resource-based industries such as timber and mining provide valuable jobs to Navajo workers. Navajo employed off the reservation or in towns on the reservation return to matrilineal family homes in remote areas as often as possible—every weekend or during vacations, depending on distances—in order to participate in family activities. Navajo in need of medical attention freely combine biomedical care and treatments administered in state-of-the-art facilities across the reservation with traditional care and treatments administered at home or in hospitals or clinics. Most Navajo claim more than one religious affiliation; many of those who have adopted non-Navajo religions still participate actively in the dozens of extant traditional ceremonies that may be held for themselves or for members of their extended families (Frisbie 1992; Frisbie and Tso 1993). These healing rituals focus primarily on an individual patient and his or her restoration to harmony, but by extension they affect all of the patient's relations—members of his or her extended family, clan relatives, and aspects of the cosmos.

This study is based on observations made during Navajo ceremonies and on consultations with Navajo experts. I spent the summers of 1991, 1992, and 1993, as well as short periods during other seasons, consulting with Navajo religious practitioners, elders, and professional scholars. Together we investigated the philosophical underpinnings of Navajo cultural constructions of the human body, personhood, and effect.[3] When I began research in 1991, I focused on the significance of the designs found on Navajo women's traditional handwoven attire—two-piece dresses, wearing blankets, and sashes. This work led me to study the role these textiles play in contemporary ceremonies, and from there to examine how the system governing effect interweaves with Navajo cultural constructions of the human body and personhood. In response to the directives of members of the Tso and Billie extended family, who sponsored my research and acted as research directors, as well as to the directives of other Navajo people with whom I collaborated, my focus and methodology shifted as the project progressed.

I sought out and consulted with men and women of all ages and a variety of backgrounds, in recognition that individuals in any society have different degrees of understanding of their "culture" related directly to issues of knowledge, power, and access. In similar fashion, I acknowledge that all ethnographers have their limits and that all interpretations made by outsiders are provisional (Rosaldo 1993:8). Anthropologists, like native people themselves, are positioned subjects who are prepared to know certain things and not others; therefore, as an anthropologist I had limited access to knowledge, which affected my understandings.

Who am I as a positioned subject, and what am I prepared to know? I am a middle-aged woman who went to the field with children. Unbeknownst to me when I started the project, in the view of my Navajo hosts this put me in a stage of life advantageous to my research. Being a mature woman gave me access to discussions of childbirth, conception, and menstrual restrictions that a man could not have gained. Being the mother of two healthy children put me in the fourth stage of life and gave me some credibility. Being the mother of a prepubescent daughter gave me direct access to study the Kinaaldá, the puberty ceremony.

To conform to the Navajo pedagogical system, which requires that learning be accomplished by doing, I allowed my methodology to be guided by my Navajo hosts. I did the things they said I must do in order to learn about the things I was interested in. While doing day-to-day activities such as chopping and cleaning vegetables, searching for a ceremonial practitioner, driving to a border town for groceries or automotive parts, or doing laundry, I gained knowledge through interactions with Navajo people. Owing to my sponsorship by the Tso and Billie extended family, my work falls within a contemporary anthropological methodology suggested by Barbara Tedlock (1991:69) to replace the problematic notion of classic "participant observation." This book is neither an ethnographic "memoir" centered on my personal experiences and reactions to doing fieldwork nor a "monograph" centered on the Navajo as "others." Rather, it strives to present all the contributors—myself, Navajo consultants, and our families—together in a single "narrative ethnography" highlighting the character and process of the ethnographic dialogue.

My work with Navajo people began by acknowledging tribal control over access to intellectual property. Before leaving for the field, I contacted the Navajo Nation Historic Preservation Department (NNHPD), obtained an ethnographic fieldwork permit, and devised consultation consent forms to comply with the NNHPD requirements. Every consultant was asked to sign a form agreeing to work with me voluntarily and stating whether he or she wanted a fee and whether he or she wanted his or her name used in this work. The name of each consultant who chose this option is used throughout the book. Those who chose not to have their names cited are referred to simply as "anonymous elder," "anonymous man," or "anonymous woman," followed by a fictitious location.

My daughter, Ragen, accompanied me to the Navajo reservation for my first season of fieldwork. I decided to live at Navajo Community College in Tsaile, Arizona, for two important reasons. First, I wanted to contact Navajo experts teaching at the college in order to seek their advice and assistance, because I wanted to work within the Navajo system. Second, we left for the reservation with no prior contacts there. I knew housing was at a premium on the reservation but that affordable housing was available in the dorms at NCC. My daughter, son, Ryan, and husband, Greg, each spent variable amounts of time with me in the field during the summers of 1991, 1992, and 1993 and during numerous one- to two-week visits to the reservation during other seasons in 1993, 1994, and 1995. We alternated between living in the NCC dorms and living in a house near Wheatfields Lake rented from a member of my sponsoring family during our stays on the reservation.

It was necessary for Ragen to be adopted into the matrilineal clan of Mrs. Rosie Tso of White Valley, Arizona, in order for the family to sponsor a Kinaaldá ceremony for her. This adoption created kinship alliances between members of the Tso and Billie families and members of my family. By accepting me into their family, the Tsos and Billies extended warmth and kindness to me, my husband, and my children, and they have assisted me greatly with my work. I view my relationship with them as a lifelong commitment. They sized me up before deciding to accept my family into theirs, and I have a role to play in this relationship.

I am called on to "act as a relative" in a variety of ways. While on the reservation, I am expected to contribute food and cash to ceremonies and to provide transportation. While I am witnessing or assisting with ceremonies, my observations are often interrupted by requests such as "Go check on some coffee" or "Go heat up some water." When not in the field, I am expected to contribute cash to family needs, such as the funeral of Nakai Tso, who died in November 1993 at the age of 104. I am asked to send classified ads when someone in the family is looking for "a good used truck," and to sell arts and crafts on a regular basis.

The contacts I have made since 1991, and the generosity of my host family and other Navajo people, allowed me access to numerous ceremonies and other family events. Guided by my host family, I have witnessed and participated in several Kinaaldá and healing ceremonies where I analyzed the Navajo concepts of the body and personhood revealed by the manipulation of the bodies of patients and their kin during treatment. My observations were clarified and augmented through interviews.

All interviews were tape-recorded and transcribed to ensure acquisition of correct Navajo terminology and, more importantly, to enable me to use people's own words in this book. I found that open-ended interviews worked best; I simply introduced the focus of my research and let the consultants discuss what they considered the most important aspects of the topic. As we went along, I generated questions in response to specific terms and information mentioned. I always brought a list of questions based on prior interviews and used it to fill in gaps. Interviews with elderly people were conducted in Navajo with a younger relative acting as translator. Having family members act as translators worked well because they were familiar with the consultant's speech and could usually understand and translate regional variations in dialect or antiquated phrases. These translations were verified and refined by Wesley Thomas.

Direct quotes from interviews are presented throughout this book, followed by the consultant's name, the location of the interview, and the date of the interview (in the form of month/day/year). The majority of these excerpts appear exactly as they were transcribed, including false starts and grammatical errors made by myself or by the Navajo people with whom I consulted. In some cases, for the sake of clarity, false starts or repetitions are replaced with an ellipsis. Near verbatim quotes from interview transcriptions are used as part of an effort to present all of us as real, multifaceted human beings within the negotiated and contested context of the interview experience.

In several cases, at the conclusion of an interview session, family members of the younger generations who had gathered around thanked me for coming and asking their grandmother or grandfather the questions discussed. For example, at the close of an interview with Mrs. Irene Kee of Crystal, New Mexico, one of her grandsons commented, "Thank you for coming and asking my grandmother about these things. She is telling stories we have not heard before." He had never heard these stories because no one in the family knew or thought to ask about them. This kind of thanks helped alleviate the discomfort I felt because of my interfering in people's lives every day to ask probing questions.

In addition to interviewing, I conferred at regular intervals with key people such as Harry Walters at NCC and Wesley Thomas from Mariano Lake, New Mexico, about what I was learning. They made sophisticated sounding boards because Walters is trained as an anthropologist and Thomas is a graduate student in anthropology. They both, therefore, are conscious of, and sensitive to, dialogues and issues current within the discipline. As we reviewed information I had received, they offered additional explanations, pointed out possible correlations, filled in gaps, and suggested further avenues of inquiry. Wesley Thomas verified and clarified translations, adding notes where pertinent. Harry Walters cautioned me when I strayed into areas of "guarded" knowledge, such as information about ceremonies that could be used for witchcraft, and steered me in other directions. Nowhere was his influence more evident than in my developing understanding of the profound intricacies of the diverse stories that make up the Navajo oral tradition.

Navajo oral history is central to this work because it serves as a philosophical charter with explanatory and predictive powers. This oral history consists of compressed metaphoric accounts that are interpretable on twelve different levels of analysis, each differentiated by degree of abstraction. These levels imbue the philosophical system with tremendous flexibility and adaptability. How the explanatory and predictive powers of the twelve levels of knowledge help contemporary people cope with the uncertainties of daily life is explored throughout the book.

Multiple levels of interpretation are documented as they were shared with me, but it is beyond my degree of comprehension to give a full exegesis of all twelve levels of abstraction for any one topic. As Oscar Tso explains in the following excerpt from an interview conducted on a hot August afternoon in his son and daughter-in-law's garage in Many Farms, Arizona, multiple levels of understanding are acquired throughout a lifetime of incremental gains and learning by "doing."[4]

> OT See, as you begin to acquire an understanding, and as you grow in knowledge, these people will tell you a story, kind of like a general story. And then, later on you begin to have questions. Like the way you question me. And then they will tell another story. This time it will be in more detail. And then maybe another time, you have another question and it is going to be, you know, at a level even deeper than maybe the first two times. . . . And when you obtain the level of a time when somebody will sit down with you and begin to recount things, in very minute detail and they will sing some songs for you, and there will be prayers that are said right along. . . . And that is where you are going to begin to have a full understanding of where these came from. Who said what, and just in what ways that some of these things were done.
> MS Uh-huh.
> OT And some of the songs and some of the prayers were just something that was done. Something that was, that somebody said, you know, and then that is how you gather some of that knowledge. So, so, I am not too sure I can really have a full understanding of what level I am sharing some of these things with you. I think you have heard it at a general level. Maybe I am at a point where it

is more specific. And then what I tell you, you are going to have a very limited understanding of it, and then when you can reach a level where you are at the prayers and songs level you are going to have a totally different understanding of what we are talking about.

MS Well see, I agree with you and one problem when I am trying to do an interview is trying to make up ideas for questions. . . . Because what I think might be important to ask about may not be what is really important. And so I can see that you have an understanding of what I am going through, trying to learn about this. So maybe you would want to just tell me what you think is important about the Kinaaldá, in terms of Navajo women.

OT See, I could sit here and begin to determine what is really important in terms of education. . . . In terms of maybe writing a paper or getting some of this knowledge on a piece of paper. But then again, I would, it is going to be very in-depth [chuckles]. Probably sit there all day and not cover too much. So I would probably have to be very general in my explanation. . . . Even every day of the week for the next few weeks, I wouldn't, it wouldn't be enough. . . . So along with everything that we mean to consider we need to see probably a couple of Kinaaldá ceremonies and participate and see, and kind of just go through the motions of going through a Kinaaldá, you know. To begin to really understand. (Oscar Tso, Many Farms, Arizona, 8/9/92)

When a Navajo shows interest, elders will begin with a story at level one, the most general level. Gradually, as the hearer's understanding becomes more sophisticated, elders repeatedly retell the story at increasing levels of abstraction. In like fashion, my queries were initially dealt with at level one, and as my understandings became more sophisticated, Navajo elders and others offered explanations at increasingly abstract levels. At the most abstract levels, the origin and creation stories are told in the form of songs and prayers. As a result, usually only Navajo people of advanced age who have specialized ceremonial knowledge have access to, or understanding of, the stories at their highest levels of abstraction.

What Navajo people taught me—through verbal explanation and the experience of "doing" in ceremonial and secular contexts—about Navajo theories of life and about their ideas concerning the human body and personhood is described in this work. My goal in presenting these materials is not to construct a composite version of Navajo philosophy. The narrative serves as a platform for the distinct voices of the Navajo individuals and families who opened their world to me and my family. To foreground Navajo voices, several chapters focus on the way contemporary Navajo people draw on their philosophical system to deal with specific problems faced at various points in the life cycle—problems that are fundamental to the attainment of full Navajo personhood.

Personhood is developed gradually in the Navajo world by controlling the influence of various substances and events on the body and parts of the body such as umbilical cords, voice, hair, and menstrual blood. The complex manipulations of the body and parts of the body necessary to becoming a Navajo person are framed around the critical events in the life cycle of a Navajo, from conception through puberty. The choices Navajo people make in an effort to control, contain, or harness the power manifested in effects is the connecting thread running through each of these chapters, which include personal narratives by Navajo consultants, summaries of the philosophical premises pertinent to specific circumstances, and various options from which people choose.

During the course of this project, I often found myself asking the questions that few younger Navajo ask anymore. This asking opened doorways for communication between myself and members of the Navajo families with whom I visited. People answered many of my questions, generated new ones, and often asked me questions. What should be done with the answers to all these questions is problematic. Navajo culture has many areas that should remain private. Views vary among families and regions about what types of things should be made public. This variation creates a constant tension between many Navajo people and scholars from outside. Fundamentally, many Navajo people consider it dangerous to transfer knowledge to those who cannot cope with it adequately. They believe such carelessness can lead to abuse of knowledge and result in danger to the whole community (Pinxten and Farrer 1990:243).

As I noted earlier, I was cautioned by Harry Walters and others when I strayed into areas of "guarded" knowledge. I took their guidance into consideration when faced with the difficult task of deciding how to edit problematic materials out of my book while maintaining clarity and cohesion. I tried to be sensitive and respectful, but undoubtedly there are individual Navajo who will object to some of the things I decided to leave in. I bear ultimate responsibility for the contents.

MOLDED
IN THE
IMAGE OF
CHANGING
WOMAN

CHAPTER I

COMPARATIVE VIEWS ON THE BODY, PERSONHOOD, AND EFFECT

Sadie vigorously rubbed the yucca root as I poured the hot water into the basket. Next Sadie gently washed Ragen's hair in the warm sudsy mixture, carefully collecting the rinse water in a pan under Ragen's head. With her wet hair streaming around her face and shoulders, Ragen jumped up and ran clockwise out of the hooghan into the pre-dawn chill. She ran down the hill toward the east followed by a small group of people who were yelling so that the Holy People would hear. . . . At the conclusion of the public portion of the ceremony, Sadie guided me in the proper disposal of the shampoo rinse water. She told me to dispose of it just outside the door. She cautioned, "Pour it gently. Do not let it splash." Sadie said this was so no harm would come to Ragen. Sadie instructed me further that after the required holy period, Ragen's hair must be washed at dawn and the rinse water saved. She told me to pour the rinse water around the perimeter of our home so that Ragen would always be drawn back home. (Field notes 7/26/92)

Sadie Billie's instructions on disposal of the shampoo rinse water marked a turning point in my field research. I was perplexed by Mrs. Billie's concern for my daughter's physical and emotional well-being. How could tossing out shampoo rinse water harm Ragen's body? How could the placement of the water have the effect of drawing her home? I came to realize that Mrs. Billie's instructions made sense only within the framework of a set of assumptions about the nature of the human body and personhood very different from my own. To find answers to my questions, I began to explore the rules governing *effect* in the Navajo world. Navajo ideas about how various substances and events can affect people offer insight into more general anthropological questions about the construction of the body, self, and personhood.

The extensive ethnographic accounts we have of Navajo culture and society refer again and again to the effects of events on the health and well-being of individuals, their loved ones, and their unborn children. These events can include observing the construction of a sandpainting (Kluckhohn and Wyman 1940: 61 – 62), hearing certain songs (Hill 1936:9; Wyman 1938:98), being molded at birth (Bailey 1950:75) or at puberty (Frisbie 1993 [1967]:13), coming into contact with Anasazi ruins (McPherson 1992:119 – 21), menstrual blood (Bailey 1950:10 – 11), or lava said to be the petrified blood of monsters (Reichard 1950:22, 81), witnessing a fatal accident (Haile 1938:25), doing other people's laundry (Hill 1936:18; Reichard 1950:35), wearing secondhand clothing (Mitchell 1978:35 – 36), or simply drinking breast milk (Wright et al. 1993:788). Despite the prevalence of brief allusions like these in the literature, no attempt has been made to clarify the underlying logic—the interconnecting Navajo systems of rules—governing *association* and *effect*.[1]

In this book I focus on the complex interweaving of the cosmological, social, and bodily realms that Navajo people navigate in an effort to control, contain, or harness the power manifested in various effects. The complex rules defining who or what can affect what or whom under specific circumstances—rights, prerogatives, and agency—are explored as a means of determining what these effects tell us about the cultural construction of the human body, self, and personhood in the Navajo world. I offer my explanation through an analysis of three metaphorical constructions in bodily and social experiences: homology, complementarity, and synecdoche. These concepts structure the complex relationship of parts to the whole in a world constructed according to paradigms set forth in the Navajo origin story. Parts share similar structure (homology). Wholes are made up of dual integrated components (complementarity). And every part is equivalent to the whole, so anything done to, or by means of, a part is held to take effect upon, or to have the effect of, the whole (synecdoche).

My analysis presents some complex, contested points of view about the human body, personhood, and effect as they are understood and lived in the modern Navajo world.[2] To place the analysis in context, I first provide a brief overview of the history of anthropological studies of effect and the body. Then I turn to more recent work on the body, self, and personhood based on the cultural constructionist point of view and on metaphoric analysis of such constructions. Constructionist analyses of the Navajo concepts of association and effect offer significant insights into the complex interweaving of philosophy and action.

CLASSIC ANTHROPOLOGICAL PERSPECTIVES ON THE BODY AND EFFECT

Interest in the rules that govern association and in the effect events can have on the health and well-being of people has a long history in anthropology. Victorian scholars, attempting to understand all known human beliefs and behaviors, sought to reduce complex phenomena to underlying laws or to fit these phenomena into grand evolutionary paradigms (or both). They investigated the effects events purportedly had on people under the rubrics of magic and religion. Three "laws of sympathetic magic" were observed in societies throughout the world: similarity, opposition, and contagion. Because of their seeming universality, these "laws" were believed to be windows into the human mind, representing fundamental principles of human thought (Tylor 1974 [1871]; Frazer 1959 [1890]; Mauss 1972 [1902]).

The "law of similarity" maintains that "like produces like" (Frazer 1959 [1890]: 5). Things that resemble one another share fundamental properties—if rain is needed, pouring out water will produce it. The "law of opposition," closely tied to the law of similarity, maintains that opposites work on opposites (Mauss 1972 [1902]:64, 71). The "law of contagion" maintains that "things that have once been in contact continue ever afterwards to act on each other" (Frazer 1959 [1890]:5). This is the law of most direct concern in this book, for it is based on the principle of synecdoche—the identification of the part with the whole.

The principle of synecdoche holds that people, objects, and other entities that have contact may influence each other through the transfer of some or all of their properties. The part stands for the whole. "Teeth, saliva, sweat, nails, hair represent a total person, in such a way that through these parts one can act directly on the individual concerned, either to bewitch or enchant him. Separation in no way disturbs the contiguity; a whole person can even be reconstituted or resuscitated with the aid of one of these parts: *totum ex parte*" (Mauss 1972 [1902]:64).

Put another way, "the personality of a being is indivisible, residing as a whole in each one of the parts" (Mauss 1972 [1902]:64). Connection remains in force even after separation. Therefore, the effect continues after the physical contact has ended, and the effect may be permanent. Moreover, this connection can extend the physical boundaries of the person to include "everything which comes into close contact with the person—clothes, footprints, the imprint of the body on grass or in bed, the bed, the chair, everyday objects of use, toys and other things" (Mauss 1972 [1902]:65). This extension of personhood on the basis of synecdoche is crucial to my analysis of Navajo views on the construction of the human body and the rules governing effect.[3]

Classic anthropological investigations into such effects have tended to focus narrowly on restrictions surrounding exposure to menstrual blood (Durkheim 1897; Stephens 1962; Young and Bacdayan 1965; Douglas 1966; Weideger 1977) and on the use of parts of the body, bodily fluids, and offal in witchcraft (Fortune 1932; Evans-Pritchard 1937; Middleton and Winter 1963). Anthropological studies of menstruation and menstrual substances, based largely on the pollution model promulgated by Mary Douglas (Buckley and Gottlieb 1988: 3–50), have focused on limitations placed on women's activities to the exclusion of other explanations for menstrual restrictions and prohibitions. To date, studies of witchcraft and sorcery have tended to focus on the roles these practices play in social control (Walker 1989), maintenance of social distance and economic distinctions (Lindenbaum 1979), relief of psychological tensions (Morgan 1936; Kluckhohn 1944), and the reasons for the existence of such "bizarre" behaviors among millions of contemporary people (Walker 1989:6; also Luhrmann 1989).

There are several problems with these classic studies. For instance, in most cases the ideologies and rituals associated with these parts of the body and bodily substances have been extracted and analyzed separately from their cultural contexts. Focused on menstrual blood and the parts of the body used in witchcraft, but slighting the other bodily substances that can affect people, these studies have tended to highlight the polluting or dangerous effects of substances and ignore their potential beneficial influences. Research on the Navajo is no exception (see Morgan 1936; Dyk 1966 [1938]; Wyman and Harris 1941:59; Kluckhohn 1944; Bailey 1950; Reichard 1950:35; Keith 1964; Wright 1982). As a result, previous studies did not fully explore the complex rules defining who or what can affect what or whom under particular circumstances, or what these effects might tell us about the cultural construction of the human body and personhood in the societies under investigation. Such analyses have predominated because until relatively recently the body's centrality was assumed and unproblematized, or, as some have argued, largely ignored (Farnell 1995:4–10), by anthropologists.

Yet for pioneers in the anthropology of the body, the human body was the symbol par excellence—a universally important means of metaphoric expression, communicating information for and from the social realm. Scholars such as Mary Douglas and Victor Turner found that bodily conditions were inextricably linked to classifications of the world, but they took very different stances on the relationship of the body to the world. In their analyses, the body, bodily boundaries, and bodily products either mirror the world (Douglas 1966, 1970) or classify it (Turner 1967). Believing that bodies universally reflect the social worlds in which they are found, Douglas looked exclusively at how societies impose form onto the body (1966). In contrast, Turner considered "the human organism and its crucial experiences" to be the "*fons et origio* of all classifications" (1967:90) and postulated that all people everywhere use concepts and color associations derived from bodily experiences and products—white (breast milk, semen), red (blood), and black (feces)—as metaphors for understanding and classifying the world.

Human bodies and cultural classifications of worlds are indissolubly linked in all societies. In many cases, however, the metaphoric process is the reverse of that postulated by Turner. For example, in the Navajo world, "symbolic statements about the supernatural-natural world provide the basic paradigm for interpreting bodily processes of health and illness" (Lamphere 1969:282). Accounts of the construction of the Navajo world stand as paradigms for understanding the human body and bodily processes. Thus, Navajo understandings of the body and bodily experiences are cultural constructs—not, as Turner postulates, natural or biological facts.

BODIES AND SELVES AS CULTURAL CONSTRUCTIONS

[T]he body has been, and still is, constructed in almost as many ways as there are individuals; it seems to be all things to all people. Thus the body is defined as good or bad; tomb or temple; machine or garden; cloak or prison; sacred or secular; friend or enemy; cosmic or mystical; one with mind and soul or separate; private or public; personal or the property of the state; clock or car; to varying degrees plastic, bionic, communal; selected from a catalogue or engineered; material or spiritual; a corpse or the self. (Synnott 1993:37)

Until recently, the human body remained "virtually invisible to the vast majority of sociocultural anthropologists" (Farnell 1995:4), and most anthropologists whose interests did lie in the body, health, or illness accepted that the physical body fell "naturally" into the domain of the physical sciences and outside the scope of social and cultural anthropology (Lock 1993:134). Theoretical insights since the 1970s, however, have decentered Western science in general and biomedical constructions of the body, health, and illness specifically (Lock 1986; Gordon 1988; Rhodes 1990). As Michel Foucault demonstrated, even anatomists do not observe a universal biological body through dissection, because the clinical gaze is a cultural gaze (1973:124–47). Moreover, anatomical constructs of internal organs, such as images of female reproductive organs as inverted versions of male organs (Laqueur 1987, 1990), are cultural constructs that serve to resolve ideological problems in the social and political realms.

This disfranchising of biomedical views is rooted in the idea that the meanings attached to the body—its boundaries, substances, and essences—are constructed on the basis of cultural understandings rather than on the basis of universal physiological facts. It can no longer be assumed that "dialectics exist between an infinity of cultures and a universal biology"; rather, it has been realized that a multitude of dialectics exist "between cultures and local biologies, both of which are subject to transformation in evolutionary, historical and life-cycle time bytes, and to movement through space" (Lock 1993:146).

Cultural constructionists accept the body as culturally shaped, constrained, and invented. Focus on bodily representation of social meanings has opened up studies of the effects of substances and events and thereby generated new sensitivities that are relevant to understanding cross-cultural differences in constructions of the body and bodily experience. Accounts of fluid, boundless, and elusive bodies have proliferated.[4] Moreover, the decentering of biomedical constructs of biology and human experience has revealed the idea of the self to be yet another cultural construct, leading to new insights into variation in constructions of selves and individual experiences worldwide (Rosaldo 1984; Ewing 1990; Holland 1992; Battaglia 1995). As a result, over the last few decades, the classic anthropological opposition between the self—the awareness of oneself as a "perceptible object" (Hallowell 1955)—and the person as a social construct has blurred (see Ewing 1990:254–58).

Groundbreaking studies based on research carried out in Melanesian, Southeast Asian, and African societies shed light on the role of effect in the development of bodies, selves, or persons cross-culturally, and on how personhood can be extended to entities that might be considered "inanimate" in Euro-American worlds. Anthropological analyses acknowledging the complex role effects from exposure to bodily substances or other events can play in the development of bodies and persons, which began to appear in the 1970s, continue to offer new understandings (see, for example, Meigs 1976, 1984; Gillison 1980; Herdt 1981, 1982a, 1982b; Poole 1981; Daniel 1984; Strathern 1988; Battaglia 1990; O'Hanlon 1992; Riesman 1992). In combination, these various insights have culminated in a shift from a focus on the "body" or "self" per se to a focus on the whole *living body*, the "person."[5]

Studies such as those just cited provide models for the complex ways in which the sharing, ingestion, or expulsion of substances contributes to the building of the body and personhood. They offer fresh perspectives on how to analyze Navajo theories about the variable contributions of male and female bodily substances to the development of specific body parts.[6] They indicate ways in which personhood can shift and flow throughout a life cycle, and they illustrate how attributes can be transferred through bodily and nonbodily substances.

Cross-cultural differences in concepts of personhood abound. In many societies, personhood consists of the relations—ties and obligations—that attain among human beings and other entities (Strathern 1988:268–74). This is so in the Navajo world, where nonhuman entities—homes, birds, mountains, baskets—have qualities of personhood, where membership in the community of life is based on shared composition and structure, and where the boundaries of persons are extended by synecdoche.

"TO HAVE YOUR FEET PLANTED IN THE EARTH"

> **RL** See, and Navajo medicine men say that . . . say like I wanted to put this [up] for decoration [referring to a ceremonial basket she is holding]. OK, like I had a lot of these [and I wanted to] put them up in my house. And I couldn't find a way to hang it up. See this one has a thread.
>
> **MS** I don't know why that is there.
>
> **RL** A string OK. From what they tell me . . . you should never hang these up because, you know, you're hanging, you know. . . . You can't put a string like this and hang me up can you?
>
> **MS** No.
>
> **RL** OK, and that's the same thing. This is the breath of life, and you're supposed to, you know, handle this just like you were handling a baby or myself. I mean, you don't go hanging somebody by their hair up here! [touching the whorl at the back of the top of her head]. (Regina Lynch, Tsaile, Arizona, 7/16/91)[7]

Ts'aa', ceremonial baskets, should not be hung on the wall as decorations because they are persons who share characteristics with all other persons with whom they coexist.[8] All entities in the Navajo world consist of the primary elements moisture, air, substance, and heat, which are permeated by vibration, and they share structural features such as sunwise directionality, a trajectory of growth from the ground upward, and a series of binary oppositions to distinguish inside from outside and left from right. Relationships between and among entities are based on culturally sanctioned rules governing rights, prerogatives, and agency.

To clarify the definition of life and the parameters of personhood in the Navajo world, I consulted with several Navajo experts on these topics. I explained that Navajo people had told me and other scholars that sandpaintings were considered to be alive during a ceremony and that people consistently referred to ceremonial baskets and other entities as living persons.[9] As Mae Bekis of Tó'tsoh, Arizona, explains in the following narrative, Navajo people are taught from earliest childhood to consider phenomena such as the earth, sky, sun, moon, rain, water, lightning, and thunder to be living kin.[10]

To us the sun is a person. That is the way we talk about it. Jóhonaa'éí, we say, Jóhonaa'éí shitah, that means Jóhonaa'éí is my father.
Tł'ééhonaa'éí shitah [the moon is my father] is the same as that.
And then Nahasdzáán shimá [the earth is my mother]. We say that
in our prayer. And so they said it is a living thing to us. And we
had already accepted that way, and when my mother, my father,
my great-grandfather, they don't have it written like that. But it is
preached to us, [since] the day we were born and we were brought
up in that feeling, and that atmosphere. And so, by the time we get
old enough we already accept that Jóhonaa'éí shitah, Tł'ééhonaa'éí
shitah, Nahasdzáán shimá. We already accept that. (Mae Bekis,
Tó'tsoh, Arizona, 7/28/93)

Persons such as Jóhonaa'éí and Nahasdzáán are frequently portrayed in songs,
prayers, and sandpaintings with attributes similar to those of humans. Many
researchers have assumed that references to physical traits like earth's feet or
a mountain's feet, the representation of Diyin Dine'é, "Navajo Holy People," as
rainbows with arms and feet (see, for example, illustrations in Newcomb and Reichard 1937 or Reichard 1939), or the attribution of personal characteristics such
as stubbornness, fear, loneliness, and understanding to Diyin Dine'é (Reichard
1950:58−62) are examples of anthropomorphism—the attribution of human
shape or characteristics to supernaturals, animals, or objects (see, for example,
Haile 1943:67; Gill 1974, 1981, 1983:503−5; Witherspoon 1977:29; Pinxten et al. 1983:9). But the assumption is false.

The Navajo people with whom I consulted all agreed that they recognize these
phenomena to be kin, but they emphatically denied that they consider them to be
made in the image of humans. Harry Walters of Tsaile, Arizona, clarified this point
when I asked him what defined "being alive" in the Navajo philosophy and theory
of life.[11]

HW For living things it is to have your foot, to have your feet,
planted into the earth and your head in the sky. In your Mother
Earth and Father Sky. Everything that is alive has its feet planted in
the earth and its head in the sky. Birds, plants, animals, insects,
people. So this is what determines what life is.

MS Well, then, how would a sandpainting be alive?

HW Now, when we talk about alive in our Western society we
think in terms of everything that is breathable, you know.

MS Breathing?

HW Yeah, breathing and living and thinking. You know, having all the senses of a human. You have to understand that in Western society man is the master of the universe. He is like God. So we think of everything in terms of "like man," you know, when we see something, a sandpainting figure for example, we label it anthropomorphic. You know what I mean? It is an image of man.

MS Yes.

HW And then so we cannot comprehend mountains have feet. They have eyes. . . . They think, they speak and they are alive. So, we cannot comprehend a mountain having feet because when we say something has feet we automatically try to envision that in terms of a human body, because we are conditioned that way.

MS Yes, but that is a Western view, I am trying to understand a Navajo view.

HW Yes. I know. See this is the difference in the way we think. This is the way we think, and then so, in the Navajo terms it is easily comprehended when we say mountains have feet. Because man is a part of nature. (Harry Walters, Tsaile, Arizona, 8/10/93)

To further elucidate the contrast between Euro-American and Navajo perspectives, Walters sketched the image shown in figure 1 as he went on to explain.

At the beginning of each class, I draw this. You know something like this [fig. 1]. And I ask them [his students] to get a piece of paper and write down what did they see in there? And all the non-Navajo students they put "man." The Navajo students they put "yé'ii" [deity]. You know, so this is how we see it, how we see things, you know, because in Western culture man is important. Man is God. He dominates over nature. Man is the most important thing. This is why we have the words like anthropomorphic, meaning "in the image of man." In Navajo . . . man is in the image of the Holy People. When we see something like that, it is a Holy Person, it is not a human image. See? That is the difference. (Harry Walters, Tsaile, Arizona, 8/12/93)

Similarities can be metaphorically drawn among all persons in the Navajo world precisely because all persons share structure and are made from the same elements. As Terence Turner has pointed out, such similarities are based on the abstraction of a feature from a prototype object which then serves as a common

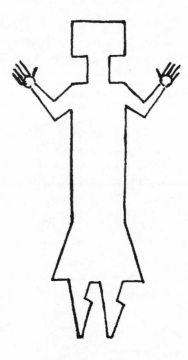

Figure 1. Sketch by Harry Walters.

feature of a class of phenomena (1991:127). For example, similarities drawn between the bottom of a mountain and the bottom of a human derive from the abstraction of a feature—base—which is part of the Navajo cultural construction of personhood. As such, it serves as the common basis of a relationship between the two things. In this case, the term "foot" is used to refer to the quality of being the "base" of all persons, including mountain persons and human persons. Shared structure and elemental composition create an intricate network of effect that links all Navajo persons.

METAPHORIC STRUCTURES AND DAILY PRACTICE

In the Navajo world, the complex network of effect makes the human individual part of and dependent on the kinship group and the community of life, including plants, animals, and aspects of the cosmos that share substance and structure. Many authors have asserted that since interconnection among all aspects of the world is a fundamental reality, the Navajo worldview is holistic (Reichard 1950; Witherspoon 1977; Farella 1984). Study of the relationships of parts of the body to each other and the relationships of parts to wholes—within human bodies and persons, among human and nonhuman beings—offers an important way to elucidate the philosophy and theories governing the Navajo cultural construction of the human body and personhood. Understanding the relationship and integration of beings and entities in the Navajo world hinges on understanding the organizing metaphoric concepts of Navajo thought: homology, complementarity, and synecdoche.[12]

Metaphor and structure are inextricably linked, because metaphor is always defined as an aspect of the structure of relations in the Pragueian sense of the term (Turner 1991:152). Yet in this analysis, the shared structure evidenced in metaphors—homology, complementarity, and synecdoche—is a means rather than an end. This study is concerned with structure insofar as it is based on the metaphoric structures linking cultural constructions. Yet it is not reductionist. Elucidation of the structural aspects of these constructions and the relationships between them is necessary to understand the framework within which contemporary Navajo people make choices to solve problems. Structure simultaneously informs daily life and is reproduced in it, because human behavior represents interaction among individual actors who consider options, make choices, and negotiate within the context of powerful structural systems. Within the theoretical framework of practice theory (Bourdieu 1977; Ortner 1984, 1989; Comaroff 1985; McCloskey 1993), we can consider decisions made by Navajo people about controlling and manipulating the potential positive effects of events on their lives while simultaneously limiting the negative effects.[13] These decisions are shaped by several powerful structural systems that individuals must navigate, including the Navajo and the Euro-American cultural systems.

Action, in turn, affects structure. As will be seen later, practice and the structural system interact and respond to each other in complex ways. Practice reproduces the system, for example, when a family plans and performs a traditional puberty ceremony for a young woman at the onset of menstruation. The system changes in direct response to practices imposed from outside, such as mandatory attendance at boarding schools, when rules shift to allow a family to postpone the ceremony until summer vacation.

Metaphoric constructs acquire significance in the Navajo world in the process of human action, that is, as aspects of complexes within which human action takes place.[14] Formalized notions of the human body, personhood, and effect in the Navajo world are not purely descriptive of a static, preordained social world. They are tools that real people use in constructing and reconstructing a world that adjusts values and goals inherited from the past to contemporary problems and desires. In my work, I seek to understand the complex interplay of structure and agency that elucidates people's choices as they grapple with the puzzles of life.

As social beings, Navajo people use their understandings of, or access to, the Navajo philosophical system to actively make choices on a day-to-day basis to maximize positive, nurturing effects while minimizing debilitating or negative effects on themselves, their loved ones, and their world. Within the context of this philosophical system, Navajo people recognize themselves as persons who are part of a larger entity—the Navajo universe. Since the Navajo view their universe as existing prior to humans, humans can logically be considered only to have been made in the image of the universe that preceded them, and not the reverse. Thus, to understand the Navajo cultural construction of the human body and personhood, we must turn our attention to the construction of the universe and to the special characteristics of life within that world.

The space within which Navajo life is lived is structurally organized on the metaphoric constructs—homology, complementarity, and synecdoche—that interconnect all entities in the Navajo world. Interconnection among all aspects of the world is a fundamental Navajo reality, but this interconnection is inherently neutral in terms of relative power and dominance. Power, based on knowledge, must be used to transmit effect between or among entities. Navajo people maximize or minimize effects by manipulating their knowledge and power. The collection of vivid narratives known as Navajo oral history is the core of Navajo ancestral knowledge.

CHAPTER II

ANCESTRAL
KNOWLEDGE
IN THE
CONTEMPORARY
WORLD

The Navajo basket has a lot to it as far as the history and the story behind it. . . . What I learned when I was small was that, my grandmother used to make these, and I know that when she would start it, they start right here in the middle. . . . That is what she calls hajíínáí, which means emergence. That's where, in the Navajo tradition, the Navajo people emerged from under the earth. . . . And it goes round and round. The Navajo strongly believe that the world goes round and round. The world is round, our life cycle goes around. . . . So, it's like life is a circle, that's what it represents. . . . It's kind of like the history of the Navajo culture and of what it has, of all the sacred elements and so forth that we have. . . . Yet it still goes round and round. And then way at the top here, this is what they call Diné, which is "the people." (Jennifer Jackson, Window Rock, Arizona, 7/10/91)[1]

After the first frost and before the first thunder—when the ground is fully frozen—Navajo elders use ceremonial baskets to teach history. The designs on the baskets represent the mountains, rainbows, clouds, and other features of the Navajo sacred landscape (fig. 2). Beginning at the center, the place of emergence, a grandmother carefully recounts the major events that befell the Navajo ancestors in each of the subterranean underworlds through which they traveled, their emergence onto the earth's surface, and the processes used by the Diyin Dine'é, the Holy People, in the construction of the world. From there, her finger moves outward along the spiraling coil as she talks. The circular movement of the spiral delineates simultaneously the passage of time and the cyclical nature of life. The

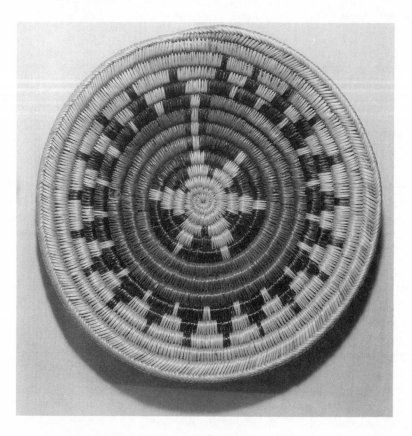

Figure 2. A Navajo ceremonial basket, or *ts'aa'*. From center to rim, the design symbolizes the place of emergence, the earth, the sacred mountains, the rainbow, black and white clouds, and contemporary Navajo people. Photograph by Greg Schwarz.

story continues, vividly recalling the course of the Navajo people up to the present. At the end of her narrative, the grandmother's finger rests on the stitches along the outer rim, which represent the Diné, the contemporary Navajo people.

Contemporary Navajo turn to the stories making up Navajo oral histories as the most important sources of information about their world, for these stories contain the ancestral knowledge that is a charter for life.[2] The Navajo origin and creation stories describe the preparation of the physical world, the creation of its inhabitants, and the delineation of the Navajo role in that world (Spencer 1947: 12). They establish an ethnic identity for all Navajo, defining meaningful relationships among individual members of the community and between the community and the cosmos (Zolbrod 1984: 25). These narratives tell more than simply where the Navajo came from and where they have been; they constitute a philosophical system that underlies the cultural construction of every aspect of the Navajo world.

Contemporary Navajo people turn to their oral history for guidance on matters of current concern because it is a philosophical wellspring for explaining the nature of life, the world, and all living things. The usefulness of the narratives stems from their being compressed metaphoric accounts that encode numerous messages at twelve levels of knowledge differentiated by degree of abstraction. These multiple levels of abstraction allow for great flexibility and adaptability in interpretation. Ancestral knowledge is considered a fundamental element of present reality, "not an objectified, distanced, inert position of wisdom or truth" (Pinxten and Farrer 1990:249). For Navajo, their history is "not an attribute or vehicle of an objectified representation of knowledge about reality." Rather, it is "the process of what is constantly in the making" (Pinxten and Farrer 1990:249).

The Navajo believe the universe preceded human existence. Thus, to understand the structural principles of Navajo philosophical orientation underlying "the process of what is constantly in the making" and the cultural construction of the world, it is necessary to consider, first, Navajo views of the universe and their place in it. In all of the several hundred versions of the Navajo origin story transcribed to date, each subterranean world is referred to by color, with a progression from dark to light.[3] Most accounts have three or four worlds—black, blue, yellow, and white (Yazzie 1971:9). Each underworld is portrayed as being in some state of chaos and disorder, resulting in the need for travel into the next world. The journey upward culminates in the emergence onto the earth's surface at the *hajíínáí,* "place of emergence," in this world. Often referred to as the "glittering" world (Yazzie 1971:17), the present world is more accurately called a world of *'áłíílí,* "supernatural or magical power," in recognition that "it is imbued with wondrous aspects and qualities which defy scientific knowledge and understanding" (Harry Walters, 3/24/95).

Several distinct types of beings coexist in the Navajo universe, including the Diyin Dine'é, the Nihookáá Dine'é, or Earth Surface People, animals, plants, rains, and mountains. Humans are not separate from other beings or aspects of nature in terms of power and dominance. All beings and aspects of nature are *ałk'éí,* "those who should be treated with compassion, cooperation, and unselfishness by the Navajo"—in other words, as kin (Witherspoon 1975:37). The Navajo consider themselves to be the Nihookáá Dine'é, having been created on the earth's surface by Asdzáá Nádleehé, "Changing Woman," the most highly revered of all Navajo Holy People and the inner form of the earth. She directed them to live within the geographical area demarcated by their four sacred mountains (O'Bryan 1956:112). The rules governing the web of relations between and among all beings and aspects of nature constituted the charter given to the Navajo by the Holy People. This web of relations forms the core of Navajo social life.

The common elements that permeate all Navajo oral traditions combine to form the Navajo worldview—a paradigm for ritual action and space structured on homology, complementarity, and synecdoche. For this reason, these histories offer a means by which to understand the cultural construction of the Navajo world, including the human body, personhood, and effect. To understand Navajo views of their place in the world, we must go deep into the womb of the earth, back to the beginning, to the first underworld, for, by Navajo accounts, the story of their origin contains the essence of all that exists or is ever possible.

ORIGINS

In Navajo they say like, whatever that goes on within your world it is moving. It is just like a flow, everything is in flow. There are no solid objects or anything. Everything . . . goes through trans-formation. It goes through manifestations. There is wear and tear, there is, but there is no addition or there is no loss to anything. It is just a transformation. You are in that. You are participating in that, so everything is alive. So that is how the Navajo would inter-pret. (Hanson Ashley, Shonto, Arizona, 7/27/93)[4]

Life began deep in Mother Earth in the First World, the Black World. Small in size, this world was much like a floating island in a sea of water mist. "It had four cor-ners, and over these appeared four clouds" (O'Bryan 1956:1). The columns of colored vaporous matter at each of the cardinal directions—white in the east, blue in the south, yellow in the west, and black in the north—were primordial, contain-ing within themselves the elements fundamental to life—moisture, air, substance, and heat. As Hanson Ashley remarked, these elements are finite in quantity and in a constant state of flux. They have been continually formulated and reformu-lated in a perpetual process of transformation since the time of the First World.

Where the white column and the black column met in the east, a male being was formed. He was accompanied by an ear of white corn made of white shell. This ear was perfectly shaped and completely covered with kernels. Simultaneously, where the blue column and the yellow column met in the west, a female being was created. A perfect ear of yellow corn made of abalone shell came into being with her (Goddard 1933:127; O'Bryan 1956:1; Yazzie 1971:9). Accordingly, white corn is a symbol of male fertility and yellow corn is a symbol of female fertility (Yazzie 1971:9). These beings are considered by many to be Áłtsé Hastiin, "First Man," and Áłtsé Asdzáán, "First Woman," the Diyin Dine'é who directed generative processes in the first and subsequent worlds (O'Bryan 1956:1; Yazzie 1971:9).

First Man and First Woman were humanlike "only in that they were male and female and they were attracted to each other" (Witherspoon 1977:141). The other beings dwelling in the First World were thought of as Air-Spirit People (Zolbrod 1984:35) or Mist Beings (O'Bryan 1956:2; Yazzie 1971:9). They had no definite form or shape but were to change into humans, animals, birds, reptiles, and other creatures in this, the present world. First Man, First Woman, the Mist Beings, and all other beings in the First World and all subsequent worlds were each animated by Sạ'ah Naagháí (male) and Bik'eh Hózhǫ (female), the primordial life-giving forces of the Navajo cosmos.[5]

In the last underworld, the first male and female beings with humanlike form were created.[6] Diyin Dine'é laid a sacred buckskin on the ground with its head facing west. On top of it they placed a perfect ear of white corn and a perfect ear of yellow corn with their tips facing east. Over the corn a second sacred buckskin was carefully spread so that its head faced east. Then the White Wind from the east blew between the buckskins. Removal of the top buckskin revealed that the white corn had been transformed into a man and the yellow corn had been transformed into a woman. The White Wind had given them life (Zolbrod 1984:50–51).[7]

They lived as man and wife and had five sets of twins. The first twins were neither entirely male nor entirely female—they were *nádleehé*.[8] The other sets of twins each consisted of an entirely male person and an entirely female person who initially lived as husband and wife. After a time they ended these incestuous marriages and married Mirage People (Zolbrod 1984:51–53). First Woman grew concerned when these marriages dissolved easily. Seeing the need for marriage to guarantee offspring and the continuation of life, she developed a plan to strengthen the bond between men and women to ensure enduring marriages (Zolbrod 1984:53). She created genitals and sexual desire to enable men and women to attract each other for a lifetime.

> She planned that it would be hard for men and women, once attached, to separate again. She decided that both men and women should have medicine to attract each other. Then she made a penis of turquoise. She rubbed loose cuticle [epidermal substance] from the man's breast. This she mixed with yucca fruit. She made a clitoris of red shell and put it inside the vagina. She rubbed loose cuticle from a woman's breast and mixed it with yucca fruit. She put that inside the turquoise penis. She combined herbs and waters of various kinds which should be for producing pregnancy. She placed the vagina on the ground and beside it the penis. Then she blew medicine from her mouth on them. . . . "Let them shout," she said. The penis shouted very

loud, but the vagina had a weak voice. "Let them have intercourse
and try shouting again," she said. When they tried again the penis
could not shout loud, but vagina had a good voice. (Goddard 1933:
138–39)

To add a finishing touch, Coyote extracted "four hairs from his left beard" and "placed them with the genitalia of man." He extracted "four more from his right beard and placed these with the genitalia of woman" (Haile 1981:38). Following their construction, these organs were distributed to young men and women only upon their reaching maturity, for the specific purpose of enabling them to conceive and give birth to healthy offspring. The powers of sexual desire had not been known before, and they proved to be a double-edged sword, for they ultimately led to the separation of men and women, the loss of reproductive capacity, and the birth of monsters.

First Man, First Woman, and their progeny flourished until lust led to adultery, which in turn led to a conflict between First Man and First Woman. During this quarrel it was revealed that each felt the other sex was inferior and that each sex was capable of existing without the other. Men and women decided to live apart. During the separation, the sexual desire created by First Woman became ever stronger, leading the men and women to seek pleasure by new means. "So strong did it become that members of both sexes indulged in masturbation. The women sought to satisfy themselves with long stones and thick quills. They attempted intercourse with cactus or with bone. The men, meanwhile, tried to relieve their longing with mud, or else they used the flesh of freshly slain game" (Zolbrod 1984:63; see also Stephen 1930:99; O'Bryan 1956:8; Yazzie 1971:30; Haile 1981:25). Realizing that they could survive without the other sex but that they could never flourish because they could not reproduce, men and women decided to reunite. Shortly after the reunion, a flood necessitated the journey up into the next world.

At the place of emergence, First Man and First Woman built a sweat house in which they thought and sang into existence the world as the Navajo now know it (Witherspoon 1977:16–17). Once their plans were made, they built and conse-crated a ceremonial *hooghan,* a traditional Navajo home, in which to create pro-totypes for all life on the earth's surface (Wheelwright 1942:62). The hooghan was a microcosmic structure of the Navajo world, which, on the cosmic plane, was comprised of Nahasdzáán, "Mother Earth," and Yádiłhił, "Father Sky." The four support pillars of the hooghan were identified with the cardinal points, and in the creation ceremony its floor represented the earth's surface (Gill 1981:52).[9]

The prototype world constructed on the floor of the first hooghan as a micro-cosm of the larger world serves as a paradigm for Navajo cosmology. Seven points are specified in the Navajo worldview: east, south, west, north, zenith, nadir, and center. To strengthen the earth, First Man and First Woman made and placed a mountain at each of these critical points. The mountains were constructed of soil that First Man had gathered from the corresponding sacred mountains in the last underworld when all life forms were forced by flood to escape into this world; he had kept the soil in his medicine bag in anticipation of this purpose (Matthews 1994 [1897]:74–75; Goddard 1933:130; O'Bryan 1956:23; Wyman 1965: 91; Yazzie 1971:13). The following mountains mark these directions in Navajo sacred geography: east, Sisnaajiní, or Blanca Peak; south, Tsoodził, Mount Taylor; west, Dook'o'oosłííd, San Francisco Peak; and north, Dibé Nitsaa, La Plata Peak. Dziłná'oodiłii—Huerfano Peak, or the mountain "around-which-moving-was-done—and Ch'óol'į́'í, Gobernador Knob, the place where Changing Woman was found, were placed in the center.

One of the four foundational principles of Navajo education and philosophy was linked to each of the sacred mountains at the cardinal directions—*nitsáhá-kees,* "thinking," *nahat'á,* "planning," *'iiná,* "living according to a pattern," and *sihasin,* "confidence, assurance, and security" (McNeley 1993). Then First Man assigned Diyin Dine'é to be inner forms residing within the physical form of each mountain, plant, and animal created to exist on the earth's surface (Wyman 1965: 91). A Holy Wind (McNeley 1981:22) and a set of powerful paired personages were placed at each of the cardinal directions (McNeley 1993). Early Dawn Boy and Early Dawn Girl live in the east, Blue Daylight Boy and Blue Daylight Girl live in the south, Yellow Evening Twilight Boy and Yellow Evening Twilight Girl live in the west, and Folding Darkness Boy and Folding Darkness Girl live in the north (Aronilth 1990:32). Separately or in combination, these Holy Winds and powerful personages direct all life, movement, thought, and planning on the earth's surface (McNeley 1981:6, 1993; Aronilth 1990:32; Avery Denny, 8/11/93).[10]

Once these associations were completed, each sacred mountain was ritually dressed in representations of its physical outer form. This dressing established the proper associations of colors, male or female qualities, and *ntł'iz,* or "hard goods"—precious stones and shells—with each of the cardinal directions. Finally, the mountains were ready to be fastened to the earth. Sisnaajiní, sacred mountain of the east, was fastened to the earth with lightning, associated with the color white, and dressed with white shell, morning light, white lightning, white rain, dark clouds, and white corn. This mountain is associated with nitsáhákees. Tsoodził, the sacred mountain of the south, was fastened to the earth with a great stone knife, associated with the color blue, and dressed with turquoise, dark mist, and different kinds of wild animals. This mountain is associated with nahat'á. Dook'o'oosłííd, the sacred mountain of the west, was fastened to the earth with a sunbeam, associated with the color yellow, and dressed with abalone shell, sunset light, black clouds, yellow corn, and all sorts of wild animals. This mountain is associated with 'iiná. Dibé Nitsaa, the sacred mountain of the north, was fastened to the earth

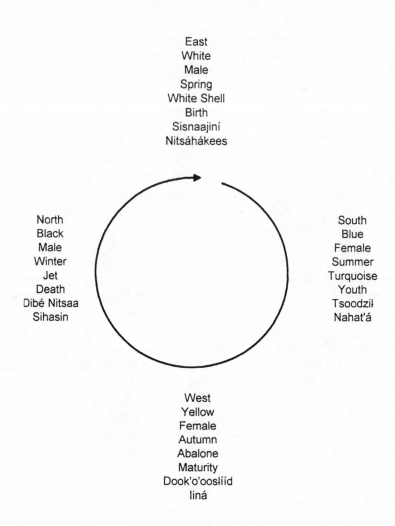

East
White
Male
Spring
White Shell
Birth
Sisnaajiní
Nitsáhákees

North
Black
Male
Winter
Jet
Death
Dibé Nitsaa
Sihasin

South
Blue
Female
Summer
Turquoise
Youth
Tsoodził
Nahat'á

West
Yellow
Female
Autumn
Abalone
Maturity
Dook'o'oosłííd
Iiná

Figure 3.   Navajo cosmology I.

with a rainbow, associated with the color black, and dressed with jet beads, night blackness, dark mist, different kinds of plants, and many wild animals. This mountain is associated with sihasin (Matthews 1994 [1897]:78–79; Wheelwright 1942:63–64; Yazzie 1971:17–18; McNeley 1993). The colors, ntł'iz, winds, and other things associated with each of the cardinal directions are the fundamental components that combine to form the most pervasive and integral aspects of Navajo cosmology (fig. 3).

After the mountains were placed, the Diyin Dine'é went on to create and place the sun, the moon, and the stars, as well as to determine all aspects of life and death within this sacred geography. The newly created world was in a state of "natural order" in which all living things were in their prescribed places and in their proper relationships with all other living things.

The perfect order of the world was disrupted because of the sexual aberrations and excesses of the last underworld. The women who had masturbated with quills, cacti, antlers, stones, and bones gave birth to misshapen creatures who grew into monsters. When the women saw that their newborns were deformed, they abandoned them, leaving them to die where they were born. At first, the women did not even tell the men about the birth of these deformed beings. The monstrous babies, however, did not die. Instead, they flourished, grew huge, and began preying on the healthy children. The birth of these monsters represents the presence of *hóchxǫ'*, "ugly, undesirable" forces in the world. When the monsters came into the world, plants, animals, and people lost their capacity for reproduction. As a result, death and destruction were everywhere.

Taking pity, the Diyin Dine'é intervened. They arranged for First Man to find Changing Woman at Ch'óol'į́'į́. One morning at dawn the people saw a dark cloud over Gobernador Knob, and they sent a message to Talking God asking him to investigate. Talking God approached Gobernador Knob from the east. He heard a cry, but he saw nothing because the cloud cover was so thick. He climbed farther, circling the peak as he went. From the south, he heard a bird cry, from the west, more birds, and from the north, a corn beetle. By now he had gone nearly full circle and had almost reached the top. From the east, he approached and saw the dark cloud with a rainbow and soft, falling rain. He looked again, and a baby girl was lying under the rainbow and rain.

This infant, Changing Woman, was the child of Sạ'ah Naagháí and Bik'eh Hózhǫ. Talking God gave her over to First Man, who took her home to First Woman. They raised her in a "miracle way." Under the direction of the Holy People, they fed her sunray pollen, pollen from clouds, pollen from plants, and flower dew so that she matured miraculously. In two days she walked, in four days she talked, and in twelve days she began to menstruate.

Her menstruation symbolized the restoration of power and fertility on the earth and was cause for great rejoicing. The first Blessing Way ceremony, the Kinaaldá, was celebrated in honor of the event. Shortly after this ceremony, Changing Woman mated with the sun and gave birth to twin sons, Monster Slayer and Born For Water. Changing Woman kept the boys close to home while they grew and hid them from the monsters so they would not be eaten. When they reached adolescence, the twins wanted to know who their father was, so they went on a quest to find him. Along the way, they met Spider Woman, who told them their father was the sun and gave them magical tools with which to reach him. When they found their father, he made them endure several trials to prove they were his children. They persevered, and finally the sun supplied them with powerful weapons to slay the monsters. They worked together to slay all the monsters except Hunger, Poverty, Old Age, and Lice. The world was saved.

Changing Woman was lonely for companionship and decided that there should be more people, so she created humans. She created the Nihookáá Dine'é here on the earth's surface. By most accounts, she did this by rubbing skin wastes from her breast, from her back, and from under her arms. She mixed this substance with ground white shell, turquoise, abalone, and jet (the ntł'iz that are vital components of Navajo cosmology), and with corn of all colors. Then she molded these materials into cylindrical forms that were ritually transformed into human beings. These beings were animated either by the breath of Changing Woman or by the entrance of Holy Winds (Matthews 1994 [1897]:147–48; Franciscan Fathers 1910:356; Goddard 1933:168; Wyman 1970:447–48; Yazzie 1971:74). The Diyin Dine'é decided to give the world over to humans and then take their places as the inner forms of the features of Navajo sacred geography.

Changing Woman became the inner form of the earth. Her continual maturation, death, and rebirth are mirrored in the changing seasons of the earth: birth is mirrored by spring, youth by summer, maturity by fall, and old age and death by winter (see fig. 3). As the inner being of the earth, Changing Woman is considered the mother of all who dwell on the earth's surface. She is "the source and sustenance of all life on the earth's surface, controlling particularly fertility and fecundity" (Witherspoon 1977:18).

When the world was turned over to the Nihookáá Dine'é, Changing Woman and the other Diyin Dine'é gave the Nihookáá Dine'é the components of their ancestral knowledge—songs, prayers, ceremonies, and stories. Together these form a charter for life, a contract between the Nihookáá Dine'é and the Holy People that gives Navajo people the right to live within Dinétah, "the area demarcated by sacred mountains," under the special protection of the Holy People for as long as they follow the guidelines established for the Navajo way of life. This charter determines how they must live in order for the world to be maintained and life to continue. Moreover, because of its compressed metaphoric nature, this body of knowledge contains seemingly limitless guidance for contemporary Navajo faced with personal or social problems.

FAIRY TALES OR METAPHOR?
THE TWELVE LEVELS OF KNOWLEDGE

> HW OK. That is level one, right there. Level one.
>
> MS Level one? OK.
>
> HW Yeah, level one, but there are twelve levels. When you get to it, it is very complicated, even for me, I know, I think I will just stay at the two levels. (Harry Walters, Tsaile, Arizona, 8/12/93)

Origin stories offer guidance to contemporary people because they compress historical knowledge and human experience into vivid narratives that can illuminate and educate. As teaching tools, or parables, they are subject to different levels of analysis. In the Navajo world the stories are useful because they contain numerous messages at different levels of interpretation, depending on the degree of analytical abstraction applied by the Navajo listener. As Harry Walters explains, all components of Navajo culture are based on four main levels of knowledge, each of which can be subdivided into three additional levels of abstraction:

> OK. I won't go into the twelve, because, uh, that is very complicated, and then, you have to know ceremonies to get into that. . . . All components of culture are based on that. If you were to categorize them [the components of Navajo culture] into philosophy, art, music, or history, things like that, it will not work. But if you put it in the four levels it will work. And so the four main ones are hózhǫ́ǫ́jí hane', and then diyin k'ehjí hane', and the third one is hatáál k'ehjí hane', and the fourth one is naayéé'jí hane'. (Harry Walters, Tsaile, Arizona, 3/20/95)

Hózhǫ́ǫ́jí hane' is the elementary level used to teach young children. *Diyin k'ehjí hane'* expands on the first level by incorporating information about the twelve Diyin Dine'é, mentioned in all ceremonies and stories, who represent different principles in nature. The third main level, *hatáál k'ehjí hane'*, includes songs and prayers associated with each episode in the origin stories. *Naayéé'jí hane'* is specifically concerned with the stories associated with Naayéé'jí, or Protection Way, ceremonies and, as such, is limited to people who have specialized ceremonial knowledge (Walters, 3/20/95). Altogether, twelve distinct levels of knowledge are encoded into each episode of the origin stories. Navajo educators draw upon these levels of abstraction to illuminate ancestral teachings.

As an experienced educator, Harry Walters knows that a learner must be able to put new information into a familiar context to grasp the lesson at hand. He turned to the Changing Woman portion of the origin narrative to illustrate to me how the different levels of abstraction can be drawn out of a single account. "Remember I told you that on level one, level one is basic elementary, you know, Changing Woman was found on the mountain, she became an adolescent after twelve days" (8/12/93). Walters was alluding to the episode in the Changing Woman story in which she was found as an infant strapped in a cradle and taken to the home of First Man and First Woman, where she was raised in a "miracle way." The following excerpt is a typical rendition of this episode as told to me by Wilson Aronilth of Tsaile, Arizona.[11]

A miracle thing happened, a child came into the world to save our people, and this child came into this world in the form of a little baby girl which they say like, this spirit called the holy spirit, we call it "Haashch'éélti'í" I think today the English translation they call it "Talking God." Myself, a lot of these English translations throws off a lot of our stories, but that's the way that I think they call it, Talking God, but in Navajo we say, "bił haayoołkááł' Haashch'éélti'í." When you say—if you understand the language, it's self explanatory—it's the holy spirit that found the child and then brought it to First Man and First Woman's home and raised it in a miracle way. She was fed with air, light, water, moisture, mist, plant pollen. Moisture and mist and pollen are one of the most natural ingredients. And she grew up miracally [sic] in twelve days, and on the twelfth day she reached her pubertyhood [sic]. She became a woman. (Wilson Aronilth, Tsaile, Arizona, 7/3/91)

Harry Walters explained that on the next level of knowledge, the story of how Changing Woman was found and raised is slightly different:

HW Level two is diyin k'ehjí hane'. It says, Changing Woman was found and she was dressed in white shell. She was not found as a baby, she was found as an embryo, an undeveloped egg. First Man brought her home and he said, "This is all there was. The baby that was crying. Nothing else." So when First Woman took it, it became a baby. Then she said, "this is . . ."

MS Did she put it in her womb and carry it, or did she just . . . ?

HW She just took it.

MS She just took it and then it immediately became a baby?

HW Uh-huh.

MS OK.

HW And she was dressed in white shell. That is why she was called White Shell Woman. (Harry Walters, Tsaile, Arizona, 8/12/93)

The difference between level one and level two is that on level two Changing Woman is not found as a fully formed baby. When Talking God climbed Gobernador Knob to investigate the dark clouds, he found that an undeveloped embryo was the source of the crying. He gave it to First Man, who took it home to First Woman, saying, "This is all there was. . . . Nothing else." The undeveloped embryo immediately became transformed into a fully formed baby when First Man put it into First Woman's arms. Important information regarding the roles of women and

Changing Woman's position in the Navajo cosmos are encoded into this version.

That the embryo developed only after being placed in First Woman's arms establishes precedents for the roles of women in Navajo society and human development. The primary culturally sanctioned role for women is that of nurturer. That is, Navajo women are to be mothers, whose most important responsibilities are to foster and sustain the development of children. Children will develop from embryo to fetus to infant, and on through all five main stages of life, only with the nurturance and guidance given by mothers. The primary relationship between mother and child is that of sustenance. On the basis of this link, the concept of mother extends to all factors in the world that contribute to the sustenance and development of human life. Therefore, as Gary Witherspoon has pointed out, the term for mother, *amá*, has a wide range of referents in the Navajo world, including "one's mother by birth, the earth, the sheep herd, the corn field and the mountain soil bundle" (1977:91). Virtually anything that contributes to sustenance and development is a mother in the Navajo world.

In a subsequent meeting, Harry Walters summarized the level four version of the finding of Changing Woman to demonstrate how subtle changes are made in story content in order to teach effectively at increasingly abstract levels of knowledge.

> The fourth level, naayééʼjí haneʼ, deals with the same [episode in the origin] story but [considers] stories that are associated with the Naayééʼjí ceremonies. Ceremonies like the Evil Way. The Crystal Gazing, Protection Way, uh, Hand Trembling, or Enemy Way. Red Ant Way, the Big Star Way, uh, or the Upward Moving Way. These are the Naayééʼjí ceremonies and then so they deal in a different [body of knowledge]. So the story would go like this, First Man heard a baby crying on the mountain, and he went up there and instead of finding a baby, he found a corn growing, it was a young corn, it must have been maybe about five or six inches high. And then underneath it was a corn beetle. And then, uh, he was surprised. And he reached down to pick up that corn beetle and it turned into an embryo, an undeveloped embryo. And then, he took that and he brought that home to his wife and he says, "This is all it was." And when she took that, it became a baby. And then so, she dressed her in White Shell and she became known as White Shell Woman. (Harry Walters, Tsaile, Arizona, 3/20/95)

At this level, the episode encodes information regarding the interconnection that exists among all Navajo persons. In this account, it was First Man who investigated the strange phenomena seen on Chʼóolʼį́į́. As he climbed to the summit, he heard a different sound at each of the four directions: an undifferentiated cry in the east, a bird cry in the south, the cries of other birds in the west, and the sound of a corn beetle in the north. Upon reaching the top, he saw a dark cloud with a rainbow and falling rain. He looked again and saw a young corn plant; again, and saw a corn beetle that turned into an undeveloped embryo as he picked it up. When he took the embryo home to First Woman, it developed into a baby in her arms. In this version, corn plants, corn beetles, and embryos are portrayed as interchangeable. It reveals that on the most abstract level of knowledge, all persons who live now or who have ever lived in the Navajo world are constructed of the same fundamental elements and structured on paradigms of directionality (sunwise movement and the trajectory of growth) and complementarity.

In both advanced versions of this episode, First Woman became the child's mother when she provided the sustenance for the embryo to develop into a baby. Once the baby was fully formed, First Woman dressed her in white shell. Thereafter she was referred to as White Shell Girl until her puberty, when she was given the name White Shell Woman or Changing Woman. White shell is the ntł'iz associated with the east, the direction also associated with dawn, spring, and, by extension, birth. Dressing the baby in this sacred material directly associates Changing Woman with the beginning of the day, the beginning of the annual cycle, and the beginning of life.

To make sure I fully grasped the lesson, Harry Walters moved on to the next episode in the Changing Woman story, the birth of the Hero Twins and their slaying of the monsters. The level one version of this episode with which I was most familiar is as follows:

> In the third underworld some of the people engaged in abuses of their capacity to reproduce. These abuses included incest, adultery, masturbation, and immodesty. The consequences of these abuses did not become apparent until the females started to give birth to various sorts of monsters that began to terrorize and devour the people. The capacity to properly reproduce was lost, and death and despair set in. To save the world and the people, First Man came up with a plan. . . . Changing Woman would save the world by first restoring the power of reproduction, and secondly by giving birth to the Twins who would slay the monsters. (Witherspoon 1987: 15)

With this version of the story in mind, I reasoned that since the "capacity to properly reproduce was lost," women had been able to give birth only to monsters after the separation of the sexes in the last underworld. Therefore, Changing Woman must have been the first well-formed entity created after the separation. I decided to ask Harry Walters if this was so.

> MS Was she [Changing Woman] the first person that was not a monster after the separation of the sexes?
>
> HW No. There were babies that were born. That is what the—
>
> MS There were healthy babies that were born?
>
> HW That was what the monsters lived on.
>
> MS But, I thought that—
>
> HW All during the time that they were there. But the monsters were born right after, right after the separation. Not all of them, there were only twelve.
>
> MS There were only twelve monsters?
>
> HW Yes, not all women gave birth to monsters.
>
> MS I thought that the women lost their capacity for reproduction due to the sexual abuses that they engaged in during the separation of the sexes. So they weren't able to give birth to babies again, until Changing Woman was born, and she is the one that brought the capacity for reproduction back to . . .
>
> HW No!
>
> MS No?
>
> HW There were babies that were born during the time when the monsters were roaming. They would stop pregnant women, and they would ask them, "When are you due?" To make sure that they were there when they [delivered], because that is what they ate!
>
> MS Oh, so they were giving birth, but the monsters were eating them all, so that is why . . .
>
> HW Uh-huh.
>
> MS They had a capacity for reproduction but the children weren't surviving?
>
> HW Uh-huh, now, see, what does that signify? See, that is the next level of teaching. Were there actually monsters? (Harry Walters, Tsaile, Arizona, 8/12/93)

What? There were no monsters? By way of illustration, Walters was walking me through the steps of reasoning he takes as a modern Navajo scholar. He and other contemporary Navajo know the monsters are metaphors for something else. They reduce this episode to the essential problem: for some reason the children were not surviving. Something was causing high infant mortality or infertility rates. What was it?

> HW Maybe they were, the women . . . they were infected with something where infant mortality was a hundred percent. That is why the population began to dwindle. See, that is another way of looking at it. That is another level. . . . Maybe because they were committing incestuous acts and all kinds of, uh, uh . . .
>
> MS Uh-huh. (Harry Walters, Tsaile. Arizona, 8/12/93)

Perhaps the women were infected with a disease that made them infertile or caused the infants to die. On this level the monsters represent the diseases or whatever was causing the high rates of infant mortality or infertility or both. They are metaphors for diseases and health problems.[12] Walters continued, "Instead of monsters. So what Changing Woman did, she set laws and said, 'Now, this is the proper behavior, moral behavior. You follow these, you will have healthy babies.' See that is another level" (8/12/93).

He had moved on to the next level of abstraction, from monsters to diseases to immoral behavior. The story of the separation and subsequent reunion of men and women in the last underworld encapsulates important information about the male-female relations of all entities. It documents that neither sex can function or properly reproduce without the other. If infertility or infant deaths were caused by the incestuous acts and other sexual aberrations committed by the people at the time of the separation, then on this level the monsters represent moral dilemmas.

The reunion demonstrates that men and women, although different, are complementary—that is, necessary parts of a whole, who have equal roles and responsibilities. Changing Woman did not simply bring back the capacity for reproduction; she established order by demonstrating the contrasting yet comple-mentary male and female principles that would come to be known, respectively, as naayéé' k'ehjigo (often shortened to naayéé'jí), "on the side of protection," and hózhǫ́ǫ́jigo (often shortened to hózhǫ́ǫ́jí), "on the side of peace, harmony, and order." To maintain the "natural order" of the world, she gave the Nihookáá Dine'é laws to govern "proper behavior, moral behavior." The monsters were born be-cause of moral aberrations before and during the separation of men and women. The knowledge given to the Nihookáá Dine'é by Changing Woman and the other Holy People when this world was turned over to them is meant to guide future actions so members of the Navajo world can avoid such problems. This knowledge enabled Navajo ancestors to have healthy children who would survive.

To make sure I understood the lesson, Harry Walters asked me to paraphrase my new understanding:

MS So, it is not that she brought back the capacity for reproduction, she gave them something that was the ability to have healthy children that would survive.

HW Yes, yes.

MS And the monsters are metaphoric for something else.

HW Yes. Uh-huh, yes, that is another way to look at it. See that is what I mean by different levels.

MS I know, I know, and most of the people that would talk to someone like me would give it to me at that level one.

HW Yeah, the elementary level.

MS But then—

HW That is going to just read like a fairy tale. (Harry Walters, Tsaile, Arizona, 8/12/93)

The gifts from the Holy People to the Nihookáá Dine'é—songs, prayers, ceremonies, and stories—continue to inform the contemporary world. Across the vast Navajo reservation, elders and teachers use the vivid narratives of Navajo oral history to teach Navajo people about their roles and places in the world. These compressed metaphoric accounts are powerful tools that can illuminate, educate, and offer solutions to the concerns of contemporary life. Because of this power, access to the various levels of knowledge, as well as to specific bodies of knowledge, is controlled by elders who limit individual exposure on the basis of various factors—age, gender, occupation—to only that which they deem appropriate.

PARTIAL KNOWLEDGE

You just have to go through it to learn it and that is how it is passed down. Information and things. You as a young person are only limited to know so much. And you are, it is like you are offered or given the stories and told by hands-on experience. Seeing it. And that is how you learn more and more about it. Because even my mother when I ask her certain things, she still really doesn't know certain things. And it is like you are given that information at certain times of your life, or when you go to the ceremonies. (Traci Michelle Begay, Many Farms, Arizona, 7/26/91)[13]

No hard and fast system by which knowledge is transferred exists in the Navajo world. Knowledge is transferred as needed. The Navajo cultural system dictates that particular parts of the human body—for example, afterbirth and umbilical cords—are more susceptible to effect than others, and that the human body is more open to effect at critical times in the life cycle—for example, at birth, at puberty, and during pregnancy. Knowledge is evoked by such occasions, as well as by illness or accident, at which times knowledge is transferred.

Individual understandings are affected by access and change over time in the altering Navajo cultural world. Access to specific forms of knowledge is restricted by elders and other concerned family members, who generally attempt to limit an individual's exposure to only that information they judge relevant to his or her stage of life—infant, child, young man or woman, man or woman, and elder. Thus, only hózhǫ́ǫ́jí hane' stories are told to young children, because they are considered too vulnerable to be exposed to the power contained in the more advanced levels of knowledge (Walters, 3/20/95). And certain bodies of knowledge, such as information about hunting and warfare or pregnancy and childbirth, are restricted by gender.

Furthermore, such information is often withheld from men and women who are perceived to have no need for it. For example, mothers and grandmothers make a concerted effort to limit a woman's exposure to information about pregnancy and childbirth until she marries, regardless of her age (Sunny Dooley, 8/21/92). On the other hand, both men and women can gain access to specialized knowledge through occupational training, such as becoming a weaver, a silversmith, or a singer. Training as a singer may conceivably allow access to the third or fourth level of knowledge—hatááł k'ehjí hane' or naayéé'jí hane'—depending on the type of ceremony or ceremonies learned. Understanding and accepting these limitations, the Navajo people with whom I am acquainted recognize their own knowledge as partial. They see and acknowledge themselves as situated subjects in a position to know certain things and not others.[14]

Within the recognized limitations of personal knowledge, Navajo people living in the modern world often cope with individual concerns by placing them within the larger cultural context of Navajo philosophy and oral history. Correlations are commonly drawn between the experiences of Navajo ancestors and the experiences of contemporary Navajo persons. In our discussions, the people with whom I consulted continually referred, directly or through allusion, to the vivid narratives that detail the problems and experiences of individual Diyin Dine'é—problems resolved by one of the numerous ceremonies or other techniques used by Navajo people today. To teach me about Navajo life and explain their courses of action in problem solving, they contextualized each of the topics under consideration within the broader framework of the origin and creation stories that make up Navajo oral history.

This contextualization is appropriate because the ancestral knowledge contained in these stories constitutes a philosophical system that serves as a charter for the Navajo way of life. This philosophy orders the world on the basis of homology, complementarity, and synecdoche, the metaphoric concepts that underlie the cultural construction of every aspect of the world within the area demarcated by the sacred mountains, including the human body, self, person, and effect. But the stories do not simply establish the paradigmatic structures upon which the Navajo world is built; they also have explanatory and predictive powers. As such, they are the philosophical backdrop many contemporary Navajo use to explain the way the world is and to guide them in assisting their children and other family members through every stage of life.

When Navajo parents want to understand how best to guide a newborn child toward full Navajo personhood, they turn to this philosophical wellspring. When a young mother wants a daughter, she turns to these narratives. When it is time for a grandmother to direct her granddaughter through the transition from childhood to womanhood, she turns for guidance to the Changing Woman stories and the rules governing performance of the Kinaaldá ceremony. When faced with illness, people routinely choose to employ traditional means and ceremonies such as Hózhǫ́ǫ́jí, (Blessing Way), Anaa' jí ndáá' (Enemy Way), or Hóchxǫ́ǫ́'jí (Evil Way)— first performed to resolve challenges faced by Diyin Dine'é—to either enhance or negate the influence of effects on individuals and, by extension, their kin. In every case, parallels are drawn between the individual concerns of contemporary people and the experiences of Navajo ancestors. Such parallels can be drawn because all persons in the Navajo world are constructed of the primordial elements of the First World, are linked by shared structure, and are related to each other as kin.

CHAPTER III

THE NATURE
OF LIFE
IN THE
NAVAJO WORLD

HW The element, the element is, it is in everything. It is holy. When you put it together in a certain composition it is human. And [when] it is put together in a certain composition, it is a tree. And [in] another certain composition, it is an insect.

MS Now, I see what you mean, OK.

HW Yes. And then . . . when those die and go back, and then we drink the same water, we breathe the same air, uh, and we eat the food from the earth. And then all of these things, the elements, come together and where they are put together there is life again. The elements are the seeds, the plants, so that is the cycle right there. See? It is a cycle. (Harry Walters, Tsaile, Arizona, 8/12/93)

The theory of life established in the actions of the Diyin Dine'é and documented in the origin stories dictates that a special kind of life exists within the confines of Navajo sacred geography. At various stages in the underworlds, the Diyin Dine'é formulated and transformed the primordial elements to create entities as needed. After their emergence onto the surface of this world, the Diyin Dine'é used these same elements and methods to construct life forms to fill the newly demarcated world. As Harry Walters explained, these primary elements—moisture, air, substance, and heat—were and are the "seeds" for all past and future creation.

The twelve levels of knowledge reveal that on the most abstract level, all persons who live now or who have ever lived in the Navajo world—hooghan, baskets, corn plants, corn beetles, humans, cradles, mountains, prayers—were and are constructed of the same fundamental elements, linked by metaphoric structures including complementarity, permeated by vibration in the form of sound or movement, and possessed of the same seven senses and anatomical components, including mind, eyes, ears, legs, and feet. Despite these many similarities, the numerous distinct types of persons in the Navajo world have individualized life cycles that are determined, in part, by degree of personal power based on knowledge, which gives agency and volition.

The elements are considered to be like seeds because, as Avery Denny of Low Mountain, Arizona, points out in the following conversation, once an individual life cycle is completed, the component elements—moisture, substance, air, and heat—return to the cosmos to be reformulated in future life.[1]

> AD So when we die we go back into the earth and then it [pointing to a drawing he did of the human body with one arrow pointing toward the sky and a second arrow pointing toward the ground] goes back into nature. That is how it works, the whole system.
>
> MS OK. So you are saying what, your body goes into the earth, and what goes into the sky?
>
> AD This one goes back into nature [tapping on the drawing]. The whole cosmic order, the whole cycle.
>
> MS The breath of life?
>
> AD The breath of life is your spirit, it goes back into what it came out of through your clan. Through your clan, it goes back into, anywhere in there. There is no heaven and no hell, there is no place that is hell in my way.
>
> MS So are all the people that ever existed in the Navajo world still here?
>
> AD Yeah. Even you, yeah [chuckles]. There is no heaven, there is no hell. Everything is just in here. You go back to where you came from. . . . That keeps us alive. Są'ah naaghái bik'eh hózhǫ́ means a cycle of life. (Avery Denny, Chinle, Arizona, 8/11/93)

Moisture, air, substance, and heat are not all that is needed for life to exist. As Hanson Ashley explains in the next passage, every life form constructed through reformulation of the primary elements is permeated by vibration in the form of sound (language) or movement. This fifth element—vibration—is also necessary for life.

> And then they talk about the elements. There are four, four elements. But then again they talk about another one, they say five elements. The fifth one is the sound. You know, any, like all these four elements, they have some kind of sound. . . . Like the fire has

a sound, water has a sound, air has a sound, the substance somehow it creates a sound. So the fifth one is the sound itself, that vibration, OK. The vibration is the . . . essence of all the other elements. The vibration can go through anything. So they believe that that vibration has to be there within the human body. You have to have that in order to keep your body, body, to be vibrant, in order to react to all the other elements. (Hanson Ashley, Shonto, Arizona, 7/27/93)

The sounds and vibrations connected to the primary elements in the First World constitute Áłtsé Saad, "First Language." This language still exists. It is spoken by animals and newborn humans, but, as Ursula Knoki-Wilson of Ganado, Arizona, notes, it is unintelligible to contemporary humans: "There were, I guess, mostly vibrations. And there was sound too. They were not sounds that we are familiar with in terms of audible sounds the way our ears register it. But there were sounds. Mind sounds I guess they are called. There is a sound connected with the elements. All of the elements" (Ursula Knoki-Wilson, Fort Defiance, Arizona, 7/29/93).[2]

When I asked Harry Walters for clarification about these sounds, he explained that the primordial elements produce language because they themselves are alive.

> MS And did those four elements have sounds?
> HW Yes, yes they have sounds. They speak, they hear, they listen, they understand. (Harry Walters, Tsaile, Arizona, 8/12/93)

Being alive, these elements have the same seven senses as all other life forms in the Navajo world: the capacities to see, hear, taste, smell, touch, know, and speak. The sense of knowing gives one the capacity to have awareness of oneself in the world, to internalize and understand information about the world, and to think and to organize thoughts. The sense of speech gives one the capacity to externalize thoughts (Wesley Thomas, personal communication 11/12/94) as well as to control and manipulate power based on knowledge.

The fundamental living elements take a variety of forms when they are formulated and reformulated, depending on the particular entity under construction. This variety includes, but is not limited to, the following manifestations: Moisture can take the form of water, rain, mist, snow, blood, or saliva. Air can appear as wind, breath, or voice. Substance can take the form of soil, pollen, skin, cornmeal, ntł'iz, wood, or stone. Heat can appear as sunlight, zigzag lightning, sunrays, or fire. Vibration can take the form of song, prayer, speech, or melody. Individual persons such as baskets, hooghan, cradles, looms, songs, and masks are formed from a variety of manifestations of these basic elements. Regardless of the particular forms these elements take, one thing remains constant: some type of moisture, air, substance, heat, and vibration must be included in the formulation for life to exist. Consider, for example, the construction and use of baskets, hooghan, cradles, and looms.

BASKETS

> MS People have told me that baskets are like people. And that they should be treated with respect, as a living entity. So, I thought maybe you could explain to me a little bit about what, how do I say this? What is the essence that gives something life?
>
> UKW Because they came from nature. Even, a basket is just a material thing but what it is constructed from is from nature. Once upon a time, the reeds that went around for the bindings, to go around in the basket, once upon a time, were alive. In terms of having a breath, the wind within it, or the spirit within it. And that spirit is still, resides in there, even though it is inanimate, it still . . . the essence of spirit still resides in there. Everything in nature has it [an inner being]. . . . Even inanimate objects. Like, [pause] but when, when umm, like the basket . . . what it symbolizes is what is alive. It embodies a whole philosophical life within it. In addition to the fact that it was truly alive at one time. . . . The entire basket just represents the mind holistically. The whole entire, and then it represents the emergence of man. Umm, our emergence from our beginnings. (Ursula Knoki-Wilson, Fort Defiance, Arizona, 7/29/93)

Navajo oral history records the construction of four primordial baskets, *ts'aa'*, in the First World and the vital role basket persons play in ordering Navajo creation, philosophy, and life.[3] The Diyin Dine'é combined their "mysterious powers and colors" to create the first sacred baskets from the fundamental living elements. Each individual basket was identified and named according to the material from which it was constructed.

> *Black Jet Basket, Turquoise Basket, Abalone Shell Basket and White Shell Basket. This is the reason why there are black, blue, yellow, red and white colors in the basket. Sometimes you can only see black and red. . . . The Holy People blessed it [the basket] with good thoughts, ideas, thinking and planning. . . . The purpose of why this basket was made was to create and keep all creation in order. To keep the direc-*

*tions, thoughts, ideas, thinking and planning in order. To keep na-
ture, the Holy People's laws in order, so they won't be confusing. So
there could be East, South, West, North, and Spring, Summer, Fall
and Winter. When the Holy People wanted life to exist, they used
this basket to put their children together, to produce life (Aronilth
1985:206–7).*

The attributes of contemporary basket persons document and present the laws
of the Diyin Dine'é. The designs on the basket are a visual record of Navajo history
from the emergence through every phase of life in this world. They record the
critical events in the construction of every aspect of the Navajo universe and in
Navajo history. As a visual record of the "natural order" of the Navajo cosmos, the
designs on baskets serve as mnemonic devices by which life can be ordered.[4]

The structure basket persons share with other persons in the Navajo world is
evidenced in the process of their construction and use. These shallow, coiled baskets range in size from approximately twelve to fourteen inches in diameter and
two to three inches in height. They are characterized by having a two-rod-and-
bundle foundation. The rod and bundle are constructed of two sumac twigs and a
cluster of yucca fibers; the coils consist of dyed and undyed sumac splints (Whiteford 1988:37). The actual number of coils varies from basket to basket, but
Navajo experts agree that baskets should ideally have a total of twelve coils from
center to rim. These twelve coils represent the twelve layers or levels of knowledge
(H. Ashley, 7/23/91).

The basket maker, who sings a specific song during the process of construction,
is careful to begin with a butt end at the center and to place the butt end of each
subsequent rod against the tip of the preceding one. This assures that the sumac
rods lie in the direction in which they grew (Tschopik 1940:449). The homology
between baskets, hooghan, and the universe is explicitly drawn by Irene Kee of
Crystal, New Mexico, in the following explanation of basket construction and the
importance of the designs on the basket.[5]

> From here the start point is begun here. It is done sunwise. Follow-
> ing the direction of the sun. That is how it is done. It began like
> that. Woven in that direction [running her finger along the spiral
> of a basket]. New ones [rods] are added here and it continues here,
> and finally it ends here [touching the opening in the basket de-
> sign]. This opening is always here. It is the doorway. This is made
> according to the hooghan and the universe. It is made according to
> the thinking of Talking God. He stated to make the basket sunwise
> and make the ending parallel with the opening of the basket. The
> opening of the basket has to be the same location where the coiling

ends. It is the same with our homes. We enter from and go out in one direction. We live that. In the western part of the hooghan, we conduct washing hair ceremony during Blessing Way ceremonies. All Navajo ceremonies are related to this basket. It has a purpose. It is utilized in multiple areas within our culture. That is how it is. It is not made without purpose. It has a purpose, the designs have purpose. (The words of Irene Kee, Crystal, New Mexico, 8/3/92, translated by Wesley Thomas)

The design layout characteristic of Navajo ceremonial baskets consists of five concentric panels around a center. The center is surrounded, consecutively, by a band of white terraced triangular forms pointing away from the center; a band of black inverted terraced triangular forms; a red band; a band of black terraced triangular forms pointing away from the center; and a band of white inverted terraced triangular forms. These panels are not continuous for the circumference of the basket. As Mrs. Kee pointed out, they are intersected by a distinctive break in the design that connects the panel of white terraced triangular forms nearest the center with the rim of the basket, where the coiling ends. This opening in the design, the "way out," must face east throughout a ceremony. Ceremonial practitioners use the place where the rim is finished to ascertain the correct directional placement tactiley when the basket is full or the light in the hooghan is dim (Matthews 1894:202; Tschopik 1940:450).

When viewed from the concave surface, the spiral produced by the coiling of the rods, as baskets are sewn, appears to be expanding in an "antisunwise" direction from the center outward (Stewart 1938:26; Tschopik 1940:452; Fishler 1954:211). This is in direct contradistinction to the proper ritual order and the Navajo view of the way the world operates: namely, sunwise. This direction of coiling can be explained, however, when the context of its use is further illuminated. A fundamental aspect of every Navajo healing ceremony is a cleansing of the mind and body to facilitate the ritual return to the beginning of the world. Through this process a state of balance or harmony is restored. The patient's relationships with all members of the community of life are redefined through the ritual. The counterclockwise direction of the basket spiral represents the return from the contemporary world (the outside edge), through Navajo history (the twelve coils), and back to primordial time (the center of the basket), which is returned to during all ceremonies (H. Ashley, 7/23/91).[6]

To facilitate a cure, the patient is ritually returned to the exact point in Navajo history when the rite being performed for her or him was originally conducted.

HW When you are a patient, you know, you go back to that, to the beginning. During a ceremony, it goes back to a time in history where that, where that law and order was developed, so you reen-act, you go back to that.

MS OK.

HW And then, you place yourself back, back at that time.

MS Like the first underworld?

HW Yes.

MS That far back?

HW Yes. Well, different periods in time, in history.

MS OK. . . . So, do you go back to the time in history when the person that is often referred to as the hero of the text that is in-volved with the ceremony—

HW Yes.

MS to when those events occurred?

HW Yes!

MS So, if it's like a Naayéé'jí ceremony then it goes back to when Monster Slayer was actually fighting the monsters and things like that?

HW Yes.

MS With the Kinaaldá, they go back to the time when . . .

HW Changing Woman.

MS Changing Woman, OK, I understand that.

HW Yeah, you go back to that. (Harry Walters, Tsaile, Arizona, 8/10/93)

In this context, analogies are drawn between the Diyin Dine'é for whom the ceremony was first performed and the patient for whom it is currently being conducted.

HOOGHAN

At the rim of the place of emergence, Talking God directed First Man and First Woman in the construction of a hooghan (Mindeleff 1898:489). As in the case of baskets, the living elements moisture, air, substance, heat, and vibration were formulated to construct hooghan, whose structure, process, and use followed the paradigms established in the construction of the world. The four main support poles were constructed of the ntł'iz associated with each of the cardinal directions (Aronilth 1985:181). Each quadrant of the hooghan is referred to as the realm or world of a particular female member of the Diyin Dine'é, and the associated pole

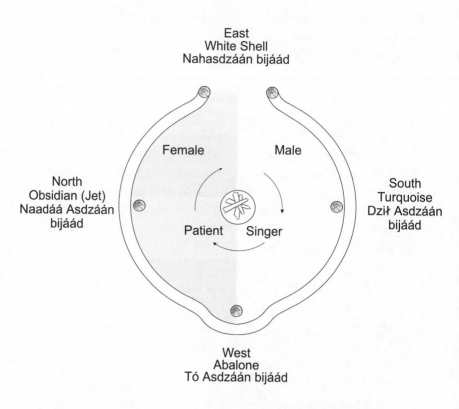

East
White Shell
Nahasdzáán bijáád

North
Obsidian (Jet)
Naadáá Asdzáán
bijáád

Female

Male

Patient   Singer

South
Turquoise
Dził Asdzáán
bijáád

West
Abalone
Tó Asdzáán bijáád

Figure 4. Floor plan of a *hooghan,* the traditional Navajo home. Drawing by Greg Schwarz.

is referred to as that woman's leg. The eastern pole, constructed of white shell, was set first. It is referred to as Nahasdzáán *bijáád,* "Earth Woman's leg." The southern pole, constructed of turquoise, was set second. It is referred to as Dził Asdzáán bijáád, "Mountain Woman's leg." The western pole, constructed of aba-lone, was set third. It is referred to as Tó Asdzáán bijáád, "Water Woman's leg." The northern pole, constructed of obsidian, was set fourth. It is referred to as Naadą́ą́' Asdzáán bijáád, "Corn Woman's leg" (Haile 1942:47; Aronilth 1985: 178; Jett and Spencer 1981:22–23). Last, a fifth pole was set next to the east-ern pole to demarcate the doorway, which must always face east (fig. 4).

The Diyin Dine'é instructed the Navajo in the construction of two styles of hooghan, *hooghan bikạ',* the "male hooghan," and *hooghan ba'ááe,* the "female hooghan."[7] Hooghan bikạ' were originally designed to be used exclusively for praying, singing, making plans, and ceremonial purposes, while hooghan ba'ááe were originally designed to be used as places for children to be born and nurtured in, as well as locations in which families might eat and rest (Aronilth 1985:

179–81). The distinctive shapes of male and female hooghan were modeled after the two central mountains of Navajo sacred geography. The peaked roof of hooghan bikạ' mirrors the profile of Ch'óol'į́'į́, where Changing Woman was found, and the more gently rounded roof of hooghan ba'ááD is an image of Dziłná'oodiłii (Williamson 1984:152; Nabokov and Easton 1989:326).

Modern hooghan are modeled on the prototypical forms constructed by the Diyin Dine'é, but the fundamental concepts governing shape, directional orientation, and order are reinterpreted with accessible materials such as wood. After a suitable site has been found, a sacrifice is made to Asdzáán Nádleehé, as the inner being of the earth. Trees are cut to form the poles, and other building materials are gathered. Two poles are laid on the ground tip to tip and a circle is drawn around them. The ground within this circle is excavated six to twelve inches down to form a level floor. The four main support poles are set in their proper places following the cosmologically prescribed sunwise order—east, south, west, and north. As in the case of the sumac rods used in basket construction, particular attention is given to the trajectory of growth. Special care is taken to stand the hooghan poles up in the direction in which they grew (Aronilth 1985:180). Ntł'iz, corresponding to the materials used for each pole in the prototypical hooghan, are placed in the bottoms of the postholes. Accordingly, white shell is placed in the eastern posthole as that pole is raised, turquoise in the southern posthole, abalone in the western posthole, and obsidian in the northern posthole (Williamson 1984:160; Nabokov and Easton 1989:327).

The newly constructed hooghan, consisting of two of the fundamental elements—moisture and substance—is incomplete and cannot be used until a Hooghan Da'ashdlishígíí, House Blessing ceremony, is performed. The new hooghan is animated when it acquires air, vibration, and heat during this ceremony. It is imbued with the breath of life (air and vibration) through song and prayer, and it attains the substance of heat as a fire is lit at its center.[8] After this ceremony, male and female hooghan are alive and ready for full life cycles. In the words of Wilson Aronilth:

> *A male hooghan has a mind, thought, thinking, body, spirit and soul like us. It can see, feel, think, hear and grow like us. It has love and respect like us. It wants to be kept clean, not dirty. This male hooghan doesn't use bad thoughts, [bad] feelings and dirty language, so we were told to use good wisdom, good thoughts, good language inside of this hooghan, not talk about someone in a bad way. (Aronilth 1985:180)*

Female hooghan have special roles during their life cycles because they are considered to be mothers (Aronilth 1985:183). Earth Woman and Mountain

Woman, associated with the eastern and southern quadrants of the hooghan, respectively, represent the sources of building materials needed to provide shelter. Water Woman and Corn Woman, associated with the western and northern quadrants, represent the sources of sustenance needed by the inhabitants (Jett and Spencer 1981:23). As Wilson Aronilth explains:

> *A female hooghan is our mother. . . . A female hooghan has a mind like us. It can feel, see and grow like we do. It has love and feelings like us. For this reason, sometimes if you go away from home, somewhere to work or go to school, maybe for two weeks or over a month, or a year, the feeling, the spirit of the home will miss you. Probably you will feel the same way. Time comes when you come home, this home is really glad to see you, so will you. . . . Also when you are inside this home, be kind, show respect towards people, use good words when you talk. Don't criticize your relatives and friends from inside of your home. . . . This home doesn't feel good when it is dirty and not kept clean. It doesn't like it when you use bad words inside it. This home provides a place for you to sleep and rest and eat and enjoy yourself, just like the way your [birth] mother takes care of you. (Aronilth 1985:183)*

To show respect for one's hooghan mother, one must follow strict rules governing movement within her. Tradition dictates that upon entering, all persons must move within the space sunwise—east, south, west, north. And they must follow rules governing the use of interior space in certain contexts. Hooghan interiors are never subdivided physically, but they are subdivided socially. The south side of the interior is prescribed as male, and the north as female. Cooking, weaving, and other domestic chores were traditionally completed in the area designated by gender (Jett and Spencer 1981:22–23).[9] During a ceremony, the religious practitioner sits on the right-hand side of the patient, who occupies the northwestern quadrant of the interior space (Lamphere 1969:288; and see fig. 4). These positions remain constant regardless of the sex or gender of either the patient or the religious practitioner (Thomas, 2/12/92).

Formerly, properly constructed hooghan were the only places that could be "sanctified" for ceremonial use (Haile 1942:45). Hooghan remain the location of choice for ceremonials, and most families maintain one for such occasions even when the majority of their members live in modern housing. Most hooghan constructed today are of the female variety and are used for ceremonial as well as domestic purposes. If a family chooses to use a residential hooghan for a ceremony, articles related to domestic activities—looms, weaving tools, cooking equipment, and so forth—are temporarily removed. Beds, couches, and tables are removed or rearranged to shift the layout of the interior space from domestic to ceremonial. Accordingly, single mattresses or mats are placed in the southwestern quadrant for the singer and in the northwestern quadrant for the patient to sit upon. Pillows, blankets, and mats are placed around the walls on the north and south sides for family members and visitors to sit on during the ceremony.[10]

When hooghan are not available or convenient because of road conditions, ill health, or other reasons, ceremonies are held in alternate structures. Regardless of the type of structure employed, participants adhere rigidly to Navajo cultural rules governing the sanctification of space before commencement of a ceremony and the use of sunwise movements within the sanctified space for the duration of the ceremony. The shapes of modern dwellings and the placement of fixtures such as doorways and wood-burning stoves necessitate minor adjustments to this system on a case-by-case basis.[11]

The structural principles hooghan share with other persons are revealed in the processes of their construction and use, which follow ritually prescribed tenets. Owing to these shared principles, the Navajo hooghan is a homologue of the larger world, mirroring the orientation of all Navajo cosmology (see fig. 3). The attributes of hooghan persons make them physical representations of Navajo cultural conceptions governing the organization and use of space. As such, the physical attributes of hooghan correlate directly with attributes of the Navajo universe. This correlation is demonstrated in the following ways.

Both the universe and the hooghan share a circular, domelike shape dominated by the four cardinal directions. The sunken floor and slightly spherical roof of the hooghan correspond to Navajo images of the earth and the sky. At the center of the hooghan's ceiling is the smoke hole. This is his or her breathing hole, from which prayers emerge (Griffin-Pierce 1992:92). The placement of this opening corresponds to *yá ałníí,* the "zenith of the sky." At the center of the floor is the fire pit, the placement of which corresponds to *ni ałníí,* the "nadir of the earth." The zenith is believed to be a hole in the sky, and the nadir is considered to be the center of the earth, through which the Diyin Dine'é emerged (Pinxten et al. 1983: 10–11). The hooghan's eastward-facing doorway is its "way out." Furthermore, the ritually correct direction of movement within a hooghan—sunwise, or east, south, west, and north—correlates with the sun's daily movements.

CRADLES

Like baskets and hooghan, *'awééts'ááł,* cradles, are constructed from the primordial elements and share structure with all Navajo persons. Cradles made today of cedar and oak are modeled after the first cradle found with Changing Woman. When found, she was strapped into a cradle made of rainbows, lightning, and

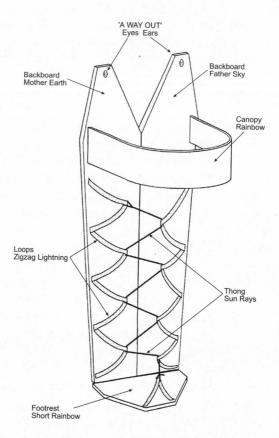

'A WAY OUT'
Eyes Ears

Backboard
Mother Earth

Backboard
Father Sky

Canopy
Rainbow

Loops
Zigzag Lightning

Thong
Sun Rays

Footrest
Short Rainbow

Figure 5. The traditional Navajo cradle, or *'awééts'áál*. Drawing by Greg Schwarz.

sunbeams (Fishler 1953:149; Wyman 1970:513). After she was taken to First Woman, Talking God instructed First Man to construct a cradle of wood. The backboards for cradles, which were formerly cut from the branches of a live tree (Ursula Knoki-Wilson, 8/10/92; Walters, 8/18/92), should be split from a single board so that they are mirror images of each other when laid side by side (Sadie Billie, 6/28/92). As is the case with the materials used in constructing baskets and hooghan, particular attention is given to the trajectory of growth in the placement of these boards. Special care is taken to arrange them so that they lie in the direction in which they grew, from the foot of the cradle upward, to parallel the direction in which the child will grow. These materials are animated with song and prayer during the process of construction. The cradle maker sings a song naming each part, from the bottom to the top, as he or she assembles the cradle (Nakai Tso, 8/8/92).

The special significance attributed to each part of the wooden cradle demonstrates that it is a homologue of the Navajo universe (fig. 5). The longitudinal back-board on the left-hand side represents Mother Earth, and the longitudinal back-board on the right-hand side represents Father Sky. The steamed wooden canopy arched over where the child's head will rest represents a protective rainbow (Mustache 1970; Mae Bekis, 8/5/92; N. Tso, 8/8/92; Knoki-Wilson, 8/10/92; Walters, 8/18/92; Sunny Dooley, 8/21/92). Buckskin loops, which are used to lace the child securely in place, run up both sides of the backboards. The loops represent male zigzag lightning, while the thong that is laced through these buckskin loops from top to bottom represents either sunrays (Mustache 1970; Bekis, 8/5/92; N. Tso, 8/8/92; Knoki-Wilson, 8/10/92; Dooley, 8/21/92) or female straight lightning (Walters, 8/18/92). The footrest and the board attached behind the longitudinal backboards under the arched canopy represent short rainbows (Mustache 1970; Bekis, 8/5/92; N. Tso, 8/8/9; Knoki-Wilson, 8/10/92; Walters, 8/18/92; Dooley, 8/21/92). The hole at the top of each longitudinal backboard is a "way out," or, in combination, these holes represent the cradle's eyes (N. Tso, 8/8/92) or ears (Dooley, 8/21/92). Some people believe these holes provide a means for the child to have prophetic vision (Knoki-Wilson, 8/10/92). Altogether, when a child is laced into a cradle, she or he is symbolically nestled in the protection of the Navajo cosmos.

LOOMS

Navajo weavers construct their intricate tapestries on an upright *dah'iistł'ǫ́*, loom. The loom is a powerful ally; together, its shed rods, heddles, batten stick, and other tools enable the weaver to weave textiles to be worn or sold. These woven products can be used to fight off cold, hunger, and poverty (Aronilth 1985: 197–98). The construction of the loom has precedent in Navajo oral history. It is said that

> *Spider Woman instructed the Navajo women how to weave on a loom which Spider Man told them how to make. The crosspoles were made of sky and earth cords, the warp sticks of sunrays, the healds [sic] of rock crystal and sheet lightning. The batten was a sun halo, white shell made the comb. There were four spindles: one a stick of zigzag lightning with a whorl of cannel coal [jet]; one a stick of flash lightning with a whorl of turquoise; a third had a stick of sheet lightning with a whorl of abalone; a rain streamer formed the stick of the fourth, and its whorl was white shell. (Reichard 1968 [1934]: frontispiece)*

As is true for baskets, hooghan, and cradles, all requisite elements of life are present in the loom—moisture in the form of a rain streamer and sky; substance in the form of earth, rock crystal, white shell, jet, turquoise, and abalone; and heat in the form of sunrays, sheet lightning, and zigzag lightning. The loom is animated when it acquires air and vibration from its maker in the process of construction. The maker sings a song and says prayers as he constructs the loom, thereby imbuing the loom with a breath of life.[12] A loom can "see, feel, move, and grow just like all creation. So it is considered holy" (Aronilth 1985:198).

In addition to demonstrating the need for some form of each of the primary elements in the construction of loom persons, the description recorded by Gladys Reichard establishes that looms are homologues of the Navajo world. The directional orientation of the loom is established in the process of use. Looms are assembled so that weavers face east as they sit at the device. This placement orients the loom within the framework of the seven points integral to Navajo cosmology. The top of the loom indicates the zenith of the sky, and the bottom crossbar represents the nadir of the earth. The weaver indicates east with the direction of her or his gaze, the vertical beam on the right indicates south, west is behind the weaver, and the vertical beam on the weaver's left-hand side represents north. Weavers are cautioned to include a "way out," from the center to the right selvage—toward the south—in the design of textiles (Bennett 1974:7–8; Aronilth 1990).[13] Such openings enable a weaver's energies to move on to future undertakings. If a weaver concentrates all of her creative and physical energies on the manufacture of any one textile without including a way out, she risks losing her vision and even her mind (Franciscan Fathers 1910:294).

LIFE CYCLES

> MS Maybe you could tell me a little more about this that you are talking about, transformation? There is no addition, and there is no loss? There is just change?
>
> HA Uh-huh.
>
> MS So are you also saying that there is no static condition, nothing ever just stays the same? . . .
>
> HA Nothing stays the same, everything moves, everything is in a process. That is how the Navajo would say that. They use the seed like if you put it in, the seed in the ground, I mean, and then it grows. That is why they use . . . a corn stalk as an analogy. It will grow to the extent of its life, then the seeds will form. So that is the way that it is in human life, they say. You are actually growing. You are growing, you are growing until your life gets to the full-

ness. But what happens [is], you just go through the transformation. (Hanson Ashley, Shonto, Arizona, 7/27/93)

As Hanson Ashley noted, analogies are frequently drawn between the life cycle of a corn plant and those of other types of persons in the Navajo world. Alluding to creation story episodes in which Changing Woman was found as a corn plant and in which corn played a fundamental role in the construction of the first Nihookáá Dine'é, Harry Walters points out that a direct correlation exists between corn and the human body:

> HW We are corn people. Uh, uh, we are made from corn, this is the tassel, you know the hair. [Holds the hair up at the top of his head].
> MS Hair is like the tassels of the corn?
> HW Yes, and then, uh, the blanket that we wear is the, you know, the shawl that covers you is like the [wraps himself with his arms].
> MS The shawl is like the husk of the corn?
> HW Yes, the husk of the corn. . . . Therefore, when you are having the ceremony, you are never without a blanket. . . . So, uh, corn, when the corn becomes ripe. When it is ready to be eaten then, you know, you use that. (Harry Walters, Tsaile, Arizona, 8/10/93)

Such analogies demonstrate the continual process and change essential to the Navajo world, where all life begins and ends with transformation. On an elementary level, all artifacts are alive because they are constructed of the primordial living elements—moisture, air, substance, heat, and vibration. Furthermore, every individual life cycle is a process of transformation—creation or birth, growth, maturity, decomposition, and reformulation. Despite these similarities, variations in life cycles were readily recognized by the Navajo people with whom I consulted, many of whom pointed out that the primordial living elements take on a special form of life when they are formulated in persons, such as baskets, rugs, songs, feathers, masks, or grinding stones, who are constructed or used for specific purposes. Ultimately, the specific trajectory of transformation evidenced in every individual life is determined by personal knowledge, power, and agency, as well as by the type of person one is.

Like corn, most plants, animals, and humans are born, mature, and die, after which their elements are reformulated into new life forms. But different types of persons—mountains, Diyin Dine'é, sandpaintings, *jish* (medicine bundles), hooghan, cradles—have different types of life cycles.

The sacred mountains have lived continuously since they were constructed by the Diyin Dine'é. Changing Woman, who was alternately found as a corn plant, a corn beetle, an undeveloped embryo, or a child, is born, matures, dies, and is reborn annually, as reflected in the seasonal changes of the earth. A sandpainting is made for a specific segment of a ceremony, after which it is dismantled and its components returned to the earth (Reichard 1950:343–44; Parezo 1983: 14–20; Griffin-Pierce 1992:55–56). A jish is constructed when an apprentice masters a ceremony. When the practitioner discontinues practice of the ceremony, the jish can either be passed on to a new apprentice or dismantled and its elements returned to their sources. Throughout its life cycle, a jish needs regular exercise in the form of ceremonial use. If it is not used, its power declines (Frisbie 1987:103).

Individual hooghan who are regularly maintained by their family members often live for generations. Formerly, hooghan were abandoned only if a family member died inside the dwelling.[14] In the contemporary world, hooghan are frequently disassembled by family members and moved to new locations, or they are dismantled and the parts reused in new dwellings (David Harrison, 8/18/92).[15]

A cradle is constructed shortly after the birth of a child. When the child outgrows the cradle, it is disassembled. Cradle parts are stored until the birth of another child, when they are reassembled for the use of the younger sibling. A cradle can continue to be passed down from sibling to sibling provided each child sustains healthy growth while in the cradle (Kee, 8/3/92). If a woman is not going to have any more children, the cradle is disassembled and the parts are placed outside under the protection of a rock outcropping or in another area where rain and hard wind will not reach them (Sadie Billie 8/8/92).

In addition to variations in individual life cycles, some Navajo experts believe, as Avery Denny explains in the following account, that certain forms of life can exist only within the confines of Navajo sacred geography. To illustrate this point, he proposed two hypothetical situations: What becomes of a song recorded on an audiocassette tape when it is removed from the area demarcated by the sacred mountains? And what becomes of an eagle plume when it is removed from this area after being stolen?

> MS So, what I was trying to find out was, what is it that makes something alive in the Navajo view?
>
> AD OK, hmm, let's say this tape right here. What I am talking [saying] in there is, it sounds alive [chuckles]. In these four sacred mountains, it is. If you listen to it here, it will be alive.
>
> MS Uh-huh.
>
> AD But once you take it out, then it, the "spirit" that is in that song, would all vanish . . . once you leave these four sacred mountains.

And then if I had a feather like this, an eagle plume, like this, and then this is made for me. . . . I talk to this and then this is what I believe. And then this feather would recognize me. . . . It is going to be alive and then we would communicate right here. But if somebody else came along and then took it, steals it. Once it gets in the wrong hands, that, the sacredness or the spirit of that feather, it is going to come back to me. And then this is just going to be, just another old feather. (Avery Denny, Tsaile, Arizona, 10/8/93)

The "spirit" in the song or the feather, which Avery Denny said would return to him if the song or feather was removed from the area demarcated by the sacred mountains, is the inner being, or "breath of life," that animates all Navajo persons. To clarify the significance of the departure of an entity's inner being, I asked what would happen to a basket if it were sold to someone living off the reservation. In response, Denny told me that in his opinion, a basket person could not live after removal from the Navajo sacred geography because its inner being would return to its maker. But, as he adds in the following narrative, such entities are readily reanimated upon their return to Navajo sacred space.

AD There is no life to it, it is just a design. But once it [the basket] goes back into the four sacred mountains . . . it comes back to life. Or, if it was brought back to that woman that wove it, and then that automatically, that spirit is going to go back into it. It would recognize [her, the weaver].

MS What if it was used in a ceremony? But not by the woman that wove it. Would it become alive during the ceremony?

AD Yes. It would be. But once it leaves the ceremony, if it was for a patient, and then that [patient], she would have belief that this is a sacred thing, but then it will, her, the way that she [the weaver] understands this pattern that she did, it will help the patient to heal, too. And then when the medicine man gets it, when the medicine man gets it, it will separate. Just like the weaving part will go back to the lady [the weaver], and then the healing part will go to the patient, but then when it gets into the medicine man, her or his belief is going to go in there. Then it is his [the ceremonial practitioner's]. That is how it works. But then if he [the ceremonial practitioner] takes it to Gallup [New Mexico] to sell it, it [the inner being] comes back to him [the ceremonial practitioner]. This is nothing but a basket, but if somebody else buys it again for a ceremonial purpose, for a reason, for a purpose, when it gets into that ceremonial hooghan, that spirit [inner being] is going to go back in there again.... It works like that [chuckles]. (Avery Denny, Tsaile, Arizona, 10/8/93)

Unlike the basket sold in Gallup, New Mexico, in Avery Denny's example, many nonhuman Navajo persons continue to live when they are removed from their sacred geography, even when they are placed in less than desirable living conditions, such as museum storage rooms or exhibit cases. Alfred Yazzie of Fort Defiance, Arizona, and his wife, Alice, made a special trip to the Field Museum of Natural History's Native American collection in the autumn of 1993 because they had been told that some sacred beings of the Navajo people were confined there. The Yazzies were distressed to find sacred Yé'ii Bicheii (Talking God) masks hanging in a display case and other masks and medicine bundles "imprisoned" in sealed vaults in museum storage areas. "When we saw the sacred masks and the medicine bundles they have locked up here, we were very sad to see them treated this way.... My wife broke down to see these Holy Ones, who are still living, longing for their people. They need to be re-blessed and returned to the Navajo people" (*Navajo Times,* September 23, 1993, p. A-1).[16]

Central to understanding the retention or loss of life in a mask, basket, or other artifact taken outside of Navajo sacred geography are notions of power based on knowledge, purpose, and agency. On an elementary level, the principle of synecdoche dictates that anything which is made or used for a specific purpose is alive insofar as it is an extension of a person with individual agency. But as Hanson Ashley explains in the following narrative, not all things in the Navajo world have agency. Objects such as a cup or a piece of paper have no personal volition or agency; rather, they are only temporarily animated in the process of use by the agency of the individual who is using them.

OK. Like this paper. If you just leave it there, you know, that is it. But once you move it then it becomes alive. Somehow it supports your, [it] supports you in some way. Or maybe I am just fiddling around with this paper, somehow it calms my nervousness, or something is taking place to comfort me. Or let's say if I have a cup here, you know, those are used in some way. It supports me. . . . They are alive, because you are part of that, they are part of you in some way. So the way you see your world, yes they are alive, but it is you that, you have to make it to say that it is alive. . . . And if you separate yourself from it . . . then they are just materialistic. That is it. There is nothing. They are just solid. But if you kind of, if you feel, or you understand, that you are participating in that process and you are part of that, then the understanding is that, yes, they are alive. So it is just a matter of the way that you think about things. (Hanson Ashley, Shonto, Arizona, 7/27/93)

Unlike the cup or the piece of paper in the preceding example, rug, sandpainting, and basket persons, like looms, cradles, and hooghan, are initially imbued with life by their makers during the process of construction. On the basis of the principle of synecdoche, this process forms an inalienable connection between maker and product. Moreover, as Harry Walters points out, an individual artifact can take on a life of its own through use in a ceremonial context.

> HW When it's being manufactured, a part of the artist also goes, they give it, a part of it, you give it, uh, uh, life.
>
> MS Uh-huh. Part of manufacturing is giving it life?
>
> HW Yes. Yeah, giving it life. The same way with weaving a rug. The same way with doing a sandpainting. So there is a strict guidance that you follow in that because a part of you will go into that basket. . . . So you have to make it just right. . . . You don't do things like put it on your head, throw it around, or spin it around like that, because if you do that a part of you is already in there. Even though if the basket is not finished. A part of you is still, is in there. It will have, because you are working on it, you and the basket are the same. Your inner being is also part of [it], [your inner being] is going into that basket.
>
> MS So part of your wind goes into the thing that you are creating?
>
> HW Yes.
>
> MS And then does the basket get its own wind later? Or does it just have part of your wind?
>
> HW Yeah . . . after it is used, then it becomes the medicine man's or whatever. Then it has a life of its own.
>
> MS Does it acquire its own wind?
>
> HW Yes.
>
> MS That is very helpful. (Harry Walters, Tsaile, Arizona, 8/10/93)

Ultimately, degrees of power based on knowledge, purpose, and agency determine whether an entity can live only within Navajo sacred geography—the basket in Avery Denny's example—or whether it can live anywhere—the masks and medicine bundles at the Field Museum. For, as Harry Walters noted, artifacts, such as the basket in his example, acquire "a life of their own" when they are imbued with knowledge through the process of being used in a ceremonial context.

Navajo persons, such as this hypothetical basket or the masks and medicine bundles in the Field Museum, have personal power based on knowledge, which gives them agency and volition. They have power and agency because they are Navajo persons who are integral to ceremonial healing. In the following narrative, Walters contrasts a ballpoint pen with a pair of grinding stones to illustrate that although everything in the Navajo world is made up of the same fundamental living elements, not all things are equally important. Things made for a ritual purpose are imbued with power and agency because the process of their construction "represents a ceremonial order . . . a history" (Walters, 8/10/93).[17]

HW Now, this pen will not [have power and agency]. Even though it is [constructed of the fundamental elements]. . . . It is not important, you know?

MS Yeah?

HW It is important, yes, but not something that is used in a ceremony. Something that has been set in motion . . . by the Holy Beings to be a part of a ceremony, or a teaching, [or] a healing process. Those are considered to be more sacred.

MS OK.

HW Because there are some history, philosophy, art, healing, all of those [which] are part of that. But basically, everything has an inner being, you know, the rocks, petals, everything. But there are some things that have been used, for example, the stone back there [points to a set of grinding stones].

MS Uh-huh.

HW Now before it was shaped like that if it was just a stone. It was just a stone. It had an inner being. But it has been touched. It has been altered. It has been made, you know, a part of. What do you call it? It has been given a special inner being to serve a purpose.

MS OK. So all things have an inner being, but things that have been used in a ritual context, a ceremonial context, in an important context are given an additional inner being?

HW Yes.

MS Like that stone or a basket or a sandpainting?

HW Well, not an additional inner being, they always have an inner being . . . but they have been initiated in a special way. . . . Its power has been harnessed to do something that is to be respected. It can be used for healing. It also, at the same time because of the male and the female thing, the warrior and the peace, it can also be destructive. So, that is . . . where they take extra care because the peaceful side, there is no problem, it is the naayéé'jí side. It also acquired that side. (Harry Walters, Tsaile, Arizona, 8/10/93)

Artifacts made for specific ritual purposes are imbued with additional power during the process of initiation and use. In the act of initiation, these persons are infused and entrusted with the particular type of knowledge associated with the ceremony for which they were made or in which they are used. This knowledge becomes a permanent aspect of the person. Such knowledge equals power, which gives agency and volition. Because of this association, elderly Navajo are reluctant to give away their hard-earned knowledge; it equals power for them just as it does for the various types of persons constructed by humans for ritual purposes and imbued with power during initiation and use—baskets, jish, masks, grinding stones.

No Navajo will ever tell all that he or she knows about any one topic to any one individual. To do so is risky. To Navajo people, knowledge is a source of life-enriching and life-sustaining power, because in the Navajo world an individual's knowledge can be used to exert power on reality. "Any particular item of anyone's knowledge is therefore a part of that person's power. Transfer of knowledge is, by consequence, a giving away, and so a loss, of power" (Pinxten and Farrer 1990:249).

As a result of the direct relationship of knowledge to power, a diversity of opinions exists regarding what, when, where, how, and for how much various types of information should be shared among Navajo people, as well as with outsiders. As Sadie Billie notes in the following summary of her father's views on the sharing of knowledge, a fee of some form—livestock, jewelry, cash—must accompany every exchange of knowledge in the Navajo world as a form of protection for all parties involved.[18]

He wanted to say that when something is shared like this, he said even in the past . . . I guess not everybody was the same. They all knew differently. And let's say this person wanted certain information from another person that they didn't know, he said that when they exchanged things like that, he said there was always a fee involved. He said, it's not just now. . . . At that time he said it was like livestock or jewelry and stuff. He said it's not new to do that, he said even with small ceremonies when they conduct these, even if it was your relative [who conducted the ceremony], you still had to pay them. And I guess it plays as a protection for that person that is performing the ceremony or telling the story. (The words of Nakai Tso, paraphrased by Sadie Billie, Tsaile, Arizona, 7/10/91)[19]

The protection attained through the exchange of valuables—livestock, jewelry, cash—for knowledge extends beyond the individuals directly involved, to their families (Ruth Roessel, 7/26/91).

Time and again, Navajo consultants reiterated that giving away knowledge, even under the protection of such exchanges, shortens life. When Wesley Thomas and I approached Archie Begay of Upper Greasewood, Arizona, for an interview in August 1993, Mr. Begay refused. Hastiin Begay said he did not want to share his stories because to do so would shorten his life. He noted, as support for his belief, that all the "medicine people" who told stories at Navajo Community College in Tsaile, Arizona, during the early 1970s had since passed on (Begay, 8/11/93). Clearly, to Archie Begay, knowledge is one power that keeps him alive.

When I asked an elder from Ganado, Arizona, to tell me the story he had learned about the designs on the ceremonial basket, he became agitated. As he explains in the following excerpt, his understanding of the basket cannot be shared in full because it has personal significance; it is knowledge that sustains his life.

> We have our stories. In it we have prayers, songs, white corn, blue corn, mixed corn. We have pollen from each of these corns which we offer. We are made of it. First, Changing Woman and the Holy People did it. Created us. That was the reason why our prayers were strong and powerful. The Blessing Way ceremonial prayers. The prayers of Christians seem to have no pattern and are presented without purposes. The Navajo prayers included turquoise and white shell is mentioned, they are interwoven into the prayers. That is how we prayed and sang. We have left it behind. . . . I have to quit here. We are talking about something I was asked and had no intention of talking about. Many people have asked me for this particular information. This information is a portion which sustains my life as an individual. That is the reason why we cannot continue with it. . . . That will be all. (The words of an anonymous elder, Ganado, Arizona, 7/10/91, translated by Wesley Thomas)

After making this statement, the elder abruptly ended the interview. I was disappointed, remembering the effort his granddaughter had made in arranging it, but, understanding the ramifications that such an exchange could have on him—transfer of knowledge equals a loss of life-enriching and life-sustaining power—I did not press him to continue.

Navajo elders such as this man from the Ganado area prize the agency and volition given by knowledge of the Navajo philosophical system because of their understandings of themselves as parts of a larger community of life sharing in a special form of existence established in the charter between the Navajo and the Holy People. They acknowledge that all members of this community of life are constructed of the same fundamental elements, share structure, and relate to each other as kin. This association is exquisitely demonstrated in the elder's explanation about the strength and power of Navajo prayers. As he points out, Navajo prayers have special power for Navajo people precisely because the elements from which Navajo people and all other forms of life in the Navajo world are made—substance (in the form of turquoise, white shell, and pollen), heat, moisture, air, and vibration (in the form of voice)—are interwoven into the prayers.

Changing Woman, in constructing the Nihookáá Dine'é, followed the fundamental principles governing the construction of all life in the Navajo world. As a result, the human body is a homologue of the Navajo universe. It is composed of the same primordial elements as all other Navajo persons, and it shares the same structure, including sunwise direction and complementarity.

FOUR WINDS

—Pauline Escudero Shafer (Apache)

Asleep . . .
Surely there was a thing
to remember . . . turning skies
red rock
or the Wind

Wake
Begin to recollect
The rush of the Mother comes
from the soles up . . . Breathe
this rocking heat
as it vibrates the world into being
Breaking crystal silence
Ringing colors
Ringing time
Making all things spin outward
Shaking free
from the inside out
Finding hands to touch prickly brush
Feeling sand between the fingertips
Conceiving each step
in perfect harmony

Until a song rises up whirling
a breath of four Winds
and rain
Weaving blue skies red echoes
of red stone black night
dotted with white corn flecks
Weaving these strands over
and under

To finally throw open fast
above you
and cradle you my child
with these rainbow dreams
Which are not dreams but
a way home
that begins with the Wind
from the soles
up

CHAPTER IV

THE CULTURAL CONSTRUCTION OF THE NIHOOKÁÁ DINE'É

A complete individual is from the sole of his moccasins, kétł'ááh, you know, kéyah, is land, kéyah, earth. Kétł'ááh means more the attachment, like the earth to you. It is a word that is used with affection like a mother and infant relation, you know. So this is important, it is a connection between you and your mother. This is why little children, you don't slap them on their feet. You don't tickle them on the soles of the feet, it is a vital point, it is where, it connects you to your mother. . . . So, the prayers always say . . . from the bottom or soles of your feet. And then all the way up to the point where my feather emerges. Meaning the strand of hair where the swirl is like that, that is the top of your head. And then so, they take that and then they attach a feather to it. So, from the soles of your feet to the strand of hair that you attach a feather to, it makes a complete individual. (Harry Walters, Tsaile, Arizona, 8/12/93).

Navajo people are explicitly linked to Mother Earth and Father Sky. The complete Navajo person is made up of several integrated parts: the physical outer form, the inner form, the body surface, the body print, the power of movement, garments, hair, the "anchoring cord," and the "feather of life." The physical outer form is animated by the inner form, which is made up of intertwined winds. The individual Navajo person is connected to Mother Earth by his or her body print and "anchoring cord," and to Father Sky by the "feather of life" at the top of his or her head.

The first Nihookáá Dine'é were constructed on the earth's surface out of the primordial elements used to construct all life in this world—moisture, air, substance, heat, and vibration in the form of sound (language)—according to the paradigms established in the construction of the world at the place of emergence. In addition to these elements, powerful influences linked to the four cardinal directions and to an individual's clans are involved in the conception, growth, and development of every Navajo. The structural features shared by all persons in the Navajo world, first evidenced in the construction of baskets, hooghan, cradles, looms, and the first Nihookáá Dine'é by the Diyin Dine'é, continue in the action and process of contemporary living—developing, thinking, and being. These features are attention to the trajectory of growth, a pathway, or "way out," that enables factors to move from inside to outside, and a binary division of the person that distinguishes left (male) from right (female). Directional orientation is evidenced in attention to the trajectory of growth during manipulations of the body in ceremonial contexts, as well as by the sunwise movement of Holy Winds entering the body and by human thought and actions in a variety of contexts. The need for a "way out" is evidenced in ceremonial contexts as well as in day-to-day activities involving creative processes.

THE CONSTRUCTION OF THE FIRST NIHOOKÁÁ DINE'É

From the beginning of the basket, when the earth was created, when the universe was created, when the sun was created, when Changing Woman came into being, turquoise basket existed, white shell basket existed. They were used then. Obsidian basket and crystal basket were used. The Holy People used these baskets to create us. We were created as the first Earth Surface People. The Diné. . . . Changing Woman, who was found on the top of Ch'óol'íí, created us. After her Kinaaldá and after she gave birth to the twins, after the twins killed the monsters and other beings. . . . Changing Woman and the Holy People did it. Created us. (The words of an anonymous elder, Chinle, Arizona, 7/10/91, translated by Wesley Thomas)

Nihookáá Dine'é consider Changing Woman, the inner form of the earth, to be their mother because she constructed them here on the earth's surface from her own flesh, corn, and the "hard goods" (ntł'iz) associated with each of the cardinal points in Navajo cosmology.[1] Navajo oral historians recount several different processes of generation that brought these beings into existence, including transformation of figurines or corn, asexual creation from Changing Woman's flesh or a mixture of other materials or both, and, eventually, heterosexual reproduction, the means by which Nihookáá Dine'é continue to multiply. Systematic comparison of these seemingly disparate generative processes reveals threads of continuity that can be used to explain Navajo beliefs about the makeup and functioning of the human body. The fundamental living elements—moisture, air, substance, heat, and vibration—take a variety of forms in individual accounts.

> The Holy People are the ones who planted us here on the Earth by their handiwork. They did this by using their great powers in planting the first seed of White Corn and Yellow Corn. Through the image of White Corn a male being was made. Through the image of Yellow Corn a female being was made. The Holy People also had with them the four sacred minerals. With the seed of white shell, turquoise, abalone shell and black jet, the human body was made. These four minerals were used for creating all parts of the human body. We are a seed, a plant, in the eyes of the Holy People. We are the flesh and the seed of the Holy People. (Aronilth 1990:33).

In most versions of this portion of Navajo oral history, the substance used in the creation of humans was Changing Woman's own flesh, rubbed from the surface of her breast, back, shoulders, sides, and arms (Matthews 1994 [1897]:148; Franciscan Fathers 1910:356; Fishler 1953:91; Wyman 1970:447, 633; Yazzie 1971:74). Other accounts document the use of substance composed of a mixture of Changing Woman's skin wastes and ground white shell (O'Bryan 1956:166), a mixture of Changing Woman's flesh and the power from the primordial medicine bundle and the corn stalk (Wyman 1970:239), or a mixture of ground white shell and corn of all colors (Goddard 1933:168).

According to these accounts, Changing Woman rubbed skin wastes from various portions of her body and molded this substance, alone or in combination with ground corn and ntł'iz, into soft cylindrical or round forms. For example, in an account told to Aileen O'Bryan by Old Man Buffalo Grass in 1928, "the White Bead Woman wished now to have her own people. . . . She took a white bead stone and ground it to powder. She put this powder on her breasts and between her shoulders, over her chest and on her back; and when this powder became moist she rubbed it off her body and rolled it between her fingers and on the palm of her hand. From time to time a little ball dropped to the ground. She wrapped these little balls in black clouds. They arose as people" (O'Bryan 1956:166–67).

Alternatively, the first Nihookáá Dine'é are said to have been constructed of ears of corn or figurines of ntł'iz. In the following account, Nakai Tso tells how the first humans were constructed from turquoise and white shell figurines.

> It is retold that White Shell Woman made four persons. She placed them and spoke a word for each person. They spoke. . . . The sun entered the house of White Shell Woman. People tell these stories.

The sun was not aware that he entered the house of White Shell Woman. He picked up the tobacco container and prepared the pipe, then he lit the tobacco. While he was smoking, he heard this song. [Sings part of a song]. The song was sung by White Shell Woman when the sun entered her home. . . . I do not want to be accused of making up stories. Here White Shell Woman prepared and rolled a "cigarette" then she smoked it. The sun, all this time, just watched her. She smoked her "cigarette." The prepared four, turquoise and white shell figurines, were near her. She spoke to the figurines. They rose up. She spoke for them. "I am not returning, I am staying here," she said. "You four will return to where I came from. You will become humans, so you, my children, have to return to where I came from," it is said. The figurines arose and were sent on their way. (The words of Nakai Tso, Tsaile, Arizona, 8/8/92, translated by Wesley Thomas)

In other accounts, the first humans are said to have been constructed of substance consisting of ears of white and yellow corn (Matthews 1994 [1897]:136), a turquoise figurine in humanlike form coupled with white corn and a white shell figurine in humanlike form coupled with yellow corn (O'Bryan 1956:102–3), or the white shell and abalone shell images of corn mentioned in the following account.

Then First Man and First Woman . . . made an image of a man of the ear of white shell corn, rounded at the end, with which First Man came into existence. Then they made an image of a woman of the yellow ear of corn made of abalone shell, rounded at the end, with which First Woman came into existence. . . . Then he [First Man] began to sing and in the morning they began to move and breathe. The newly created pair couldn't get up, however. They invited the holy ones in vain. Finally, they sent messengers to the Sky with hard substances [ntł'iz] as a fee. Then smoke [Holy Wind] came and blowing through the new pair, passed each other and came out. This made the body hairs and air came out (the pores of the skin). Six women and six men, twelve all together stood up. Thus Navajo were made. (Goddard 1933:146–47)

In these accounts, heat is introduced to the process of creation as a result of either the friction of grinding, carving, or otherwise shaping figurines (Goddard 1933:146–47; O'Bryan 1956:102–3; Nakai Tso, 8/8/92) or the friction of rubbing epidermal substance off Changing Woman's body and molding it (Matthews 1994 [1897]:148; Franciscan Fathers 1910:356; Fishler 1953:91; O'Bryan

1956:102; Wyman 1970:447, 633; Yazzie 1971:74), grinding it (O'Bryan 1956:166–67), or mixing it with other materials (Goddard 1933:168; Wyman 1970:239). Heat might also be introduced as the warmth of sunlight (Goddard 1933:143–47) or of smoke (N. Tso, 8/8/92). Moisture is introduced when the primordial forms are covered by, or wrapped in, a variety of different manifestations of moisture, such as "the four clouds and the four vapors" (O'Bryan 1956:103), "a dark cloud" and "dark fog" (Wyman 1970:633), "black clouds" (O'Bryan 1956:166–67), or "a layer of rising haze" (Wyman 1970:240).

The first humans were animated by the air and vibration of Changing Woman's breath (Wyman 1970:633), by her voice in the form of speech (Franciscan Fathers 1910:356; Wyman 1970:448; N. Tso, 8/8/92) or in the form of song (Goddard 1933:168), by the combined song of Changing Woman and Talking God (Fishler 1953:91), by the combined song of Changing Woman, Talking God, and other Diyin Dine'é (Fishler 1953:91), or by Holy Winds (Matthews 1994 [1897]:137; Goddard 1933:147; O'Bryan 1956:102–3). The Holy Winds slipped between the buckskins, blankets, or sheets of moisture covering the modeled Nihookáá Dine'é and entered their bodies. Talking God raised these coverings several times to check on the progress of their animation.

> *Once again did he raise the top skin and look in. But this time he did not lower it. This time he held the two skins apart for a longer while. For this time he saw that the white ear of corn had been changed into a man. And he saw this time that the yellow ear had likewise become a woman.*
>
> *It was the wind that had given life to these two Nihookáá Dine'é, or five-fingered Earth Surface People. . . .*
>
> *Nítch'i the Wind had entered between the heads of the two buckskins and had made his way through all four legs of both, thus transforming those ears of corn into two mortals.*
>
> *It is the same wind that gives those of us who dwell in the world today the breath we breathe.*
>
> *The trail of that very same wind can actually be seen in our fingertips to this day. That very same wind has likewise created our ancestors ever since.*
>
> *That very same wind continues to blow inside of us until we die.*
> (Zolbrod 1984:287)

The multiple levels of understanding presented in these diverse accounts reveal that the Nihookáá Dine'é are simultaneously constructed of Changing Woman's flesh, ntł'iz, and corn. Regardless of what form the fundamental elements—moisture, air, substance, and heat—take in individual accounts, on the most abstract of the twelve levels of knowledge inherent to Navajo philosophy, all humans can be interpreted as being constructed of the same fundamental elements, linked by metaphoric structures (including particular directionality and complementarity), permeated by vibration in the form of sound or movement, and possessed of the same seven senses and anatomical components as all other persons in the Navajo world—birds, corn plants, mountains, cradles, corn beetles, or homes.

The first Nihookáá Dine'é were not made to live as individuals; rather, they immediately were matched and paired to found the Navajo social order. It is generally agreed that Changing Woman selected men and women from the first Nihookáá Dine'é to live as husband and wife and thus established the four original clans of the Navajo and the practice of clan exogamy (Matthews 1994 [1897]: 148; Reichard 1950:28; O'Bryan 1956:167; Wyman 1970:458, 634; Yazzie 1971:74; Aronilth 1985:83). Many accounts, such as the following version told by Wilson Aronilth, detail the specific part of Changing Woman's body from which each clan was formed.

> As she rubbed the upper portion of her right breast, she created a female. Then she rubbed the upper portion of her left breast and made a male. They became the Towering House Clan [Kinyaa'áanii]. She made them brothers and sisters and to be related as a clan.
>
> Then Changing Woman rubbed her back and made a man from her right side. As she rubbed her left side of her back, she made a woman. This created pair became the Near The Water Clan [Tó'áhaní]. They became related as one clan.
>
> Next, Changing Woman rubbed her arms and the upper part of her right arm became a man while the underside of her arm down to her waist became a female. These became the Bitter Water Clan [Tódích'íí'nii]. She paired these two to be related by clan as brothers and sisters.
>
> Finally, Changing Woman rubbed her left arm on the upper part and formed a man. Next, she rubbed the underside of her left arm all the way down to her waist and formed a woman. These became the Mud Clan [Hashtł'ishnii] and these two were then related as brothers and sisters by clan.
>
> This came to pass that Changing Woman then made four pairs by rubbing her flesh from various parts of her body, switching them around and matching them until she laid them down as man and wife. (Aronilth 1985:83)

There is no consensus in the various accounts of this episode about exactly which clans originated from Changing Woman's flesh, or which clans originated from which parts of her body, but members of the clans believed to have come from her flesh take special pride in their sense of being members of an original clan (Wyman 1970:34).[2] Once paired, these men and women were directed to go forth to where Changing Woman's sacred cornfields were in the east, within the sacred mountains of Dinétah, and increase their numbers through heterosexual reproduction (Aronilth 1985:83). As a result, the creation of Nihookáá Dine'é in the contemporary world begins with the traditional Navajo wedding ceremony, sexual intercourse, and conception.

THE FORMATION OF NIHOOKÁÁ DINE'É
IN THE CONTEMPORARY WORLD

Our lives are like the corn plant—the seed is planted in the earth and the power of the sunlight is what makes you grow. When conception occurs, the female represents the earth and the male represents the universe. When they come in union during the sexual act it is sort of reliving the whole plan of creation. So that is how they teach it. The seed is planted and the power of the sun and the universe is what makes it grow. (Ursula Knoki-Wilson, Chinle, Arizona, 8/10/92)

Navajo people understand and explain creation and conception both metaphorically and physiologically. They use the metaphorical accounts to go beyond simple descriptions of physical or biological events and to convey the complexities of Navajo philosophy. Ursula Knoki-Wilson uses the corn plant metaphor to explain human conception. This account acknowledges the Navajo sense of intimate connection to, and dependence on, the universe. Navajo people consider every individual act of human reproduction a reenactment of the creation of the universe.

We believe that we come out of Mother Earth. From the Father Sky. They are facing one another, in between there we are the child of the Holy People, and in there we have mountains that we live by. That is our body and soul, that is our flesh and blood, too. And then there is the water. Nahasdzáán áádóó Tó Asdzáán [Mother Earth and Water Woman], that is how we, we believe that that is where we come from. Áádóó, eiya ei Nílch'i dóó [and, the wind also]. We have the spirits, the four spirits of the four directions, that would be like dawn, midday, evening, and then darkness. The spirits in those areas and then the spring, summer, fall, and winter. In these areas there is a spirit of the Holy People. These Holy

People that is what gives us life. . . . The Holy People made it so people can be born and live the full extent of their life as a human being. We have 102 years old, that is how far we have to go. So, there is a road of life. It is set aside for us that on these sacred mountains we are going to go on our road of life to make our complete cycle. (Avery Denny, Chinle, Arizona, 8/11/93)

First Woman designed the means for human reproduction—so people could be born and live the full extent of their lives as human beings—at the same time that she created sexual desire to ensure that men and women could attract each other for a lifetime. "Then she made a penis of turquoise. She rubbed loose cuticle from the man's breast. This she mixed with yucca fruit. She made a clitoris of red shell and put it inside the vagina. She rubbed loose cuticle from a woman's breast and mixed it with yucca fruit. She put that inside the turquoise penis. She combined herbs and waters of various kinds which should be for producing pregnancy" (Goddard 1933:138–39).

Despite references to reproductive fluids such as "herbs and waters of various kinds" in many oral accounts on the subject, the Navajo theory of human conception was never fully explicated by any of the numerous prior ethnologists who wrote on this topic (Leighton and Kluckhohn 1947:1; Bailey 1950:18; Reichard 1950:29–30; Witherspoon 1975:24). Indeed, fundamental misinterpretations have been promulgated in the anthropological literature over the years. In one of the earliest accounts of Navajo views of the process of human conception, Dorothea Leighton and Clyde Kluckhohn wrote that "according to Navajo belief, conception results from the union of the male fluid with menstrual blood or other secretions of the female. Most Navahos seem to feel that menstrual blood is the principle basis for the fetus" (1947:1).

Leighton and Kluckhohn's findings were corroborated by Flora Bailey, who conducted the most complete investigation to date on Navajo sex beliefs and practices.[3] In 1950 she noted that her consultants offered a variety of explanations in answer to the question "What starts the baby?" or "What is the cause of conception?" Yet Bailey saw as a "common core" running through each explanation "the fact that intercourse is necessary, and that there is some important connection between menstrual blood and conception" (Bailey 1950:18). In publications following Bailey's pioneering study, Leighton and Kluckhohn's phrase "or other secretions" was dropped, and the Navajo theory of human conception was simplified to "the man's water (semen) and woman's blood (menstrual) make the baby" (Witherspoon 1975:24).

More recent analyses of native theories of conception and of the significant roles various substances can play in the construction of the body or individual body parts (Poole 1981:126; Battaglia 1990:38) served as models in my own research as I developed questions about the Navajo theory of human conception—a theory involving "fluids" other than those recognized in biomedical models of human conception.[4] Contemporary Navajo educators and philosophers believe that human conception occurs as a result of the mixing of the reproductive fluids— "herbs and waters of various kinds"—during sexual intercourse between a man and a woman. The sex of a child is determined by the type of fluid the 'íígąsh, or sperm, contacts in the mother's womb. Combining 'íígąsh with tó ałtahnáschíín results in a male child, and combining it with tó biyáázh results in a female child (Walters, 8/18/92). Tó ałtahnáschíín, "all different kinds of waters come together," is identified as male, while tó biyáázh, "child of water," is identified as female (Aronilth 1990:33).[5] If a male child is conceived, the 'atsągstíín, or the embryo from conception to birth, and the placenta will lodge on the left side of the mother's uterus; a female embryo and placenta will lodge on the right side. This positioning is believed to be virtually infallible; indeed, traditional Navajo midwives determined the sex of a child by ascertaining to which side of the mother's womb the placenta was attached.[6]

The Navajo theory of conception clearly distinguishes the act of conception from the development of the fetus in the womb. After conception, blood from the mother's body and both types of fluid contribute to the child's growth and development in the womb. The growing fetus is nurtured by blood supplied by the mother—the blood that would have become menstrual fluids if conception had not occurred (Knoki-Wilson, 8/10/92; Walters, 8/18/92). In addition, tó ałtahnáschíín and tó biyáázh each play a fundamental role in the proper development of the fetus, for they foster the development of contrasting aspects of the person—male/female, warrior/peaceful (Aronilth 1990:33).[7]

Conception and the subsequent development of the child involve more than bodily fluids from the mother and father. They involve the whole cosmic order. Powerful influences from the sacred mountains are called into action by the traditional Navajo wedding ceremony.

> As the Diné people we always go back to the four sacred mountains, that is part of our biggest belief. We believe that there is no other place on this planet where there are the four sacred mountains, the four directions, where there are four cardinals [the four cardinal points], where there is dawn, and blue daylight, and evening yellow twilight, and then the folding darkness. That is how we believe. And there is white shell and then minerals, you know. And then there is turquoise, and then the abalone shell, and then the black jet. And then through there, we find that is where our thinking, our thoughts, are. And then our planning throughout the whole, our life. And then our life, how we are going to live this life.

And then how we are going to have integrity and strength and faith and prayers and songs has to go with it. Then according to that, from these creation, we believe that our Holy People, the Holy People, created us from these areas. (Avery Denny, Chinle, Arizona, 8/11/93)

The actions of bride and groom during the wedding ceremony, particularly the consumption of cornmeal mush out of a ceremonial basket, call upon the powers associated with each of the four cardinal directions to assist with the conception and development of the couple's future children. Nihookáá Dine'é were given the marriage ceremony by Changing Woman. When the time came for the first marriage between members of the four original clans, Changing Woman said,

HW "You take a basket. This basket will be used," like that. "It has a history in it, hajíínáí, and then there are the six sacred mountains and then the rainbow inside which is your 'agáál, I mean your means of travel, the rainbow is what gives us movement." There is rainbow in here [points to the bottoms of his shoes] underneath our shoes, you know, the soles of our feet. And uh, "And then the clouds. There are two forms of clouds. K'os diłhił ááhdiłhił, male and female clouds. . . . Dark cloud and then ááh, ááh means foggy, foggy, dark fog."

MS Which one is female?

HW The dark fog, the one that covers up the whole sky, you know. "And gentle rain." That is what, that is female. And then so that is what those, the outer terrace, is what it is, those clouds.

MS The terraced designs on the basket?

HW Yes, uh-huh. "And then that also represents male and female rain, because rain represents birth. The beginning of new life." Without rain, you know, there would be no procreation and so it is a necessary part of creation. And so. And she said, "Use this basket." (Harry Walters, Tsaile, Arizona, 3/24/95)

Throughout Navajo history, the marriage ceremony has been performed exactly as Changing Woman directed. It continues to be performed in this manner today.[8] After the marriage arrangements are made, a date is set for the wedding ceremony. The bridegroom and his family arrive at the bride's home at sunset on the appointed day. When entering the hooghan prepared for the ceremony, the groom walks sunwise around to the west side, where he sits on blankets spread there for the couple to sit upon. The bride enters a short while later, holding a fire poker and a ceremonial basket. As a physical embodiment of the world constructed at the place of emergence, of Navajo history, and of Navajo philosophy, the ceremonial basket plays a profound role in this melding of two lives and the subsequent creation of new life.

> The basket is our life. That is where we come from, that is why you have to have a holy matrimony and eat from the basket. That is what gives life. So, it is alive. See it is alive, it is living. To have the holy matrimony you have to have a wedding basket, from that wedding basket is going to come a child, out of that is going to come a child. A child is going to be born. That is life. (Avery Denny, Chinle, Arizona, 8/11/93)

The basket carried by the bride contains a specially prepared cornmeal mush made from water and ground blue corn (Fishler 1954:206), white corn (Roessel 1993a:44), or white corn mixed with yellow (Witherspoon 1975:17). Moving sunwise, she sets the basket down before the groom and takes her place on his right. The father or the maternal uncle of the bride precedes her as she walks to her place. He carries a container of water, a ladle, and a bag of pollen. The bride takes the ladle and pours water over the groom's hands as he washes them; the groom then pours water over the bride's hands as she washes hers. This washes away the past and symbolizes the fact that from this point forward the couple will share life together (Roessel 1993a:44).

The bride's relative then adjusts the ceremonial basket so that the opening in the design is oriented to the east, toward the doorway of the hooghan. He takes a pinch of pollen from his *tádídíín bijish,* or pollen pouch, and draws a line with it from east to west across the mush. With another pinch of pollen he draws a line across the mush from south to north. Finally he draws a complete line with pollen around the circumference of the mush, from the opening in the basket's design sunwise—east, south, west, north. The groom takes a fingerful of mush from the place where the pollen lines intersect at the eastern edge of the mush. He eats this, and then the bride dips from the same place. Subsequent fingerfuls of mush are taken from the south, the west, the north, and the center by both groom and bride. As Harry Walters explains in the following passage, each pinch of cornmeal mush eaten from the basket has singular significance.

> The reason that they take the cornmeal from the four directions is because you are saying that, "All the knowledge that lies to the east, we want that in our marriage. All the knowledge that lies in the south, we want that in our marriage. All the knowledge to the west, all the knowledge to the north." And where the pollen crosses in

the center—the direction from the east to west is male, the direction from the north to south is female. And then so, when you take, you know, pinches [of] the cornmeal from where the male and female [lines of pollen] cross it is for the children that you are going to have. The grandchildren, the great-grandchildren you are going to have. That is what it signifies. (Harry Walters, Tsaile, Arizona, 3/24/95)

Consumption of the pinches of mush taken from each of the cardinal directions ensures that the type of knowledge associated with each particular point in Navajo cosmology will become incorporated into the marriage. Consumption of the pinches of mush taken from the center—where the lines of pollen drawn across the mush from east to west (male) and south to north (female) intersect—guarantees that the marriage will be blessed with fertility.

After the bride and groom have eaten mush from each appointed place, the basket is passed to the relatives and friends in attendance, who eat the remaining mush. Consumption of this mush notifies the Holy People of the union of the bride and groom and their respective clans in marriage.

When they do this, when they eat like this [referring to the groom and bride eating cornmeal mush from the ceremonial basket during the wedding ceremony], then when they have sex, when they have sex then automatically, this is your clan, right here is your mother's clan [pointing to the sacred mountain of the east on a sketch he has made], and then your father's clan, and then your maternal and the paternal grandparents, their clan, in these four areas, you know. And then you are going to make a connection like this, all these connections, all these connections. . . . When they unite in the holy matrimony, the four clans, they have this meal. Then it would seed. The sperm of these four sacred mountains, they come into working, they work together. . . . They go to work as they witness all of this, the holy matrimony, all the prayers and the songs that goes with it, all these Holy People they are notified so when they [the newlyweds] have sex, when they have sex, then it goes into action. . . . Out of this whole creation of the whole cosmic order of life, of the Mother Earth and the Father Sky, of all these four sacred mountains that I mentioned, evening, yellow, morning, the twilight, morning, dawn, blue daylight, yellow evening twilight, and the black jet, or darkness, folding darkness. And then spring, summer, fall, and all, this whole cycle of this, everything that is created in between the Father Sky and the Mother Earth they all got notified, they go into action, so when they have sex, this white shell and the abalone shell [pointing again to his drawing], they make contact here. They make contact in a mysterious spiritual way that nobody can explain. It happens, they fertilize the egg. (Avery Denny, Chinle, Arizona, 8/11/93)

The powerful personages from each of the cardinal directions, who are notified of the marriage by the eating of corn mush during the wedding ceremony, must contribute to the child's growth for proper development to occur. These influencing personages, who govern the timing of development not only in the womb but continuously throughout life, work as pairs. Early Dawn Boy and Early Dawn Girl, from the east, direct the child's physical growth and development (Aronilth 1990:32; Denny, 8/11/93). Blue Daylight Boy and Blue Daylight Girl, from the south, supervise the child's learning and knowledge (Aronilth 1990:32; Walters, 1/20/95). Yellow Evening Twilight Boy and Yellow Evening Twilight Girl, from the west, guide the child's social life, love, and unity with family. Folding Darkness Boy and Folding Darkness Girl, from the north, govern the development of the child's awareness and make sure the child has proper rest (Aronilth 1990:32).[9] These entities consistently influence all Navajo children. Personal heritage comes into play in regard to inherited substances and lifelong influences from the clans from which one descends.

The profound influence of the clan system in the Navajo world cannot be overstated. As Avery Denny told me, "to us the clan system is the foundation of our generations" (8/11/93). Navajo people refer to themselves as "born of" their mother's clan and "born for" their father's clan. They also reckon descent through their maternal grandfather's clan and their paternal grandfather's clan.[10] A lifelong connection exists between every Navajo and the clans from which she or he descends. Navajo people distinguish four types of "blood" that run through every individual's system, one type from each of the clans with which she or he is associated.

And then through the clans, the four clans. Your mother's clan, your father's clan, and then your maternal grandfather's clan and paternal grandfather's clan. You represent four people. Through your mother's clan, you were born for your father's clan, and then your maternal and paternal grandfather. So you represent four bloods, there are four types of blood in your system. So through that, OK, if you want to look at it like this again, your mother's clan, your mother's clan through her genes or through your blood flow of your mother or your grandmother. (Avery Denny, Tsaile, Arizona, 10/8/93)

Through this shared substance—one of the four types of blood—each clan influences the development and functioning of a bodily system—the digestive, the skeletal, the nervous, or the respiratory system.[11] As Avery Denny explained these associations:

> The nervous system, the skeletal, and then your digestive system and then your respiratory system. There are four, so you have four bloods and then you have the four clans, everything is four. So, everything is four in your body. So, the vital parts, you can't separate the heart from one another, or the lungs this way, and say that, that is the one, the main one. It all works together as one. Just like this natural order. . . . Your mother would be your nursing, you're fed on your mother's milk, so that is your digestive system. And then your father is the one that gives you that support to stand up, that would be your skeletal system. . . . Your respiratory system would be your paternal grandfather, meaning he is the one that is going to teach you how to pray and all that stuff. And your maternal [grandfather] would be your nervous system. (Avery Denny, Tsaile, Arizona, 10/8/93)

In addition, each of the clan categories reckoned by Navajo people is associated with a cardinal direction—mother's clan with the east, father's clan with the south, maternal grandfather's clan with the west, and paternal grandfather's clan with the north. Clan members have responsibilities regarding the principle of Navajo philosophy—nitsáhákees, nahat'á, 'iiná, or sihasin—associated with their respective cardinal point.[12] The principles of Navajo educational philosophy supervised by the clans are the fundamental tenets of Navajo life. Nitsáhákees refers to the development of awareness, up to the level of planning. Nahat'á refers to action based on thought, or the carrying out of plans. 'Iiná refers to the act of living according to a pattern established by the Diyin Dine'é. Sihasin refers to the confidence, assurance, and security gained from spirituality (Walters, 8/12/93; McNeley 1993). "Your mother gives you the thinking, your father gives you the planning, your maternal grandfather will give you the life to live, and stand for what you believe, and then your paternal grandfather teaches you how to pray, have hope and songs" (Denny 10/8/93). Therefore, nitsáhákees is associated with the mother's clan, nahat'á with the father's clan, 'iiná with the maternal grandfather's clan, and sihasin with the paternal grandfather's clan (see fig. 6 for a summary of these associations).

The intimate relationship between mother and child reinforces the responsibility of the mother's clan for training children in nitsáhákees—the development

East
Early Dawn Boy   Early Dawn Girl
Physical Growth and Development
Mother's Clan
Digestive System
Nitsáhákees
Sisnaajiní

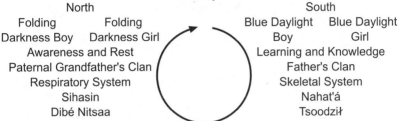

North
Folding   Folding
Darkness Boy   Darkness Girl
Awareness and Rest
Paternal Grandfather's Clan
Respiratory System
Sihasin
Dibé Nitsaa

South
Blue Daylight   Blue Daylight
Boy   Girl
Learning and Knowledge
Father's Clan
Skeletal System
Nahat'á
Tsoodził

West
Yellow Evening Boy   Yellow Evening Girl
Social Life, Love, and Unity
Maternal Grandfather's Clan
Nervous System
Iiná
Dook'o'oosłííd

Figure 6. Navajo cosmology II.

of awareness up to the level of planning. A child acquires initial awareness and thinking through the flow of substance from her mother's clan.

> Through your blood flow of your mother, or your grandmother, they are the ones that teach you that mind, or thinking, is the one that gives you that intelligency [sic] to, for you to realize a mother's love. She is the one that teaches you how to love yourself. . . . She is the one that is going to be carrying you for nine months in her womb. And she is the one that is going to give you birth, and then she is the one that is going to feed you, and raise you. So she is the one that knows love for you. So, through your mother you learn how to love. Through your mother's blood she teaches you how

to love. Even if your mother is not here. Your mother is gone, but you already have that blood in your system so she is the one that teaches you how to love and then through that you learn how to love yourself, because you love your mother. That is how you take care of yourself. And then through that understanding, and then you are not alone, you have all these mothers. Just like Mother Earth and the Water [Woman], that is your mother, too. . . . You call them "Shimá" then that is how you use shimá, in that way you talk to Mother Earth and then that Water Woman, or Tó Asdzáán. . . . Then through that you learn how to communicate with people. Through that you learn how to love your mothers, and then you love to take care of this Mother Earth and then that water and then the mountains. They are all your mothers. So, that is how you respect them. And they are the ones that clothe you with how they are dressed and then that is how you, that is your clothing, or, whatever is blessed or endured with those mountains and this Mother Earth, and they are the ones that give you that appearance, or that character, or the personality, and then your appearance. So, you have to, in that way, you have to take care of yourself, watch what you say, watch where you go, because you represent your mother. (Avery Denny, Tsaile, Arizona, 10/8/93)

The role of the father's clan is to instruct children in the proper order of the world. Nahat'á—action based on thought, or the carrying out of plans—is associated with the father's clan. A child learns to plan and put his thoughts and his surroundings in order through the flow of substance from his father's clan.

Your father's blood teaches you how to, you say like, put things in the right places, in the right order. Maybe clockwise and then all these other ways called, through the natural cosmic order of life, you put things in the right order. So, if you stand in the center you would already know that it is clockwise, and this is east and north and all that stuff. It teaches you that the sun comes up and then it goes this way and then the darkness comes this way. Everything that your father teaches you is true. Teaches you, or it trains you. Teaches you how to say, "Dad," and then he is going to say, "Shawéé' shiyázhí," too. And then you found out this Father Sky is your father, and then some of these are your fathers, and then nature is your father, and then that is how you respect those natural resources, or natural order. Some of them are your fathers. So, you say, "Dad. Dad. The sun is my father, even the Father Sky is my father." So that is how, and then when you look into them, it teaches you how things are in order, and then you will never be lost. So if you have a dad he could buy you a little toy and say, "Here son this little toy is yours and then when you finish playing with it put it back in this place right here. And then put your shoes in the right place, put your—" and then you just watch him, what he does. And then after he is finished with working with something, he will put it back, put it away in the right order. Same here, everything is in the right order. It teaches you that. (Avery Denny, Tsaile, Arizona, 10/8/93)

The role of the maternal grandfather's clan is to instruct its children in the proper pattern of life according to the Navajo way. It is this clan's responsibility to instruct children in 'iiná—the act of living according to a pattern established by the Diyin Dine'é. Clan members accomplish this by teaching children about their history. They teach a philosophy for living by recounting Navajo oral history. This process allows children to place themselves in a context, to envision their own lives within the time frame of the entire history of the Navajo people.

And then through your maternal grandfather's blood, he is already gone, he is not here with you, but in your blood. He is the one that teaches you about your history, about your heritage, or about where you come from. Meaning, if you are a Navajo, you kind of look back and then there is that emergence place, and then all these events there, the ceremonial records, the timeline. It is just like a timeline. You look through all this and then your maternal grandfather is going to train you how to have curiosity or questions. . . . And then it is going to teach you, or train you how to look this way, where you are going to be at twenty-five, thirty, or forty years. And then how are you going to raise your kids. And then you are going to be a grandfather. You will be where he was, for you, and then how are you going to greet your grandchildren, and all this. And then some of these natural [phenomena], or just like Talking God would be your grandfather, and then through that, you know, it trains you about your history, where you are going to go, it is like that. (Avery Denny, Tsaile, Arizona, 10/8/93)

A child acquires spirituality through the flow of substance from his paternal grandfather's clan. It is this clan's responsibility to guide the child to sihasin—

confidence, assurance, and security. Clan members accomplish this by instructing the child in ceremonial matters. A child gains confidence, security, assurance, and, ultimately, peace of mind through acquired faith and belief.

> OK. And then through your paternal grandfather's clan. He is going to teach you, or that blood is going to teach you, to understand your spirituality. Meaning, you are going to have a prayer and a song. You are going to have a belief, you are going to have faith, or something like that. It is going to teach you how to say . . . "May I walk in beauty, beauty before me, beauty behind me, below me, above me, all around me." . . . Your grandfather is going to say, "Come on grandchild, say this, say this. Pray for yourself, come on pray for yourself. Have a ceremonial belief," or something like that. So, he is the one that is going to teach you to say "Hózhǫ́ n, ." And then that is going to be your nalí's, your paternal grandfather's clan, they are the ones that are going to teach you how to have a ceremonial belief. And then he is the one that is going to tell you to learn these prayers, and learn these songs, and then he is the one that is going to say, "Try to have a ceremony for yourself, try to think like this." (Avery Denny, Tsaile, Arizona, 10/8/93)

Many elements and factors contribute to the construction of Nihookáá Dine'é— 'ííghsh, tó ał'tahnáschíín, tó biyáázh, blood from the mother's body, the influences of the powerful personages associated with the cardinal directions, and the influences carried in the four clan bloods. Individually or in combination, each of these contributes to the growth and development of every contemporary Navajo person from the moment she or he is conceived, through every stage of life for the full extent of her or his life as a human being.

THE CONSTRUCTION OF NAVAJO PERSONS

> MS Well the other thing I wanted to ask you to do, being an artist will make it a lot easier, is to draw what you called the complete individual. And you said there was a strand of hair, with the feather connected to the sky.
>
> HW Uh-huh.
>
> MS So, I wondered if you would please try to draw out the Navajo conception of the complete individual, and include the vital parts of the body. You know what we were talking about the other day?

Which parts are considered the most vital? And also the placement of the mind.

HW Uh-huh [he begins to sketch] . . . OK the genital point, the heart, the eyes, the mouth, the let's see, on the back side, the back side is the liver, and then the throat right here, the eyes, the mouth, the throat, the voice box. The heart, and then the back is the liver, and then there are rainbow in here [indicating the knee and elbow joints]. Rainbow is what gives us movement.

MS In the joints?

HW Yes. You look at the sandpainting and a short rainbow is right there, it is what gives us movement. And then down here [pointing again to his sketch], we stand on a rainbow. (Harry Walters, Tsaile, Arizona, 8/12/93)

As Walters spoke, he sketched the image of the complete Navajo person shown in figure 7. A Navajo is made up of the physical outer form (which is animated by an inner form), the body surface, the hair, the garments, the capacity for movement, the body print and anchoring cord (which connect the individual to Mother Earth), and the "feather of life" at the top of the head (which connects the person to Father Sky). The physical outer form, or Navajo body, is divided into layers from its center outward and by binary divisions that distinguish inside from outside and left from right. The body surface accumulates lifelong protection through painting, blackening, bathing, and the application of other ritual paraphernalia in ceremonies. Hairstyle and garments serve to identify a person's age, gender, and condition. The body print is the impression left in the ground by the hands, the feet, or the reclining figure. It reflects the intimate relationship of the person to her world. The feather represents a person's confidence, assurance, and faith in his or her own abilities.

The physical outer forms, or bodies, and other aspects of contemporary Nihookáá Dine'é are constructed of the same fundamental living elements as those used in the construction of the first Earth Surface People: "Our whole body, such as our arteries, veins, flesh and bones, are made up of beautiful white shell, turquoise, abalone shell, black jet, red beads, and sacred banded rock. . . . The red blood is also identified as a glittering coral mineral and the blue blood is identified as a turquoise stone" (Aronilth 1985 : 147).

The rain, clouds, rainbow, white corn, yellow corn, and ntł'iz used in the construction of the original Nihookáá Dine'é correlate directly with the parts of the human body and other aspects of the person in the contemporary world.[13] 'Atsiighá, "the hair on the head," is composed of male rain, female rain, and the moisture of clouds (Aronilth 1985 : 145−48, 7/3/91; Regina Lynch, 7/16/91;

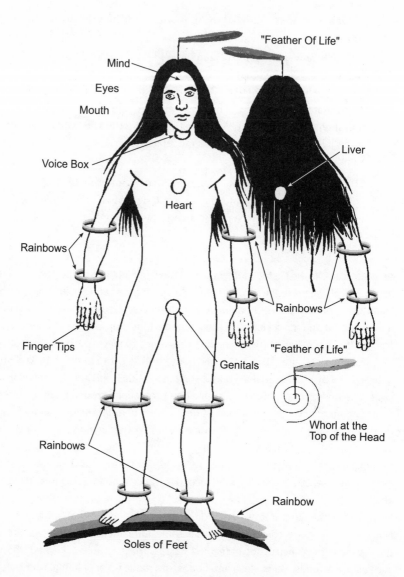

Figure 7. The complete Navajo person, or *diné*. Original sketch by Harry Walters; redrawn by Greg Schwarz.

Jean Jones, 7/25/91; Mae Bekis, 8/5/92). The flesh of contemporary Nihookáá Dine'é is a mixture of sacred white and yellow corn and dirt from the mountain soil bundle (Aronilth 1985: 145–48). *'Atsoo'*, "the tongue" (Aronilth 1985: 147), and *'agáál,* "the moving power," at the joints and under the soles of the feet are constructed of rainbow (Walters, 8/12/93).[14]

Nááts'íílid, "rainbow," plays an important role in communication, movement, and transportation, owing to the make-up of both 'atsoo' and 'agáál (Walters, 8/12/93). Communication by means of spoken language became possible through the "mysterious power" and "blessing" of Talking God when, "by his power, he inserted the sacred rainbow into our mouth. This became our tongue and our words and then the words began to become effective with the mixture of moisture and of a little water. For this reason, the spirit, roots and foundation of our language is this rainbow beam and Talking God" (Aronilth 1985: 147).

The *nááts'íílid 'agod,* "short rainbow," in the joints provides Nihookáá Dine'é with the capacity and power to move. The spirit of rainbow is called the sacred transportation of the Holy People and Nihookáá Dine'é (Aronilth 1985: 195). Rainbow in one form or another provides simultaneously the power for movement and safe conveyance to Nihookáá Dine'é on and off the reservation, beginning while a child is in the cradle.

The footrest of the Navajo cradle consists of short rainbow (see fig. 5). The child stands on it throughout her time in the cradle, and it provides a secure means by which to transport her. Once out of the cradle, Nihookáá Dine'é stand and travel on rainbows while within the area demarcated by the sacred mountains (see fig. 7). Nihookáá Dine'é who live or work outside of Dinétah carry a specially prepared *nááts'íílid 'agod'i,* "short rainbow being," with them to ensure safe movement. Wesley Thomas of Mariano Lake, New Mexico, told me that his short rainbow being maintains a continuous link between himself and his mother's home, regardless of how far he may travel.[15] As he explains:

> One end is rooted within Navajo sacred space and the other is temporarily rooted wherever I am. Should I travel, I do so by rainbow. It provides the energy for modern technology, as my mode of transportation. When I return home to the reservation, the rainbow retracts with me. At home I have a particular ceremonial to revitalize and reenergize the rainbow. It is reblessed. The 'agod'i I have is retied and secured during this ceremony, so it will not become undone when I am away from home—during my travels away from Dinétah. (Thomas, 11/29/94)

Most parts of the physical outer form found between the soles of the feet and the top of the head are made of one of the ntł'iz associated with the cardinal directions in Navajo cosmology—white shell, turquoise, abalone, and jet. *'Azooł,* the windpipe, (Hill 1938: 124; Haile 1947; Lang and Walters 1972: 61), *'alizh,* the urine, (Haile 1947), *'ajóózh,* the vagina, (Reichard 1950: 31), and *'ííghgháátsiighąą',* the spinal cord (Haile 1947), all consist of white shell, the precious shell of the east. *'Azid,* the liver (Hill 1938: 124; Haile 1947), *'acho',* the male genitalia or penis (Goddard 1933:138–39), and the blue blood traveling to the heart (Mustache 1970; Aronilth 1985:145–48) all consist of turquoise, the precious stone of the south. 'Acázis, the pleurae, are abalone (Hill 1938:124; Haile 1947), the hard good most commonly associated with the west. In addition, 'ajéí, the heart and lungs (Hill 1938:124; Haile 1947; Lang and Walters 1972: 61), and 'adátsoo', the clitoris (Goddard 1933:138–39), are said to be red coral, a material often associated with the west. 'Anáá', the eyes, are composed of jet (Haile 1947), the precious stone of the north.

Opinions often vary regarding exactly which parts of the body are made from which ntł'iz. Consider, for example, the composition of blood, brains, fingernails, and toenails. Wilson Aronilth considers red blood to be a "glittering coral mineral" (1985:145–48), whereas Curly Mustache, an elder from Tsaile, Arizona, states that it is composed of pyrope, a type of garnet (1970). Father Berard Haile was taught by his consultants that 'atsiighą́ą', the brains, were made of abalone (Haile 1947).[16] In contrast, Mae Bekis was taught that the brains were made of white shell: "And then they said that we have what we call a white shell that has not been dropped, that has not been touched by anything but the Holy People, that sits in the forehead of her [Changing Woman's] head" (8/5/92). Curly Mustache specifically stated that "all our nails (fingers and toes) are said to be all polished, beautified White Shell beads" (Mustache 1970).[17] As he explains below, Wilson Aronilth believes 'aláshgaan, the fingernails, and 'akéshgaan, the toenails, are made from a combination of materials to fulfill an important communicative function.

> Our toenails are said to be made out of a beautiful polished abalone shell and white shell that are interwoven together. This is the very reason why the White Shell Boy controls us from the East direction, the Abalone Shell Girl controls us from the West direction. We communicate with these two Holy People through a mysterious power of a holy beam. Also, moisture and a mixture of air and water is what our toenails are made with. This is why it continues to grow and for this reason we are told to keep natural. (Aronilth 1985:146)

In addition, the specific materials from which parts of the body are composed can vary from person to person. For example, some experts believe 'awoo', teeth, are made from a combination of white shell and white corn (Aronilth 1985:145–48), but others believe that teeth are made of either white shell or white corn alone (Mustache 1970), rather than in combination. As Curly Mustache explains: "Our teeth are said to be White Corn Kernels. These are said to be imitation White Shell Beads. This is the reason why our teeth do not last too long. There are very few who do have the real White Shell Bead teeth. This lasts a lifetime. It is foretold this was granted by White Shell Woman to certain people" (Mustache 1970).

These materials make up all components of the physical outer form—internal organs, flesh, bones, muscles, and skin. These components do not form a solid mass; rather, they interconnect to form an intricate series of layers with spaces between them: "The body is composed of skin, flesh, bones, and internal organs— all considered layers, each tissue carefully fitted to those next to it. Nevertheless, between the layers are interstices ('atatah [sic]) through which ghosts [winds] may travel. They enter the body where there are whorls—for instance, at the finger tips [sic] and hair spirals—as frequently as through orifices—mouth, nose, ears" (Reichard 1950:31−32).

The purpose of these 'atá't'ah, "the interior recesses, pockets, and folds," between the internal organs and the layers of the body surrounding them—skin, flesh, bones—is to allow air to circulate throughout the body. Air, one of the living elements essential to life, enters Nihookáá Dine'é shortly after birth in the form of the first gulps of air taken by newborn infants and the entrance of inner forms— the Holy Winds (Walters, 8/18/92; Bekis, 7/28/93; Denny, 10/8/93).

THE INNER FORM

When you were born and took your first breath, different colors
and different kinds of wind entered through your fingertips
and the whorl on the top of your head. Within us, as we breathe,
are the light breezes that cool a summer afternoon,
within us the tumbling winds that precede rain,
within us sheets of hard-thundering rain,
within us dust-filled layers of wind that sweep in from the mountains,
within us gentle night flutters that lull us to sleep.
To see this, blow on your hand now.
Each sound we make evokes the power of these winds
and we are, at once, gentle and powerful.

—*Luci Tapahonso,* from "Sháá Áko Dahjiníleh: Remember the
Things They Told Us"

As it did in the creation of the first Nihookáá Dine'é, air plays a pivotal role in the animation of every contemporary human being. Wind gives life and breath to Earth Surface People. In the Navajo view, the entrance of air into an infant marks the beginning of life for every person; a newborn is not considered to be alive until he breathes and cries.[18] The winds that enter the body at birth animate the outer body, leaving it partially during dreaming and permanently at death.

The locations of entrance and departure of the winds are evidenced on the body surface by the whorls on the fingertips, on the bottoms of the feet and toes, and at the top of the back of the head (McNeley 1981:35; Walters, 8/18/92; Bekis, 7/28/93; Denny, 10/8/93). The whorl at the top of the back of the head mirrors the spiral at the center of a ceremonial basket. In each case, the spiral marks the entrance of the "breath of life," the animating winds into the person.

RL OK. See this, where your hair starts here?

MS Uh-huh.

RL That's your breath of life here—

MS The whorl on the top of your head?

RL Yeah this [points to whorl on top of her head]. . . . So this is what they call . . . your thinking, your knowledge of what you're made of. So actually, this is, like a little baby, they say the soft spot here? [She points to the fontanel.] But after they get to a certain age, it grows together, but we as Navajo this circle here [pointing again to the whorl at the top of the back of her head], is the representation of the basket here, that's where it starts, where life begins, the breath of life.

MS And what about the whorls on your fingers and your feet?

RL I was told they're the same thing. . . . We think that way, everything in the Navajo thinking is done clockwise in the circle, OK. Everything that is done that way is, you know, because the circle has to do with well-being. (Regina Lynch, Tsaile, Arizona, 7/16/91)

Winds also mark the internal components of the body. For example, as Hastiin Mustache points out in the following account of how the winds entered Changing Woman shortly after she was found, winds leave their circular imprints on the muscles. According to Curly Mustache, all the Holy People assembled to deal with a matter of critical concern:

The infant was not crying like it should. What shall we do? They all were concerned. The Black Wind was asked to perform his ritual on the infant. Black Wind went to the infant and entered into her right foot through her body to the tip of her head. Making a whorl encircled there where he came up. This is where the hair center spot is now, as we see it on our heads. The Blue Wind then went through the hair center spot and came out on the bottom of our toes and our fingers have circle imprints on them. Our muscles also have circle markings on them which we do not know, or see them. This is exactly how it was told long ago. We all can see the imprints on the tip of our fingers and toes. The White Wind went into the infant's left foot and came out where the Black Wind first came out. . . . Yellow Wind entered the infant on the top of her hair center spot and came out on the bottom of her right foot. . . . The infant began to cry faintly. (Mustache 1970)

Once an infant breathes and cries, the constitution of its body begins to undergo transformation. Navajo infants are soft at birth. After the child emerges from the birth canal, internal contact with air through respiration, along with contact between air and the outer surfaces of the child's body, begins to firm the infant.

MB When the baby is born there are Holy People there, and they want the baby. "I want my feeling in the baby. I want mine." And there isn't only one, starting with Coyote. . . . And so, there is different breath that goes into the baby when it is born. And the baby is usually real soft. That is why when you see a big baby, until it gets contact with the air when it comes out, then it forms, like the head is kind of hard?

MS Uh-huh.

MB But at first it is just really soft.

MS So what is it that makes it hard? The air?

MB It is the air. The contact of air into the baby. [Whispering] That makes it form after it is out. And there it has to do with the Holy People again. And they are the ones that contacts, you know, the wind. Well it is the air that contacts with the body, with the flesh, and then that is when the baby [becomes firm]. I have seen it, I have. Well, I don't know if, I, uh, with my song, that is the way it goes. My song goes that way.

MS For when the baby is born?

MB Uh-huh.

MS And there are no Holy Winds that come into the baby at conception or during the time that it is in the mother's womb?

MB No, uh-unh. No, not until it is completely out. And it contacts with the air, then it is. I don't know if the other way is different. In your way. I don't know. (Mae Bekis, Tó'tsoh, Arizona, 7/28/93)

The air entering the child permeates its interior, filling the pockets, recesses, and folds of the internal layers. This process gradually makes the child's body firmer. The bodies of young children remain malleable for the first year or two, and Nihookáá Dine'é return to this soft, malleable state at critical times in the life cycle, such as at puberty and extreme old age (Walters, 8/18/92; Bekis, 7/28/93

E. Yazzie, 12/5/93). For best advantage the infant's body is molded by female relatives shortly after birth. Additional molding occurs during puberty, when the body is again malleable (Knoki-Wilson, 8/10/92; Walters, 8/18/92; Denny, 8/11/93).

Once air fills the outer form to capacity, fine hairs emerge from pores all over the surface of the body (Reichard 1950:497). These fine hairs and pores are necessary to the proper functioning of the body, "for it is through these that air comes out of the body" (O'Bryan 1956:103; see also Goddard 1933:147). These fine body hairs are likened to *nanise' bikétł'óól,* "the vegetation roots," in Mother Earth's body: "The tiny 'hair' on our arms, legs and body are the representation of 'vegetation roots.' We communicate with moisture, mist and a mixture of water and air through this and this is how our physical body breathes. For this reason, we are told not to cut the tiny hair on our arms and legs" (Aronilth 1985:147).

The air circulating in, through, and out of the body maintains the constant connection of individual Nihookáá Dine'é to their world. Small winds form over the entire surface of the body wherever air flows through the tiny hairs and pores. These animating winds make moving, talking, and thinking possible.

> We are covered with winds, which enables us to do what we want. What it is supposed to do, it works our minds for us. So that we can move, we can talk, we can think, you know, and that is what it is all made of, is from the winds. And it is not just one, because if it was one then you would only have like one fingerprint. But because there is seven different kinds, and then in seven different directions when it entered us, that is why you got the, you know, different fingerprints. It is not just one type of, one whorl, or one spin. It is just a number of them and they all go in different directions because of that. And that is what makes us, you know, our minds and our spirits, and it makes all of that up in one person. Or in each individual. (Anonymous woman, Upper Greasewood, Arizona, 8/13/92)

The individual natures of the specific winds that enter a child after birth determine what kind of personal characteristics he or she will have. There are many different kinds of winds that may enter a child.[19] According to Hastiin Mustache, once a child is born, various types of winds vie to enter it. The natures of the particular winds that enter the child ultimately determine its health, personality, and habits. When, as in the situation described in the following passage, an unwelcome wind enters a child, he will develop undesirable characteristics despite all efforts on the part of his parents.

> *The Smooth Wind was very fast. Before he was given permission [by the Holy People] he got into the child first. These are the unfortunate*

ones who are unhealthy and are always sick. Although some heal-
ing ceremonies are performed for them. The people who have been
granted the Good Winds are blessed with everything good. These
people are sometimes the least appreciative. What they are gifted
with does not satisfy them and they fail to care for them. They are
careless. They are the troublemakers. All these have been discussed
and approved by the Holy People long ago. Well competent intelli-
gent parents do not always have children raised according to their
standards. Some become delinquents. This is why the whole human
race differs. We cannot make them all turn to good people. There is
always the bad, half and half. Some people are blessed with valuable
possessions. Others cannot seem to get a hold of them some way or
the other. (Mustache 1970)

Regardless of the particular types of winds that enter an individual, homology between Nihookáá Dine'é and other persons in the Navajo world—hooghan, deer, corn plants, baskets, birds—is evidenced in the sunwise direction of the markings of the entrance of the winds at the fingertips, the bottoms of the feet and toes, and the whorl at the top of the back of the head. The direction of the hair growing from this portion of the scalp demonstrates the proper direction for human thought—sunwise. Hair grows sunwise because hair is a physical embodiment of thought.

HAIR, MOISTURE, AND THOUGHT

When the human beings were made by the Holy People, at the beginning of time, we were directed not to cut our hair. It is rain. It comes from the black cloud. When it is raining you would see sheets of rain, that is human hair. . . . That is why the hair tie was created for Navajo people. It is used to keep our hair tied. When a ceremony is being conducted for you, your hair is untied. When you are not a patient in a ceremony, you are not to have your hair untied. But today, everyone is like that [with hair untied]. According to the stories of how we were raised, these same stories are not acknowledged by the young people today. (Anonymous elder, Chinle, Arizona, 7/10/91)

Hair, which is composed of male rain, female rain, and the moisture of clouds (Aronilth 1985:145–48, 7/3/91; Lynch, 7/16/91; Jones, 7/25/91; Bekis, 8/5/92), is affiliated with the mind and thought. Hair is a physical embodiment of thought and lifelong knowledge (Aronilth, 7/3/91; Lynch, 7/16/91; Bekis, 7/28/93; Knoki-Wilson, 7/29/93). The direction of Nihookáá Dine'é thought is sunwise—east, south, west, north—because Talking God dictated that all Nihookáá Dine'é would think according to the plan for life embodied in the ceremonial basket.

> This [basket] is made according to the hooghan, sunwise. The house blessing are done with this basket. You start from this side, then this side and this side. It is all done according to the sun. The way it travels. At the end, the last part you take and distribute the cornmeal out the front door. There are very important stories related to these baskets. Talking God, Yé'ii Bicheii, instructed, "This is how it is to be made," he said. It was constructed according to him. He continues that, "The thinking process of us all will be sunwise. The thinking process of humans will be in rows and in sequences. The process will continue to the ending part of the basket." That was according to Talking God. (The words of Irene Kee, Crystal, New Mexico, 8/3/92, translated by Wesley Thomas)

The direction of human thought mirrors the direction of the coiling in ceremonial baskets and in the whorls marking the entrance of winds into Nihookáá Dine'é—at the top of the back of the head, on the fingertips, and on the bottoms of the feet and toes. In each case the spirals go sunwise. As Mrs. Flora Ashley of Shonto, Arizona, points out in the following conversation, a direct correlation exists between the spiral of the basket, which is representative of Navajo philosophy and the history of the Navajo people since their emergence onto the earth's surface, and the clockwise spiral of human thought.[20]

> FA Well, this basket is a representation of our orientation, our livelihood. That is what it is. Start out from the center, means that it is your thought process again. And, it is also the entrance of our emergence. That is what that is.
>
> MS So the center represents the emergence—
>
> FA Uh-huh, all through your thought process.
>
> MS Through the underworlds? And the individual thought process?
>
> FA Uh-huh. It is your livelihood, the emergence, and your thought process. Everything goes clockwise. That is the way our thought process is. We think clockwise. That is why we don't, there is no such thing as [a] deadline, and we don't have a linear mind. We

always, everything has to be.

MS You don't have a linear mind? You mean like Western?

FA Our thought processes. Uh-huh.

MS Western is linear, right. ·

FA Uh-huh. So—

MS Navajo is? How would you describe Navajo?

FA Clockwise spiral, I guess that is what you would call it. (Flora Ashley, Tsaile, Arizona, 7/29/91)

The hair growing out of the 'atáá'ha'noots'eeí, "the point at the top of the back of the head where the hair assumes a concentric spiral growth pattern," is one's "feather of life." Individual feathers are distinctive. Holy People use these feathers to identify individual Earth Surface People. As an elder from Lukachukai, Arizona, told me: "The feather of life is her thought and her livelihood. This portion of hair hanging over the forehead contains her thought and her livelihood-to-be. This hair extends from the swirls, where the hair originates from. The swirls are from the wind which first entered her body when she was born. From that it created her feather. She is known by that, her own individual feather of life" (anonymous elder, Lukachukai, Arizona, 8/13/92, translation by Wesley Thomas).

Because of its importance, the Holy People directed the Nihookáá Dine'é in strict rules regarding manipulation of the hair at specific stages in the life cycle. For example, a child's hair should not be cut before it begins to speak a language of the Earth Surface People such as Navajo or, more recently, English, instead of Áłtsé Saad, the language of the First World (Lynch, 7/16/91; Jones, 7/25/91; Agnes Begay, 7/26/91; Dooley, 8/19/92; Bekis, 7/28/93), or until after the fontanel closes (Bekis, 7/28/93; Knoki-Wilson, 7/29/93). Cutting of the hair before this time risks impairing the child's development (Knoki-Wilson, 7/29/93; Walters, 8/10/93). In addition, hair must be carefully groomed daily to contain and control one's thoughts.

They tell us that while you are living as an earthly human being you should never untie your hair and let it hang down loose, you should always tie it, and like the way it is illustrated here [pointing to a diagram of the traditional hair bun like that in figure 8]. Tie it clockwise. . . . That way you would have a real solid, strong mental and emotional and philosophical and psychological thought and thinking and feeling. That's what they said. . . . The only time that they untie our hair is when we live to the full extent of our life. When death takes our life then they untie it and utilize that traditional comb or brush . . . and they separate our hair from the middle

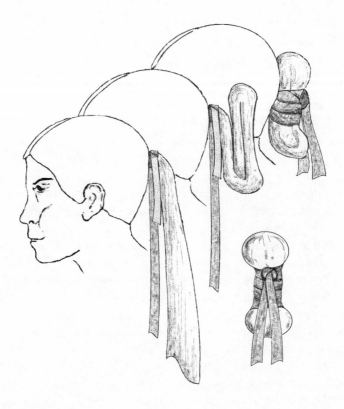

Figure 8. The traditional Navajo hair bun, or *tsiiyééł*. Drawing by Greg Schwarz.

and they make our hair just loose and straight. That's how they put our body away. You should never bury somebody with their hair tied. So, for that reason, they say you shouldn't just let your hair loose while you're living. Only, for certain special participation in ceremonies. (Wilson Aronilth, Tsaile, Arizona, 7/3/91)

The Holy People directed all Nihookáá Dine'é to wear their hair in the *tsiiyééł*, or traditional hair bun, shown in figure 8. When I asked women what the relationship was between thinking and the hair bun, they told me the bun helped to contain and control one's accumulated knowledge so that one could think effectively and not have one's thoughts "scattered." As Sunny Dooley of Vanderwagen, New Mexico, explained:

SD [Women] tie their hair down at the nape of their neck and pile all of their knowledge into a bun, you know. . . . It just represents all the knowledge that you have to accumulate and you hope to tie it together so that you can use the knowledge effectively and just not let it be, you know [makes hand motions around head].

MS Scattered?

SD Scattered, and be a scattered brain kind of thing. (Sunny Dooley, Gallup, New Mexico, 8/21/92)[21]

Or worse, as Ruth Roessel of Round Rock, Arizona, pointed out, leaving your hair unsecured risks having your thoughts literally "blow away." Mrs. Roessel told me the purpose of the bun was to "just have your hair folding back to your head, and that is where all the thinking is developed, and if you have your hair hanging down and blown on, and there is hardly any, any, you know, thoughts into your head and it is blown away [chuckles]. That is the whole idea, I guess" (7/26/91).[22]

Wearing your hair in the traditional bun demonstrates that you are "thinking in the proper way" (Dooley, 8/19/92), that you are "strong and the mind is good" (Jones, 7/25/91), that the "mind is all set" (H. Ashley, 7/23/91), and that your "thinking is controlled" (Bekis, 7/28/93). When thinking becomes uncontrolled, illness will likely ensue. An ill person's thoughts must be realigned in order for health to be restored. Mae Bekis gave the following account of the way she realigns a patient's thoughts during the Blessing Way ceremony.

MB When you wash up your patient, you know, you use a regular brush. That was, you know that has been brought down. I have one of those brushes. You use that, you don't use a hair brush that we have around here that is from the store.

MS Oh, you use the grass brush?

MB You use the grass brush. And they said that when you are brushing their hair all their thinking, all the things are put together back in place. And that is where you comb all that together. To, back here [indicating the nape of her neck] and make their bun. You put all their thinking back together. (Mae Bekis, Tó'tsoh, Arizona, 7/28/93)

The traditional Navajo hair bun contains and controls a person's "feather of life," the connection to Father Sky extending from the top of his or her head. In doing so, it embodies a person's thought, knowledge, and material wealth. "The bun is the tied feather of life. Your thought is enclosed and it also contains your planning capabilities. It contains your material wealth and knowledge. We have left that whole concept behind. We have done that as Navajo. Other people, non-Navajo people, have always had short hair. They operate on a different system, unlike Navajo" (anonymous elder, Lukachukai, Arizona, 8/13/92, translation by Wesley Thomas).

As this elder notes, many Navajo no longer wear the distinctive bun every day. Pressures from the outside world, such as grooming requirements at government-run boarding schools and dress codes for government employees, have taken their toll over the last fifty years. As a result, the majority of Navajo people today do not wear the traditional hair bun on a daily basis, but it is still recognized as a strong symbol of ethnic identity among contemporary Navajo. As Jean Jones of Rock Point, Arizona, told me: "The Holy People, they know us for that" (7/25/91).[23]

STRUCTURAL HOMOLOGY

> MS Do you know, is there a certain side of the body that is considered male and female?
>
> OT Yeah.
>
> MS Can you tell me about that?
>
> OT OK, the right side, well, the right side is the representation of your mother, from your mother's side. And your left is from your father's side. So if you want to consider anything male, then it is your left side.
>
> MS OK, is that the same for men and women?
>
> OT [Nods his head.] Same as that cradle board, you know [indicating a cradle hanging on the wall].
>
> MS Yeah. I noticed that.
>
> OT The right side, if you laid down, your right side would be Mother Earth and your left would be Father Sky, you know. Same thing, you know?
>
> MS So it is the same thing with the human body?
>
> OT Uh-huh, yeah. There is, uh, you know, it is a, there are aspects of something from your father's side and something from your mother's side. So your left side is a representation of your father's side, or you can consider that the male. The male side of you. (Oscar Tso, Many Farms, Arizona, 8/9/92)

The sunwise directionality of the whorls at the back of the top of the head and the wrapping of hair in the bun serve to identify Nihookáá Dine'é as living entities functioning within the "natural order" of the Navajo world. Structural homology with other persons in the Navajo universe also includes attention to the trajectory of growth, a pathway, or "way out," enabling factors to move from inside to outside, and a binary division of the person that distinguishes left (male) from right (female). Like cradles, grinding stones, and hooghan, humans are divided laterally into male and female sides.

The structural homology shared by all persons in the Navajo world is demonstrated by an infant in a cradle lying on the floor of a hooghan with its head to the east. The backboards of the cradle have been carefully placed to ensure that the trajectory of growth of the tree from which they were cut is maintained in the completed cradle. The direction of growth is from bottom to top, correlating with the future growth of the child. As Oscar Tso pointed out, while lying in a cradle, a child has the female side of its body on top of Mother Earth, the female side of the cradle, and the male side of its body on top of Father Sky, the male side of the cradle (see fig. 5). When the child is placed with its head toward the doorway of the hooghan (east), the female and male sides of its body and the female and male sides of the cradle correspond with the female (north) and male (south) sides of the hooghan.

The binary structural division shared by all persons in the Navajo world reflects a fundamental principle of Navajo philosophy and cosmology—duality. An underlying aspect of Navajo philosophy is that any "whole" is a combination of parts. As John Farella has noted, "on whatever basis Navajos bound an entity, it is not in terms of homogeneity. Wholes seem to be composed of two parts which are in a sense complementary and in another sense opposed" (1984:176). In fact, "what Anglos call the pairing of opposites, Navajos conceptualize as the halves of a whole, with each half necessary for completeness" (Griffin-Pierce 1992:66). The Navajo with whom I consulted used information about the body and personhood to elucidate the nature of dualism in the Navajo world. Navajo views on the cultural construction of the human body and personhood reveal that Nihookáá Dine'é embody the essence of duality—the pairing of contrasting but complementary components to make a whole.

Complementarity delineates and informs all aspects of the Navajo world, including human relationships and the human body. As Harry Walters explained: "Everything is in terms of male and female in the Navajo. This is the duality. There is a male part and then the female counterpart in everything, you know, even us. I am a man, but my left side is my male side, my right side is my female" (8/18/92).

Pairings such as life and death, hunger and satiation, hózhǫ and hóchxǫ, night and day, and male and female exist on all levels of the web of interconnection formed by the relationships of persons to each other and to the universe: the cosmic, the social, and the individual levels. As Walters noted, this complementarity establishes a base paradigm found throughout Navajo cosmology in which male and female are paired in myriad homologues. On the cosmic plane, the universe consists of Mother Earth and Father Sky. Since their reunion in the last under-world, men and women have been considered necessary counterparts. Being complete, a couple represents a stronger entity than does a single person. Therefore, on the social level, no man or woman is considered to be complete or whole unless he or she has a counterpart of the opposite gender (Dooley, 8/19/92).[24]

On an individual level, every person is regarded as a whole possessing both male and female aspects or qualities, a pairing that is demonstrated in the actual composition of the human body. As Wilson Aronilth explains, "we are divided right in half from the tip of our head down to our feet. One side of our body is male and the other side is female" (1985:147). The left-hand side of the body is considered male while the right-hand side of the body is female (Aronilth 1985:147; Annie Kahn, 7/8/91; McPherson 1992:44; Nakai Tso, 8/8/92; Oscar Tso, 8/9/92; Knoki-Wilson, 8/10/92, 7/29/93; Walters, 8/18/92, 8/10/93, 8/12/93; H. Ashley, 7/27/93; Bekis, 7/28/93; Denny, 8/11/93, 10/8/93).[25]

In our discussions, English-speaking Navajo consultants consistently used the terms "male" and "female" to refer to the contrastive sides of the body. The English term "male" literally translates into Navajo as *biką'*, "its male sexual partner," and "female" literally translates as *ba'áád*, "its female sexual partner."[26] These terms, biką' and ba'áád, are commonly used to make biological sexual distinctions among domestic or game animals such as sheep, goats, and deer, and they have been used by prior researchers to refer to male and female aspects and qualities.[27] But I was told that according to current usage, these terms are considered impolite in reference to human companions. When I sought clarification on this point, Ursula Knoki-Wilson used humor to enlighten me about why it was inappropriate to use the terms ba'áád and biką' to refer to one's spouse or companion. She explained that ba'áád and biką' were used to distinguish biological sexual differences but that you should address your companion by "the relationship, not by the biological difference" (Knoki-Wilson, 7/29/93). Accordingly, she said,

> I wouldn't call my husband "Penis." And he wouldn't call me "Vagina" in our relationship. He would call me "Honey" or "Sweetie," or whatever. So in Navajo it is the same thing, the "ba'áád dóó biką'ii" kind of determines the biological difference. In sexual terms. They are not the bodily terms for the body, but they connote a sexual difference between the sexes. . . . In our relationships we call them companions . . . but when they are in ceremony and ritual, you know, they might be making a sandpainting and they will refer to it as "ba'áádii" and "biką'ii." And that is appropriate because they are describing the sexual difference there, the biological difference, [the] gender difference. (Ursula Knoki-Wilson, Fort Defiance, Arizona, 7/29/93)

When I asked people what Navajo terms they would use to refer to the respective sides of the body, a variety of terms were mentioned. For specific reasons explained later in this chapter, Harry Walters used the term *naayéé' k'ehjigo*, "on the side of protection," for the male side and *hózhǫ́ǫ́jigo*, "on the side of peace, harmony, and order," for the female (8/18/92). Hanson Ashley told me he preferred the terms *dinego*, "the man's side," and *asdzáángo*, "the woman's side," to connote the concepts of masculine and feminine respectively (7/27/93). Avery Denny uses są'ah naagháí to refer to the male side and bik'eh hózhǫ́ to refer to the female because at the most abstract level of knowledge, the level of songs and prayers, these terms encapsulate all that is male and female (8/11/93; see also Benally 1994:24–26).

In the following account, Curly Mustache elaborates on this binary division of the body and correlates human veins with their counterparts in the body of the earth:

> *It is said that half of our blood veins are blue, the other half red. I do not recall which side is red. It divides right in half from the head down between our legs. The two colors join in the middle. Each side of the blood veins do their work for the body. When it comes together it just automatically turns to its own color fast. All these blood vessels are called "earth veins" (Nahasdzáán bits'oos). When digging in the damp ground you will find these long worms, which we call earth worms. The blood flows in these throughout our system. The fluid that we call blood has its work to do to purify our system to keep us alive. (Mustache 1970)*

The red—coral or pyrope—veins found on the right-hand side of the human body are female. The blue—turquoise—veins that run through the left-hand side of the human body are male (Aronilth 1985:147).

The interworkings of the complementary components of the body are further refined to form a complex system of checks and balances, with female parts of the body controlling male parts of the body and male parts controlling female parts. For example, as Hanson Ashley explained, nerves from each side of the brain crisscross at the back of the neck so that the right side of the brain (female) controls the left side of the body (male), while the left side of the brain (male) controls the right side of the body (female).

They talk about the human body and in Navajo they say like on the right, the right side of the body is feminine, on the left side is masculine. And then they talk about the brain, [the] right side is female, the left side is male. But somewhere in the back of your head, it crisscrosses there, so the right side of the brain takes care of the left side of the body. And then the left side of the brain takes care of the right side of the body. So they believe that it crisscrosses somewhere. So that is the way, that is the same way that they do things, like in traditional ceremonies, there are a lot of things that they do and they always have this, the cross, or the crisscross motions. (Hanson Ashley, Shonto, Arizona, 7/27/93)

This division—left side male, right side female—correlates with the placement in the mother's womb of male and female embryos, respectively. In addition to contributing to the development of the complementary male and female components of the body in utero, the fluids tó ałʼtahnáschíín (male) and tó biyáázh (female) foster the development of distinctive qualities that are associated with each of these contrasting, yet complementary, sides (Aronilth 1990:33). As Ursula Knoki-Wilson explains, these contrasting sides and qualities are regarded as aspects of personhood rather than as purely physical attributes: "What I learned is they say that your right side is your female side and the left side is your male side. And so they teach you that, you know, you're always balanced in that way psychically. That you are, you know, you respect both, the male and the femaleness within you. . . . It is more like psychic energies that they are referring to rather than, you know, the actual physical dimensions" (8/10/92).

On one of the twelve levels of knowledge, the left-hand side of every individual is naayééʼ kʼehjigo, "on the side of protection," the "warrior" side of the person, while the right-hand side is hózhǫ́ǫ́jigo, "on the side of peace, harmony, and order," the female or "peaceful" side of the person (Walters, 8/18/92). This division is not unique to humans; every living entity in the Navajo world has had naayééʼjí and hózhǫ́ǫ́jí components since the first underworld (Knoki-Wilson, 7/29/93; Walters, 8/10/93; Denny, 8/11/93). These contrasting aspects of personhood caused perpetual problems in the underworlds because the ability to control them did not become available until after Changing Woman was found.

> HW It began in the First World, yes. There, First Man and First Woman had two minds. But they didn't know it, they didn't know how to control that. That is why, uh . . .
>
> MS When you say two minds, you mean they had two sides to their minds?
>
> HW Two sides—
>
> MS Or was it two minds?
>
> HW They were deceitful, they were cheats, they were evil on one side. All of us are like that, we are like that, we are like that.

MS Yeah.

HW We are like that. But, then they let this, the negative evil side take over. They didn't know how to balance that see, each time, in each world, you know, it goes like this. It was, actually Changing Woman was the one that showed us how to use that. How to balance, that, the two minds, the two sides. (Harry Walters, Tsaile, Arizona, 8/12/93)

Changing Woman gave the Nihookáá Dine'é the knowledge necessary to control and balance the naayéé'jí and hózhǫ́ǫ́jí sides of life through thoughts, songs, prayers, and ceremonies.

Naayéé' k'ehjigo, the warrior side, represents the essence of masculinity, whereas hózhǫ́ǫ́jigo, the peaceful side, represents the essence of femininity in the Navajo world. Fundamentally, there are no mutually exclusive characteristics associated with one side or the other; instead, the contrast between sides reflects dual facets of every trait or aspect of personhood. There are aggressive and passive, protecting and blessing facets to all personal characteristics, including creativity, developing, thinking, and feeling (Walters, 8/18/92). For example, Ursula Knoki-Wilson told me that the warrior side is associated with "shielding," "wisdom," and "emotional release," while the peaceful side is associated with "nurturing," "analytical thought," and "being in touch with one's emotions" (8/10/92). Shielding and nurturing are necessary components of fostering development; wisdom and analytical thought are two parts of thinking; and connection and release are both aspects of experiencing emotion. One or the other of these dual facets may come to the fore in direct response to any situation in which an individual may find himself.

There are male (warrior) and female (peaceful) reactions appropriate to every situation:

HW Suppose that you are walking down the street and somebody throws a punch at you? You know, you put out your hand to protect yourself. Whether you are male or female, that is your male side. Your warrior side reacting. And so this is what I mean by male and female characteristics. . . .

Now, if you are in a war, say even though you are not a soldier in the military and you are running, and then you came upon an enemy, you know, somebody you don't know. But he is an enemy and he has a gun in his hand. And you see a gun there and you pick it up and shoot him. Now, that is your warrior side reacting in a warrior way. See?

MS Give me an example of how the female side reacts. Or what the female side does.

HW And then, let's say you're a soldier in enemy territory and then after you have driven off the enemy then you find women and children. And then do you go and gun them down? No. You leave them alone. That is your female side, your [peaceful] side reacting, you know. (Harry Walters, Tsaile, Arizona, 8/18/92)

These contrasting sides are not viewed as separate. Indeed, in our discussions, Hanson Ashley took exception to my choice of words when I explained how I had learned that the body was "divided right in half from the tip of the head down to the feet," and to my repeated references to the sides of the body as the "male half" and the "female half."

HA I guess to say half male and female that is—[shakes his head].

MS That's wrong?

HA That is the wrong way to say it in English.

MS How would you say it?

HA In Navajo "ałheesilá," ałheesilá, when you say ałheesilá, is a umm, OK, what is the best way? There is interaction, OK. (Hanson Ashley, Shonto, Arizona, 7/27/93)

Later, catching himself using the term "divided," Ashley pointed out that in his opinion, use of this term was misleading because it tended to highlight the distinction between the sides of the body rather than the more important consideration, the complementarity of the sides of the person. He told me: "OK anyway that is how the body is umm, is divided, not necessarily to say they are divided but, it is just two 'hemispheres' you might say, or two different oppositions that have to interact. And like for men, for men there are certain times that you are going to react like a woman they say. There are certain times. You have that, the woman's characteristics, sometimes it comes out" (7/27/93).

In an effort to clarify the relationship between the male and female "hemispheres" in the Navajo model, Ashley turned to concepts he believed would be familiar to me—components found in the biomedical model of the human system. He made an analogy between the sympathetic and the parasympathetic nervous systems found in the biomedical model and the male and female "hemispheres" referred to in his own explanation to illustrate how the contrastive sides interrelate.

HA Just to give you an illustration, like umm, talking about this, I am thinking medical, they use the term sympathetic nervous system, and there is parasympathetic nervous system. There are two systems.

MS OK.

HA [The] sympathetic nervous system is in control when you are awake and [the] parasympathetic nervous system is resting, but when you go to sleep then that nervous system [the parasympathetic] activates, and the other system [the sympathetic] retreats, and it rests again. So they alternate. But they are not separate really, but it is just a two [part] system that interacts and interacts.

MS So that is a better analogy, that there is a male system and a female system,

HA Right, there you go.

MS That are both necessary . . .

HA It is both, yes! (Hanson Ashley, Shonto, Arizona, 7/27/93)

Avery Denny also made an analogy to a biomedical concept—the immune system—to explain the purpose and functioning of these complementary aspects of the person. He told me that on the most fundamental level of Navajo philosophy, the sides of every individual represent Są'ah Naagháí and Bik'eh Hózhǫ́, the parents of Changing Woman, who are the animating forces of the entire Navajo universe. The male side is są'ah naagháí because of its protective role, and the female side is bik'eh hózhǫ́ because of its blessing role.[28] As Denny explained:

Są'ah naagháí means protection, and then bik'eh hózhǫ́ is Blessing Way. Meaning that your body has its own immune system to fight off any kind of disease or sickness. We Diné believe that we have that kind of, są'ah naagháí bik'eh hózhǫ́, is the one that is separated like a male and a female, inside our body. So, if I was a man then my left side of my whole body, it represents a male. That is where I hold the bowguard and the bow and arrow. And then on the right side, I hold the corn pollen. And then I say "Hózhǫ́ násháádóó." That is Blessing Way. So, in that way my body is in balance, like Protection Way and then Blessing Way. So, any kind of disease, or sickness, or cold, ever comes into my body, or if I am into it, then my left side of my body is mainly just, it would protect the right side. And then over here too. They crisscross to take care of one another just like a man and a [woman], a male and a female. To have that balance. Blessing Way, protecting. Protection Way and then Blessing Way depend on one another inside the body. So, that is what we believe, są'ah naagháí bik'eh hózhǫ́. It works like that. (Avery Denny, Tsaile, Arizona, 10/8/93)

Time and again, Navajo with whom I consulted stated that they do not consider one side of the person, or one facet of any particular characteristic, more significant than the other; both sides and facets are necessary for harmony, balance, and health to exist. This was reiterated when I inquired whether treatment differed if a health problem was limited to one side of the body or the other. I was told that although the distinction between sides is readily acknowledged on a philosophical level, and Navajo people are conditioned from early childhood to perform certain activities with one hand or the other (and certain activities are done to one side of the body or the other in ceremony), Navajo people do not routinely make a conscious differentiation between the experiences associated with the right or left sides of their bodies (H. Ashley, 7/27/93; Knoki-Wilson, 7/29/93; Walters, 8/10/93; Denny, 10/8/93).

MS In terms of healing, I am wondering, are there different treatments depending on if the illness or ailment has affected the male or the female side of the body? For example, what if someone is having paralysis on their right side? Is there a different treatment than if it was paralysis on the left side?

HA OK, now I need to go back on that. You don't treat your body to be male or female. If you are a man you don't treat it that, "My right-hand side of my body is a female," you know, you don't do that. You know, in your mind you don't have that. But in the story, you understand that. That there is [a distinction]. But in real life, in reality, you don't treat it that way. So when there is a sickness, when there is a sickness, and then if there should be, let's say, if your left-hand of your body is ailing or the right side of the body is ailing. You don't say, "Oh, it is my female or male part that is sick," or whatever. You don't think that way. But, within the ceremony, they have that. Whatever spirit that they talk about, or let's say they make a sandpainting, there has to be two. There has to be male and female figures within the sandpainting. That has to do with the body, OK. So, but in reality you don't think of it that way, but through ceremonial, and through the stories, it is understood. So through songs and through prayers, you know, it is in there, it is mentioned. Male and female. (Hanson Ashley, Shonto, Arizona, 7/27/93)

In combination, the naayéé' k'ehjigo and hózhǫ́ǫ́jigo aspects of the individual contribute to the development and maintenance of a physically, emotionally, mentally, and spiritually harmonious person. To be whole and remain harmonious, all

Navajo must respect both the maleness and the femaleness within themselves (Knoki-Wilson, 8/10/92). Fundamentally, the purpose of all living entities in the Navajo world having male and female sides is "to have respect for both, the power of both dimensions. And [to] perpetuate the feeling of harmony and balance. And that there is unity, that there are physical differences, but then you also have unity. [Pause]. So, you know, it is an important concept especially when it comes time to do healing work. I mean herbs have to have come from male and female herbs and certain waters have to have male and female put together for ritualistic work and things like that" (Knoki-Wilson, 7/29/93). Indeed, when illness occurs as a result of imbalance, or when a new stage of life is broached, the naayéé' k'ehjigo and hózhǫ́ǫ́jigo aspects of the individual play important roles in ceremony.

HOMOLOGY AND SYNECDOCHE IN PRACTICE

OT A bowguard is worn on the left. And then when there are prayers that are going to be taking place, there are certain things that you hold on your left, and certain things that you hold on your right.

OT Anything for protection you hold it on your left side.

MS Both men and women?

OT Yeah. And anything that is good, you hold it on your right side. Well, like uh, like protection ceremony they usually have paraphernalia that are, they say ádináályééł. Ádináályééł means something that you take around yourself for protection. Ádináályééł is something that you hold up to say prayers.

MS So what you would wrap around you . . .

OT Or take around you for protection is the ádináályééł. It is, like you might hold an arrowhead on your left. Which is a form of a weapon. . . . So that is kind of like a protection, so you hold it with your left hand, you never hold it in your right. Tádídíín, you hold it in your right.

MS Uh-huh, yeah I noticed that at the Kinaaldá everyone used their right hand to make the tádídíín blessing. And, um, I think you were explaining to me that when you take the first pinch of the tádídíín it goes in your mouth. And the second one goes on the top of your head. And you said those represent two things?

OT No, there are three things. One thing that you take in for your physical, and then one goes on top of your head, then the other one to pray [motions out away from his body when referring to the third].

MS OK, so did you say that the one that goes in your mouth is to represent your physical development and growth?

OT Uh-huh.

MS And the one that goes on the top of your head is your mental development and growth?

OT Uh-huh.

MS And then the third one, which, you are right, I had forgotten to mention, was where you go from east to west. Do you always go from east to west? Or do you go away from you?

OT Yeah, you kind of make an offering, you know, like away from you, [demonstrates] like that, you know. You're offering something to something like nature. So you are kind of going like this [spreads imaginary pollen out in front of his body]. It is not that something is going to go away from you or anything. That is how you are praying, make an offering. (Oscar and Opal Tso, Many Farms, Arizona, 8/9/92)

Reflective of the protecting and blessing aspects associated with the respective sides of the body, certain activities are done exclusively with, or to, the right or the left side of the body. Anything having to do with blessing and good will involves the right hand and side, regardless of the handedness of the individual (Walters, 8/12/93; Denny, 10/8/93). As illustrated in Oscar Tso's example, the tádídíín bijish, or pollen pouch, is held with the left hand, but the fingers of the right hand must be used to pinch the pollen that gets applied to the tip of the tongue and the top of the head, and the same fingers are used to make the offering (Oscar Tso, 8/9/92; Walters, 8/12/93; Denny, 10/8/93). In addition to using the right hand in prayer, Navajo people extend their right hands in greeting.

MS I noticed that when greeting, people shake hands with the right hand.

HW Yeah, because you are extending good will.

WT Handshakes are on the right hand.

HW Yeah, handshakes, and then mountain soil, you always hold it there, in your right hand. Mountain soil, prayer sticks, things that are related to good will. Prayer sticks, offerings, white shell, turquoise, abalone, jet, and those kinds of things. That is good will. (Harry Walters and Wesley Thomas, Tsaile, Arizona, 8/12/93)

In contrast, certain activities are done exclusively with the left hand. A man holds his bow with his left hand and wears his k'eet'oh, or bowguard, on his left arm (Oscar Tso, 8/9/92; Walters, 8/12/93; Denny, 10/8/93).

> AD If you are in the male way, you hold that bow on this side [indicating his left] and you have that bowguard. Even if you stretch this to use [motions as if drawing a bowstring with his right hand to shoot an arrow], but this is already your shield, already your protection.
> MS You hold the bow, and the k'eet'oh on your left arm?
> AD Uh-huh, yeah. (Avery Denny, Tsaile, Arizona, 10/8/93)

In Protection Way ceremonies, protective materials such as arrowheads or armor must be held with the left hand or worn on the left side of the body (Walters, 8/12/93; Denny, 10/8/93). As Harry Walters explains:

> HW Things that are weapons, arrowheads, you hold in your left, and a stone knife. "Anáályééł," you know, for protection and, those kinds of things, bow and arrow, you hold in your left hand.
> MS And is there anything else that you can only do with your left hand?
> HW [Pause] Ahh, things that are from Naayéé'jí, the Protection Way ceremony, are associated with the left. In the Protection Way ceremony they have charms, you know, you always wear it on the left. (Harry Walters, Tsaile, Arizona, 8/12/93)

The trajectory of growth—from the soles of the feet to the top of the head—and the distinction between the masculine and feminine sides of the body are carefully observed in the manipulation of the human body in all ceremonial contexts. According to Sunny Dooley, "when you have any kind of blessing done, you never go from the head down, you always go from this way up [indicates from her feet upward], because that is how nature grows. Trees don't just develop. They grow from that way, you know, they go from [motions from her feet upward], and so you always encourage growth upwards, whatever blessing" (8/21/92).

A variety of materials may be ceremonially applied to patients, including herbal mixtures, ashes, sheep fat, pigments, pollen, cedar smoke, and an assortment of accouterments such as sashes, moccasins, handwoven textiles, shoulder straps, or braided wristbands and anklebands made of yucca. These artifacts served as the clothing or armor worn by Diyin Dine'é during the critical junctures in Navajo history that are returned to in the process of the specific ceremony. These materials are used to dress the patient in the image of a particular member of the Diyin Dine'é.

Every substance or artifact with which a patient is ceremonially painted or dressed provides a layer of lifelong protection to the surface of the body (Walters, 8/10/93; Denny, 10/8/93). Such a layer is acquired, for example, when a young woman is adorned with items of traditional female attire such as a sash, moccasins, a handwoven dress, or a hair tie as she is ritually dressed in the image of Changing Woman during her Kinaaldá. Another example comes from a critical point in the Hóchxǫǫ'jí, the Evil Way ceremony, when the patient is dressed in shoulder straps that have protective materials such as arrowheads, deer hooves, bear claws, shells, and ntł'iz attached to them. As Harry Walters explains, in this context these artifacts are used to dress the patient in the image of Monster Slayer, thereby instilling lifelong protection:

> HW To protect, you know, just like a coat of armor that he, like a soldier, will put on. There was a ritual involved in that, so, then even if you take it off, you still have the armor.
>
> MS You always wear it?
>
> HW Yes.
>
> MS You always have it?
>
> HW You always have it.
>
> MS As a protection?
>
> HW Yes, just like the yé'ii mask when you, once you put it on, and then you take it off. You have been initiated, and then you are blessed with that. You have certain [privileges]. You can dance in it. When there is a ceremony involving someone to be dressed in a yé'ii to treat the person you can do that.
>
> MS Uh-huh.
>
> HW Otherwise, you can't do this. That is what it symbolizes. The place, when you put that armor on, and then after the prayer is said, and then you can take it off, you always have that protection.
> (Harry Walters, Tsaile, Arizona, 8/10/93)

Individuals acquire an additional layer of protection each time such items are ceremonially applied to them. As a result, people accumulate multiple layers of protection during their lifetimes.

Each protective layer, which is beneficial to the person to whom it is ceremonially applied, can cause grave harm to the uninitiated. For example, snakes are painted onto the feet and big toes of patients as a means of protection during Na'at'oyee, the Shooting or Lightning Way ceremony (Reichard 1950:645–48; Bekis, 3/22/95), the Diné biniłch'ijí, or Small Wind Way, and the Níłch'ihjí, or Wind Way (Bekis, 3/22/95). As Mae Bekis points out in the following passage, harm can result from the simple act of an uninitiated person's wearing the footwear of someone who has been ceremonially painted in this manner.

> Even the shoes like if uh, if uh, somebody was initiated with some singing, you know, like Lightning Way and uh, when they do the painting on their patients, like Lightning Way and they have a, you know, they use a snake as a painting for their patients. Right here [points to the place on her own body]. . . . On the [outside of the] calf. And then on your big toe, under here [pointing to a sketch she is making of the body painting]. From the nail down is the head of a snake that is coming down and then the tip is the tongue here. The forked tongue? And then they said, it does an imprint in your shoes. And you are not supposed to wear [the moccasins or other footwear of] anybody that is initiated like through Lightning Way, Wind Way, the Small Wind Way and all of this. You are not supposed to wear somebody's shoes like that because the imprint, it puts an imprint forever on the shoes. It just, you know, the black paint that they use? It makes an imprint inside of your shoes and it imprints deep into your skin. . . . And they said the black paint that they use, it is a, it is just a clay. The black clay, but it imprints on your body in your flesh and they said it stays a long time in there. Even on [places her hand on her chest]. They put it on you, on your chest too. And then they said, that imprint stays within you as long as you live because you are initiated. (Mae Bekis, Tó'tsoh, Arizona, 3/22/95)

Once application to the patient is complete, the pigment, pollen, ashes, herbal mixture, or other substance is passed sunwise to all members of the family and others in attendance. Individuals apply each substance to their own bodies in the same manner as the singer applied them to the patient's body, or such applications are completed by an assistant to the singer. When a seriously ill person needs a ceremony but cannot be present—for example, if he or she is hospitalized in a comatose state or in intensive care—articles of the individual's unlaundered clothing are used in place of the entire person.[29] This clothing is laid out and "worked on" during the ceremony. Harry Walters explained why this method of treatment is effective:

HW [It is because] that clothing has touched you, that is a part of you. See?

MS Yeah, uh-huh. So if they have that piece of clothing there, when let's just say, when the herb is passed, would someone sprinkle the herb on the clothing?

HW Yes, everything that is done.

MS And would they blacken it?

HW Everything that is done to the patient would be done to that.

MS As if it was the person?

HW [Nods his head.] They lay them out, shoes, socks, trousers, shirt, even a hat.

MS Of the person that can't come?

HW Yes. (Harry Walters, Tsaile, Arizona, 8/10/93)

An absent patient derives benefit through treatment of his or her garments because the sweat, sloughed-off skin cells, and other bodily substances that become attached to articles of clothing when they are worn make the garments part of the person.

Depending on the nature of the ceremony, the singer starts with either the right or the left side when applying blessing or protecting materials to the patient. Manipulations begin on the right and move to the left during ceremonies associated with blessing, such as the molding and painting of a young woman during her Kinaaldá. Application of materials starts on the left and moves to the right in healing and protection ceremonies (H. Ashley, 7/27/93; Walters, 8/12/93), as in the portion of the Hóchxǫǫ'jí described in my field notes:

> The singer and his assistant took the patient out by the ash pile north of his mother's hooghan and had him strip down to his shorts. When they walked over to the ash pile I was directed to enter the hooghan and watch from the window or door. The singer's assistant twirled a bull roarer in front of the patient, to the north. The singer carefully helped the patient bathe in the water prepared with a herb collected from the base of a tree that had been struck by lightning. Once he was done washing they turned to enter the hooghan. I sat down and awaited their entrance. I sat on an old sofa on the south side, I noticed neat piles of ash at each of the cardinal points around the woodstove.
>
> The singer, his assistant, and the patient entered. The patient took his position on the west side of the hooghan to the left of the singer. The patient sat with his legs and arms outstretched. His feet were

flexed and his hands were lying on his legs with the palms up. The singer began a series of songs, using a gourd rattle. After one or two songs he stopped and crushed some herbs into water in a coffee can and then put the bull roarer in this. Then he dug through his paraphernalia bag [an old suitcase] and removed some arrowheads, herbs, and rocks. . . .

Next, the patient was treated with ashes from the piles around the fire with an eagle feather fan. The singer began a new series of songs as he dipped the fan into the ash pile on the east. Starting on the patient's left, the singer tapped the patient on the soles of his feet with the feather fan. He dipped the fan into the ash pile on the south and tapped the patient's knees and palms. He continued singing. Next, he dipped the fan into the ash pile on the west and tapped the fan against the area over the patient's heart and on his upper back. Then he dipped the fan into the ash pile on the north. With this ash he tapped the fan on the patient's shoulders, on the sides of his head, along the crest of his head from the nose backwards and then on the top of his head. Finally, the singer made a clockwise circular motion around the patient's head with the fan, concluding his song as he clapped the feather fan to the north [the patient's left]. In each case, the singer started on the left and moved to the right [left sole, right sole, left knee, right knee, etc.] tapping twice at each location. (Field notes, 8/8/93)

A Hóchxǫ́ǫ́'jí ceremony is required to restore health when a person has been infiltrated by harmful factors as a result of contact with the death of a Navajo. Such malevolent factors can enter at numerous locations on the body.

UKW They enter through the fingertips and the palms of your feet, they say.

MS Both hands and both feet?

UKW Uh-huh.

MS They can enter either side?

UKW [Nods her head.] Well they can enter anywhere in the pores too. (Ursula Knoki-Wilson, Fort Defiance, Arizona, 7/29/93)

The singer motions his eagle feather fan clockwise over the patient's head, raises it upward to the smokehole, and then claps it sharply to the left of the patient to direct the harmful factors leaving the patient. Some Navajo are of the opinion that the singer directs his motions to the left of the patient at this juncture in the ceremony because negative elements must leave the body through the fingertips of the left hand (Knoki-Wilson, 7/29/93). Others are of the opinion that malevolent factors are perceived to be leaving the body from the left side at this point in the ceremony only because of the patient's position in the hooghan, not because the fingertips of the left hand provide the point of departure (Walters, 8/10/93). A patient sitting on the west side of the hooghan facing east has her or his left side to the north. Therefore, the singer motions to the left as he uses his eagle feather fan to drive the malevolent factors leaving the patient's body out of the hooghan to the north. A clear passage or "way out" must be provided for the flow of personal creative powers on a day-to-day basis as well as for the expulsion of harmful phenomena in such ceremonial contexts.

As Flora Ashley explains in what follows, because of the paradigm established by the Diyin Dine'é through their emergence out of the underworlds, the need for a "way out" is universal in the Navajo world. Navajo people must provide a "way out" in all artifacts they manufacture because in the process of construction the artifact becomes both part of its creator and a conduit for creative processes and thoughts. As a result, an artisan who neglects to include a "way out" in an artistic product risks blockage of her or his thinking and creative powers.

> FA We always have an opening. Because we breathe every day. And we want our artifacts to breathe with us too. And then, they also tell us that somewhere you do it unfinished, like it might have an unfinished place, in order that your whole cycle is not done yet.
> MS Uh-huh.
> FA That is what it means. And then when . . .
> MS Hnn, OK, so is this [pointing to the break in the design on a ceremonial basket], what is called the atiin [road], is that the opening?
> FA Uh-huh, this is your path of the life here. If you close it then you are just blocking up your own path. So, there is always a path in every, a passage through everything, because of the emergence. Because we believe there is always another "way out." There is always an "out" somewhere. So, when you make this basket the weave at the end [must be at the opening in the design].
> MS Uh-huh.
> FA They say that you are supposed to complete it in one day. The last round. So they start it real early so they can complete it before the end of the day. And if you don't do it they say it might give you blindness. Yeah, that is what they told me. (Flora Ashley, Tsaile, Arizona, 7/29/91)

The "way out" may take a variety of forms, depending on the item under construction. As Mrs. Ashley pointed out, it can be found as the distinctive break in the design of the ceremonial basket that is likened to the doorway of a hooghan. As Irene Kee notes, openings such as these are necessary because of the nature and direction of human thought. The clockwise spiral of human thought can go only forward, never backward.

IK Our minds were constructed so that our thinking would be progressive, not in reverse. It will always be forward, similar to the sun. It moves only forward, never backward. He [Talking God] told us that is how it will be done. The ending part of the basket ends here [pointing to the end of the outermost coil on a basket she is holding] and the opening part of the basket is in the same location. When your house door is locked and you are inside, you cannot exit through any other place except when you open your house door. You cannot exit through any part of the wall. It is not possible. There is always an opening. From there you are able to continue thinking and be progressive. This was made according to the Talking God.

LT Well I guess all this clockwise, the way they do it this way . . .

MS Uh-huh.

LT You have to do it that way so that it will keep your mind open. It is the way the mind goes. It has something to do with your mind.

MS Shá bik'ehgo [sunwise], is the way that your mind goes?

LT Uh-huh, and then it goes, it goes straight out and if you don't have this [pointing to the break in the design of a ceremonial basket] then you're all closed in, I guess. This [the opening in the basket design] is just like your mind is wide open. (Irene Kee and Lillie Tsosie,[30] Crystal, New Mexico, 8/3/92. The words of Mrs. Kee translated by Wesley Thomas.)

Openings can also take the form of breaks in the designs of woven textiles that provide pathways from the center to the edge, or they can be the untying of a woman's hair during childbirth to prevent complications in the delivery. As Ursula Knoki-Wilson makes clear in the following account, in each case the opening provides a pathway for human thought so that it can continually move forward to new undertakings.

MS I know that when a basket is woven they have to have that passageway from the center to the rim. And I know that in weaving, women are supposed to put these two yarns all the way out, which is called by some women a "way out?"

UKW Uh-huh.

MS And what I have always wondered is, do men also have to include a way out? Like if they are a silversmith? Or is this only something women do?

UKW No, men do it too. In anything that you do that is creative, you know, like your artwork, you are supposed to put it in.

MS Anything creative?

UKW Yeah, anything you do you are supposed to leave a pathway for . . . And that is what, I guess, in a way, you know, it has to do with your body too. You know, they say if you get anything stored inside it is, that is not the natural way so you have to let them go. It is sort of like you have a spiritual pathway that is connected to your inside, to the outside too. So they say anything you do if you don't include a pathway, you are shutting yourself off from the power of spirit. So that you have to do it. (Ursula Knoki-Wilson, Chinle, Arizona, 8/10/92)

An opening is incorporated into every ceremonial sandpainting, and silversmiths must incorporate them into their work as well (Jonah Nez, 7/1/92). A "way out" is needed to ensure that all of an artist's thoughts and creativity will not be locked into any single artifact. As D. Y. Begay, a weaver from Salina Springs, Arizona, notes in regard to the contrasting line frequently woven through one corner of a rug's selvage: "It is for us [weavers]. There are times when I go somewhere or I'm with a group, and I can't think of anything but my weaving. I want to be working. My mind gets so totally taken up with weaving that it is hard to think of anything else. When both mind and body become so absorbed, a weaver may become trapped. We add the line to give us 'a way out'" (quoted in Jacka 1994:24–25).

This pathway guarantees that the artist will be able to move on to future endeavors, but the flow of a person's creativity can still become blocked if the person does not put his or her special skills to constructive purposes. As Harry Walters points out in the following passage, noteworthy skill as a potter, painter, weaver, or silversmith is considered a gift from the Holy People. If they misdirect the rewards gained by means of their gifts, artisans can develop creative blocks that render them unable to work.

HW You come to a period that you can't do anything, you come to a block. And then to get beyond that you have a ceremony done for you so that your creativity will keep on flowing. . . . You can come to a block, you know, in silversmithing. It is a gift. Being able to do that, to be a weaver, to be a fine silversmith. It's a gift and, uh, you treat it with respect from the Holy People. You know, uh, if the money that you get, you blow it on booze and things like that, you know, if you come to that, you know, you will stay that way.

MS You will get a block and then never be able to create again?

HW Yes, yes, and then, but when the money that you get, you use it to help your family, to buy food and things like that, the way it was meant to be. And that is the way that it should be. And then the block is telling you that you have been blessed with this gift and you have not acknowledged where it came from. You know that is what it is. (Harry Walters, Tsaile, Arizona, 8/10/93)

A lifelong connection exists between artifact and maker. In addition to being a conduit for an artist's creative powers, in several ways every artistic product is literally a part of its maker. Artifacts are imbued with life through the entrance of the maker's wind (Walters, 8/10/93), and the designs in artifacts are extensions of the individual artist because they are physical embodiments of the maker's thoughts (Bekis, 7/28/93). The lives of weavers and other artisans producing for the off-reservation market are further complicated by the fact that actual parts of their bodies are incorporated into their works of art in the process of manufacture. For example, as Mae Bekis explains in the following narrative, oil from a weaver's hands and her saliva and hair all inevitably become integrated into yarn as it is carded and spun, and into the textile as it is woven.

This man that is doing it [referring to a ceremony being performed in the local community] down here, he can do a sing, a Weaving Way singing too. Because you are thinking, a lot of your designs, you are thinking away. And that will affect you later on, too. Just the memory. . . . There are some ladies that can get affected by that. And they said it is just thinking away. And then you sell your mind away, your thinking. . . . By selling the rugs. And then you never know how they keep it and how they take care of it, and all that. . . . And, you know you may think, "My hand is clean," but you have the body oils on your loom, on your [rubs her fingers together as if rolling yarn between them], when you're, and even sometimes you get to [motions running yarn through her fingers and mouth], you know, fiddle with it, the yarn. . . . And you get your saliva on it, and it is sold with your saliva and it has all the body oil, and everything, and your thinking. Your hair, you know, gets in the way, gets caught in it. It is in it. And nobody knows where they take it and all that, so. That is why it affects them. (Mae Bekis, Tó'tsoh, Arizona, 7/28/93)

As a result of the lifelong connection between a weaver and the parts of her or his body—oils, saliva, hair—and her or his thoughts contained in the designs of the textile, weavers frequently need ceremonies to rectify problems that develop after their textiles have been sold. Because, as Mrs. Bekis cautioned, when textiles are sold to strangers, "you never know how they keep it and how they take care of it, and all that."

The situation resulting from incorporation of various parts of a weaver's body—hair, saliva, body oil, or thoughts—into handwoven products is not unique in the Navajo world. It is a single example among many of the fact that, in the Navajo world, the boundaries of the self—the awareness Navajo people have of themselves as perceptible subjects—and those of the person—the social construct based on culturally sanctioned rules, prerogatives, and agency—are extended beyond the confines of the skin by the principle of synecdoche. It dictates that every part is equivalent to the whole, so anything done to, or by means of, a part takes effect upon, or has the effect of, the whole. The principle of synecdoche, coupled with the other structural principles that govern construction of the human body, plays an important role in the attainment of full personhood in the Navajo world. As will be seen in the next chapter, children must be assisted by parents and other kin at critical points in the life cycle to foster and develop the fundamental elements of personhood—awareness, relations, agency, and obligations among human beings and other entities—which are structured on the principles of homology, complementarity, and synecdoche.

CHAPTER V

BECOMING
A NAVAJO

The agreement that was made on top of Ch'óol'íí was that the baby would not become a mortal until the age of eight. And in between that time, from the time that it is conceived until the time that it is born, it is still a magical child. It is still a child that is capable of miracles. You know, that kind of thing. And they say that the Holy People are still instructing the baby even through the womb as it emerges and it cries. And the Holy People finally leave the child, somewhat detach themselves from the child, is what I should say, when it laughs. And so, when the baby first laughs, that is when you give them a huge party and you're sort of illustrating your competence to the Holy People that we're going to be all right, we're going to be good relatives, we're going to be good nurturers, we're going to be good parents. (Sunny Dooley, Gallup, New Mexico, 8/19/92)

Children must be assisted in the process of attaining full Navajo personhood. The teachings of the Diyin Dine'é dictate that particular parts of the body—afterbirth, blood, umbilical cords—are more susceptible to effect than others, and that the human body is more open to effect at critical times in the life cycle—in utero, at birth, at puberty, and during pregnancy. Previous anthropological analyses acknowledging the complex role effects from exposure to bodily substances or other events can play in the development of bodies and persons offered me insights into Navajo views on the developmental nature of the human body and personhood (Meigs 1976, 1984; Gillison 1980; Herdt 1981, 1982a, 1982b; Poole 1981; Daniel 1984; Strathern 1988; Battaglia 1990; O'Hanlon 1992; Riesman 1992; Wright et al. 1993).

Theoretical insights gained from pioneering work in Melanesia emphasize the ongoing construction of the human body. In some Melanesian societies, the body is revealed as a collection of "substances and flows from a number of sources momentarily come together" (O'Hanlon 1992:603). Contrary to the complete body posited by Western biomedicine, this type of Melanesian body, like the Navajo one, is subject to fundamental alteration during the life cycle. Alterations occur through physical manipulations and ingestion or expulsion of bodily substances. Traditional wisdom offers guidance for family members on fostering developing Navajo persons through manipulations and treatments at each of the critical points in the life cycle.

Navajo people seek knowledge and make conscious decisions based on this knowledge regarding how best to control and manipulate the potential positive effects while limiting the negative effects of diverse substances, actions, and events on the development of persons. Consideration of the various methods used to influence children—prenatally and throughout childhood—reveals that Navajo individuals can be affected by contact with other persons (human and nonhuman alike), with various substances, or with dramatic events. Effect can be transferred through a variety of means, including person-to-person contact, contact with bodily substances such as blood, exposure to the sensitive portions of a ceremony, or exposure to another person's death.

The prenatal period is a time of intense susceptibility. As a result, precautions are taken by both parents throughout the gestation of a child. After birth, children are carefully bathed and molded to take advantage of the body's malleability at this time. In addition, Navajo parents and grandparents carefully manipulate parts of the child's body, such as the blood associated with childbirth or the umbilical cord, and this manipulation has lifelong effects on the child.

> MS Are there any special rules regarding the disposal of a baby's first bathwater? The water from the first bath?
>
> UKW Yeah, they are not supposed to just, you know, splatter it all over the place. They are supposed to pour it real gently to the earth. In a safe [place], you know, like maybe underneath a healthy bush or tree, something like that. But they are not supposed to splatter it anywhere.
>
> MS Oh? I guess what I was thinking about was the fact that at birth the child is usually covered with some blood.
>
> UKW Uh-huh?
>
> MS And so that would be in the bathwater.
>
> UKW Yeah.

MS Is there any danger associated with the blood involved in childbirth?

UKW Well, blood is not supposed to be burned. Because they say if you burn blood then it invokes fever, because it is sort of like living tissue and you burn your living tissue, so to speak. . . . So if you splatter it then the living tissue would get bruised, so to speak, then your body would, the baby's body would suffer, you know, sort of like trauma from that. So they are supposed to gently pour it.

MS So the blood from the birth, which is no longer actually attached to the body, is still considered to have an influence over the body?

UKW Yeah. (Ursula Knoki-Wilson, Chinle, Arizona, 8/10/92)

Synecdoche and the rules governing effect demand that all parts of the body clearly belong to someone. In the Navajo language it is impossible to say simply "leg" or "umbilical cord" because parts of the body must always be possessed; the term for every part is inalienable from a pronominal prefix. For example, the stem for umbilical cord, -ts'éé', cannot occur in speech without a prefix such as shi-, "my," ni-, "your," or 'a-, "someone's," to designate possession. Such identification is critical because the principle of synecdoche dictates that parts of the body, bodily fluids, and offal offer the potential for positive or negative effect throughout a person's life. Parts of the body and bodily substances can affect the health and welfare of the individual and, by extension, her or his kin and community, long past detachment or elimination.[1] As Mae Bekis of Tó'tsoh, Arizona, explains in the following passage, because of this lifelong connection individuals must demonstrate personal responsibility over parts of their own bodies and bodily fluids, and, as Ursula Knoki-Wilson also noted, adults must demonstrate responsibility over those of children.

MS I have noticed when I am visiting in homes and they are trimming hair, like a little child's hair or one woman trimming another woman's hair, that they sweep up the hair and put it in a little bag. And the same with nail clippings. How is one supposed to dispose of those things?

MB I was always told that when you trim your hair you are supposed to burn it. Not all of it, just part of it, you know, burn it and put a little water on it and then rub it together and put it back on your hair. That is to restore, [to ensure] keeping your hair all the time. . . .

MS And then what do you do with the rest of the trimmings?

MB Then the rest, you can burn it. You can't throw it away because if you threw it away outside it would be blowing around by the wind and then who knows that it can be picked up by the rats, mice, the snakes and they will make a nest and then you will have a headache and nobody will know why you have a headache. Or the birds pick it up for their nest somewhere up on the tree or, uh, up into the highest pine tree, or way up into the rocks, you know. And you wouldn't know where your hair is and they say, they say it can give you headaches.

MS Will it affect your thinking?

MB Yeah. That is why they say, "Be careful with your hair. Always burn it."

MS Uh-huh. How about nail clippings? Like when you trim your nails?

MB Nail clippings, always burn it too, you know. And they say, that the Crow picked it up, this is just part of a story, they said that, "Way long time ago the First Lady had cut her nails and then the Crow picked it up and said it was a precious heshi [ground shell beads]." And so, they said, from there on they said, "Don't throw your nails away," you know, they say, "Always burn it to dispose of it." (Mae Bekis, Tó'tsoh, Arizona, 3/22/95)

Within the framework of practice theory (Bourdieu 1977; Ortner 1984, 1989; Comaroff 1985; McCloskey 1993), we can consider decisions made by Navajo people about controlling and manipulating the potential positive effects while simultaneously limiting the negative effects of events on their lives. The Navajo system—the paradigms established by the Holy People—governing the cultural construction of the human body and personhood simultaneously informs choices and is reproduced in practice through the actions taken to guide children toward full personhood. Practice, in turn, affects the system, because the Navajo system of beliefs is not a static set of rules that are blindly followed. Contemporary parents use methods passed down from their elders for attaining lifelong effects on children—the placement of umbilical cords or the selection of someone with particular skills to mold an infant at birth or a young person at puberty—as tools rather than as restraints. They actively manipulate the cultural system inherited from the past to influence the development of their children along lines that conform to current values and goals and respond to the problems and demands of the modern world. Family members guide children through every step toward personhood in the Navajo world. One of the first steps is determination of sex.

WANTING A DAUGHTER

Well, I had two boys and my husband and I wanted a daughter really bad. And my mother told me that this one woman that was a relation to us, she said, "You can go see her and she will tell you about how to go about it." So we went there, but she was very ill and she didn't really know [the woman was not coherent, owing to illness]. . . . I guess her daughter knew of the way that she was doing things, you know, [how to] perform that small ceremony for a woman to have a daughter. But it was just a brief one. It didn't take more than ten minutes. The way she told us was to, they call it hadahoniye' [aragonite], it's a long rock, you know, it's real narrow, it would be the size of my finger and they're like that [indicates the size of her little finger]. And it has kind of a different version of color in it. I know my dad has quite a bit of those. And I guess it's picked only from certain areas of the reservation, or where sacred places are going to be. She told us to grind it on a stone, put it in water and drink it. So we just did that, my mom did that. And then she knew of something that was passed on from her mom, she barely remembered, and it was sea shells where they had an opening in it [referring to small shells of the genus *Cypraea*]. And she told me to wear that all the time around my waist. I had one around my waist all the time. One in my pocket or in my purse. And every so often she told me to rub it against my stomach, you know, rub it on. So I did that for the nine months that we had my daughter. Then my daughter was born, and you know, it was really unbelievable! I had her in the hospital and I kept looking at her. I had to open her legs and make sure she was a girl! I was really, I was that desperate. It really made me feel good. (Sadie Billie, Tsaile, Arizona, 7/10/91)[2]

The sex of the child is said to be determined at the time of conception by the type of fluid with which the father's sperm merges in the mother's womb. If the man's sperm combines with tó ał'tahnáschíín, a biologically male child is formed; if it combines with tó biyáázh, a biologically female child results (Walters, 8/18/92). This sexuality is not immutable. Navajo can and do influence the sex of their unborn children. Parents who have a sexual preference take action and often pursue all avenues to influence the outcome of the sex of the child. If a pregnant woman has a preference for either a male or a female child, she will ask her family to hold a Blessing Way ceremony for her sometime in the first trimester of the pregnancy and have the ceremonial practitioner refer to the desired sex in all pertinent passages of prayer (Wyman 1970:337; Wilson 1980:17). The practitioner would say, "May I give birth to Pollen [Boy or Girl], may I give birth to Cornbeetle [Boy or Girl], may I give birth to Long-life [Boy or Girl], may I give birth to Happiness [Boy or Girl]!" depending on which sex is desired (Wyman 1970:337). Alternatively, women seeking a child of a particular sex are directed to ingest, wear, or apply to their bodies various substances that can influence the sex of the child prior to conception or during gestation.

When I inquired about the means available to Navajo women wishing to influence the sex of an unborn child, women initially demonstrated mild reticence to discuss these matters, and they tended to frame descriptions of specific methods with qualifying statements. Consider, for example, the following conversation I had with Mrs. Louva Dahozy of Fort Defiance, Arizona.[3]

> MS What about if a woman wanted a girl, like if she had four children, four boys, and she wanted a girl? Was there any special thing that women could do?
>
> LD They did a lot of things. I don't know if that worked or not, but they did a lot of things like that.
>
> MS Like what?
>
> LD Like the grandmother would say to the girl that is married that they have to eat certain things, and stuff like that.
>
> MS What kinds of things?
>
> LD Like from the sheep, certain parts from the sheep that she would eat so she can have a girl or a boy whatever she wants, I guess. (Louva Dahozy, Fort Defiance, Arizona, 8/19/92)

Comments such as Mrs. Dahozy's that she did not know whether such methods worked or not indicate that these consultants could not or would not verify the accuracy of the methods. I sensed that women were often reluctant to verify the effectiveness of these methods with testimony from personal experience because they expected disapproval on my part. Navajo women are conditioned to be shy about sharing traditional techniques such as these because in the past, they or their female relatives experienced ridicule from non-Navajo for using such "unscientific" methods.

Once women felt assured I was not seeking to ridicule them, I was told of a variety of methods, including the ingestion of various parts of animals. Indeed, the "parts from the sheep" alluded to by Mrs. Dahozy came up repeatedly, for in many families, women desiring female or male children are directed to eat specific parts of sheep.

The parts from the sheep are effective, I am told. It is up to the Holy People, they are the ones who put the sex of children in order. If you are blessed you will have a child of one sex and the next one will be of the opposite and the third of still another sex. I think that is how it is. I think of that often. The sheep's stomach, the smaller one, the sheep has two [stomachs]. The intestine that is connected to this stomach is used. Girls are constantly told to eat this part, so they will have male babies. That was what we were told. "Eat the kidneys, both of them," we were told. "Eat the kidneys, so you can have a female baby," we were told. That is how the sheep were helpful and useful in making male and female babies. That was how it was done, by our ancestors. . . . When you butcher, you can remove the windpipe and eat that part. Then the woman can have a male child. (The words of Irene Kee, Crystal, New Mexico, 8/4/92, translated by Wesley Thomas)

As I discussed this topic, my ignorance of sheep anatomy became readily apparent to the people with whom I consulted. In some cases, my ignorance hampered initial clarification of which parts of the sheep were deemed influential. When Mae Bekis tried to instruct me on the exact organs of the sheep that should be eaten, I was at a loss regarding to which anatomical part she was making reference.

MB If you want to have a boy, there is some, uh, it is inside the sheep, it is kind of an intestine. There is a little bag like that [indicating three to four inches with her fingers] and it has a, we call it 'ach'íí', it is intestine coming from it. They said eat a lot of that. It is a little bag, it is just like a stomach.

MS [Looking puzzled] A little bag about the size of your fist?

MB It is just like a stomach, but is has a little, it has got a lot of meat on it about that far.

MS Uh-huh, about four inches?

MB Uh-huh, and they said, "Eat a lot of that if you want a boy." I don't know if it is true. (Mae Bekis, Tó'tsoh, Arizona, 8/5/92)[4]

Other women with whom I consulted used biomedical terminology when referring to the organs of the sheep considered beneficial. Use of this terminology also led to some confusion on my part.

MS Have you ever heard of a treatment to have a boy? Like if a woman had six daughters?

UKW Yeah, the only one I heard about is you are supposed to eat a certain part of the sheep, you know, there is that little, I guess it is the spleen that is attached to the stomach.

MS Oh, that is what it is? It is the spleen?

UKW Yeah. It is the spleen.

MS Oh, yeah. Somebody told me about it but I couldn't think what part of the body it was.

UKW Yeah, it is the spleen, they are supposed to, you know, cut it open and sort of stuff it with the omentum, the greater omentum of the sheep. Just a little piece of it.

MS What is the greater omentum?

UKW It is that little fat sheet that goes over the stomach.

MS Oh, oh, OK.

UKW The adipose tissue that goes over the stomach, that one.

MS Your medical terminology! I will look it up when I go home.

UKW Yeah, it just, they take a little piece of it and stuff it into the spleen and then they eat that. (Ursula Knoki-Wilson, Chinle, Arizona, 8/10/92)[5]

In addition to ingesting the intestine, spleen, and windpipe to ensure having male children, and the kidneys to guarantee female children, women are often directed to ingest substances taken from significant places in the landscape, such as the ground aragonite mentioned by Mrs. Billie (7/10/91). The sex of unborn children can also be influenced through ingestion of materials "scraped" from places in the landscape with special features such as likenesses to human male and female genitalia:

LT If a woman came to you who has five daughters and wants a boy baby and asked for your help, how would you reply to that question? Do you know anything in that area?

IK There is something available that will help that. At Blue Ridge Mountain, there is a rock. It is shaped and huge [demonstrating the size with her hands]. I am told it resembles a man's penis. It is standing there erect! It is scraped. Particles from the rock are used. Closer and toward us, there is a water which runs out, there is a small rock. It is about this size [indicates an arm's width]. The rock resembles the knees of a woman. Right in the middle there is a perfect resemblance of the thing we pee through as women. It sits there. It is scraped too. A shaving of the rock is done, too. The powder part of it is mixed with water and drunk by the person who wants a female child. If the woman wants a male child, she has to use the powdered rock from the previous mentioned rock. It really resembles the sexual organ of a man, I tell you! [Laughs] It really resembles it. . . . I remember seeing that with "Mud Lady" a while back. We visited those rocks. It really actually resembles a lying woman. I was told you can even apply the powder from the rock to horses. If you want a female horse, you apply the powdered rock to a female horse, so she will have a female baby horse.

LT If she wants you to show her where it is, will you remember where it is, still?

IK It has been a very long time since I have been there. I do not know. If people found out there was water available, they might have placed a drinking trough for the animals. Even maybe, those rocks are stolen by the white people. (The words of Irene Kee and Lillie Tsosie, Crystal, New Mexico, 8/4/92, translated by Wesley Thomas)

"Like produces like." The correlation in form between these rocks and male and female genitalia—penis and vulva—ensures the effect of drinking particles scraped from these rocks. The shape of *Cypraea* shells also contributes to their influence. The serrated edges characteristic of the openings of these shells are said to look just like the vulvas of female infants.[6]

That is helpful, too. The one she has in her hands [referring to a large abalone shell with several small *Cypraea* shells in it], especially if a female baby is wanted. The female baby is small, it [the child's vulva] is like that. That is what I was told. . . . Yes these [as I hand the shells to her]. My maternal aunt, tried. She tried. Finally, at the end, she was given a girl. I do not know what she did. Look, it really does resemble a little girl [pointing to the serrated edges of the opening of a Cypraea shell]. You can file this portion off and consume it, it would help. A girl baby will be given to you. (The words of Irene Kee, Crystal, New Mexico, 8/4/92, translated by Wesley Thomas)

As Sadie Billie remarked, women can also be directed to wear, or apply to their bodies, a variety of substances to ensure having a child of the desired sex. Drilled white shells are frequently tied to a young woman's sash at her Kinaaldá to make sure that she will have female children (Agnes Begay, 7/26/91; Kee, 8/4/92;

Dooley, 8/21/92). And, as Mrs. Lillie Tsosie of Crystal, Arizona, explains in the following passage, women are also told to wear white shell while they are pregnant to guarantee having a daughter (Annie Kahn, 7/7/91; Sadie Billie, 7/10/91; A. Begay, 7/26/91; F. Ashley, 7/29/91; Kee, 8/3/92; Walters, 8/18/92; Dahozy, 8/19/92; Mrs. Joe McCabe, 8/19/92).

> One of my friends told me that, she lives in that house [indicating a house south of her home], she has a little girl, after she had two boys. They are teenagers. She said she used to wear that [white shell], she had a little tiny one, about that small [indicates about three-quarters of an inch in length]. She said she used to wear that all the time when she was getting pregnant. She had a little girl.
> (Lillie Tsosie, Crystal, New Mexico, 8/4/92)

Women are directed to wear turquoise in a similar manner while pregnant to ensure having a boy (Kahn, 7/7/91; F. Ashley, 7/29/91; Walters, 8/18/92).

A more aggressive approach involves the application of white shell or pollens directly to the body. As Mrs. Billie noted, her mother directed her to rub the white shell against her abdomen regularly throughout her pregnancy (Billie, 7/10/91). Alternatively, women who desire daughters are told to grind the white shell and apply it to the surface of their bodies while pregnant.

> **MB** This one [holding up a *Cypraea* shell] if a lady is pregnant.
> **MS** Uh-huh?
> **MB** You use this one. Grind it, [whispering] if you want a girl.
> **MS** Oh, that is if you want a girl?
> **MB** You grind it and then you put it on yourself and you can have a girl.
> **MS** And you rub it on yourself?
> **MB** Uh-huh, all over, outside, your body. That is what it is for.
> (Mae Bekis, Tó'tsoh, Arizona, 8/5/92)

Specially prepared pollens can also be applied to the body to influence the sex of future children. As Harry Walters explains:

> Water comes in two forms, male and female forms. One is tó biyáázh, tó ał'tahnáshchíín. All water is like that. Even the one that comes from the sink, you know, comes in that form. Tó biyáázh is dew. Sometimes when there is a fog, in the wintertime, you know, when the fog lifts, you see these little white crystals on the trees

and grass. Those are tó biyáázh. The female. And then the medicine men go out there and then they sprinkle corn pollen on it,
and then they sprinkle it on a dish, you know, the water collects
on that. And then, when it dries it just leaves the pollen. So that,
the pollen, is used on the woman if she wants to have a female. A
female child. . . . And then tó al'tahnáshchíín is water that comes
in many forms like rain, lakes, streams, things like that. Those are
tó al'tahnáshchíín. Again, you also go to that, and collect some,
sprinkle water on it, let it dry. And then if you want to have a male
you use that. (Harry Walters, Tsaile, Arizona, 8/18/92)

The Navajo women with whom I consulted demonstrated a sense of empowerment gained from possessing esoteric knowledge, largely unknown to men, that
enabled them to influence the sex of their unborn children. They have knowledge
of a variety of specific means that can be used to influence the sex of a child before
conception or during pregnancy, including the application of pollens or white shell
directly to the mother's body, the wearing of white shell or turquoise, the ingestion
of aragonite, white shell, or particular parts of sheep, and the power of prayer.
These are only a few of the ways in which a fetus can be affected, for fetuses are
considered to be extremely malleable and susceptible to effect.

PRENATAL SUSCEPTIBILITY

The nature of an illness or problem contracted by a child while in the womb is often
patterned after the cause; that is, like produces like. In the 1940s, Leighton and
Kluckhohn were told that if a parent broke a pot, the child's fontanel would not
close properly, and if a pregnant woman inverted a rug on the loom, her child
would become inverted in the womb (1947:14). During the same era, Flora Bailey
was told that if a woman used a six-prong weaving fork while pregnant, her child
would be born with six fingers or six toes, and if she cut or sawed the edge of an
old cooking pot, the child would be born with a harelip (Bailey 1950:41, 42). As
Irene Kee explained, she learned from personal experience why many of these
restrictions are still observed today:

Both the man and woman together have many things to observe.
The pregnant wife has restrictions, so does the father-to-be. Making pottery is forbidden. It cannot be made. Also, battens and other
weaving tools are forbidden to be made by either [parent]. The
fingers of the weaving fork cannot be made, so you cannot cut and
create or reproduce any form which duplicates any part of the hu-

man anatomy. The prongs of the weaving fork resemble the fingers of a child. A spindle cannot be made, too. If one is made it will affect the mind of the baby. It happened to one of Joe Begay's [fictitious name] daughters. It took a long time for that to be corrected. It was finally done in the Farmington [New Mexico] area. That is where they found out it was caused by the creation of a spindle. People say you are not to do patchwork on torn or worn clothing or blankets. I think they are telling the truth. You are never to sew your clothes while wearing them. That is forbidden. Look at [him, indicating one of her sons], he has a patchlike pattern on his body, which is very obvious to anyone and everyone. I did that. I sewed while I was pregnant with him. It has affected him. My mother scolded me. She insisted that I undo the sewing, but I did not. She scolded me continuously because of that and for a long time, too. (The words of Irene Kee, Crystal, New Mexico, 8/4/92, translated by Wesley Thomas)

Unborn children can also take on the characteristics of animals to which they are exposed in utero. In the past, pregnant women were cautioned against looking at a dead animal for fear the child would take on its attributes. If a pregnant woman saw a dead bear, her child would be born clubfooted; if she saw a dead duck, the child might have webbed hands or feet (Bailey 1950:34).

Navajo women are still warned to avoid dead animals while pregnant. This precaution has been complicated in the contemporary world by the widespread adoption of pickup trucks and high-speed highway travel. As Sunny Dooley points out in the following account, in the contemporary world, exposure to road kill is a recognized hazard.

SD They say that when your child is within you anything can affect the child. So that when it is born, it takes on those characteristics. And my mother says the reason why children are so volatile today is because so many pregnant women drive by highways where they see dead dogs or dead animals on the highway. And those, like, "łééchąą' bik'ehgo." Is how you would say it, meaning "you are similar to a dog." You know, kind of like, you know what I mean?

MS Oh, I see what you mean.

SD Then the child takes on those characteristics of the dog. You know, meaning that they growl, they have umm, and they bark, they are lazy and you know they just don't do anything. And she says, "Maybe that is why children are like that today."

MS Who knows?

SD And there are actually ceremonies to correct that. You know, so you can undo the fact that "łééchąą'gi," the "like as," you know, whatever it is that you are "like as." It can be undone. (Sunny Dooley, Gallup, New Mexico, 8/19/92)

Precautions must be taken by all Navajo of childbearing age to prevent exposure to death or events of a traumatic nature. Such exposure can negatively affect the mother during delivery or the child before or after birth, or even prior to conception. "If a woman sees a dead person or the bones of one other than a Navajo while carrying a child, the child when it grows up may have bad luck in the form of disease which could only be cured by anadji [*sic*] or War Dance [Enemy Way]. The same ill luck would be attracted if a man saw such things when his wife was pregnant" (Reichard 1950:115).

Birth defects or childhood illnesses are frequently attributed to violation of precautions on the part of either parent. As Mae Bekis explains in the following personal narrative about her exposure to a solar eclipse while she was pregnant, and her daughter's exposure to a lunar eclipse while the daughter was pregnant, it makes no difference whether such violations are committed willfully or unknowingly. Problems with the eyes or the ears of the unborn child that may result from such exposure are prevented or rectified after the birth of the child through the performance of a ceremony in which a sandpainting of an eclipse of the sun or an eclipse of the moon—whichever shone on the pregnant woman—is followed by a sandpainting of a full sun.

> **MB** Like when I got pregnant, there was an eclipse and I walked outside. It already shone on me. And so, after I had the baby, I have to do something for the baby. And they have a tádídíín that they use. And it was given to my baby with some songs so it won't affect, they said it will affect the ears or the eyes, the earache or the blindness later on in life. . . . The father, the sun, already knows that this is done for us and then it won't in any way it won't affect [the child]. Like [my daughter], I guess when her little boy, she was over here and she said, "Mom did you see the eclipse?" This was during the night and she said, "It is partly gone." I guess she looked up there. And just lately her baby had an eye problem and the doctor said it is not red eye [pinkeye, conjunctivitis], it is just some flu or a pollination. And so her baby has to have something done. And they had a hand trembler and [she] told her that she saw the eclipse. . . . So they did that for her and the baby.[7]
>
> **MS** What type of ceremony did they have to do?

MB It has to do with the Lightning Way. See, they usually print the sun [or the moon, depending on the circumstances] as an eclipse. They put it down in the sandpainting. And then they have to sit on it and get some medicine. They have to drink some medicine. . . . [In a situation such as that experienced by her daughter] You use the moon eclipse as, you know, dark all over and then the next morning they do the sun.

MS As an eclipse?

MB No. The same, the moon eclipse and the sun. I guess it is just the shadow that crosses or something?

MS Yeah.

MB And so they have to use both of it. During the night they use an eclipse, the next day it is full, it is just a regular sun they use.

MS So during the night they have an eclipse of the moon sandpainting?

MB Uh-huh, uh-huh.

MS And then during the day?

MB The day is the sun, it is clear. (Mae Bekis, Tó'tsoh, Arizona, 7/ 28/93)

Illness can also result from a parent's unavoidable exposure to a dangerous situation, as is illustrated in the following account told by Sunny Dooley. In this case, harmful effect was transferred to a child through her father's sperm.

SD Also what is interesting is that men, the father of the child, can affect their baby. It was really interesting for me to hear one time, just recently, that not only women can transmit, like fetal alcohol syndrome, like if they drink, but also the sperm of the male can too. If they are abusing or misusing drugs [it] can also affect the baby in the same way. Or that if they do certain activities, their sperm counts go down and all this kind of stuff. And I was explaining this theory to my mother. And she then said, "Well of course!" And then she told me, "That is the reason why you had to have a Squaw Dance [Enemy Way], was because when your father was away in Kansas on the railroad, you know, he saw an accident. It happened over there where a white man was killed, right in front of his face. And he came back and made love and created you, and so that particular traumatic experience affected every part of him, even his sperm," you know.

MS Yeah, of course.

SD I mean it sounds weird.

MS No, no.

SD And then, "So when you were born it did not manifest itself until you were six or seven. Then you would just have nosebleeds and pass out." She took me to like PHS [Public Health Service clinic or hospital] and they couldn't find anything. I mean like they pulled out my boogers and everything, and I just remember being at PHS crying my eyes out, because it hurt so much. And they wanted to do surgery on my nose. And my father said, "No, you are not going to do surgery on my daughter's nose!" [Chuckles] So they took me to a hand trembler. And then the hand trembler told my parents that my father saw, you know, this accident. [The hand trembler said] "Somewhere in a city, and it is affecting your daughter, and you still had that essence about you when you came back to be with your wife and that's why," you know. And so then I had to be in an Enemy Way ceremony and all this kind of stuff. (Sunny Dooley, Gallup, New Mexico, 8/19/92)

In many families, even when neither parent is known to have been exposed to a potentially harmful event such as an eclipse or a fatal automobile accident, a Blessing Way ceremony is routinely conducted as a prophylactic measure in the last trimester of pregnancy to ensure that the child will be healthy and the delivery fast and without difficulty (Kluckhohn and Leighton 1974 [1946]:212; Wyman 1970:335–37; Stewart 1980:11–12; Hartle-Schutte 1988; Kahn, 7/7/91; Sadie Billie, 7/10/91; Bekis, 7/28/93).[8] This ceremony may also be conducted to correct existing problems. For example, as Mae Bekis explains in the following account, this important ceremony has the power to restore health to a damaged fetus, even one that has been affected by venereal disease.

MB Well, like I had one patient down here [indicates west with her lips], she was having problems, you know, and I guess she had VD [venereal disease] to start with. And then, so the doctors in Farmington told her that her baby was going to be deformed, you know, and she was going to have a hard time. And she was crying and she said, "I want a good baby. I want to have a fully formed baby." And so, I guess at first she didn't really believe it but her mother told her about the Blessing Way and all that, that can be done for her. And so she came over, her and her mother, and then she talked to me on it. And then, in front of her mother she didn't say much about the VD, but after I started the sing, for her, when I went down there [to the patient's home], her mother was out of sight and she told me what her problem was. And she had the VD to start with, when she started having [conceived] the baby. And then, the doctors told her that she might have a breech baby, she might have a deformed baby. And so she was really scared to have her baby. And then I told her, I said, "In prayer," I said, "I'll have this all forgiven and see how your baby is going to come out." And then I did the sing for her. And we had to pray, you know, her and I had to pray. And I said, "Just follow me about the prayer." And then on the fourth day, when she was going to wash up [after the required four-day holy period], at four-thirty in the morning, she started her pain.

MS Ohh.

MB And then at seven o'clock she had her baby. They delivered it in Farmington and this, the doctor that had told her, "The baby is going to be this and that," they called him, but he was still on his way from Aztec [New Mexico] and she had the baby. And she said the baby was perfect.

MS Ohh!!

MB She didn't have any problems. She said, "All I thought about was the song that you were singing, and that you were telling me about." And then she said, "All this time," she says, "every time I had the pain, I was thinking of the song that you were telling me about," she said. And when she had her baby, "It was perfect," she said.

MS That is wonderful. (Mae Bekis, Tó'tsoh, Arizona, 7/28/93).

Once a Blessing Way ceremony has been performed in the last trimester of pregnancy to facilitate the safe delivery of a healthy child, no further preparations are made. Family members return to their usual routines, quietly awaiting the birth of their newest relative.

BIRTH

This White Shell Girl, later to be called Changing Woman, was the one who did this [set the precedents for Navajo childbirth]. She was given two boys, the first is called Monster Slayer and the second is Born For Water. That is how my story goes. When the children were about to be born, First Woman and First Man were confronted with what needs to be done. They wanted advice and were creating confusion among themselves when their first child was to be born. They did not know it was going to be twins. Talking God came to their front door. He instructed First Woman and First Man to place a beam inside the west side of the hooghan. "Place a red sash belt over it, draping it evenly on both sides of the beam. She will hold onto the belt and will give birth doing that. I cannot be involved as I am afraid of the menstrual blood." With that statement he left and went on his way. They don't know where, probably went back to his own home. The first was a boy. Then another boy fell out again. First Woman bathed the baby boys and placed them within the softened cedar barks. Just like what they did with their mother [Changing Woman] when they first found her. She prepared her grandchildren really nice then. (The words of Irene Kee, Crystal, New Mexico, 8/4/92, translated by Wesley Thomas)

In the process of giving birth to the twins, Changing Woman established precedents for the Navajo birthing process. Up to the late 1930s and early 1940s, most Navajo women bore their children at home (Lockett 1939:15; Leighton and Kluckhohn 1947:15; Bailey 1950). Children were born in their mother's or grandmother's hooghan, except in excessively hot weather, when birth took place outside under the protection of a *chahash'oh*, a brush shelter designed for summer use. At the onset of labor, an experienced female relative or a midwife was called. The family took care in selecting the midwife or female relative who would supervise the birth because her condition could affect the child. A woman had to be physically fit in order to serve as a midwife, for if she had any physical ailments they would be transferred to the child through her hands as she facilitated the delivery and cared for the newborn (Dooley, 7/21/93).

The midwife or female relative who was called on to assist with the birth supervised preparation of the hooghan for the delivery. Under her direction, a large pot of water was placed on the fire or stove. A sharp utensil for cutting the umbilical cord and strings with which to tie it were placed in this water and allowed to boil for at least an hour (Wilson 1980:18). As in Mrs. Kee's narrative of the birth of the twins, a red sash (*sis łichí'í*) was wound sunwise and suspended from a ceiling beam or a supplementary support pole on the west side of the hooghan, between the fire and the back wall. This sash was for the woman to grip while in labor. To offer greater support, a knot was tied in a sunwise direction near the lower end of the sash. Corn pollen was placed along the sash from the top to the bottom after it was suspended (Bailey 1950:56). All applications on the sash and the mother during the process of birth were made downward—from the top of the head to the toes. Such applications moved in reverse of the usual ceremonial order—from the soles of the feet to the top of the head—because they were intended to facilitate delivery of the child (Wyman 1970:336).

A shallow excavation, approximately four inches deep and two feet across, was made where the sash touched the floor. Warm sand or soil was placed in this excavation and covered with a sheepskin. These materials were intended to catch the maternal bodily fluids released during childbirth. At the onset of labor, the parturient woman untied her hair bun, removed her jewelry and anything else that could be seen to "tie" or bind up the child in the womb, and then knelt on the sheepskin on the western side of the hooghan, facing east (Kahn, 7/7/91; Rosie Tso, 7/14/91; Knoki-Wilson, 8/10/92; McCabe, 8/19/92; Dooley, 8/21/92).

When called upon to assist with births, midwives would first ascertain whether the position of the child was correct. They used a variety of means, including hand trembling, to diagnose problems. Leighton and Kluckhohn report that in the 1940s, if a woman's labor was protracted, all women and long-haired men in the immediate vicinity were asked to let their hair down. If this did not reconcile the problem, all horses and other livestock in the surrounding area were released (Leighton and Kluckhohn 1947:15). If these actions failed, a ceremonial practitioner was called in to diagnose the problem. The "Unraveling" ceremony was frequently employed to correct any "tying in" of the baby in the womb. This condition was thought to result from inappropriate acts by the parents during the pregnancy. The child was "untied" or freed for quick and easy birth through the ceremonial act of unraveling. The proper technique for unraveling was demonstrated for Flora Bailey by an elderly consultant, and Bailey described the process as follows.

> She removed the hair string from her hair, held the end, and made a loop, holding the two ends together but not tying them. Then she did a crochet stitch with her fingers and made several such stitches (the number is not significant) looped on the string. Holding both ends, one in each hand, she pressed the unraveler four times (though again she declared the number was insignificant) against my abdomen, each application being slightly lower than the former. Finally with a flourish she pulled the end and neatly unraveled the string. She then insisted that I make the knots and unravel the hair string against her body. She seemed pleased at my success. (Bailey 1950:61)

In addition to such ceremonial methods for aiding childbirth, active assistance was given through massage and manipulation. In uncomplicated births, the midwife and other people in attendance assisted the laboring woman by administering herbal infusions and comforting touches and words until the delivery. The delivering mother pulled against the knotted end of the sash during contractions. A second assistant grasped the parturient woman from behind, gently applying downward pressure on her abdomen during contractions (Bailey 1950:63; Wilson 1980:19; A. Begay, 7/26/91; F. Ashley, 7/29/91). The midwife knelt facing the mother, prepared to guide the child as it emerged from the birth canal.

Often, women went into labor when no midwife or knowledgeable female relative was available to supervise the birth. In such situations, like the one described in the following account by Mrs. Agnes Begay of Many Farms, Arizona, neighbors were frequently called on to help.[9] Knowledgeable about birthing practices or not, these people did the best they could under the circumstances.

> **AB** One time I was asked to help. There was a lady having a baby across the wash over here [indicates west with her lips]. My husband, late husband, you know, we went over there. And there was only a man that was the lady's husband there. He didn't know what to do. So he told, he said [for Mr. Begay] to hold around here [indicates the waist]. "Just push it down like this." And when the baby came, he said, "Mrs. Begay take the baby out." And when I opened her skirt, the baby had something covered over her face!
>
> **MS** Oh, yeah?
>
> **AB** It really scared me and I said, "This is not a baby! There is something born here!" I said [chuckles]. And then the husband went over there and tore that thing off of it. I think, I know how you call those?
>
> **MS** Veils [cauls].
>
> **AB** Uh, I think so.
>
> **MS** That is very rare.
>
> **AB** And then the baby started crying right there. I never forget that. (Agnes Begay, Many Farms, Arizona, 7/26/91)

Once the baby was born, the woman supervising the birth ascertained that the child was breathing and stimulated it to cry with a gentle, circular, sternal massage. She then cut and tied off the umbilical cord, wrapped the child in an expendable blanket or sheep pelt, and placed it with its head toward the fire to rest, while all present waited for the afterbirth to be delivered.

Following safe delivery of the placenta, the child was bathed in warm water, wrapped in a blanket or sheep pelt, and handed to its mother, who would greet the child while shaking his or her right hand (Stewart 1980:11; Wilson 1980:20). Care was taken in selecting the woman who would bathe the child, because her personal attributes—industriousness or laziness—were transferred to the infant (Bailey 1950:75). The mother was given an herbal drink and cornmeal mush to regain some strength. The child was given an herbal emetic made from juniper and pinyon to cleanse its system of the amniotic fluids. The mother's abdomen was wrapped with a layer of warm, damp cedar (Waxman 1990:192) or spun wool (Lockett 1939:17) held in place by a tightly wrapped sash (Lockett 1939:17; Waxman 1990:192).

The midwife or attending female relative dipped her right forefinger into a mixture of pollen and water and administered a pollen blessing. Next, the woman who bathed the child shaped it by means of gentle molding. She pulled on the child's nose to lengthen and straighten it, she pressed on its forehead to flatten it, and she pressed and shaped the arms and legs to "make them stiff" and facilitate future walking (Bailey 1950:75; Begay 1974:7). The bathed, blessed, and shaped child was then placed at the left side of its mother, with its head facing east toward the fire (Leighton and Kluckhohn 1947:17; Bailey 1950:77; Begay 1974:7). This would continue to be the child's regular sleeping position throughout infancy. Infants were placed in this position to allow the heat of the fire to penetrate the child's skull and thus aid the closure of the fontanel (F. Ashley, 7/29/91; Knoki-Wilson, 8/10/92), and to promote the development of a "nice round head" (A. Begay, 7/26/91).

After making the mother and child comfortable, the woman who supervised the birth rolled the afterbirth, together with all other materials stained with blood or amniotic fluid, up in the sheepskin on which the delivering mother had knelt and removed them from the hooghan. These materials were hidden in the upper branches of an isolated tree (Leighton and Kluckhohn 1947:16; Bailey 1950:70), disposed of in a shady place, or buried to avoid grave harm to the child (Bailey 1950:70−72). A child remained in quiet isolation with its mother for four to fourteen days after birth. Once the family was assured that the infant was healthy and would live, they introduced him or her to the extended family and began to prepare clothes and a cradle for the child.[10]

A gradual shift toward hospital births began in the 1930s (Leighton and Kluckhohn 1947:15). The actual time frame varied from area to area, depending on when individual hospitals and clinics were built on or near the Navajo reservation, on road conditions, and on a family's physical proximity to a hospital or clinic (Waxman 1990:192−93).[11] This shift gained momentum in the 1950s in response to dramatic changes in the Navajo world, including increased school attendance and pressure from health care professionals for hospital births (Begay 1985:91; Waxman 1990:194−98). By the mid-1980s, 99 percent of all Navajo deliveries occurred in hospitals (Boyce et al. 1986). Despite this trend, traditional techniques for assisting births and caring for newborns and mothers have not been forgotten. Indeed, many such practices are presently incorporated into the birthing experience in modern hospitals across the reservation (Waxman 1990: 187–203; Knoki-Wilson, 8/10/92; Hardeen 1994:20–24).

Traditional sashes hang in the birthing rooms at the Indian Health Service hospital in Chinle, Arizona, available for laboring women who wish to use them. Many Navajo mothers, even young women never exposed to home births, find comfort in pulling against these sashes during the later stages of labor (Waxman 1990: 198). Family members are free to burn cedar for smudging, make pollen blessings, or use any other materials they deem beneficial. Ceremonial practitioners are frequently called in to diagnose problems by means of hand trembling or crystal gazing and to perform ceremonies to rectify problems when needed.

During her many years of service on the maternity wards of reservation hospitals, Ursula Knoki-Wilson has witnessed the use of numerous Navajo practices to facilitate births. Of utmost concern are shielding and protection prayers, for, as she notes, many Navajo consider hospitals to be like "haunted houses." "Some of them will come in and do shielding prayers and chants from Blessing Way. Shielding chants and prayers. If they suspect that, well you know, in the hospital there are, it is sort of like a 'haunted house,' and there are spirits that live in there. So you have to do shielding to protect the mother and child" (Knoki-Wilson, 8/10/92).

In addition to wanting shielding and protection prayers, women who choose to use the sash belt provided in each of the birthing rooms at Chinle hospital or who bring their own sashes to other birthing centers often have a short pollen blessing performed before the birth. This procedure represents the beginning of the child's journey on the pollen path of life.

> UKW And some of them will do blessing of the sash belt. They sprinkle corn pollen on it and that represents the baby's journey.
> MS In what way does it represent the baby's journey?
> UKW Well just from the actual act of being born. (Ursula Knoki-Wilson, Chinle, Arizona, 8/10/92)

In addition, family members may bless the woman in labor with specially prepared pollens or medicines designed to expedite her labor. If a delivery is protracted or exceptionally difficult, family members frequently call in a ceremonial practitioner to diagnose the problem through hand trembling.

> Sometimes if they don't know why the baby is not being born when it should be or whatever, they will do a hand trembling ceremony to maybe diagnose which way the baby is lying. If the baby's head is coming first, or if the bottom is coming first, or something. Is the baby lying in the right direction? Something like that. Or, maybe

it is related to some other thing, you know. It could be anything, the mental state of the couple. Maybe they committed some [violations of] taboos that they weren't aware of, or that they don't remember. So they will do a hand trembling to find out. And then the couple is supposed to focus on that, whatever it is that they find out, so that they can relax their minds, which then affects relaxing their bodies. And so I have seen them do that. (Ursula Knoki-Wilson, Chinle, Arizona, 8/10/92)

If this diagnosis indicates that the child is "tied up" by the umbilical cord or by inappropriate behavior on the part of either parent, the ceremonial practitioner may perform an Unraveling, or "Untying," ceremony (Waxman 1990:197).

UKW They allow them [ceremonial practitioners] to come in to do whatever. One ceremony they do is called the "Untying" ceremony. If they suspect that the baby is not coming down as easily as it should, they say that the baby is hung up on the umbilical cord. So they will do this ceremony called the Untying ceremony. And they will make motions over the woman's body.

MS And do they actually untie something?

UKW Yeah. They get a rope and put knots in it and then they straighten them out over the woman's abdomen. They do that. (Ursula Knoki-Wilson, Chinle, Arizona, 8/10/92)

Alternatively, a ceremonial practitioner may "chase the baby out" by means of "singing-the-baby-out" songs from the Blessing Way and an eagle feather fan (Knoki-Wilson, 8/10/92; McCabe, 8/19/92).

Once the child and placenta are safely delivered, hospital staff bathe the child in warm water, wrap it in a blanket, and hand it to its mother. She shakes her newborn's right hand in greeting, saying, "Yá'át'ééh shiyázhí" (Welcome, my little one), to acknowledge to the child and the Holy People that this child is hers (Wilson 1980:20; Begay 1985:117; F. Ashley, 7/29/91). A relative in attendance may give the child an herbal emetic at this time. Once the child has vomited up the mucus and amniotic fluids it swallowed while in the womb, a pollen blessing may be administered, which is followed by the first molding. A female relative dips her right forefinger into pollen and administers it to the child's mouth to foster its physical development and to the top of the child's head to foster its mental development. Then, saying a brief prayer, she spreads pollen in front of the child in offering (Wilson 1980:20; Oscar Tso, 8/9/92). I was told this is done as a notification to the Holy People that a new "track" on the pollen path of life is starting on the earth's surface.

> FA They give corn pollen to the baby to acknowledge them that there is another new life, to the Mother Earth and the sky. To all the nature, so they can be aware there is a new human, a new track is starting so that is what they do.
>
> MS A new track?
>
> FA Uh-huh, well we always say, when we represent ourselves we always say, "There is going to be tracks on the Mother Earth."
>
> MS Footprints?
>
> FA Footprints. I guess that is what you would call it. (Flora Ashley, Tsaile, Arizona, 7/29/91)

Molding, the process used by Changing Woman in constructing the first Nihookáá Dine'é, is used today by mothers and grandmothers to further the development of personhood in newborns. The bodies of Navajo infants, which are soft at birth, gradually become firm after emergence from the birth canal, owing to internal contact with air through respiration and contact between air and their outer surfaces (Bekis, 7/28/93). While his or her body is in this semifirm state, the newborn infant is massaged from the feet upward.

> MS Do you know if infants are molded after birth?
>
> UKW Yeah, they get massaged.
>
> MS And can you tell me about that?
>
> UKW They just massage them "head to toe." Mainly just they pull on their arms and just a regular massage.
>
> MS Do you know why they do that?
>
> UKW It stimulates their bodies. I guess, it sort of molds them for life, too. So they can accept life's challenges or something.
>
> MS Do you see any association between that molding and the molding that is done during a girl's Kinaaldá?
>
> UKW It is sort of a reinforcement of being ready to accept the challenges, for her [the kinaaldá, or pubescent girl] it would be the challenges of motherhood.
>
> MS Uh-huh. And for the infant it is?
>
> UKW It is for this life's journey. (Ursula Knoki-Wilson, Chinle, Arizona, 8/10/92)

To promote physical beauty and strength, the child's head and facial features are shaped after his or her arms and legs are stretched (Walters, 8/18/92). Young mothers are taught by their female elders to continue this molding regularly once they take the child home. "They usually say try to get up with your baby early in the morning, about four o'clock and just keep them straight, you know stretch them. So it can, it is just the same as the molding at the Kinaaldá. They said, just wake up with them early and then, you know, pray with them and mold them and all that, and on the process of growing. And that is how ours was" (Bekis, 7/28/93).

As both Ursula Knoki-Wilson and Mae Bekis remarked, the molding of infants immediately after birth foreshadows the molding of adolescents during their puberty ceremonies. Additional molding will occur at puberty when the body returns to the soft state characteristic of newborns and is again malleable (Knoki-Wilson, 8/10/92, 7/29/93; Walters, 8/18/92; Bekis, 7/28/93; Avery Denny, 8/11/93; Elizabeth Yazzie, 12/5/93). In each case, the young person is molded to encourage his or her physical strength and to prepare him or her for the inevitable challenges of this life's journey.

Once the newborn is attended to, a grandmother concerned about her daughter's speedy recovery offers advice on breast-feeding and postpartum care, including manipulation of the new mother's body. To control blood loss and to aid recovery from childbirth, she may bind her daughter's abdomen with a layer of warm, damp, cedar branches held in place by a tightly wrapped sash (Waxman 1990: 192; Sadie Billie, 7/10/91; A. Begay, 7/26/91; Tsosie, 8/4/92; Knoki-Wilson, 8/10/92). This is done as soon as possible after childbirth, in the hospital or immediately after the mother and child return home. As Sadie Billie explains in the following narrative, this binding quickens the return of the uterus and the mother's body to their previous sizes.

> She never really told me why she did that until after. I had to start asking her questions. And umm, she just told me also to breast-feed and she didn't really give me the reasons why. . . . But I went along with what she told me and I breast-fed all my children. And she did the same thing with the sash belt. She had a real wide one she wanted me to wrap around myself. And she said it would like, it wasn't until like maybe three or four months down the road that she told me she did that to keep myself in shape. To get the uterus to get back to the normal size real quick. And she said that if you don't do that then your stomach will begin to hang. . . . My second child I didn't, I was kind of like away from her a lot and I didn't use that sash belt. So I kind of have bulges in my stomach and she knew that right away. So with my daughter, umm, she said it was hard

for me to get back to the way I was before I had my children, you know, flat tummy and stuff like that. So what she did was, when she was going to wrap me with the sash belt she would get the cedar, the green, I guess it would be called green cedar. She would get whole, you know, get branches off and warm them up. And as she's wrapping me she put them [indicates laying them horizontally around her waist]. . . . The juniper trees and she would break off like maybe that many pieces [indicates four with her fingers] and she would put it into the ashes. Not the coals but the ashes portion of it, but it would be warm, and as she's wrapping me she'd put them in between those [layers of the sash] and wrap me. It was very uncomfortable, but she'd make me do that to get back into shape, you know, to keep my, it took a little bit longer because she said I was really not fit, you know, I had really gone out of shape with my second child. . . . I had to wear that sash for six weeks straight, not taking it off, even going to bed with it. She made me wear it. And that did help, I mean it really did! And I am glad I did that. . . . So that was her way of keeping in shape and keeping your original measurements. (Sadie Billie, Tsaile, Arizona, 7/10/91)

In addition to allowing these kinds of practices to be performed for mother and child in the hospital, staff at reservation hospitals are sensitive to family concerns over the care and disposal of parts of the body important to the mother's postpartum care and to the safety and future of the child.[12] Particular concern focuses on the placenta, the water used in the child's first bath, the child's first stool, and umbilical cords.

Since a newborn's body is covered with blood and amniotic fluids when it emerges from the birth canal, special rules govern disposal of the water from a baby's first bath. The blood is treated with reverence because it is considered to be part of a person, essentially constituting "an undeveloped human" (Walters, 8/18/92). The water used in a baby's first bath must be carefully collected and disposed of to avoid harm to the child, which can result from careless handling of the water. The bathwater must not be splattered or incinerated, because the blood washed from the child's body is living tissue and a connection remains in force between the child and this tissue even after it is detached from the child's body (Knoki-Wilson, 8/10/92).

Substance from the child can affect the mother as well. Hospital staff consult with mothers or their relatives before disposing of the child's first stool, since many Navajo mothers use this material for personal benefit. Often Navajo mothers spread their newborn's first stool (meconium), which consists of intestinal secretions and fluids swallowed while in the womb, on their own faces to remove any dark pigmentation (melasma gravidarum) resulting from the pregnancy (Begay 1985:117; Waxman 1990:197; Hardeen 1994:20). Hospital staff also show cultural sensitivity in decisions regarding the disposal of the afterbirth and the umbilical cord. "Nurses routinely ask mommies if they want to take the placenta home. If they do, then the nurses just wrap them up in a plastic bag or something and put it in a paper sack and give it to maybe one of her relatives, or herself when she is discharged. They take it home so they can bury it" (Knoki-Wilson, 8/10/92).

Placentas are taken home from the hospital to be buried so they can "become one with Mother Earth again" (Knoki-Wilson, 8/10/92). Placentas are most frequently buried in a hole two to three feet deep in the ash pile north of the family hooghan (Bekis, 8/5/92; Knoki-Wilson, 8/10/92; 7/28/93; Elizabeth Yazzie, 12/5/93) or in a badger hole (Walters, 8/18/92). The placenta can also be placed in a live bush (Walters, 8/18/92), buried beneath a juniper or pinyon tree, where it is "put away" with a cornmeal blessing (Dooley, 8/21/92), or placed in another location of special significance to the family. If the child remains in the hospital for an extended period because of complications in childbirth, prematurity, birth defects, or illness, hospital staff will save the umbilical cord when it falls off and give it to the mother to take home with the child (Knoki-Wilson, 8/10/92).

UMBILICAL CORDS

When the umbilical cord has dried so that it can be taken from the infant, it must not be thrown out where an animal might get it, as it is considered part of the child and has symbolic control over its destiny. (Newcomb 1940:29)

The teachings of the Holy People governing the cultural construction of personhood dictate that the umbilical cord be placed in a location considered by the parents and grandparents to be most beneficial to the child's future. When the family wants a boy to be good with livestock, parents or grandparents bury his cord in a sheep, cattle, or horse corral (Newcomb 1940:29; Leighton and Kluckhohn 1947:17; Bailey 1950:74), tie it to the tail or mane of a horse (Newcomb 1940:29; Knoki-Wilson, 8/10/92), or tie it to a sheep (McCabe, 8/19/92).[13] A boy's cord is buried in the family fields when it is desired that he be concerned with farming (Newcomb 1940:29; Bailey 1950:74; Bekis, 7/28/93). A girl's cord is buried underneath the place where the loom is erected in the hooghan if the family wants her to become an expert weaver (Newcomb 1940:29; Leighton and Kluckhohn 1947:17; Bailey 1950:74; Knoki-Wilson, 8/10/92; Walters, 8/18/92; Dahozy, 8/19/92). A family in need of a shepherd will bury a girl's cord in the sheep corral to ensure that her thoughts are with the livestock (Bailey 1950:74; Bekis,

7/28/93). They bury a girl's cord inside the hooghan—or, if they do not live in a hooghan, outside near the home—when they want the girl to become a good homemaker (Newcomb 1940: 29; Knoki-Wilson, 8/10/92; Bekis, 7/28/93).

Many contemporary parents and grandparents continue to bury the umbilical cords of new family members under looms or in corrals to actuate the development of good weaving and herding skills. While recognizing the importance of traditional skills, other Navajo, concerned over the ways in which Navajo life is changing, believe that to succeed in today's world their children and grandchildren will need additional skills. Elders who wonder how to guarantee that their grandchildren will acquire such skills turn to Navajo theories of the body and personhood for answers. Knowing that proper placement of the umbilical cord can promote proficiency in weaving or livestock management, these people wonder whether the Navajo system can also be used to foster new skills such as those required to be a good student in the Western educational system. As Mae Bekis explained, these elders devise ways to test the Navajo system to see whether it can be relied upon to influence their children and grandchildren in the desired ways: "And then my brother up here, he said, he wanted to see if it really works. And so he put his granddaughter's cord, they are just small, about like that [indicates about the size of a quarter] after it dries out. He said he put it in a dictionary. And he said, 'That girl is never out of a book. Her nose is into the book all of the time.' So he thinks it is true" (7/28/93).

Regardless of the particular place selected by the family, it is of the utmost importance that a child's dried and detached umbilical cord be anchored to something of substance—a horse, a cradle, a dictionary, a loom, or Mother Earth—and not lost or left somewhere inside the home, for children will seek out their unanchored cords. As Mae Bekis explains, a problematic situation has arisen in her family because she misplaced her grandchildren's umbilical cords during a move back to the reservation from Colorado:

> When it is dried up, they say that if you keep it in the house, the baby would be nosing around to find its cord. . . . I have a granddaughter and a grandson, I lost their cords. My daughter told me to bury it somewhere out here. And I lost them, and whenever she brings them, they [her grandson and granddaughter] are looking, looking everywhere. I say, "Your cord's not here anymore," I say, "I lost them somewhere in the process of moving." But they're always digging, digging, digging. (Mae Bekis, Tó'tsoh, Arizona, 7/28/93)

In extreme cases, loss or misplacement of a cord can result in lifelong disorientation or antisocial behavior. Bailey was told by a consultant that if a boy's cord was lost, "the boy runs around and is no good" (1950: 74), and Leighton and

Kluckhohn were told that if the cord was kept in a sack in the hooghan, the child would steal (1947:17). To avoid such problems, parents and grandparents take great care in the placement of umbilical cords. The majority of people with whom I consulted stated that in their families the cords of new members were buried in auspicious places. I was told that umbilical cords were intended to be buried because this "anchors the baby to the earth" (Knoki-Wilson, 8/10/92).

Burial of the cord in the earth anchors the child to the "belly button" of Mother Earth and establishes a lifelong connection between an individual and a place, just as the cord anchors a child to its mother in the womb and establishes a lifelong connection between mother and child. The presence of this anchoring cord is evidenced by the spirals on the human body. The spirals found on every Navajo represent an anchoring force that forms a continuous connection from the earth to the person. This connection traverses the body, beginning at the navel and continuing to the spirals at the back of the top of the head, from which it extends out of the top of the head (Wyman 1970:135–36). The spirals at the navel and the top of the back of the head demonstrate the path of this connecting cord, which is most frequently anchored to Mother Earth. As Sunny Dooley points out in the following conversation, a direct correlation exists between the spirals found on the human body and the spiral found at the center of the ceremonial basket, which represents the "belly button" of the earth.

> SD This particular crevice at the bottom right here [pointing to the spiral at the center of a ceremonial basket], they will say it is the "belly button" of the earth. And, umm, the umm, I don't know what you call it, but on the top of your head? Up here.
>
> MS The spiral, the whorl that is on the top of your head?
>
> SD This, the whorl, that is where that particular thing concludes. So it is sort of like a beginning and the ending for that. . . . It just represents that you are blessed with life, because this is like a basket of life. And you are living within the belly button of your mother the earth. So, it is sort of like a bottom and a top. It is not really considered a bottom or a top, but it is just an entity, that, you know, like when you think of a screw? Maybe, like you are screwed into the earth? Do you know what I mean?
>
> MS I see, OK, so the spiral represents your being screwed into the earth. I like that. (Sunny Dooley, Gallup, New Mexico, 8/19/92)

The act of burying a child's umbilical cord securely "screws" or anchors that person to a particular place. Where one's cord is buried is one's true home. As a result, Navajo people associate deep-felt senses of belonging with the places where their cords are buried, and many feel it is contrary to the "natural order" for the connection between individual and place to be severed under any circumstance. This sense of anchoring, and the spiritual and historic nature of the connection to one's home, are implicitly understood in the Navajo world. Contemporary Navajo from all walks of life find occasion under a variety of circumstances to refer to the places where their umbilical cords are buried, whether they are politicians seeking reelection or individuals facing relocation (see Schwarz 1997b).

Placement of a child's umbilical cord has a profound effect on the child's future occupation and personal proclivities. It also establishes a child's relationship to his or her physical landscape, anchoring the individual to Mother Earth and to a specific place. A few months after the umbilical cord becomes detached from the body, the next step on the path to personhood is taken. This occurs shortly after the child's first laugh, when a small celebration is held that establishes the child in relationship to her or his social landscape. During this ceremony, children are anchored within the complex network of kin by the initiation of reciprocity in the form of a small gift of natural salt from the child to each member of his or her extended family.

FIRST LAUGH

At the end of the second day the baby laughed for the first time and there came a man Atsé hashke [sic], the First Coyote, who said: 'I was told that my grandchild laughed for the first time." A woman came saying: "I was told that my grandchild laughed for the first time." She was the Salt Woman. First Woman took charcoal and gave it to the Coyote saying: "This is the only thing that lasts." So he painted his nose with it and said: "I shall know all things. I shall live long by it." And First Woman also gave the Coyote salt. He swallowed it and said: "This shall be my meat. It will make my meat taste good." And satisfied with his gifts he departed. It was the Salt Woman who first gave the gift of salt to First Woman. Then the two Yei [sic] returned for their gifts. One was given white bead moccasins, and the other decorated leggings. They took them and went away satisfied. Now that is why all persons present receive a little gift when a baby laughs for the first time. (O'Bryan 1956: 73)

When infants are near the age of four months, relatives begin to joke about the need to be cautious in their presence, because the person who makes the baby laugh for the first time is obligated to sponsor a ceremony in honor of the event (Oscar Tso, 7/14/91; Traci Michelle Begay, 7/26/91; Mae Bekis, 8/5/92). When family members with well-paying jobs drop by for a visit, elders gleefully hand them the baby in the hope that the child will laugh and thereby secure an affluent sponsor. Members of the family who are not working are cautious about contact with a child of this age.

> MS What is their obligation?
>
> TMB They just have to do all the work. They bring the food and everything, and they do all the preparation and stuff for the child and everybody who is there. . . . So, you are always careful when you meet little ones. You always ask the mother, "Well has she laughed yet?" Because you don't want to make them laugh. (Traci Michelle Begay, Many Farms, Arizona, 7/26/91)

The First Laugh ceremony ('Awééʼ chʼídaadlóóhgó bá naʼaʼnʼę́ę́ʼ) celebrates the child's initial expression of emotion. Navajo people describe emotion variously as "there is a feeling of sighing in the heart, or there is some type of expression where you sort of like empathize with someone" (H. Ashley, 7/27/93), or as a "thought that is connected to how one feels" (Knoki-Wilson, 7/29/93). The child's first laugh marks its preliminary step toward expression of this type of thought, empathy, and emotional development. Relatives use the occasion as their opportunity to anchor the child's emotional life firmly within his or her social landscape by initiating the child into the complex network of communication and reciprocity that operates within extended families.[14]

> They talk about the emotion. How it develops is, uh, you probably heard about the Navajo they honor this, when a little infant, a child is born and later, their First Laugh? [I nod my head.] Then a child first laughed. The child will laugh and then cry. That is where that emotional development starts, they say. So it has something to do with crying and then laughing, that is what it is, they say. So in Navajo they say that is the beginning, that is where it initiates, the emotional being, or the emotional aspects of the humanity, that is where it initiates. When the baby first laughs and then cries, and then that is when they do a ceremony for them. And that is what it is, they honor that. That is where the emotions begin, so I would say, the first cry and the first laugh, that is what emotion is. That is where the development starts, or initiates. (Hanson Ashley, Shonto, Arizona, 7/27/93)

Expression of emotion through laughter or tears is an important component of communication in the Navajo world. When people express thoughts that demonstrate empathy for others, they often do so through tears or humor. In the Navajo world, one is not to cry without a purpose. Crying with no purpose is associated with needing or desiring something to happen. For example, if a child cries when he or she is injured, the tears that are shed are recognized as deriving directly from the physical pain. But if a child cries for no apparent reason, it is believed that his or her action will create another reason. As a bodily substance, tears have the power to affect those present during their expulsion. A connection, or bond, is built between persons who share tears.

I learned about the significance of sharing tears at the end of the summer of 1992, when it was time for me to depart. As we drove out to her mother's home so I could say my farewells, Sadie Billie warned me emphatically, "No tears. Crying will make all of us sick!" She explained that tears expressed at a departure affect everyone present and make them long for the departed. As it turned out, despite Mrs. Billie's warning, everyone present cried. Sharing of tears is an established element of departures and reunions in the Navajo world.

Emotion and tears are mechanisms for simultaneously defining and reinforcing the kinship system and personal attachments. Family members cry openly when a relative prepares to leave home. There is no stigma associated with crying on such occasions, for the shedding of tears at a departure has a purpose. It demonstrates how hard it is for family members to stretch their ties across physical separation. It is accepted that every separation involves strong emotions, but established limits are enforced to avoid complications. Consider, for example, the emotions expressed at funerals and at reunions.

At funerals and during mourning, family members cry openly up until the time the body is buried. On the fourth day after the interment, the close kin are advised to stop crying (Reichard 1928: 141 – 43; Shepardson 1978: 387 – 88); otherwise, they will be anticipating another purpose—that is, another death. Up until the 1960s, wailing often occurred when female relatives were united after even a short separation (Franciscan Fathers 1910: 510 – 11; Thomas, 3/6/94).[15] Women used such crying episodes and the resultant sharing of bodily substance in the form of tears to rekindle their kinship relations.

Like the expression of tears, humorous expression unconsciously informs everyone present at a departure or a reunion of their inalienable bonds. Navajo humor centers on subtle puns and commentary about the inevitable frailties of human nature (Leighton and Kluckhohn 1947: 234). Joking relationships exist between certain categories of relatives, among whom patterned teasing is the norm (Reichard 1928: 72 – 73; Kluckhohn and Leighton 1974 [1946]:98). On a daily basis, Navajo people rely on their finely tuned skills of wit and humor to associate with each other without ill will or attempts at domination (Leighton and Kluckhohn 1947: 110). In Navajo social interactions, "humor lubricates the rhythm of life and transforms difficult and frustrating situations into bearable and even pleasant ones" (Witherspoon 1977:184).[16] A child's first laugh initiates its lifelong involvement in the daily interchange expressed through humor and reci-procity—an involvement that formally commences with the First Laugh ceremony.

Throughout this rite, the sponsor holds and acts for the baby. With the assis-tance of this adult, the child will first apply a protective layer of natural rock salt to the outside of its own body and then give a token amount of the salt to each of its relatives, as well as to close friends of its family who are in attendance. The type of rock salt used in this ceremony is a rare commodity, found only at a few loca-tions near Dinétah. "It is a natural salt that they get either from Zuni or Salt Lake City, and it has, it is not iodized or it doesn't have anything on it. It is just natural salt" (Bekis, 8/5/92). This type of salt has many powers.[17]

Because of its powers, this special form of salt, when it is applied to the body or ingested, lends strength and protection. As Wesley Thomas explains in the fol-lowing account, before giving portions of the rock salt to each of his or her rela-tives in attendance, the sponsor helps the child rub salt on its own body, taking care not to get any salt on the child's hair, for this will cause premature aging.

> The rock salt is placed in the left hand for a male child and in the right hand for a female child. The adult holding the child takes the hand in which the salt is held and brushes it against the right side of the child's body, starting with the soles of the feet and moving upwards. The salt is rubbed against both sides of the body: the soles of the feet, the legs, the torso, the back, and the face. Care is taken to not touch the hair with the salt. If the hair is touched with the salt then the hair will turn white before it should, because the child will age too quickly. The purpose of the First Laugh ceremony is to ensure that the child will be generous, not greedy, that they will be generous and productive. My mother told me it is so "wealth will seek him." (Wesley Thomas, Seattle, Washington, 1/21/95)

Once the child's body has received a protective layer of natural rock salt, the child gives a token piece of the salt to every relative and friend present at the ceremony. In some families it is placed in the palm of the baby's right hand by the sponsoring adult, "and you give that from the baby, you know, you put it on their hand. Right on the palm of their hand and give it out" (Bekis, 7/28/93). Relatives walk up individually to accept their first gift from their new relative. As they receive their individual portions of rock salt from the baby, relatives of all ages ingest a small amount. "All the little kids and everybody puts some in their mouth" to ac-quire strength and protection. (T. M. Begay, 7/26/91)

As Wesley Thomas noted, this giving is designed to encourage generosity and to guarantee that the child will not grow up to be "stingy." A small token of natural rock salt may be given out alone or, when finances allow, "when they give it out, some of them give out gifts for the baby. So, they said, the baby won't be stingy in the long run" (Bekis, 8/5/92). In such cases, the salt and gifts are placed in a ceremonial basket, and with the help of his or her sponsor, the child hands these to each relative who files past.

LD When the baby first laughs, that is when they use the basket again.

MS Oh, the baby's First Laugh.

LD Yes, they put food in it and that is where the baby would give out food that she will be, that the baby will be generous the rest of her or his life.

MS And do they also use the special salt?

LD Yes.

MS How do they use that?

LD They just give you a little bit. I don't know what that represents, but any way it was always, it has to be in there, in the basket and then other foods. . . . In the basket with the rest of the food, a little food, and then. Today they do more than that, they really go all out and have a big feast and then they really get, give out more stuff. Of course we are, there is plenty to give now these days than what they [had] in those days. . . . So as they are growing, they have ceremonials each time that something happens, you know, like the First Laugh, and then the girl going to womanhood, and all this, and then at the wedding. They make [a] big wedding, when they get married, again. So all through your life you are special. (Louva Dahozy, Navajo, New Mexico, 8/19/92)

As Mrs. Dahozy mentioned, distribution of the rock salt and small gifts is followed by a large meal for all relatives and friends in attendance. To offset the sponsors' expense and increase the net effect of the entire event, parents and grandparents sometimes contribute a sheep (Leighton and Kluckhohn 1947:29) or other food and supplies needed for this meal (Kahn, 7/7/91).

The First Laugh ceremony celebrates the child's preliminary step on the path to emotional development. Family members celebrate this event by firmly anchoring the child within the complex system of reciprocity and communication vital to Navajo social life, thereby demonstrating to the Holy People that they are going to be "good relatives" (Dooley, 8/19/92). The next step on the path to

Navajo personhood is triggered by the child's first words. The Diyin Dine'é directed that children may have their hair cut when they demonstrate initial control over their thoughts and voices by speaking a language of the Nihookáá Dine'é.

HAIR AND VOICE

SD Up to this point in time the Holy People are still . . . seventy-five percent involved in the development in the child, OK. Any minute they can still take the child away from you. But they [children of this age] have come to a point now where they are picking up the earth language [a language spoken by Earth Surface People] which is Navajo, you know, they are starting to pick up Navajo. And so that means they are getting a little bit further away from the Holy People, because before then it would be the Holy People that would console them. . . . That is why they say that when a baby is sleeping and it is smiling it is having a good time with the Holy People, you know, that is [he or she is] actually being visited by them and they are being playful with the child. And so, you let your child sleep a lot because you want as much interaction as possible between that particular child and the Holy People. So when the child starts picking up the language of the Earth [Surface People] then that means that that distance is getting a little bit wider. And when they really start speaking complete sentences that means that the Holy People have now ascended, back upward and you now have a majority of the responsibility of teaching them the proper language of the Earth [Surface People]. And so, when that happens, the separation comes once again by exposing the child's head, by shaving it and then leaving the little sprig at the tip of the head for the boys and at the nape of the neck for the girls. And so, that is the reason for that. And that particular sprig of hair that is still left is still that connection with the spiritual side of life. A sprig is always left. It is not completely balded off, because they say if you completely cut it off you have severed the tie. And so if your child grows up to be unbelieving in anything it was your own fault.

MS So that is the tie with the Holy People?

SD Right.

MS What a beautiful thought. (Sunny Dooley, Gallup, New Mexico, 8/21/92)

The Holy People directed the Nihookáá Dine'é in strict rules regarding manipulation of the hair at specific stages in the life cycle because it is a physical embodiment of thought and lifelong knowledge (Wilson Aronilth, 7/3/91; Regina Lynch, 7/16/91; Bekis, 7/28/93; Knoki-Wilson, 7/29/93). Opinions vary from place to place and from family to family regarding the Holy People's specific directives concerning hair. Dorothea Leighton observed: "Another practice founded upon beliefs connected with the supernatural is that the hair a baby is born with must be cut off" (Leighton and Kluckhohn 1947:17). In contrast, several of the elders and educators with whom I spoke insisted that a Navajo person's hair should never be cut under any circumstances (anonymous elder, 7/10/91; Walters, 8/10/93).[18] As Harry Walters points out, according to the traditional teachings he has been trained in, hair should never be cut because of its connection to the mind and its direct influence on development.

> HW These things grow from your head [touches his hair], your mind, this is where it is. And, generally you are not supposed to cut your hair anytime. You know, you are not supposed to. When you do . . . you are cutting off some of that. This is part of you, you know, your development.
> MS Part of you. Yes.
> HW It is part of you and then when you cut it, you are cutting off that piece. So, to do that to children when they are, [shakes his head] not only to children, you are not to ever cut your hair. (Harry Walters, Tsaile, Arizona, 8/10/93)

While acknowledging these beliefs, most of the people with whom I consulted recognize that in the modern world Navajo people tend to wear their hair short for a variety of reasons, but they were emphatic that a child's hair should not be cut before a certain point in its development. This point is determined by familial tradition and practice.

Many say a child's hair should not be cut before he or she begins to speak a language of the Earth Surface People such as Navajo or, more recently, English, instead of Áłtsé Saad, the language of the First World (Lynch, 7/16/91; Jean Jones, 7/25/91; A. Begay, 7/26/91; Dooley, 8/19/92; Bekis, 7/28/93). But precisely when a child begins to talk is subject to interpretation, and so others use the closing of the fontanel as the marker (Bekis, 7/28/93; Knoki-Wilson, 7/29/93).

> UKW Some people say, "You don't cut their hair until the soft spot closes." Some say, "You don't cut the hair until the baby talks." Well,

what does talk mean? You know, does it mean it's OK when he says "gaga" or "dada" or "mama," and then that is talking, you know?

MS Yeah.

UKW And so it's a little bit, it's subject to interpretation I guess. Umm, so, I guess the important thing is when the fontanel closes. That is mostly what people agree on. (Ursula Knoki-Wilson, Fort Defiance, Arizona, 7/29/93)

The timing for the cutting of a child's hair is critical because both hair and fontanel are associated with development, and together they form a vital link to the Holy People. I was told that cutting the hair before the established time risks impairing the child's lifelong development (Bekis, 7/28/93; Knoki-Wilson, 7/29/93; Walters, 8/10/93).

When I pressed individual consultants for further explanation about the relationship of hair to thought and development, I often faced genuine surprise on their part. Most Navajo people do not question the directives of their elders or analyze the culture in which they live. They just live it. People indicated that they saw no reason to ask why something was the way it was. As Ursula Knoki-Wilson emphasizes, for them the Navajo world just is the way it is:

MS And what special significance is associated with the closing of the fontanel?

UKW Well that is a high energy center and you're, when it is open you are vulnerable to, to many things, umm. And also, if you cut their hair before the soft spot closes then their potential for learning the language is released before, I mean it is sort of like you are closing doors on them mentally. And their mental creativity.

MS Is the hair associated with learning language?

UKW Hmm [nods her head]. Because hair is thought of as an extension of your thought processes.

MS Yeah, I knew that. OK. I understand, I think I am seeing it. See, I mean it's, you understand all of this, and I have a partial understanding and so it's hard for me to grasp it unless you explain it a little fuller.

UKW Yeah. Uh-huh.

MS So, maybe you could tell me a little bit more about how the hair is thought of as a representation or, reflecting your thought processes.

UKW Ahh, you mean why it's like that? Or?

MS Yeah, we can start with that.

UKW I don't know. It just is I guess! [Laughs] . . . They just tell us that that's, you know, "You don't cut hair because it is an extension of your thought processes so if you cut your hair you sort of handicap yourself." (Ursula Knoki-Wilson, Fort Defiance, Arizona, 7/29/93)

When I sought clarification from Mae Bekis regarding the special relationship that exists between the hair, the fontanel, and a child's connection to the Holy People, she prefaced her statement by pointing out that she did not know whether or not Navajo and non-Navajo children shared the same attributes.

MS Someone else has told me that the child's first hair, the hair that grows in like before they talk, represents their connection to the Holy People. Have you ever heard that?

MB Yeah, there is, uh [pause]. You know, I don't know if your babies are that way, our babies, it seems like there is a hole in their head right here.

MS The soft spot?

MB The soft spot, uh-huh, and then it grows together.

MS Yes.

MB And when it really grows together then our babies start talking.

MS So what does that hole? Is the hole what represents the connection to the Holy People?

MB Yes, to the Holy People, that is what they say, uh-huh. And so that hole there, and they said that is one reason why too, you can't touch the mother on the forehead, because they are one. The hole in the head and if you touch the mother on the forehead when she is in the process of laboring, they said you can cause it to, for her to faint.

MS So the mother's forehead is sort of connected somehow to the top [I touch my hand to the top of my head]?

MB Yeah, somehow to the baby, too. It is kind of funny, but—

MS No it is not funny.

MB I guess it is, you know.

MS It is not funny.

MB And the growth of your hair they said, "Your hair is, it is your thinking part." You know, you don't think with you hair, but that is what, if you cut your hair, you cut off part of your thinking. (Mae Bekis, Tó'tsoh, Arizona, 7/28/93)

The hair growing out of the whorl at the back of the top of the head forms the "feather of life" that links all Navajo people to the Holy People (Walters, 8/10/93). During the formative stages of early childhood this link is vital to the development and survival of the child. When the child begins to speak and put sentences together, this signifies that the connection between the child and the Holy People is weakening and that the child's connection to Earth Surface People is strengthening. Many families believe that cutting a child's hair at this point will have no negative impact on his or her development (Lynch, 7/16/91; Jones, 7/25/91; A. Begay, 7/26/91; Dooley, 8/19/92; Bekis, 7/28/93). But it is of the utmost importance that a portion of the hair a child was born with remains uncut to serve as a lifelong connection to the Holy People. As Sunny Dooley explains in the following passage, if all the hair is cut off, a person's tie to the Holy people and the spiritual side of life will be irreparably severed.

> SD And then when the baby first talks, up to that time, the child is still dressed in magic. Not magic, I don't know how to say it, it is not like, you know. But something most wonderful. And like you don't cut the baby's hair until after it talks. Because when it begins to talk, that means that the child has first of all forgotten the language of the Holy People, and has adopted our language of mortality. And then that is when you cut off the hair, keep it, and you leave a little "sprig" right up here for the boy [motions to the top of her head], a little "sprig" right down here [motions to the back of her neck] for the girl, because you don't ever want to completely lose that spiritual connection with the child. And right there again, you recognize this little thingamajig that is in the Navajo basket? [Points to a strip of cloth knotted through the beginning of the spiral at the center of a basket].
>
> MS So, just to back up here, you leave a sprig?
>
> SD You leave a sprig.
>
> MS For the boy on the top of the head?
>
> SD Yeah, right where, right here [touches the whorl at the back of the top of her head] where his hair begins to grow and then for a girl it is right down here [touches the nape of her neck].
>
> MS And for the girl, is it at the back of the neck? Like the nape of the neck?

SD Yeah, at the nape. And then you will notice that eventually their tsiiyééł, or their hair buns, are in those places. A woman's tsiiyééł is usually at the nape of her neck. And a man's is sometimes higher. (Sunny Dooley, Gallup, New Mexico, 8/19/92)

Practice varies from family to family regarding the specific activities done when children begin to speak a language of the Nihookáá Dine'é. In some families, the hair of children of both sexes is shaved or cut off. In other families, only boys have their hair cut at this time. And in some cases, the cut hair is burned and applied to the child's body (Bekis, 7/28/93). In Sunny Dooley's family all of a child's hair is shaved off except for a "sprig" of hair at the whorl at the top of the back of the head on boys and at the nape of the neck on girls. In other families, the hair of children of either sex is cut at this time rather than shaved (Knoki-Wilson, 7/29/ 93). Whether cut or shaved, now as throughout the remainder of the child's life, all cut hair is swept up and carefully disposed of to avoid potential harm to the individual through its manipulation by rodents, birds, or snakes (anonymous woman, 3/17/95; Bekis, 3/22/95) or through its manipulation in witchcraft activities (Kluckhohn 1944).

Some Navajo believe that boys and girls must be treated differently. While it is acceptable to cut or shave a boy's hair when he begins to speak an earth surface language or after his fontanel closes, many are emphatic that a girl's hair should never be cut (Jones, 7/25/91; A. Begay, 7/26/91; Bekis, 7/28/93).

MB The baby's hair is not cut until they start talking really good. That is about two, three years, but there is some slow kids, some fast, you know. Like our grandkids. J. D., he started talking real good when he was only two years old. But we always cut his hair though because his hair is, he is half-breed. He is right there [points to a photo on the wall]. And it was just kinky, curly. And then it would get real dirty, and then when it grows his head is just big. So we always trimmed his hair, but it never slowed him down.

MS And when the baby first talks do you cut all the hair off the baby?

MB No, just leave some. And then we burn it, and then put it with a little water and sprinkle it back on their hair.

MS So, the hair you cut off, you burn?

MB Uh-huh.

MS You mix the ash with water, and then . . .

MB Mix the ash with water—

MS And then you rub it on their hair.

MB And then you rub it on their hair and the body. So, they say it has to do with the thinking. I don't know what part, but anyway they said, "So it will think better," you know, "good and all that." And that is how, but the girls you never cut their hair.

MS You never cut their hair?

MB We never cut the girl's hair. And after the Kinaaldá, they cut it, themselves, they did it. I told them never to cut your hair, because that is the growth, you know. Like the First Lady, or the White Shell Lady she never cut her hair, she never put make-up on. So, I always tell when there is a Kinaaldá, I say, "Never put make-up on your face because it just, you are already made good, you know, just like the White Shell Lady." And I say, "You are yourself, you are nobody else. You are just yourself." And so, the girls, well my girls never cut their hair until after their Kinaaldá. And then after they had their babies, they start cutting their hair. (Mae Bekis, Tó'tsoh, Arizona, 7/28/93)

Cosmic as well as personal consequences may result from the cutting of a Navajo person's hair. Because it is composed of rain and the moisture of clouds (Aronilth, 7/3/91; Lynch, 7/16/91; Bekis, 7/28/93; Knoki-Wilson, 7/29/93), long hair embodies moisture. A woman's hair is said to "bring rain," and some elders blame lack of rainfall or droughts in the contemporary world on the fact that so many Navajo women currently wear their hair short.

JJ They say that you weren't supposed to cut your hair when you're a woman, but nowadays we cut our hair. . . . They say that it brings water, that it brings rain. And then they say that your thinking and your mind is tied up with it. . . . When you're wearing it right you are strong and your mind is good. . . . Wearing it up all the time.

MS Brings the rain?

JJ Uh-huh.

MS Oh.

JJ That's right, they say it's used to bring the rain.

MS And you always need rain out here.

JJ Yeah, we're running out of rain [chuckles as she shakes her head]. No more rain! (Jean Jones, Rock Point, Arizona, 7/25/91)

A child's hair is cut when it utters its first comprehensible words in a language of the Earth Surface People, when its fontanel closes, or both. These developments simultaneously demonstrate the initial stages of developing control over voice and a weakening of the child's connection to the Holy People, which is necessary to its becoming an earth surface person. A child's hair is cut when its thoughts begin to be framed on an earth surface language so that all the thoughts contained in its hair bundle stem from Navajo or English. In many families, male and female children are treated differently when they utter their first words. As will be demonstrated in the following chapter, this contrast in treatment is also evident in the steps taken by family members to guide children through puberty into young adulthood.

CHAPTER VI

BECOMING
A YOUNG
MAN OR
WOMAN

Changing Woman comes back to visit us as a Navajo people when we do Kinaaldá. We invite the spirit of Changing Woman to come back here, and sort of reassure her, yes, we are still living by the rules that she has given us, that we still are respecting womanhood, that we still are respecting those ways that she gave us. (Sunny Dooley, Gallup, New Mexico, 8/21/92)

The next step on the path to Navajo personhood occurs in response to the change in a boy's voice or the onset of a girl's menstruation. At these times, manipulations of the body closely follow the themes established in the treatment of newborns. In addition to the types of actions performed on newborns—bathing, molding, and administration of a pollen blessing—during puberty ceremonies young men and women may be dressed in specific attire, painted with various substances, and expected to run, to participate in sweat bathing, or to grind corn. Concern continues to surround care and disposal of certain parts of the body—hair, blood, skin cells in bath and shampoo rinse water. Timely manipulations of the body—molding, running, or painting—are performed to take advantage of its malleable condition at this time. In addition, a fundamental theme of the female puberty ceremony is rejuvenation through a transfer of reproductive powers from the kinaaldá to Mother Earth.

Following patterns similar to those demonstrated in the care and disposal of umbilical cords, family members, responding to the onset of puberty, collectively make decisions to adjust the paradigms established by the Diyin Diné'é governing the cultural construction of the human body and personhood to fit contemporary desires and goals. As a result, practice simultaneously reproduces and alters the Navajo cultural system in complex ways.

"WHEN A BOY'S VOICE CHANGES": THE MALE KINAALDÁ

No particular moment marks the transition from boyhood to manhood. When the Navaho were even more mobile than they are now, the boy had to be trained for activities which took him away from home—hunting, war and trading. Young boys then submitted to rigorous physical training for their self protection. . . . Nowadays there is little formal training; consequently the boy's life goal is but vaguely defined. (Reichard 1950:39)

The Navajo female puberty ceremony is well documented in the ethnographic literature (Franciscan Fathers 1910:446; Reichard 1928:135–39; Wyman and Bailey 1943; Leighton and Kluckhohn 1947:76–77; Keith 1964; Frisbie 1993 [1967]; Roessel 1981:80–100; Begay 1983) and in the popular literature (Ryan 1988; Roessel 1993b; Hazen-Hammond 1995). In contrast, the literature is silent regarding any male equivalent. Indeed, ethnographers such as Gladys Reichard implied that the transition from boyhood to manhood passed virtually unnoticed, leaving one to believe that no male puberty ceremony existed in the Navajo world (Reichard 1950:39). After describing the puberty ceremony that took place when a girl first menstruated as an "extremely important social and religious occasion for girls," Leighton and Kluckhohn noted: "A boy's sexual maturity is, of course, less clear-cut than a girl's. Since Navaho customs with regard to modesty prevent noticing pubic hair, change of voice is the principal criterion. Only after this change has occurred will a boy normally take a sweat bath alone, although he might earlier join older relatives in one. Also, in the old days, and in conservative areas today, at puberty he would begin to be careful in the wearing of the breechcloth" (1947:77).

Such a void in the ethnographic literature is puzzling because many of the people with whom I consulted about the female puberty ceremony mentioned male puberty ceremonies that were performed for themselves or their male relatives (Wilson Aronilth, 7/3/91; Oscar Tso, 7/18/91, 8/9/92; Flora Ashley, 7/29/91; Mae Bekis, 8/5/92, 7/28/93; Ursula Knoki-Wilson, 8/10/92; Harry Walters, 8/18/92, 8/10/93; Elizabeth Yazzie, 12/5/93). Accounts from Navajo oral history are replete with references to activities surrounding the transformation of boys into men (Matthews 1994 [1897]; Goddard 1933; Haile 1938; Fishler 1953; O'Bryan 1956; Wyman 1970; Yazzie 1971; Zolbrod 1984). Earlier women ethnographers who studied events associated with puberty (Reichard 1928:135–39; Leighton and Kluckhohn 1947:76–77; Keith 1964; Frisbie 1993 [1967]; Shepardson and Hammond 1970; Lamphere 1977) may not have known about the male puberty ceremony because, in general—as Ursula Knoki-Wilson warned me—this knowledge is reserved for men and restricted from women.[1]

UKW Their manhood is not celebrated in the way the woman's is. They are kind of combined, because at Kinaaldá ceremonies all the puberty age boys get introduced to sweat lodge and that's where they get their—

MS Oh?

UKW They get introduced in sweat lodge ritual and then they get massaged over there.

MS They do get massaged?

UKW Uh-huh.

MS Is it like when the girl is molded where she lays on the blankets?

UKW No, they do it privately over there. We don't know what they do. Or, we don't talk about it because that is a man's. The men are not supposed to share what they do with the women.

MS OK.

UKW So you will have to ask Wilson [Aronilth] about what they do.

MS I'll ask him.

UKW Yeah. He may not tell you because you are a woman.

MS Yeah, right. I know.

UKW I meant that just as a warning [laughs].

MS I know, well I understand that is how these things work, and so that's OK. I guess if I am not supposed to know, I am not supposed to know. (Ursula Knoki-Wilson, Fort Defiance, Arizona, 7/29/93)

The bulk of all accounts dealing with male puberty derive from the adventures of Changing Woman's twin sons, Monster Slayer and Born For Water. When the twins reached puberty, they went on a quest to find their father. During this quest, they had many adventures and encountered numerous obstacles. On their way to their father's home, they were forced to navigate seemingly impassable rock canyons (Haile 1938:97; Fishler 1953:46; Wyman 1970:536; Yazzie 1971:38–42), walls or mountains of shifting sand that would suffocate all who attempted to pass (Haile 1938:99; Fishler 1953:46; Wyman 1970:535; Yazzie 1971:38–42, 52) or else burn them (Matthews 1994 [1897]:110; Zolbrod 1984:203–204), rocks that would crush all who attempted to pass (Matthews 1994 [1897]:109–10; Wyman 1970:536; Yazzie 1971:38–42, 52; Zolbrod 1984:199–200), cutting or slashing reeds (Matthews 1994 [1897]:110; Haile 1938:99; Fishler 1953:46; Wyman 1970:535–36; Yazzie 1971:38–42, 52; Zolbrod

1984:201–2), and cane cactuses that tore into travelers (Matthews 1994 [1897]:110; Zolbrod 1984:202–3).

These trials, in combination with subsequent events experienced by the twins while at the home of their father, the sun, and while slaying the monsters, established precedents for Navajo masculinity. "Their adventures establish many of the Navaho ideals for young manhood. They serve especially as models of conduct in war and can almost be called the Navaho War gods" (Kluckhohn and Leighton 1974 [1946]:182).

Some accounts of Navajo oral history allude to the performance of actions on pubescent male Nihookáá Dine'é modeled on those originally performed for the twins. Physical training to improve endurance and the acquisition of powerful songs are discussed by Stanley Fishler: "The Twins were trained in a special way in their youth to become very strong. While it was still dark in the morning, they would run to the east to meet the coming Dawn. Now the young boys are trained in the same way. White Bead Woman taught the boys songs to sing in the Dawn. . . . The Twins also ran to meet the Twilight and also sang songs while doing this" (1953: 44–45).

More recently, molding of boys in the image of deities was alluded to in an account compiled by educators at Rough Rock Demonstration School: "Finally, the Sun admitted that the boys were his children. He called his daughter, who was the child of the woman the boys found in the Sun's home when they arrived. The daughter was very beautiful; and there also was a son, who was as good looking as the girl. The daughter used her brother to mold the two boys in the likeness of his features. This molding was carried on by the People for some time, but I do not know whether it is still practiced for males" (Yazzie 1971:56).

Because of the void in the ethnographic literature, I was initially surprised during my first summer of research when consultants referred to male puberty ceremonies.

> FA In Kinaaldá they just do the whole process of initiating them into womanhood. Also, the young man, when they go through the stage of changing voice, they have puberty too, where they . . .
> MS Oh, they do?
> FA They sweat. The uncle gives them a sweat bath. And then, they give them herbs to drink and run, just like the woman does. But today nobody does that.
> MS But they used to do it for men?
> FA They used to do that.
> MS Huh? I never, a couple people have mentioned it, but I—
> FA That, a lot of people don't know about that one. So, that is the

initiation to become a, into the world of manhood. So, that is about the only thing I can tell you. (Flora Ashley, Tsaile, Arizona, 7/29/91)

In the following account, Oscar Tso recalls the four-day ceremony his maternal and paternal grandfathers cosponsored for him when his voice changed. The first two days involved fasting and running, and the second two days involved purification through the ingestion of emetics and participation in sweat bathing. This ceremony was followed by a Beauty Way ceremony a month or two later. In the sweat bath he learned songs and was instructed in his future roles as husband, father, and grandfather.

OT They built a sweat for me, and they talked to me about my responsibilities as a man. And then, what I need to do to take care of myself. They talked about how I should be when I get married. What I should know and how I should be towards a woman, because I have a mother, I have sisters. And I have to have respect for my mother, my sisters and then have that same respect for a woman that I will marry. And then all the daughters that I will have, or granddaughters that I will have. So, those kinds of things are explained to you. And then about how you need to keep yourself real strong, try to stay with one woman for a long time, you know. Have one set of children. And they can really preach, you know, and talk to you about a lot of things. And those are some things that are explained to boys. And then, how you have to be strong, what kind of herbs you have to take from time to time to purify and cleanse your body. To keep your mind and body strong, and have a sense of purpose as you go about living this life. So, I had the sweat done for me, as well as the Beauty Way, the Hoozhónee done for me.

MS OK, so the sweat lasts how long?

OT They had me, see at that point in time they had me to run. And they had me to fast. See that was involved in the sweat lodge ceremony. Then later on, then they had the Beauty Way or the Hoozhónee for me. . . . It was during the spring when they had the sweat ceremony for me. And they gathered a lot of herbs, and then had me to take it [an herbal emetic], and then to vomit a lot of this stuff. But before they did that they had me to fast two days without food and water, and then they administered this herb to me. To throw up. It will cleanse your body. And then they didn't give me food right off. They had these herbs that they gave to me to drink for another two days and water. So I fasted two days, but going without food was the full four days.

MS So, what was it that made them decide that it was time for you to have this ceremony?

OT Just the bodily change, and then the voice change.

MS Oh, the voice change, yeah that is what I have heard is really significant. . . . So two days before the sweat bath started you fasted?

OT Uh-huh, for two days, two full days.

MS Then you had your first day in a sweat. How long do you stay in a sweat?

OT Well they will sing, like, uh, depending on who is there. . . . I had two grandparents that were there, grandfathers. And they each took their time to build a sweat for me. And then they each took their time to talk about the basics of, I guess "the birds and the bees," is the way they talk about it in the English language. So they took their time and then they made sure that I remembered, or tried to learn some songs.

MS Uh-huh, so then there were four days including the sweat baths?

OT [Nods his head]

MS And how long after that did they have the Blessing Way for you?

OT I think it was about a month, or almost two months later. I am not too sure. (Oscar Tso, White Valley, Arizona, 7/18/92)

During the summer of 1992, Mae Bekis mentioned in passing that you could tell when a boy went into puberty by the change in his voice. When I asked her whether there was a male Kinaaldá, she told me that she had heard of a sweat bath ceremony that was formerly conducted, but that to the best of her knowledge it was no longer performed. She told me that in its place, contemporary families usually just had the Blessing Way ceremony for a boy when his voice changed.

MB Even the boys, you know, when their voice changes you can tell then. You can tell.

MS Is there a puberty ceremony for boys?

MB Uh-huh. There isn't, it is just their voice changes, you can tell, but you can have a regular Blessing Way for a boy if you want after their voice changes.

MS Someone mentioned to me this ceremony where there are two days of fasting and then two days of a sweat. Have you ever heard of that?

MB Yeah, I have heard of sweat, that sweat bath and things like that?

MS What they do for boys when their voice changes?

MB Boys, yeah, for them they did that, but not anymore, we don't do that.

MS But they used to do it?

MB They used to do it, but not anymore.

MS Oh, well I heard of a family that is planning one.

MB Oh?

MS And I had never heard of a ceremony for boys so I was really wondering.

MB Well, when their voice changes, you know, we usually do just a regular Blessing Way for them, for the fullness of their life.

MS So who educates them about the "birds and the bees," or whatever?

MB Well it is their father's job too. And part of a mother's too, you know, you tell them, "You are a young man now, you can make babies, so don't mess around with girls," and "You can get them in trouble." And things like that. We used to tell our boys that. But some of them I guess they don't. They don't tell their kids that. (Mae Bekis, Tó'tsoh, Arizona, 8/5/92)

Other physiological changes accompany the change of voice that marks a boy's entrance into a new stage of life. In some families the male puberty ceremony is triggered by a young man's first ejaculation, which, as Sunny Dooley explains, is likened to a young woman's first menstrual period.

The minute that the woman has her period and that the young man has his voice change, it is like another stage of life. And the same kind of ritual [as the Blessing Way performed shortly after birth], but more elaborate, happens, and that is the Kinaaldá [for girls] and that is the four-day sweat for the boys. . . . They don't bake a cake or anything, you know, but they have like a sweat, I know they have sweats. And I know that they have to go through some endurance kind of things. Mostly like running, and I know that like sometimes they will run like with a mouthful of water, for a certain amount of distance, just so that they can learn how to breathe . . . and not swallow any of the water, I mean that is pretty difficult to do. . . . I know they used to do that, and then like horse riding and, you know, arrowhead making, you know, weaponry? That kind of stuff, and like songs on how to overcome enemies. Horse songs, if they want to be ranchers, that kind of stuff. So they will, they also have a mentor, that is very similar to the Ideal Woman [the woman who guides a young woman through every phase of her puberty ceremony]. . . . The minute that a boy starts ejaculating, you know, that is when they say that is his period. And so that is when they will take him into the sweat bath and teach him his roles of man-hood. His responsibilities of manhood, and all this kind of stuff, so that he just doesn't, you know, run off and, umm, you know, violate women or that kind of thing. . . . Then that is when they take him aside and teach him his new roles and responsibilities. I think there is a resurgence of it. It was sort of like under the covers for a while and then all of a sudden we started noticing in our society that there are a lot of battered women, there is a lot of domestic vio-lence, there is a lot of child abuse. And I think that is where some-body asked the question, "Well what does a man do other than beat up women and rape them?" And then I think that is where our tra-ditional teachings came back in, to be taught. (Sunny Dooley, Gallup, New Mexico, 8/21/92)

As Harry Walters notes in the following account, a young man's puberty cere-mony, sometimes called a Kinaaldá, can be very simple.[2] The entire ceremony can consist of a single sweat bath followed by a Blessing Way ceremony. In some cases, the sweat is done during the afternoon of the second day of the Blessing Way ceremony, before the all-night sing, instead of on the day before the Blessing Way.

MS Is there a Navajo male puberty ceremony, or a Kinaaldá?

HW Yes, it is not exactly a Kinaaldá. It is when a boy's voice changes. You know, one day he has a real high voice and then one day he has a deep voice, that is when they. . . . It is a sweat house ceremony with songs and prayers. And then the father, the grand-parents, the uncles, you know, takes a sweat bath with him and then he is taught, now that he is a man, what he is expected, you know, what his duties and responsibilities are. . . . The sweat house ceremony is done first, and then after that, you know, the Blessing Way ceremony. Or else during the Blessing Way ceremony, during the second day in the afternoon before the No-Sleep ceremony

[the all-night sing], that is when they have the sweat house ceremony for him.

MS And do they have anything like running, or things that they
have to do like the girl does?

HW Yeah, yeah, he runs.

MS Which direction?

HW East.

MS What other similarities are there between the male and the
female puberty ceremony?

HW The similarity is the Blessing Way ceremony.

MS Well that is the main similarity. What else? I am wondering,
does the boy, OK, you say he runs, is the boy molded? Like the
girl is?

HW Uh [pause]. No, I don't think so. (Harry Walters, Tsaile,
Arizona, 8/18/92)

As Ursula Knoki-Wilson notes, some families incorporate pubescent boys into
female Kinaaldá, rather than holding separate ceremonies for young men when
they come of age.

UKW During a Kinaaldá, they did instruction for the boys as well
as the girls. So the boys, a lot of times they got introduced to the
sweat lodge around that time. And they, the elders would take the
boys and have a sweat lodge for them and then they would talk to
them about, you know, sexuality matters I guess. And one of the
things they told them was part of being a man was controlling
themselves and that if they were a man, they wouldn't be having
their wives have a baby every single year. You know, that they
would restrain themselves, and stuff like that. So they did a lot of
teaching related to abstinence. . . .

MS Well can we back up a second?

UKW Uh-huh.

MS Is there a male puberty ceremony? As well as the female?

UKW Uh-unh, no. They just have the girls. But they do certain
things with the boys at that time, you know. Like I said, for those
boys that haven't been introduced to the sweat lodge, they would
do it around that time. And then they were expected to participate
in the girl's puberty rite, you know, like run in the morning, and
help out with the chores and stuff like that.

MS And then their male elders would take the opportunity to talk to the boys?

UKW Yeah. (Ursula Knoki-Wilson, Chinle, Arizona, 8/10/92)

The individual accounts told to me by Navajo consultants closely parallel the episodes documented in oral history regarding the pubescence of the twins, Monster Slayer and Born For Water. When the twins found the sun, they claimed to be his sons. The sun made them endure a series of trials in an effort to prove or disprove their parentage. He caught them in a rope, raised them up, and dashed them against sharp flints (Haile 1938:101; Wyman 1970:541–43), spikes (Matthews 1994 [1897]:111–12; Yazzie 1971:54; Zolbrod 1984:208), or arrowheads (Fishler 1953:48) located on the east, south, west, and north walls of his home. He forced them into circular holes lined with flints—one in each of the cardinal directions (Haile 1938:103; Yazzie 1971:46)—and then, using each hole and a log as a mortar and pestle, tried four times to smash them (Fishler 1953:488; Wyman 1970:542–43). When these efforts failed, according to some accounts, he fed them poisoned cornmeal (Yazzie 1971:46) and then placed them in the freezing waters of an ocean for the night (Wyman 1970:543; Yazzie 1971: 54). The next day he forced them to endure an extremely hot sweat bath (Matthews 1994 [1897]:111–12; Haile 1938:103; Fishler 1953:49–50; O'Bryan 1956:80; Wyman 1970:543–44; Yazzie 1971:43–46, 54; Zolbrod 1984: 208–9). Fortunately, supernatural helpers interceded in each case. The twins' survival forced the sun to acknowledge them as his children, for only children of his could persevere through such tests of endurance.

After their ordeals, the twins were made over—washed, molded, dressed, painted—in the image of their male or female siblings, the other children of the sun (Matthews 1994 [1897]:112; Haile 1938:105; Fishler 1953:50; O'Bryan 1956:80–81; Zolbrod 1984:210), or in the image of their father, the sun (Fishler 1953:51). Alternatively, one twin was made over in the image of a male sibling and the other was made over in the image of the sun (Wyman 1970:546–48). As an elder from Lukachukai explained:

> It occurred during their visit with their father, the sun. The male twins were placed next to the other children of the sun, the female twins. The male twins were molded in the image of the female twins. The male twins were made resembling the female twins. That is the reason why the kinaaldá are molded and the practice is continued. It is said the voices of the female twins were strong, forceful, and unique. The male twins were wished to have the same characteristics, with strong physical presence. They were told they have to be like their twin sisters. So, the male twins were created and molded

into the image of the female twins. According to this event the kinaaldá is molded. (The words of an anonymous elder, Lukachukai, Arizona, 8/13/92, translated by Wesley Thomas)

In other accounts, such as the following one told to Stanley Fishler by Frank Goldtooth of Tuba City, Arizona, after enduring many trials to prove they were children of the sun, the twins were washed and molded in the image of their male siblings.

> The Twins went into the house with the Sun who said they were his boys. When they got inside, they found their two half-sisters and two half-brothers. . . . Since the twins had never been washed since they had been born, they had large callouses [sic] on their joints and dirt all over them. They were bathed and washed gently by their relatives. This is where they were shaped and massaged as if they were bread to fix them up. Their bodies were smoothed back into shape like their half-brothers for their bodies were greatly mis-shapened. (Fishler 1953:50)

In the following narrative, Oscar Tso explains that according to what he had been taught, once the twins were washed it became evident that they were in an extremely undeveloped physical condition and lacked any distinguishing features or coloration. To rectify this situation, their bodies were molded to give them a strong muscular form, and then they were painted with tobacco ash mixed with water to give them features such as eyebrows, eyelashes, and other body hair.

OT The molding process, in terms of I guess a male puberty ceremony is where I have an understanding of the molding. When the twins, visited the sun god, I mean, their brothers and sisters were the ones that molded them. And they combed out their hair and tied it into a bun, after kind of like an initiation type of a purification ceremony that they went through. And then when they were molded, they said that, you know, they didn't even have any muscular features. And when they were molded, I mean, they looked kind of like Arnold Schwarzenegger, by the time they got finished molding them!

Opal Tso [Laughs.]

MS [Laughs] Uh-huh.

OT I guess the eyebrows, and the mustache, and even the hair, you know, maybe even the colors were not really there until they went through the, see I would have to back up and talk about the, the . . .

MS Well go ahead.

OT The tobacco. And I don't know if, I would have to talk about tobacco for a long time and then the way that they used it. Anyway, yeah, they finished the purification ceremony with a tobacco that they smoked. And the ashes of that tobacco is what they put on here to [rubs his eyebrows].

MS Oh, to make the eyebrows?

OT The eyebrows, the eyelashes, the mustache and—

MS What about the hair?

OT The hair, and the parts of the body that have hairs, so. Anyway that is what they used in the molding process to make them look real nice, muscular, and somewhat human types of features, that they acquired through that molding process. So that is my understanding of the molding and I imagine that is the way White Shell Woman . . . from what I understand, it is the molding process that made her really, really beautiful. (Oscar and Opal Tso, Many Farms, Arizona, 8/9/92)

This account correlates with one recorded by Berard Haile in which the twins were attended by their siblings, the dawn children, who made the twins over in their own image. They washed the twins, rubbed their bodies with special pollen from each of the cardinal directions, molded them following the trajectory of growth—from the soles of their feet to the tops of their heads—and then dressed them in "dawn" clothing (Haile 1938:105). In an alternate account, the twins were molded in the image of their father, the sun; in this case, each twin was dressed in "flint" clothing and then given a "live eagle feather" and some specially prepared pollen. As noted in the following account of this episode, these items served as protective armor.

> The boys stood side by side and were decorated and dressed with flint shoes, socks, pants and shirts. The Sun put a "live eagle feather" in their hair to protect them from evil things. The Navaho still have some of these eagle feathers. Three or four people here on the reservation still have these. This feather is used by young men when they go to war to protect them, but some who own them now are too stingy and won't let them be borrowed by anyone.
>
> There was also corn pollen shaken off the four protection gods to protect them. If the gods had not done this, it would not happen now. Now pollen is used for protection and is put in socks or shoes like the Twins did. These kinds of pollen were used during the war to protect

warriors. There are many special rites that are done with this pollen. After the boys were dressed they stood up and they looked just like their father. They had lightning coming out of their bodies, heads, arms and legs. (Fishler 1953:51)

Once they were presentable, the sun made them endure one last trial to prove their parentage. He prepared a pipe of poisoned tobacco for the twins to smoke. They used an antidote given to them by a supernatural helper on their journey to the sun's home, which enabled them to smoke this pipe without ill effect (Fishler 1953:48; O'Bryan 1956:80). After they smoked, the sun used the tobacco ashes to mold their bodies a second time.

After that he called upon his children, the dawn children, to come to him. When they came to him, they were carrying something or other, suspended from a dawn cord. It seems that they were carrying a dawn ladle, a dawn bowl, and dawn pollen, when they approached the boys. With these things they set to work on them, rubbing them with dawn pollen, with skyblue pollen, and with evening twilight pollen. With darkness pollen they rubbed their hair. After that they began to shape them from their feet up, and made them look exactly as they themselves looked. Then, it seems, they took them to their home, where they dressed them in clothes, such as they themselves were wearing, in dawn shoes, dawn leggings, dawn garments, and dawn headbands.

"There is still one trial left," the sun said. Crystal rocks were burning there and produced a great, crackling noise. He picked up a turquoise pipe which he had, and used a white bead ram to poke around in it, then filled it with his tobacco [this was poison tobacco, but the twins survived with the help of an antidote]. . . . After they had finished smoking they set the pipe down. "Isn't this a surprise, my sons, my children! It's true! You really are my children!" he said to them. The remaining tobacco ashes he shook out into his hand, then told them to place their feet together, which they did. He then spit upon the ashes, and set to work on the boys by pressing them with it, much as their brothers and sisters had previously done. As he did this he kept up this speech, "My children, Changing Woman's children, White Bead Woman's children, my children, have care not to ask something extraordinary of me, whatever your purpose in coming may be! Should I ask you, is it this or that, be satisfied, and do not ask for more, my children, please!" he was saying and pleading, while he pressed them. (Haile 1938:105)

Harry Walters confirmed the importance of tobacco in this context and in other Blessing Way ceremonies. As he explains in the following account, when the twins arrived at their father's home they were so filthy and underdeveloped that the sun had a hard time believing they could possibly be his sons. The twins were cleaned and molded by either the sun (O'Bryan 1956:80–81; Yazzie 1971:46), their siblings (Matthews 1994 [1897]:112; Haile 1938:105; Fishler 1953:50; Wyman 1970:546; Yazzie 1971:56; Zolbrod 1984:210), or the sun's wife (Walters, 8/10/93) to give them a muscular, manly form.

> HW They were skinny and their hair was dirty, you know, matted, with dirt. They were filthy. This is why the sun did not believe that they were his sons. He said, "You could not possibly be my sons, because look at you." And then he had two daughters that were there and he said, "Look at my daughters how beautiful they are." And so, at the last sweat house ceremony, when they came out, yes they were molded, they were molded some say by the sun's wife, others say by the sisters.
>
> MS Yeah that is what I heard, was by the sisters.
>
> HW Yeah, by the sisters, and he told them to make them look handsome, you know?
>
> MS Uh-huh.
>
> HW So this is when they each became a man. They became muscular, they were handsome.
>
> MS I was also told that at that time they burnt tobacco to paint on their eyebrows and their hair. Is that what you have been told also?
>
> HW The Blessing Way ceremony has tobacco in it. Tobacco. This one is for your mind. . . . Tobacco is used in the Blessing Way but not every Blessing Way. Only when the family requests that. . . . It deals with the mind, you know. When you are alienated, feeling alienation, then that straightens up your thinking, your mind. So tobacco is used for that.
>
> MS So in the story that you were told, was tobacco used when Changing Woman's sons were molded?
>
> HW Yes, yes.
>
> MS OK. In what way was it used?
>
> HW They smoked it. They smoked it.
>
> MS Oh?
>
> HW They smoked it and then they blew it on their hands and then they rubbed it all over their bodies.

MS Rubbed themselves with it?

HW And then the sisters also smoked it. And they used that, you know, to mold the twins' bodies like that. (Harry Walters, Tsaile, Arizona, 8/18/92)

When I returned to visit Mae Bekis in 1993, she reported that during the past year, while visiting various communities to conduct Kinaaldá ceremonies or give lectures on child development, she had learned about male Kinaaldá practices in two Navajo communities. Remembering my interest, she kindly shared this information with me. While conducting a Kinaaldá for a young woman in Toyei, Arizona, she became acquainted with an elderly woman from Crystal, New Mexico, who was in attendance. This woman told Mrs. Bekis how they celebrated the onset of puberty for boys in her family.

MB I did a Kinaaldá down at Toyei three weeks ago. And then, there was this one lady she was in her eighties or nineties, who came down from Crystal. I couldn't remember her name, she was going by somebody "-baa'," you know?

MS Yeah [I nod my head to acknowledge that I understand she is referring to a woman's war name].

MB And, uh, she said that the boys do change, too. She says not as menstruation, but their voice!

MS Yes?

MB And she said that she heard that "a long time ago," this is the first time that I have heard this, and she said, "A long time ago," she said, "we used to do that," she said. "Like when we hear the boy's voice change," she said, "we grind a white cornmeal and pour it in the middle of the hooghan inside. On the west side. And then every morning when he gets up, he puts that cornmeal on his face, and we make him run and yell toward the east, so he could have a better voice."

MS Really?

MB Uh-huh, she said, "You do it four times." . . . She said that he would put a white corn on his face and would run toward the east. In the morning—

MS For four days?

MB At noon and in the evening. And they said for four days. And you can just give out something, as a gift, you know.

MS A giveaway?

MB A giveaway, do the giveaway. (Mae Bekis, Tó'tsoh, Arizona, 7/28/93)

This version of the ceremony closely parallels accounts collected by Pliny Goddard and Aileen O'Bryan in which the faces of the twins were "made white." According to the account recorded by O'Bryan:

> The Twins were washed first in a white bead basket, secondly, in a turquoise basket, thirdly, in a white shell basket, and fourthly, in a black jet basket. They learned that this had taken four days. Each day they had been bathed in a different basket. After this their sister brought them to their father who stood them all side by side, their sister between the Twins. The Sun shaped them, legs, arms, fingers and all, even their faces like their sister's. And he powdered them with white powder and their skins were made white. He put something black in a little bowl. It was hair ointment which he put on their hair. He pulled their hair down to their ankles and they had a great quantity of hair. Their sister dressed their hair for them and she dressed their persons. (1956:80–81)

In the account recorded by Goddard, the elder twin was given the name Naayéé' Neezghání, Monster Slayer. He was blackened with the coal of dark sky, and then white bow symbols were painted on his body. His younger brother was given the name Tó Bájísh Chíní, Born For Water. He was reddened with red earth, and then white hair bun designs were painted on his body. As the twins departed from their mother's home on their way to visit their father, the sun, they proclaimed:

> "Now we will start away to visit our father. Sun is our father. . . ." They started away. When they were a short distance in front of the door they discovered a white rainbow. They stepped on that and travelled with it. When they arrived [at the home of the sun] their bodies were moulded, their faces made white. "Now they will be given names," he said. . . . Sun came down. The two who were to be named stood in front. The elder he addressed as naiye'nezyani [sic] and the younger as tobadj'ictcini [sic]. . . . With the coal of the dark sky he made him black. With white clay he drew signs of the bow on him. This will ward off danger. He made tobadj'ictcini red with red earth and put on white hair frame [hair bun] signs with white clay. By means of these they will be protected. (Goddard 1933:156)

The differing colors of pigment with which the twins were adorned—black with white designs versus red with white designs—serve to acknowledge their complementary relationship to each other as the respective male and female counterparts of a whole. Naayéé' Neezghání is naayéé' k'ehjigo, "on the side of protection," the "warrior" side of the whole, while Tó Bájísh Chíní is hózhǫ́ǫ́jigo, "on the side of peace, harmony, and order," the female or "peaceful" side of the couple (H. Ashley, 7/23/91; Walters, 8/18/92). To highlight this difference, in accounts such as the following, each twin is molded and dressed in the image of a specific member of the Diyin Dine'é with distinctive ntł'iz—turquoise or white shell—representative of his warrior or peaceful aspects and qualities.

> "It is true, my children, you are my children, I see," he said to them. "Let it be done now, my daughter, you shall shape your brothers!" he told her. A turquoise stool happened to be there, one of white shell, one of abalone, one of jet, they say. The older one spoken of [Naayéé' Neezghání] sat down on the turquoise one, the younger one [Tó Bájísh Chíní] sat down on the white shell one, while he [Sun] sat down on the abalone one, and his son on the jet one. As for his daughter, the older one was shaped by her with a turquoise in the shape of an ashes-baked bread roll. And he [Sun] was saying, "Exactly like I am, just as I look," that was the guide in shaping him. The younger one was shaped with an ashes-baked bread roll–shaped white shell. As his son's looks were at the time, "Exactly like that, the same looks as he has," he [Sun] said. In that way it seems they were straightened [shaped], they were made to exceed anything in beauty, they say.
>
> Directly he clothed the older of the brothers in turquoise, the younger one he dressed in white shell. . . . After that it seems he then placed an agate, immune to injury, within them, he fixed their hearts for them, they say. Then it seems he placed nearby the flint garments that were there, even the clubs mentioned and the zigzag lightning arrows as requested. Then it seems dressing them was begun while in the meantime he was merely singing. . . . With this [song] the things in which they were to be dressed, were placed there. For the older one dark flints were placed, for the younger one blue flints were placed they say. (Wyman 1970:546–48)

Practices very similar to these are still followed by some Navajo families when boys begin to change into men. Consider, for example, the following account of a male puberty ceremony told to Mae Bekis by a father from Pine Hill, New Mexico, in June 1993, after she had given a talk on child development from birth through the girl's Kinaaldá.

> MB I was called to Pine Hill school on the fifteenth. And I brought this out among the parents. They had a parent meeting, and then they called me out there to talk about the baby, you know, how the baby is born and then go on to Kinaaldá, and all these other things right in there, the growth. And so I talked to them about it and then when we came to Kinaaldá, they asked me, "What do you do about boys?" And I said, "I haven't been doing anything about boys." . . . And then after I said that, there was a man there, he said he was on the parent advisory committee, and then he is a peacemaker [naat'áanii, working within the Navajo Peacemaker Court system], too. And he said that he done his son that way. He said, "It is still here. It is just a lot of us don't believe it anymore." He said, "It can still be done." He said he just gave gifts out on the fourth morning. He just gave gifts out for his son. And he said, "My son has a beautiful voice. And a real beautiful complexion." He said, "It has to do with complexion. You don't mold them or anything," but, he said, "He just ran toward the morning. Towards [the] east in the morning."
>
> MS Did he grind the corn?
>
> MB No, he said he didn't use the corn, but he made him run every morning, noon, and evening, for four days. And at the end of four days, he said, he just gave out some gifts for him and said that his complexion is real nice. (Mae Bekis, Tó'tsoh, Arizona, 7/28/93)

Despite profound changes in the Navajo world, many of the old methods for transforming boys into men endure. As the father from Pine Hill remarked, the male Kinaaldá still exists in the contemporary world. The ceremony is a resource available to parents facing the task of guiding pubescent boys into manhood. Today, boys are ushered into manhood by means of ceremonies in which they may run to the east while singing or yelling (Fishler 1953:44–45; F. Ashley, 7/29/91; Oscar Tso, 7/18/92; Walters, 8/18/92; Dooley, 8/21/92; Bekis, 7/28/93), sweat (F. Ashley, 7/29/91; Oscar Tso, 7/18/92; Knoki-Wilson, 7/29/93; Bekis, 8/5/92; Walters, 8/18/92; Dooley, 8/21/92), fast (Oscar Tso, 7/18/92), be purified with emetics (F. Ashley, 7/29/91; Oscar Tso, 7/18/91), be whitened with cornmeal (Bekis, 7/28/93), be molded (Yazzie 1971:56; Knoki-Wilson, 7/29/93), have a giveaway (Bekis, 7/28/93), learn songs (Fishler 1953:44–45; Oscar Tso, 7/18/92; Dooley, 8/21/92), and be educated in matters of sexuality and the proper behavior for

Navajo men (Oscar Tso, 7/18/92; Knoki-Wilson, 8/10/92; Walters, 8/18/92; Dooley, 8/21/92). This ceremony ensures that men will have physical strength, knowledge of songs, and educated understandings of male sexuality and responsibilities, as well as "beautiful voices."

FEMALE KINAALDÁ

Kinaaldá started a long time ago. The year of the beginning was never mentioned to me. Even the date was not mentioned. The initial ceremony was conducted by the Holy People. We [human beings] did not do it. So we do not know which human being was the first to have a Kinaaldá. We do not even know when humans came into being, let alone knowing who had the first Kinaaldá. In the world of the Holy People, Changing Woman was the first to have Kinaaldá in their own world. On top of Dziłná'oodiłii was where the first Kinaaldá was held. Changing Woman was found and twelve days later she matured to the stage to have her Kinaaldá. . . . After twelve days she had her Kinaaldá, so based on that, Kinaaldá were to occur after twelve years. That is the reason why Changing Woman went through this episode. She prepared herself. She ran on her own for four days. During the first day of the run she made a song, she sang for herself. During the second day, she completed the second song. The third day she made and completed the third song. The fourth day she made her final run. . . . At the end of the fourth-day run, she made and completed the fourth song. She ran with the song in all four directions. The songs provided energy for her. The songs prepared her for her existence. Through the songs she prepared and dressed herself in her moccasins, her dress, and her jewelry. That is how Kinaaldá came into being. Changing Woman worked on herself and she established how the Kinaaldá was to be. She was not assisted by anyone else. Kinaaldá were supposed to prepare themselves just like Changing Woman did. Today, everyone is involved in helping to prepare the kinaaldá for the Kinaaldá. The kinaaldá today is helped and is not independent as Changing Woman was. She was a creative person, she did everything to herself. No one molded her. Nobody was there to do the molding. No one was there to work on her. She stretched herself. She ran in the mornings during the early mornings, at the end of the each run, before she turned around, she took the time to stretch herself, her body, she molded herself during the middle of her run, before turning back home, for the final run. (The words of an anonymous elder, Lukachukai, Arizona, 8/13/92, translated by Wesley Thomas)

As soon as a girl realizes that her first menstrual period has begun, she tells her mother or grandmother.[3] Many families plan far in advance for this occasion, purchasing, making, or borrowing all necessary materials and articles of attire for the young woman to wear, such as a *biil*, the two-piece woven dress, or a velvet blouse and a satin skirt, along with a hair thong, women's moccasins with leggings (*kénitsaai*), a new shawl, and a sis łichí'í, or red sash. For example, in 1991 Sadie Billie itemized the preparations she and her mother had already completed in anticipation of her eight-year-old daughter's future Kinaaldá.

> My dad's sister . . . she would be like maybe ninety-three or ninety-six. We are in preparation to have her make one of those biil, for us, for my daughter. We have already got her a concho belt and we have the sash belt that's being passed on from my mom, that's been used to wrap me. It's going to be a wide one, but that's what we're going to use for her. And then, umm, the hair string we already have. And that was done with a small ceremony that my mom does and there are certain things that are put on there. . . . She has that prepared and it's buckskin, you know, it's cut, it's a long one, it's cut, and you use that to tie the hair. We have that and umm, she's eight now. Beginning now we're not going to cut her hair or do anything with it. We're going to let it grow out. And my mom estimates her to be like twelve or thirteen, fourteen when she's going to come of age. So, the beads that we're going to use, they were given to my dad. His mom gave it to him. We have that in preparation. On top of that we will use other people's jewelry, but that will be the basic necklace that we're going to use. And then the bracelet also comes from him, it's been given to him by his grandmother, so it's very, very old. And those are the basic things that we're going to use and then we will add some other things on top of that, but those are the basic things. And then her shoes are also being made and it's one of those, it's called "kénitsaaí" and it's being done by a man who is associated closely with my dad. . . . And that particular moccasin, we will pick it up in September. It has taken him like almost nine months to finish it because of, you know, his poor eye vision. So those are the basic things that we have collected. And we still have more to collect, you know, like the corn that we are going to use.

Of course the corn we're not going to really worry about it, but it has to be special corn that's being collected from my mom's field. Because nowadays people just go out and look for corn and stuff, but she wants to make preparations to where she did it from, you know, from her own. (Sadie Billie, Tsaile, Arizona, 7/10/91)

In anticipation of this important event, family members will dry corn and save husks from their personal fields when it is possible, or buy corn and husks when it is not. Relatives make a *bé'ézhóó'*, or a grass hairbrush, an *'ádístiin*, or a set of stirring sticks, and other items necessary for the ceremony.

Once a girl notifies her mother or grandmother of the onset of her menstruation, a quiet sense of urgency is evident in the final preparations before the Kinaaldá ceremony begins. As Sunny Dooley explained: "First of all we believe that when a young girl has her kinaaldá [first and second menstrual periods], her body is chemically changing quickly. And that is why we want to do as much as we can within like the minute she notices her period" (8/19/92). A one- or two-day delay is not uncommon while the corn is roasted, firewood is collected, water is hauled to the ceremonial site, arrangements are made with a ceremonial practitioner, and other final preparations are completed. As Mae Charley from north of Rock Point, Arizona, notes in the following account, young women are acknowledged to have a unique power while experiencing their first and second menstrual periods. To maximize its positive effects, family members make every effort to have as many preparations as possible completed well in advance, so the ceremony can be performed while the young woman is still in this special state.

The kinaaldá at the time of her actual kinaaldá she has something unique. It's acknowledged and celebrated days later when the power of the kinaaldá has already begun to change, then do we prepare her. When she has her power, she is not to eat with sugar or salt. She cannot eat hot meals. In that sacred manner she is to tend only to her corn grinding work. She is supposed to be in this condition throughout her Kinaaldá, dressing, and final day. (The words of Mae Charley, north of Rock Point, Arizona, 7/15/92, translated by Wesley Thomas)[4]

To take advantage of these special powers, every Navajo girl is ideally supposed to have a Kinaaldá ceremony at the time of her first and second period. "Back at the dawn of time, when Changing Woman was picked up as a baby from the crevices and when she had her ceremony. It was done for her four times, we are told. We are told not to do it four times, but only two were assigned to us" (Mae Charley, 7/15/92, translated by Wesley Thomas).[5] In fact, the second ceremony frequently is not performed when the girl's family lives far from the reservation or when inclement weather, limited family resources, or personal preference intervenes.

The kinaaldá's entire extended family plays a crucial role in the ceremony. Everyone who assists with the ceremony in whatever form—cooking, hauling water or wood, singing—directly influences the efficacy of the ceremony and the kinaaldá's future. Three people play special roles that have profound influence: the "Ideal Woman," the woman in charge of the cake, and the religious practitioner.

The Ideal Woman is someone selected by the girl's family to guide her through every step of the ceremony. She is selected because she epitomizes the ideals of Navajo womanhood: industriousness, ambition, good health, and knowledge of traditional ways (Reichard 1928:137; Keith 1964:28; Frisbie 1993 [1967]:359; Wright 1982:383–84; Begay 1983:47; Ryan 1988:4). She is usually someone considered to possess special gifts—for example, as Sadie Billie explains in the following passage, she may be an outstanding weaver or an expert herdswoman. She may be an aunt or other relative, as in Mrs. Billie's case, but she need not be a relative. Indeed, families often intentionally pick a prominent woman from the community who is not a relative, as a means of extending reciprocal relations to unrelated families (T. M. Begay, 7/28/91; Irene Kee, 8/3/92; Sunny Dooley, 8/19/92).

> That would be someone that you know very close. For mine it was done by my dad's aunt. She knows how to weave, she moves fast, she does things fast, she knows how to prepare cornmeal, she can herd sheep, she can shear, you know, she's swift at everything. That's the kind of person that's ideal for them. . . . You don't just select anyone to tie your hair and do that exercise for you. She guides you all the way. (Sadie Billie, Tsaile, Arizona, 7/10/91)

When the family is ready to begin, a blanket is hung over the door of the hooghan. This signifies to the Diyin Dine'é that a Hózhǫ́ójí ceremony is in progress. Practice reproduces the system—Navajo theories of the human body and personhood—when a family plans and performs a traditional puberty ceremony for a young woman at the onset of menstruation. The system, however, has altered over the lifetimes of the Navajo people with whom I consulted in direct response to changes in the Navajo world. The traditional Kinaaldá, modeled on Changing Woman's Kinaaldá, spanned four days and four nights by Navajo reckoning, with the all-night sing on the final night. Variations have developed over the last forty years that are designed to accommodate children attending boarding schools, families living off the reservation, and relatives with nine-to-five jobs.

Mandatory attendance at boarding schools, which became prevalent in the

1940s, had a major impact on this ceremony. Living at boarding schools for nine months out of the year meant that many girls were away from home at the onset of puberty or, as Mae Bekis explains in the following account, at the time of their second menstrual periods. Depending on individual circumstances, these young women often had only one puberty ceremony.

MB Sometimes the first menstrual it will stay just maybe, they said it is just seen and you are not supposed to wear a pad. It is just seen at that one time. . . . Well way back there when I did mine, I just saw it. And that was it. I was scared, but I told my mom, and so we did the cake and I didn't, she told me not to wear pads. She said, "That is just to tell you that you are a young lady now." . . . I didn't have to wear pads. And she just told me not to wash up for four days. But I didn't just go bleed, bleed, bleed, I didn't have to wear a pad. . . . And the second one, umm, we were told differently, you know, at school. In a boarding school at Shiprock [New Mexico]. And it was in the wintertime, and so I didn't do my second one because we were at school. Which was about, mine were about five months apart.

MS Yeah, that happens a lot. So, then did you have a second Kinaaldá when you came home?

MB No, uh-unh, no they wouldn't let me, you know. You, we didn't have trucks like this. This was in 1946, or '47, or '48, right around there.

MS But I mean when you came home for summer vacation?

MB No! You are not supposed to do that. Just the first time you see it and the second time you see it, that is it! Those are called the kinaaldá. . . . And after the third, fourth, fifth, that is the regular monthly, you know, periods. . . . Just the kinaaldá, the first and the second, that is the only time you have a ceremony, is the first and the second [menstrual periods].

MS OK. So girls that are at boarding school for the first two, they never have a ceremony?

MB Some of them, the second one they never had it because they were in boarding school. . . . This was way in '45 we didn't have no, it wasn't like this. We didn't have no lights in this area, as I remember. And I was, we were put in boarding schools and we got put there. We had to, my dad had to find a transportation for us, which was from the church, you know. They took us over, and they left us there.

MS For nine months?

MB For nine months!

MS Oh!

MB And it so happened that when we came back, I had my first, when I had my kinaaldá [first menstruation]. And that is when they did the Kinaaldá for me. The second time we were in school and I couldn't come home. There was no transportation, nobody could bring us home, so I didn't have my second one. My sister was the same way. And she had hers right when we came back from school, and then the second one she had it two or three months later, and we were back in school and she didn't do hers, the second one. (Mae Bekis, Tó'tsoh, Arizona, 8/5/92)

In the most extreme cases, a girl had both her first and second menstrual periods while away at boarding school. Prior to the 1960s, in a case such as this, the young woman would not have been allowed to have any puberty ceremony because, as Mrs. Bekis explained, the Navajo theories governing the development of the body and personhood extant at that time dictated that the ceremony be performed only during the first or second menstrual period, and not after that time. As the women affected by such situations matured, many of them faced problems with reproduction or general health, which they attributed to their not having had a Kinaaldá ceremony. Because they did not want their daughters and granddaughters to face similar problems, they looked for ways to adjust the cultural system to accommodate new practices. Within a couple of generations, the system had gradually adjusted to enable young women to undergo the needed ceremonies.

Today, young women from families living off the reservation can wait to have the ceremony at a convenient time, such as during a school vacation, and boarding schools are required to notify a girl's parents immediately upon the onset of menstruation, excuse the child from school, and provide transportation home so that the ceremony can be performed (F. Ashley, 7/29/91; Lillie Tsosie, 8/4/92). It is ideal for a Kinaaldá to be performed during the first or the second period, or both. If, for whatever reason, a young woman has her first and second periods before a ceremony can be scheduled, in many regions of the reservation contemporary practice allows for the ceremony to be performed at another time. If a ceremony must be done after the first or second period, it is imperative that it be scheduled to occur while the young woman is not having a menstrual period, because the blood from all periods other than the first two is potentially dangerous.

As Jean Jones explains in the next passage, school and work schedules have caused dramatic changes in the length of this ceremony within a single generation—during the span of time from her own Kinaaldá to the time of her daughters' ceremonies. To accommodate working relatives and school schedules, contemporary ceremonies are frequently shortened to two or three days, and the all-night sing is often scheduled to fall on a weekend.[6]

> JJ There's two ways you could do it. You could get her ready and then let her run three days. But the other one you could have a medicine man come in and then do the Beauty Way. She washes her hair in the basket in the morning when he comes. And then, she could run that same day and have the cake the next day . . . [and] have the medicine man come in the same day. Put all her jewelry on and then you could bake the cake that night.
>
> MS So is this a new thing to have the shortened version?
>
> JJ No. You could have [it] either way.
>
> MS It's always been that way?
>
> JJ It's always been that way. Yeah.
>
> MS Oh?
>
> JJ Like I had one done for my daughter and she had that medicine man come in and the next day she made the cake. She washed her hair that morning. And then she ran, she ran. The other one, you wash your hair early in the morning. Just let her run.
>
> MS On the fourth day? Or on the . . .
>
> JJ On . . . the next day you could just . . .
>
> MS The last day you wash her hair and let her run with her hair wet?
>
> JJ In the morning, early in the morning.
>
> MS Well, when you were young and you had your Kinaaldá which way did you do it?
>
> JJ I ran for three days and then the medicine man came in. We ground corn and then we used to run . . . for three days and then we had the cake on the third night. (Jean Jones, north of Rock Point, Arizona, 7/15/92)

In addition to modification of the length of the ceremony, other changes are evident in contemporary Kinaaldá. For example, most families have the bulk of the corn commercially ground with electronic equipment in reservation border towns, reserving only a token portion to be ground by the kinaaldá with stone tools. In addition, many families now use aluminum foil to line the baking pit, and kinaaldá are just as likely to wear tennis shoes as moccasins when they run. The

Navajo people with whom I consulted acknowledged these changes as mere modern conveniences and went on to assure me that the critical aspects of this important ceremony have remained virtually unaltered from generation to generation.

FIRST DAY

We arrived at Black Rock a few minutes after 9 A.M. with Nakai Tso. We immediately began unloading supplies. Greg and I rushed to the hooghan to place the ground corn, basket, jewelry, stirring sticks and hairbrush on the blanket at the center of the west wall. 9:25 Sadie began dressing Ragen. She directed her to put her satin skirt on over her head and then to remove her jeans from under the skirt. Next she helped her put her velvet blouse on. Ragen was told to sit down with her legs straight out in front of herself. Sadie put the right moccasin on first. When she got to the legging, she, Morjorie and Rosie discussed sewing the silver buttons onto the leggings. They decided we needed a different type of thread and it would take too long. So, they wrapped the legging on the right leg and then proceeded to put the moccasin and legging onto the left leg.

Ragen was told to stand up. Sadie tightly wrapped the sash sunwise around her waist and tied it. Jewelry: Sadie started with the jaatł'óół, or earrings, her mother had given to Ragen, next she put on three or four bracelets which people had placed into the basket, two rings, three turquoise necklaces and finally the concho belt sent by her brother Thomas Tso. Morjorie stepped up and tied a string of beads with a white shell on its end, onto the right-hand side of Ragen's sash fringes.

Sadie's mother and father began discussing something in very fast Navajo, I was unable to follow. Finally, Ragen was told to kneel down facing east to have her hair tied. Sadie explained that this was the procedure according to her mother's clan's, her father's clan brushed the girl's hair and had her run, before she would have her hair tied and be molded. They had decided to do it the way her mother's clan did it. Nakai Tso sang a song while Sadie brushed and tied Ragen's hair. As he sang, she brushed Ragen's hair with the grass brush, brushing Ragen's bangs down in the front so that they hung over her face. She brushed Ragen's hair into a ponytail at the back of her neck and tied it with the buckskin thong. Next, Ragen was told to stand on the edge of the blanket facing east, to wait while the women laid out blankets in front of the hooghan for the first molding. (Field notes, 7/24/92)

On the morning of the first day of the Kinaaldá, the young woman is dressed in the image of Changing Woman to mark her transition from child to adult. Before she is dressed, her hair is washed in yucca root suds. When it is dry, it is combed with a freshly made grass brush. Alternatively, the kinaaldá may be directed ahead of time to arrive at the ceremony with freshly washed hair so that she may be dressed immediately in traditional attire.

> During the Kinaaldá, you spread a material, you dress her with whatever you have, including wrapped moccasin, sash belt, white shell necklace, concho belt, turquoise necklaces, earrings. You dress her with everything. You prepare her and dress her with material goods. She is dressed with hard goods. She runs like that. It is done like that and it was established like that from the time of beginning and continuing. If you don't dress her, material wealth will not come her way. It is said. (The words of Mae Charley, north of Rock Point, Arizona, 7/15/92, translated by Wesley Thomas)

When I inquired about the order in which the young woman is dressed on the first day of her Kinaaldá, Mae Charley explained that she is dressed from the feet upward, following the trajectory of growth. With characteristic humor she pointed out why you must put the skirt and blouse on before the moccasins: "Dress is upward [from the feet up]. Remember when one is dressing, you dress first, then you sit, and then you put on your shoes. You don't start with your shoes first, or you'll be buck naked! You dress with your clothes first, then your shoes and jewelry. . . . It starts with the right side, always" (7/15/92, translation by Wesley Thomas).

The attire with which the kinaaldá is adorned may include a handwoven biil or a velveteen blouse and a full satin skirt, a sash, and moccasins with deerskin leggings, if these articles of apparel are available. Mrs. Charley went on to explain that she did not wear a biil at her own Kinaaldá; instead, she wore a velvet blouse with a satin skirt and other articles brought to the ceremony by her grandmother, who kept a bundle of items to be used exclusively by kinaaldá in the surrounding area.

> MC I just wore the legged moccasin. And I wore the buckskin for my hair tie. . . .
> JJ You wore a velvet top, right?
> MC Yes.
> JJ Shiny dress [a satin skirt], too, right?
> MC Yes. my grandmother's mother had everything prepared just

for kinaaldá. Everything for them to wear including legged moccasin, sash belt from long ago. Concho belt, hair tie, necklaces, bracelets. She said they were for preparation for the kinaaldá to dress in. Jaatł'óół, long turquoise earrings just for that purpose. When there was a Kinaaldá in the immediate area, she'd take her bundle there to be used for kinaaldá. Maybe my grandmother inherited it, I don't know? (The words of Mae Charley and Jean Jones, north of Rock Point, Arizona, 7/15/92, translated by Wesley Thomas)

Today, many families simply do not own or have access to these items of traditional attire. Instead, a kinaaldá might be dressed in a biil constructed of commercial cloth upon which designs have been appliquéd, or in a cotton skirt and blouse with tennis shoes and socks. Whatever may be available for the young woman to wear, the articles of clothing are applied in a prescribed order. If the kinaaldá is to be dressed in a biil, it is put on first. If she will wear a skirt and blouse, the skirt must be placed over her head, as she is prohibited from stepping into it (Agnes Begay, 7/28/91; Sadie Billie, 7/26/92), and then she may put on her blouse. Next, a red sash is wrapped clockwise around her waist. If she is to wear kénitsaaí, they are put on next. Once her footwear is secure, the Ideal Woman directs the young woman to stand so that she can be adorned with jewelry. She is first adorned with a new pair of jaatł'óół, earrings, usually given by the maternal grandmother. Following this, several bracelets, necklaces, and rings are placed on the kinaaldá, followed by a concho belt if one is available. Many people in the family and surrounding community request that the young woman wear their jewelry during the ceremony so that it will be blessed and revitalized.

From the surrounding community people would want the kinaaldá to wear their jewelry. When she is dressing they want their jewelry reblessed, necklaces, bracelets, hard goods. They want them blessed and place them on her, including necklaces. She runs with that. She wears them throughout the ceremony. The pieces of jewelry are redistributed on the last day back to the owners after they are reblessed. That's how it is done, it is said. She is molded on spread blankets and then the pieces of jewelry are redistributed with new lives. That is why they do that. (The words of Mae Charley, north of Rock Point, Arizona, 7/15/92, translated by Wesley Thomas)

Each of the components of traditional attire with which the kinaaldá is adorned —biil, sash, kénitsaaí, and hair tie—has special significance and is predicated on the dressing of Changing Woman at her Kinaaldá. As Sunny Dooley points out in

Figure 9. Reytavia Billie in traditional attire. Photograph by Greg Schwarz.

the following passage, contemporary kinaaldá are told they are dressed in this manner to emulate Changing Woman at this important time in their lives (fig. 9).

> SD Hopefully all along the way she is being told why she is being dressed in moccasins, why she is being dressed in a rug dress [hand-woven biil], why she is having this, why she has to not do this, you know. Hopefully that is all being explained to her as she does it.
> MS But why would they tell her she is dressed in moccasins and a rug dress?
> SD OK. The reason why would be because that is how Changing Woman was dressed when she did her ceremony. And she is emulating Changing Woman here on earth at this time. (Sunny Dooley, Gallup, New Mexico, 8/21/92)

When it was time for Changing Woman to be dressed, the Holy People dressed her in the finest. Shimá Sání Chaháłeeł, or Grandmother Darkness, wrapped herself around Changing Woman to cover her. Bįįh, or Deer, offered his skin for her moccasins and leggings. A Náátsʼíílid Diné, or Rainbow Person, volunteered to be her sash. And Kʼos Diłhił, or Dark Cloud, became her hair (Dooley, 8/19/92). The garments used to dress young Navajo women today represent the darkness, deer-skin, and rainbow used in the dressing of Changing Woman.

> When she had her Kinaaldá, it was a celebration . . . because for the first time . . . First Man and First Woman were given an opportunity that they had not created themselves, but [it was] a gift from the deities that ensured their longevity, that they would continue as a people. And it [the capacity that would ensure their longevity] was within her, because prior to that they were making monsters, you know, people not all there. I mean half people kinds of things. So that was what happened. And when she had her period, they dressed her in the finest, and the finest was, and is, the rug dresses [biil]. (Sunny Dooley, Gallup, New Mexico, 8/19/92)

The dark center of the biil, or "rug dress," as this style of garment is frequently called today, is Grandmother Darkness, who wrapped herself around Changing Woman. As Sunny Dooley explains in the following narrative, the center of the dress is black to represent hope.

> The dress is usually black. . . . Black is our color to the north. . . . This is sort of like a caption, that black is hope, and women are

hope. That is sort of like how we look at women. . . . Women have the ability to reproduce, and so a woman always has that hope instilled within her. So, that was the premise to preventing, you know, like abuses of women sexually, emotionally, physically, whatever, because you would jeopardize that hope. I think in all stories of Navajo, one of the underlying themes, one of the characteristics that keeps coming up and just like smacks you in your face, is the fact that we are very fruitful oriented? . . . Fruitful in the sense of reproducing to get better, to get better, to get better. You know, and so, that is a real quality. Like, I think that is the reason why women a long time ago had hundreds of children. You know I come from a large family. That is a family value. It means, if you were a woman and you were able to produce ten children you were worth the dowry, because, "Look now how much hope she has brought us." Because that meant that longevity would be ensured, and so the black is associated with that, it is representative of it. It is called k'os diłhił or "black clouds." Shimá Sání Chahałheeł, "Grandmother Darkness." And those are all things associated with the north. And they are things associated with hope, and fertility and the essential ingredients necessary to overcome and not to be subdued. And so, that was the premise for the black dress. (Sunny Dooley, Gallup, New Mexico, 8/19/92)

The triangular designs along the top and the bottom of the patterned panels of two-piece dresses are mountains and clouds (Aronilth, 7/3/91; Jackson, 7/10/91; Lynch, 7/16/91; H. Ashley, 7/23/91; Ruth Roessel 7/26/91; Bekis, 8/5/92; Dooley, 8/19/92, 8/21/92). In addition, as Wilson Aronilth explains, the terraced diamond designs frequently found on a red ground in these panels are the "four principles of clouds," while the straight lines, or stripes, on either side of the dark center panel are the "breath of life" (see fig. 9).

Now, uh, I'll talk about the design and pattern of the traditional woven dress. Those designs that you see are symbols . . . [that] represent our thoughts and our movement and our action of life. . . . Now, you see these designs? The first design under this [he points to the band of narrow stripes bordering the dark center panel on an illustration of a two-piece dress that he uses in his class on the foundations of Navajo culture], you could illustrate it, draw it out. [Following his suggestion, I begin to copy down his illustration in my notebook]. This represents the sacred mountains that the Navajo people highly value [he points to a row of blue triangular forms running along the top and the bottom of the patterned panels in his illustration], because the sacred mountains have a lot to do with the foundation of our hooghan, our livelihood, our prayers, our songs, and the way that we regulate and constitute our life. In other words the sacred mountains is the one that, is the one that regulates and constitutes our life, our birth, our generation. It's our strength, courage, dignity, and it shields us and secures us from harm, evil, and danger. Now, the other illustration of the design on this [he points to terraced diamond designs at the centers of the red panels on his illustration of a biil, located where a terraced zigzag is found in figure 9], this is the representation of the four principle of clouds. We believe that there is summer clouds, winter clouds, spring clouds, and fall clouds. Which brings moisture of life to our, the way we live. . . . And through seasons, different seasons we live and change and develop and grow. Now, these little lines like this [he points again to the narrow stripes bordering the dark center panel of the two-piece dress], straight lines, that's the air we breathe, our breath of life, that's what that is. (Wilson Aron-ilth, Tsaile, Arizona, 7/3/91)

The layout of biil and the designs most frequently found on them—mountains, clouds, and the breath of life—are the same as those found on ceremonial baskets. This correlation demonstrates that baskets and two-piece dresses are homologues and thus links dresses directly to Navajo cosmology (Schwarz 1993, 1994). For, as Flora Ashley explains, just as the basket serves as a visual record of Navajo history, the dress serves as a visual representation of the Navajo way of life and simultaneously as a means of identification between the wearer and her world.

The basket and the dress are, just like I said, the representation of our life. A lot of things we do is just telling ourselves that. It is an identification of who we are. Like to identify ourselves with our surroundings. And trying to tell the nature that we blend in with them and we are interdependent with the nature. So that is what we are trying to say. We are connecting ourselves with the nature. That is what we are trying to say. So, in our clothing and in our artifacts that is how it goes. (Flora Ashley, Tsaile, Arizona, 7/29/91)

After Changing Woman was wrapped in protective darkness, one of the Nááts'íílid Diné'é jumped up and wrapped itself around her waist to serve as her sash. Sis łichí'í, which are woven today of red, green, and white commercially manufactured yarns and cotton cordings, are modeled after the sash of rainbow worn by

Changing Woman. As Wilson Aronilth notes in the following passage, the rainbow has special significance to the path in life that Navajo women strive to walk.

When Changing Woman reached her pubertyhood [sic] it was the Rainbow Girl and the Rainbow Woman, Nááts'íílid Dine'é, the "Rainbow People," were the ones who helped with the sash belt. . . . When Changing Woman was disciplined to learn about her womanhood, she was the one that was given the first sash belt. From there she passed it on to our grandmothers. Today we have it. So the sash belt represents rainbow, the spirit of a rainbow, that's what that is. . . . The fringes of the sash belt represent the grass and the flowers that we walk in the midst of every day. That's how we say . . . "I want to walk, on the Holy People's path, meaning, I want to walk on the sacred rainbow beam in the midst of flowers and grass, moisture and pollen, of these plants. To feel good. I want to walk in harmony, in peace, in balance with all walks of life and creation." That's what the sash belt is. That's the way we were told. (Wilson Aronilth, Tsaile, Arizona, 7/3/91)

Next, Bįįh came forward to offer his hide, which became Changing Woman's moccasins and leggings. All characteristics associated with deer—swiftness, elegance, and quietness—are transferred to a Navajo woman when she wears moccasins with deerskin leggings. Sunny Dooley vividly describes this episode in the dressing of Changing Woman:

The deer came forth and he said, "I will give my hide for her shoes." And that is why we have deerskin moccasins. And the right side of the deer went on the right and the left side of the deer went on the left. And also in this particular phase they [the Holy People] made all the plans [for the world] on the deerskin, on an 'abaní', the "unharmed hide of a deer." They laid the constellations on the deerskin. And so when he offered his skin, he was the one to say, "I offer my skin, because I want her to be graceful. I want her to be most elegant. I want her to be fast and achieve. And I also want her to know, that her path can only lead to bigger and better places, and that includes the universe." And it also means that we are a child of the universe. . . . Whatever you see of a deer you can take those characteristics and apply it to a moccasin. That is so that she is fast, and swift, and quiet, and gets things done, the way the lady [who tied my hair] told me is that, "You get things done in the most quiet manner that brings the most change." You know, and so that is sort of like how they view it. (Sunny Dooley, Gallup, New Mexico, 8/19/92)

Kénitsaaí, which are constructed today of cowhide soles with deerskin or cowhide leggings, are modeled after the first moccasins worn by Changing Woman. Every part of the moccasins worn by Navajo women—the soles, uppers, ties, and buttons—has significance related to the time when the Holy People used an 'abaní', an unblemished buckskin, on which to lay out a plan for this world. As Wilson Aronilth explained:

> Now like the moccasin, I'll talk about the female moccasin, the sole represents our Mother Earth, meaning that we are here on the Mother Earth, we have a purpose here, we have objectives and goals. And we were told don't ever think, "I was born for nothing, I wish I was dead, I don't know what I want, I have no goals." You don't say that, you have a purpose and you're here to fulfill that purpose. So life is very precious. That's what that is. The upper portion of the moccasin, up to here [from the sole to the ankle], is the representation of the heavenly bodies. They say, "Look up sometime and see how beautiful, heaven, stars, and all this divine creation is." Now umm, the leggings are the representation of dawn, day, evening, and night. We say, "haayoołkááł, nahodeetł'iizh, nahootsoíí, chahałheeł," that's what that is. The moccasin shoestring is sunray, that means that our path of life is lit by a light, so we won't dim our life, so that the path could be lit, and nothing is going to interfere with our life. The moccasin buttons represent our behavior and our attitude. So, we are supposed to develop a good behavior and attitude. So that's the way that we were told and, umm, that's the significance of it. (Wilson Aronilth, Tsaile, Arizona, 7/3/91)

Once Changing Woman was dressed in a biil, sash, moccasins, and leggings, it was time for her hair to be brushed.

> SD Then they combed her hair. They combed her hair and the Dark Cloud came in and said, "And I will give you as much hair as you want." Kind of like thing, you know?
> MS Uh-huh.
> SD And so her hair became very dark and very long. And so when you see streaks of dark clouds like this [motions vertically], you

know. My mom says, "Oh, a woman with very beautiful hair must live over there." Because they say that those clouds have that affinity, they look for women that have hair like that and that is where it will rain the most. (Sunny Dooley, Gallup, New Mexico, 8/19/92)

Like Changing Woman, a contemporary kinaaldá, once she is fully dressed, is directed to kneel facing east to have her hair brushed and tied. The Ideal Woman brushes the young woman's hair with a grass hairbrush while the ceremonial practitioner or an elder in attendance sings a combing song. As Flora Ashley explains, a lifelong relationship exists between a woman and the grass hairbrush used during her Kinaaldá.

> FA They call it "bé'ézhóó'," but I don't know what the name is, I am not good at naming plants and those things. And they use that to brush the girl's hair. They don't use a regular brush. They use that brush because that was our brush before the [commercial] brush came. And I have one that my grandma gave me. It was made just especially for me. It was nice and fresh. They brushed my hair with it and they gave it to me to keep it. Now, my hair is getting shorter and shorter. That thing, it was like that [indicates between twelve and fourteen inches in length and two or three inches in thickness], you know, I had long hair and a lot of hair. Now, it is going this way too [indicates the brush is getting shorter and thinner]. And at the end, it is amazing, it is going shorter and shorter too! And it is getting thinner and thinner! [My grandmother] told me, "This is the representation of your hair. It will wear with you, and it will wear with your hair." And surprisingly, it is just there in my house and it is doing that!
>
> MS Interesting. You don't still use it?
>
> FA I don't use it.
>
> MS But it is still shrinking?
>
> FA [Nods her head.] So, that is amazing too. How that thing is just sitting there but it grows with me. (Flora Ashley, Tsaile, Arizona, 7/29/91)

The kinaaldá's hair is brushed out and tied in a ponytail at the nape of her neck. The hair is held in place with a special thong cut from an 'abaní' or a mountain lion skin, depending on family preference. Some hair is carefully combed forward over her face. This treatment of the hair is said to prevent baldness (Sadie Billie, 7/24/92; Kee, 8/3/92; Bekis, 8/5/92; Mrs. Joe McCabe, 8/19/92; Dooley, 8/19/92).

As Mae Charley explained, "This much is left. You cannot brush it aside, you let it hang and cover, it is said. It has always been like that. If you brush the hair sideways, it causes baldness. You are scolded if you brush it aside" (7/15/92). The hair that is brushed forward grows directly out of the 'atáá'ha'noots'eeí, the point at the top of the back of the head where the hair assumes a concentric swirl. This hair is significant because it is the kinaaldá's "feather of life."

> It is her feather. Either one or two separate strands of hair are left hanging. That is her feather of life. . . . The hair in the forward part is not long and it is usually not tied with the rest in the back as part of the bun. Even among males a small portion of the hair in the forward part of the hair is left hanging or is hanging to the side. . . . Sometimes only one group or strand of hair is left to symbolize the kinaaldá's feather. This set of strands is intentionally separated from the rest of the hair and brushed into place. That becomes her feather. (The words of an anonymous elder, Lukachukai, Arizona, 8/13/92, translated by Wesley Thomas)

The position of the young woman's feather of life during the Kinaaldá signifies that she is in the process of a ceremony that marks a transition from one stage of life to another. As Oscar Tso explained after consulting with his father, having the feather of life hanging down over the face serves to mark the girl as an initiate.

> The parting of the hair is to signify that that young person, that young lady has reached her puberty and is having that Kinaaldá ceremony. And it is kind of a marking or an identification type of a thing too. Not necessarily to other humans but to the gods. So, this very nature could recognize, "Hey," and say that, "This person is having her puberty, she is into womanhood, and she has gone through the initiation, has gone through the procedures." It is kind of set aside to say that from there on she is a, she is a . . . I guess, through the initiation one of their children has gone through into a different stage of life, you know, ready for womanhood, too. (Oscar Tso, Tsaile, Arizona, explaining a point raised by his father, Nakai Tso, 8/8/92)

Once her hair is securely tied at the nape of her neck, the kinaaldá is directed to stand inside the hooghan while her female relatives spread out the blankets and other textiles upon which she will be molded. While she stands fully adorned, female relatives may come forward to tie strands of beads with white shells, or perhaps a string of small bells, to her sash. If family members intend to make chííh dík'óózh, a protective medicine, after the Kinaaldá ceremony, they attach a small pouch filled with a mixture of ground red ochre and natural salt to her sash. Her elders direct her to spit saliva into this pouch after each run. If the family has not had the opportunity to collect the herbs and other materials necessary to make chííh dík'ǫ́ǫ́zh, they will tie a small pouch with a pinch of chííh dík'ǫ́ǫ́zh to her sash belt instead (Begay 1983:53; field notes, 7/24/92, 7/16/93).

FIRST MOLDING

That is for preparation. If that is not done the kinaaldá will not grow properly. When you are older your body will be in a proper form, not all lumpy and awkward. During the Kinaaldá, she is stretched, she is pulled and massaged. She seems to be strengthened and all her limbs are pulled in all directions. Your limbs are stretched and lengthened in all directions and seem properly placed there, as they should be. Your waist is tightened and your head is pushed back so you would not be hunched in your old age. The stretching and massaging is to mold your body into the shape designed by nature. . . . When you have your Kinaaldá you are back into your infancy stage of life. Your body is in a stage of softness. You are thought of as a newborn baby. Your body feels like that. That is why your body is molded to create strength and durability in your limbs and body. Some kinaaldá really have straight hands, limbs, and bodies. You can see that. The curved body parts are strengthened and lengthened through the Kinaaldá ceremony. . . . You start moving toward womanhood. . . . You keeping growing old. When you become a very old person, aged, when you are dying of old age then it is considered that you have returned to your infancy again. You become a baby again. . . . You become white, very white. You become small again. . . . That is the only way, when you become old. When you die of old age that is the only time that happens. You return to your infancy stage, people say, I guess. I have yet to experience it. (Elizabeth Yazzie, Mariano Lake, New Mexico, 12/5/93. Interviewed by Wesley Thomas)

At puberty, every Navajo returns to the soft, malleable condition characteristic of newborns. At this time, a young woman's body is considered "very sensitive and fragile" (N. Tso, 8/8/92). She is molded to reap as many lifelong benefits as possible from this temporary condition.

She is molded to be in the image of Changing Woman, meaning that the four aspects of her life are balanced. Her spiritual, her emotional, her intellectual, and her physical. Those four entities have to be in balance and congruent to grow with one another. Because, you know, you can be physically very well developed, and then be intellectually undeveloped. [Laughs] I think. . . . And also another thing was, they are being formed so that she has a straight back, that she has a good shape, and so, you know, that she has a nice body. (Sunny Dooley, Gallup, New Mexico, 8/19/92)

A kinaaldá is molded so that she will become "a wonderful, healthy, and strong woman" (Kee, 8/4/92) who will be in "proper form" (Elizabeth Yazzie, 12/5/93), have a "good figure" (Bekis, 8/5/92), "won't have any health problems" (Charley, 7/15/92), have "good posture and health" (N. Tso, 8/8/92), and will "accept the challenges of motherhood" (Knoki-Wilson, 8/10/92). Also, as one elder explains, molding ensures that the kinaaldá will acquire a fine, strong voice: "This is for her to have a fine voice, for her voice to be forward and strong, she will be physically strong and her appearance will be outlined with muscles. When she works—she will be strong and sturdy, her being will be well. These are the reasons why it is done" (anonymous elder, Lukachukai, Arizona, 8/13/95, translation by Wesley Thomas).

In addition to physical strength, endurance, and a fine voice, numerous other skills and characteristics are transferred to a kinaaldá while her body is in this malleable condition. A girl's family seeks to have transferred to her those traits they believe she will need to live a rewarding and satisfying life.

The first molding of a kinaaldá takes place inside the hooghan or outside in front of it, depending on family preference. Women pile up blankets, buffalo hides, deerskins, and sheepskins for the young woman to lie upon. As these items are spread out, people toss between the layers personal belongings such as car keys, purses, or wallets that they want blessed. If the molding is to be done outside, the kinaaldá is directed to walk sunwise out of the hooghan to the middle of the pile of materials and stand facing east (T. M. Begay, 7/28/91; Sadie Billie, 7/24/92; field notes, 7/16/93) or west (Frisbie 1993 [1967]:31, 64; Begay 1983:55; Kee, 8/3/92), again depending on family practices. As Traci Michelle Begay of Ganado, Arizona, recalls in the following description of her first molding, the kinaaldá is directed to lie down carefully, prone, on top of the piled materials with her arms spread out at her sides, her legs straight, and her chin resting on the pile so that her gaze is forward.

They took me out and then they laid down blankets, after blankets, after blankets, on it. And people that wanted their things blessed I guess, they threw like their purses, their coin purses, their jewelry, their money, their, even their blankets. And they just piled it up, over and over, all their belongings. . . . They did it outside facing towards the east. And then the buckskins. They laid the buckskins down. And all those things. And then I went down and I had to be careful how I went down, I remember that. I had to come down to my knees without touching the ground or anything, carefully, without any abrupt movements. I had to do it smoothly, somehow lay down on the buckskin, and my arms were stretched straight out from my sides. . . . My chin had to rest on the thing [the pile of blankets and other materials]. I couldn't keep it sideways or anything. It had to go straight forward. And my feet had to lay straight, not inward or outward. They had to lay straight. (Traci Michelle Begay, Many Farms, Arizona, 7/26/91)

The kinaaldá is molded by the Ideal Woman, who is recognized by the family as having the skills and characteristics they want instilled into the young woman. The family is careful in choosing the person who will perform this important task, because effect is transferred though the hands of the Ideal Woman as well as through any objects she may use to mold the kinaaldá. As Irene Kee explains, the Ideal Woman may use a variety of objects to mold the young woman, including mountain lion or cougar paws.

Every part of her body is massaged. It is hoped that she will become strong and healthy, with that idea in mind the back bones are massaged. The massager is informed to put pressure on her hips, push them together so she will look lean and tall. As though she was pulled out of something. Her legs are pulled so she will be a very tall lady. Her hair is massaged so she will have long hair. Water from the tloo'leeh' [unidentified grass] is used, her hair is massaged while wet with tloo'leeh'. That was how it was done back then. If you have the mountain lion paws or cougar paws you massage her body with it, so she will be a very strong woman. Where are they? These paws, are they available now? No, there are none. Those animals who are waddling on the mountains, the black ones [bears], none of their belongings can be associated with the ceremony. If they are used, the kinaaldá will become a ruthless person. You can tell by observing those animals, they are very short-tempered. It does not take much to upset them. I guess the cougar is the same, the cougar is considered to be a very strong animal and the strength is wished for, for the kinaaldá. The paws of the cougar are massaged on a horse which has just been castrated. The blood from the horse is equated with first menstrual blood of the kinaaldá, because of that reason the horse is massaged with the cougar paws. The horse has just experienced releasing its first blood, the horse is considered to be in a malleable state. The horse will never tire, just like the cougar. He will run without tiring easily. The cougar is constantly moving, you want your horse to do the same. The cougar is always hunting and watching, but only his paws are used and useful for the kinaaldá and for horses, too. Certain plants are not brought near the kinaaldá, like the aspen leaf, even on a windless day, they are forever shaking. If it is brought near a kinaaldá or a horse, the action or motion of the leaf will transform into the kinaaldá and the horse. They will behave as such, shaking constantly and continuously. That is what I was told. (The words of Irene Kee, Crystal, New Mexico, 8/4/92, translated by Wesley Thomas)

Practice simultaneously duplicates the system and alters it. Many elders use Navajo theories governing the cultural construction of the body and personhood to instill skills perceived as necessary to life in the contemporary world. In the past, a fine weaver, a good sheepherder, or a good mother was usually asked to serve as the Ideal Woman. Today, it is just as likely that a woman will be selected for her business acumen or successful career.

SD I know in this day and age they look for like a good career woman [chuckles].

MS Oh, well that is good.

SD Like I know one lady in Shiprock who wanted some woman who had a good job, and this kind of thing, you know.

MS Well, times change.

SD Times are changing.

MS That is true. (Sunny Dooley, Gallup, New Mexico, 8/19/92)

In Traci Michelle Begay's case, the family asked a woman known to be a good administrator to perform this important task. "And they made sure that . . . the lady that they get to mold has some type of gift. Or has something very important about her that they want, they want their daughter to have that image. Or want that strength drawn from them. . . . The woman that did my first one was Margaret. . . . She is an administrator in Fort Defiance [Arizona]. She came out and did it for me" (7/26/91).

The Ideal Woman often uses a flat, smooth object to mold the kinaaldá—for example, a weaving batten if she wants her to become a distinguished weaver, a textbook or a pack of pencils if she wants the young woman to become a scholar: "They put a lot of blankets down on the ground and then they mold her, so she will have a good figure. . . . They use pencils or books, but a long time ago, they used to use weaving tools. Where they said, 'She is going to be a good weaver,' and nowadays we want to educate our kids, that is why we use books and pencils to mold her" (Mae Bekis, 8/5/92).

The Ideal Woman carefully follows the trajectory of growth as she molds the kinaaldá. She begins with the young woman's feet and legs and then moves up her body toward her head. She concentrates on the kinaaldá's middle section and shoulders. As the young woman is molded, the Ideal Woman calls out each characteristic sought for her. While molding her feet she may say, "Let her be swift and graceful as a deer." While molding her legs she may say, "Let her have strength." If the family wants the kinaaldá to acquire exceptional weaving skills, the Ideal Woman will mold her hands and arms with a weaving tool while saying, "She will be a good weaver." While molding her head she may say, "Let her have knowledge and think wisely." Finally, while pulling on her hair she may say, "Let her have long, thick hair."

STRETCHING

> After they mold her, she stretches other kids. The other kids line up, she stretches them and that way they will have a good life too. And older people are very interested in a kinaaldá, because they say that by that touch, that is the first puberty [menstrual period] that the girl has had, so that is why they want to be touched by her and to get rid of their aches and pains. So that is why they always, even the older people line up, and then they get touched by kinaaldá, by the girl. (Mae Bekis, Tó'tsoh, Arizona, 8/5/92)

Once the first molding is completed, the kinaaldá is directed to stand and walk to the center of the piled blankets and face east or west, depending on family practice. All the children in attendance line up on the side of the piled blankets to await their turn. One by one they walk across the blankets and stand in front of the kinaaldá. The kinaaldá places her palms along the sides of their heads and then, following the trajectory of growth, she "stretches" them upward, "so they can grow and become tall. That is the reason why they are stretched. . . . So they will become tall. . . . It is like a healing ceremony. The kinaaldá conducts healing with her Kinaaldá, on the children. Everyone participating is blessed and it is a joyous occasion" (anonymous elder, Lukachukai, Arizona, 8/13/92, translation by Wesley Thomas).

The kinaaldá blesses the younger children with her touch "to help with the growth of the person" (Kee, 8/3/92), so that the child will grow tall, straight, and beautiful. The touch of the kinaaldá is powerful because "she represents the best physical specimen of a woman, you know. She has been endowed with these powers through the ceremony and all that. So, this is a special time of her life. She possesses these powers, so she passes that on to the people. You know, it is like Miss America, going over there and hugging children, things like that" (Harry Walters, 8/18/92).

This "passing on" of her power to foster growth and development is a profound act of generosity. The act demonstrates the kinaaldá's unselfishness and her willingness to share all that she possesses with her family and friends.

> **MS** Could you tell me a little bit about the power that the girl has when she stretches children and lays hands on the elderly?
>
> **SD** Well I think at this time, I personally believe that she does have power, because first of all she has invited the spirit of Changing Woman into her life. She has been recognized by the gods, she has been blessed and prayed for, she has been blessed and sung for. . . . And this is sort of like at the point in time where it is, you know, she has unbridled energy that can be transferred into a lot of possibilities and so the best possibility that we can think of is to encourage that same kind of maturation in the younger kids. And then also into our older people because, you know, it completes the cycle. It is this conservation of energy kind of thing again, you know. She is like in the middle and she gives some over there to go on, to become old people. And then the old people get it so that they can kind of feel the cycle being completed, so that they can leave. Do you know what I mean?
>
> **MS** Oh, I see, OK.
>
> **SD** And then also so that they can feel good and get well, and, you know, that kind of thing. But I think the underlying theme of a Kinaaldá is so that she becomes generous of spirit, that she just becomes this most generous person. Not saying giving your dog and everything away, but, that in whatever she does she remembers that it must be shared because if it wasn't for Changing Woman, I don't think we would have been around today. (Sunny Dooley, Gallup, New Mexico, 8/21/92)

As Sunny Dooley commented, the kinaaldá's generosity extends to elderly people as well as to children and young adults, because the elderly are an important part of the cycle of life, and an essential element of the Kinaaldá ceremony is rejuvenation of this cycle. Elderly people suffering from arthritis or other aliments may ask the kinaaldá at any time during the ceremony to massage their aching shoulders, backs, arms, and hands to extract the pain. Precedent for this practice exists in Navajo oral history:

There was a time when "Old Age" molded and massaged a kinaaldá. This person was slow, and had a hard time moving, and had white hair. He was one hundred two years of age. That was considered the end of human life. . . . Old Age Person with a cane once arrived at a Kinaaldá. Old Age staggered, with back pain, body pains all over, Old Age came upon the Kinaaldá site. Old Age was instructed to mold the kinaaldá. Old Age was asked to bless the kinaaldá, he acknowledged and accepted the request. A blanket was laid for the kinaaldá, the kinaaldá lay on top, and Old Age Person massaged and molded the kinaaldá. Old Age helped kinaaldá get up, at the same time, Old Age came to life with energy, like the kinaaldá. Before Old Age had a hard time getting up off the floor. Old Age told kinaaldá, "Now it is your turn to massage and mold me." Kinaaldá repeated the molding pattern which Old Age had conducted, by pulling and stretching Old Age Person's arms. At first Old Age Person cried out with pain. The pains lessened as the kinaaldá continued to mold the Old Age Person. When Old Age Person got up, the cane was discarded and he took off walking without the cane. By this event, Old Age was blessed by the kinaaldá; so today, elderly people participate in the Kinaaldá, so they too can have their pains discarded. (The words of an anonymous elder, Lukachukai, Arizona, 8/13/92, translated by Wesley Thomas)

Once the stretching is completed, the kinaaldá is instructed to put on her shawl after removing it from the top of the pile. She must wear this shawl at all times throughout the duration of the ceremony, except while running. Once she has her shawl on, she carefully picks up the next article on the pile and returns it to its owner, who thanks her profusely. She turns sunwise to return to the pile for the next item. This continues until every blanket, shawl, buckskin, or other article is removed from the pile and returned to its owner. Next, the kinaaldá is instructed to walk back into the hooghan, moving sunwise around the wood-burning stove or fire, remove her shawl, and then start running to the east from the hooghan doorway.

RUNNING

So she would be a swift person. It was necessary, a long time ago, during the time of enemies being around, warring was happening. So, she could run without tiring. It gives her endurance, it provides energy, so she will not hesitate. It will make her energetic and attentive, like the Holy People were when they lived on the earth. That is the reason for running. . . . Also, when one runs in the early morning, the Morning Gods will know and recognize you. Your morning runs are noted by the Morning Holy People. When you start running, the Morning Holy People will have already noticed you. When a kinaaldá first runs, the Holy People are aware of it and they tell one another, "That person is running so we would notice. She wants and needs us. Let us all go and help her," they would say to one another. They say that about us humans. They are available to help—anytime. They recognize you when you run in the mornings, when they, too, are about. That is why one is to run every morning according to traditional teachings. (The words of an anonymous elder, Lukachukai, Arizona, 8/13/92, translated by Wesley Thomas)

A kinaaldá may be expected to run once a day, at dawn (Bekis, 8/5/92; Elizabeth Yazzie, 12/5/93), twice a day, at dawn and noon (Jones, 7/15/92), or three times a day, at dawn, noon, and sunset (Sadie Billie, 7/24/92; Kee, 8/3/92), depending on individual family practices. Changing Woman ran in all four directions; some women recalled relatives who ran in two or more directions in the past (F. Ashley, 7/29/91; Charley, 7/15/92; Elizabeth Yazzie 12/5/93), but today most kinaaldá run only to the east. Because she must increase the distance with each run, the kinaaldá is advised to limit her first run to a reasonable distance, turn sunwise around a healthy bush or other plant, and then retrace her steps back to the hooghan. No matter how tired she may be on her return run, she must speed up as she nears the hooghan. She is followed by a stream of children and adults who run along beside or behind her for as far as they are physically able. No matter how strong an individual runner may be, those running with a kinaaldá must never overtake her, for it is believed that anyone that runs in front of a kinaaldá will age before her.

It was said, you cannot run in front of kinaaldá. You only run after her. . . . When you run in front of her, your hair turns white first, and you age quicker, too. Before the kinaaldá even begins to show her age. If someone overturns her position or places themselves in front of her on her run, even if one is younger than the kinaaldá, that person will age quicker than the kinaaldá. That is why the taboo dictates that runners run after or behind her at all times. (The words of Mae Charley, north of Rock Point, Arizona, 7/15/92, translated by Wesley Thomas)

If individual runners accompanying the kinaaldá become spent, they must stop and wait for her to pass them on her return. Once she has passed, they join the runners following her and return to the hooghan with the group. The kinaaldá is directed to make no sound as she runs. She is told to breathe steadily though her nose and try to maintain a constant pace. In contrast, the people running alongside or behind the kinaaldá are directed to yell. They do this to notify the Holy People so that they may acknowledge the kinaaldá as she silently runs.

It took three days. . . . I ran three days, each day was increased in distance. You run for a short distance, the next day you increase it, the noon run is increased, keep increasing each run until the final day. By three days you have to run a long distance. It increases your vascular capacity and your strength, that's what it is for. For muscular legs, arms. . . . With grinding corn you are preparing yourself. "Make yourself useful and fit," we were told. Running contributed to that teaching. . . . Early in the morning and then at noon. That is how it was done to the end. When the man is singing at dawn, you wash your hair and you run to the farthest distance possible and people run after you. You are not to yell yourself, but others running with you are the ones yelling. House God and the Holy People are listening to the people running after you. It is said, "The people are running after the kinaaldá." From different directions the Holy People would say that. The sunlight and the moon are listening to you and that is why there is yelling. You are not to yell it is said, only the ones running after you. Ooowwwaaaaaaaa. . . . That is how you must yell and you have to make the sound trail off and fade out. Very loud and with those distinguishing sounds, that is what was said. (The words of Mae Charley, north of Rock Point, Arizona, 7/15/92, translated by Wesley Thomas)

When I inquired why the young woman makes multiple runs during her Kinaaldá, I was told, "She runs at dawn to gain material wealth" (Kee, 8/3/92); she runs "so that she won't be lazy" (N. Tso, 8/8/92); "she runs to gain physical fitness. She runs to outrun the clumsiness of her childhood" (Dooley, 8/19/92). Kinaaldá are told to run because "you have to be strong now that you are a woman, you will bear children" (Walters, 8/18/92). And, as Oscar Tso explains, she runs to learn to accept the inevitable challenges of being a wife and a mother.

> See, a part of growing up and a part of meeting this everyday life, you know, everyday life is hard. There is laziness, idleness that sets in. So in order to meet the nature and be able to live a real clean healthy life, you know, you have to exert some energy on your part. To make yourself strong. And physical exercise of some sort like running has always been a part of building yourself up and making yourself real strong. So, you go into your womanhood and you begin to prepare for all the things like, bearing children, you have to be strong. To take care of somebody from the opposite sex, like a man. Your mind has to be strong. . . . At one time I heard that human life is kind of like they are wild. You have to mold these children. You have to provide some sort of direction to bring them up. And then I heard one time in a wedding ceremony, that men are that way too. A woman has to realize that she is going to have to, I guess in a way they say that men are wild. And you kind of have to settle them down, you kind of have to really take your time to mold them into the way that you would want them to be. . . . So you have to have that understanding, a real good understanding of the mind of a man. . . . The same thing is told to boys too sometimes, see even though these things are shared with the woman to say that men have to be molded, and have to be, I guess in a way, whipped into shape! [Chuckles] (Oscar Tso, Many Farms, Arizona, 8/9/92)

"NO MORE DOLLS FOR YOU!": DO'S AND DON'TS

> I had a lot of my aunts come over and they were real strict with me. What I could eat, what I could drink. . . . I couldn't drink any soda, or anything with sugar. I had just strictly water and maybe Navajo tea. That was it! . . . And then cornmeal, corn mush with all my meals. And rarely meat. It was rare that I really had it but, and I couldn't have any salt on any of my food. Or sugar, in any of my things. I just had to have it the way it was. And, a lot of water. I had to drink a lot of water. And they told me to stay away from kids, little kids. Playing with them. I couldn't play. I had to stay to myself, and not to hold any babies, or be around any babies. Be-

cause they thought if you are around babies then you are going to have them right away, or have lots of kids. "Don't go near any babies, or hold them. Don't look at anything [violent or hostile] or think angry thoughts, or start an argument, don't do any of that." I had to be real quiet, calm, I couldn't get upset. I couldn't use knives to cut. I couldn't actually do any cutting of anything, or piercing. I had to stay away from that blood. All of that. (Traci Michelle Begay, Many Farms, Arizona, 7/26/91)

Several food and behavioral restrictions are enforced during the Kinaaldá. Despite their variations, each restriction is premised on the belief that the kinaaldá is in a malleable state during this ceremony. Everything she does, or that is done to her, during the Kinaaldá influences her future physical strength, posture, and behavior. She is directed to remain busy and industrious throughout the ceremony to avoid becoming lazy (Ryan 1988:4; T. M. Begay, 7/28/91; Sadie Billie, 7/24/92).

When the child grows up to be a youngster about ten, twelve, or fourteen, there the Kinaaldá takes place, the first puberty of the girl. And that is when they say she became a young woman. And, "No dolls for you, and you don't play any games like climbing trees and play with your brother and things like that." We used to tell our kids that. And they are not supposed to wrestle with their brothers or, their younger brother as well as the big brothers. . . . We tell the kinaaldá that she is not a little girl any more. And, "You belong in the kitchen. You help your mother to cook and whatever. You are supposed to be in there learning." That is what we usually tell our kids, when they become a kinaaldá, and when they become a young lady. And we tell them, "No more dolls." And she is a young woman now. (Mae Bekis, Tó'tsoh, Arizona, 8/5/92)

As noted by Mrs. Bekis, the kinaaldá is not allowed to run and play with children. Instead, she is encouraged to keep herself busy helping with the typical tasks of adult Navajo women (field notes, 7/25/92; Bekis, 8/5/92). She must not sleep during the day, except on the last day when she is allowed to rest before the all-night sing. To sleep at other times would encourage laziness (Wyman and Bailey 1943:6; Sadie Billie, 7/25/92).

She is directed not to laugh. Laughter may cause the kinaaldá to become a loud woman (Frisbie 1993 [1967]:353), or deep wrinkles to form at the sides of her mouth (Wyman and Bailey 1943:6; Frisbie 1993 [1967]:353; Sadie Billie, 7/25/92), at the sides of her eyes (Begay 1983:69), or on the rest of her face (Frisbie 1993 [1967]:353). She can help with cooking tasks such as mixing dough for fry-bread or cleaning vegetables, but she must not handle sharp knives or do anything associated with animal blood (Begay 1983:103; T. M. Begay, 7/25/91; Sadie Billie, 7/25/92; Kee, 8/3/92).

The kinaaldá is not allowed to eat salted foods (Reichard 1928:136; Wyman and Bailey 1943:5; Begay 1983:69; Ryan 1988:6; Charley, 7/15/92; Sadie Billie, 7/25/92; Kee, 8/3/92; Walters, 8/18/92; Dooley, 8/19/92; Hazen-Hammond 1995:18). She is not allowed to chew gum or eat any sweets or other foods with sugar in them (Charley, 7/15/92; Sadie Billie, 7/24/92; Kee, 8/3/92; Walters, 8/18/92; Dooley, 8/19/92). It is believed that if she does so, her "teeth will become rotten" (Wyman and Bailey 1943:5; Begay 1983:69; Hazen-Hammond 1995:18) or her "teeth will fall out" (Reichard 1928:136; Ryan 1988:4). In some families, meat is also prohibited (Reichard 1928:136; Walters, 8/18/92).

All food eaten by the kinaaldá during the ceremony must be cooled before it is consumed (Ryan 1988:6; Charley, 7/15/92; Sadie Billie 7/25/92; Kee, 8/3/92), or else she may scald the bone tissue of her teeth (Begay 1983:69). The single most important food restriction concerns the 'alkaan, the "corn bread cake" baked overnight in the ground during the all-night sing. The kinaaldá cannot eat her own 'alkaan (Frisbie 1993 [1967]:353, 355; Begay 1983:151; Ryan 1988:6; Charley, 7/15/92; Sadie Billie, 7/26/92; Kee, 8/3/92; field notes, 7/17/93), because, as Mae Charley explains, the cake is an embodiment of the kinaaldá and her future potential.[7]

> The cake is her. It is for her purpose. The commercial cake is for her birthday, everybody eats that. She can't eat the Kinaaldá cake, because the Kinaaldá cake ruins the kinaaldá's teeth. They melt. A kinaaldá can't eat her own Kinaaldá cake. That is why people restricted me from eating my own cake at my Kinaaldá. I never even brushed my lips with a piece of cake. It is powerful, I was told. I think it is true. People younger than me, their teeth are melted, done, because they didn't obey the rules. (The words of Mae Charley, north of Rock Point, Arizona, 7/15/92, translated by Wesley Thomas)

THE CAKE

> In some cases the girl grinds the whole corn and cooks the corn, see. Now that she has become a woman that is like a test. . . . In the morning when they eat the cake people comment how good it is, you know. And also it signifies what kind of a woman she is going to be. . . . That means that she is going to have to learn how

to cook! It tells what kind of homemaker she is going to be. . . . Discipline, discipline, you know, goes into that. If the girl is not, you know, if she is lazy, or negatively reacts to discipline, and things like that. That can show up in there. Or the family, if the family has not properly instructed her in the ways they should, and therefore they don't work together, you know, that shows in their cake, see? . . . "They don't follow discipline," you know, "moral discipline." That is morally what it says, so that shows in their cake. . . . It represents the kind of training she has had from the family. The kind of discipline, the kind of teaching that, the practices that the family have. It shows up in the cake. And then when the cake is well done, then it also shows that she will have a great future. And then so, the family, you know, fuss and go out of their way to put out the best cake, because people will know. People are going to know from that. It is as much a reflection on the family as the girl. (Harry Walters, Tsaile, Arizona, 8/18/92)

On the first day, while the Ideal Woman dresses the kinaaldá, the woman in charge of the cake directs preparations for the 'alkaan, which will bake overnight in the ground during the last night of the ceremony. The cake is a dominant symbol, encapsulating each of the important themes of the ceremony—physical fitness, endurance, education, reciprocity, and the maximizing of potential positive effects. The cake demonstrates simultaneously the kinaaldá's past, present, and future, as well as the complementarity of male and female counterparts integral to all aspects of Navajo life.

Fundamentally, the quality of the cake is a testament to the merits of the kinaaldá's family and to the kind of woman she will become. The cake is composed of corn, water, natural and commercial sweeteners, and the energy of the kinaaldá and her relatives. Great energy is expended in planning for the cake during the weeks and months preceding the ceremony and in producing it during the ceremony itself. The kinaaldá and her female relatives break the individual kernels off the corn cobs, clean the kernels, roast and grind the corn, and mix the batter. The kinaaldá's industriousness, which is demonstrated throughout the ceremony as she roasts and grinds corn for the batter, is especially evident during the hours of arduous labor involved in mixing the batter. This effort demonstrates that the young woman understands and accepts the female role of sustenance provider and that she is prepared to feed her relatives and community. After the cake batter is mixed, female elders carefully mold and knead it, running their fingers through the hot mixture to search out and break up lumps. Male relatives and friends also invest tremendous energy in producing the cake: they prepare the pit in which it will be baked, cut and haul firewood, and collect and haul water. The completed cake demonstrates the past training the young woman has received from her family, as well as the family's commitment to the success of the ceremony and the kinaaldá's future.

Under the close supervision of the woman in charge of the cake, the kinaaldá's male relatives dig a pit southeast of the front of the hooghan. It ranges in size from seven to ten inches deep and thirty-six to forty-eight inches wide, depending on the amount of corn to be used. Great care is taken to ensure that the pit is perfectly circular and that its walls are perpendicular to the bottom, which must be level. It is essential that a fire burn in the pit for at least twenty-four hours in advance of the cake baking in order to harden and heat the pit. A reliable male relative is chosen to supervise the fire, which will burn all night on top of the cake. It is his responsibility to maintain a constant fire throughout the night, regardless of the weather, and to make sure it produces a consistent heat that will evenly cook the cake.

Ideally, the cake batter should be made from yellow corn (female), and the blessing on top of the cake should be done with white corn (male).[8] Harry Walters explained that both of these substances are necessary because they serve as hózhǫ́ǫ́jí and naayéé'jí counterparts to each other: "In the ceremony, no matter what ceremony, these male and female, warrior and peaceful nature, counterparts are mentioned along with it. So, male and female are both mentioned in all of that. So this is the reason why that, the female corn is used in the cake, you know, that has to have a male counterpart in there, which is the white cornmeal" (8/18/92).

Some families use a mixture of yellow and white corn, noting that such a mixture is best because it incorporates male and female elements into the batter.

> MS Now what color is the corn supposed to be, that is used to make the batter?
>
> SD It is supposed to be both, white and yellow corn.
>
> MS Hmm. Mixed?
>
> SD Mixed.
>
> MS Well, OK, now I have been told that yellow corn is female and white corn is male.
>
> SD Uh-huh.
>
> MS So, do you think there is some significance to the fact that the white corn and the yellow corn both occur in the cake?
>
> SD Yeah, because from this point on, you see, you endear into the kinaaldá, the girl who is becoming like the image of Changing Woman, all those qualities that you, that we think are the most ultimate, what we value. And what we value is that balance of fe-

maleness and maleness in ourselves as female women, but we also encourage that balance in men too. And so, eventually, if your daughter chooses to be, or wants to be married, you want her to have a man that is worthy of her specialness. So, that is why we have a perfect ear of white corn, and that represents that particular future potential of a partnership. Because, in the Navajo way . . . you are not considered a whole person unless you have a partner. Unless you are married. (Sunny Dooley, Gallup, New Mexico, 8/19/92)

In spite of these philosophical prescriptions, the actual color of corn used in 'alkaan is usually determined by family preference in accord with seasonal and regional availability. On occasion, dark-colored kernels, such as blue corn, are intentionally used to produce a distinctively colored cake (Kee, 8/3/92), but most of the elders with whom I consulted agreed that either yellow or white corn could be used, depending on availability (Charley, 7/15/92; Kee, 8/3/92; Bekis, 8/5/92; N. Tso, 8/8/92). "Two different kinds are used. It depends on what you want. Ground white corn is used. If there is no white corn available then the yellow corn is used. The white corn is the morning, it is part of the early morn. Yellow corn is the early evening, you see the yellowness running across in the evenings. Either one may be used for the 'alkaan. Just those two kinds. Whichever is available at the time of the event" (anonymous elder, Lukachukai, Arizona, 8/13/92, translation by Wesley Thomas).

Regardless of the color of corn used in a cake's batter, on several of the twelve levels of abstraction inherent in Navajo philosophy, every 'alkaan is recognized as a homologue of the Navajo universe, reflecting the requisite male-female complementarity in its substance and form. On one level, the cake is formed of male and female substances—yellow corn (female) or white corn (male) or both are used in the batter, and either white corn (male) or pollen (female) is used to make a blessing on top of the batter once it is in the ground. On another level, the cake is formed either as an offering for, or in the image of, a specific male or female member of the Diyin Dine'é.

The original 'alkaan made at Changing Woman's first Kinaaldá is said to have been made as an offering for the sun (male) (Frisbie 1993 [1967]:362; Haile 1938: 87, 89; Reichard 1950:409; Yazzie 1971:131), whereas the 'alkaan made at her second Kinaaldá is said to have been made as an offering for the moon (female) (Frisbie 1993 [1967]:362; Haile 1938:87, 89; Reichard 1950:409).[9] The cake itself is said to represent the earth (female), with the center of the cake representing the sun (male) (Fishler 1953:40–41),[10] or, alternatively, the sun (male) alone (Bekis, 8/5/92; N. Tso, 8/8/92). By other accounts, the cake is said to represent the moon (female), and the fire on top of the cake is said to represent the sun (male) (anonymous elder, 8/13/92; Walters, 8/18/92). Accordingly, the cake is baked at night, since that is when the moon is in the sky.

> It is made in the image of the moon, that is why it is cooked at night. That is the only time it is done. The sun is represented by the fire. The fire is the sun, and is placed on top. So, the sun, as the fire is hot and does the cooking. The bottom is the moon. The hole is dug in the image of the moon. When the moon was created, it was first placed on the ground and the first hole was dug according to the size of the moon. That is the reason why the cooking is done at night and the fire is the sun, cooking the 'alkaan. (The words of an anonymous elder, Lukachukai, Arizona, 8/13/92, translated by Wesley Thomas)

When I asked Harry Walters what significance, if any, derives from the associations made between the fire and the sun and between the 'alkaan and the moon, he reiterated the necessity for all entities in the Navajo world to have naayéé'jí and hózhǫ́ǫjí counterparts, and he confirmed that the significance lies in the fact that the sun is male and the moon is female. He explained that the cake is a homologue of the Navajo universe; therefore, it must be composed of male and female counterparts.

> HW The sun is male, the moon is female. And then the moon is not necessarily a female.
>
> MS Not necessarily?
>
> HW I mean—
>
> MS Is he a nádleehé or something?
>
> HW No, no, no. OK. Just like as I said before, you know, I am a man, but my right side is female. You're a woman, but your left side is male, see? It is necessary, you know, to have a counterpart. To be equal. To balance this [touching his right-hand side], to this [touching his left-hand side].
>
> MS OK.
>
> HW So the moon, is actually male. But he represents the female. The same way with Monster Slayer and Born For Water. See, Born For Water is not female, but he represents the female because he represents peace. He did not kill any of the enemies, any of the monsters. . . . So everything that represents peaceful, you know, everything that is nice, Born For Water stands for that. So that same characteristic also stands for female. So, you know, like . . .

MS So, in counterpart with the sun . . .

HW Counterpart, yeah.

MS The moon represents female aspects?

HW Yes. (Harry Walters, Tsaile, Arizona, 8/18/92)

When I discussed this with Sunny Dooley, she explained that as with many episodes in Navajo oral history, several different accounts exist regarding exactly whose image the cake is made in. As she describes in the following account, she was taught that Changing Woman's cake was made in the image of the sun (male) and baked under the watchful eyes of the moon (female).

SD There are all kinds of different philosophies about that, different ways of telling it. I was told that it [the cake] represents the sun, because when Changing Woman made her cake in the third world they forgot to invite the sun. And the sun was very upset [chuckles], because all the deities had come. Every person that was anybody was there, and they all sang a song. All these people sang a song. And nobody noticed that the sun had come up, because it was nighttime when they did the Blessing Way. And then when the sun came up, they say that the sun stopped in the sky, when he noticed the congregation down here saying, "Hmm, what is going on down there?" And when the sun noticed this . . . he got very angry, and he said, "Why wasn't I invited?" And nobody in the whole group knew what to say because they had completed something they thought was perfect. They did not want to be angry. They did not want to cause an argument. So they all looked at each other, and it was Changing Woman—and this is where again, they say the sun fell in love with her, because she was the one that came forward—and she said, "All of my relatives have celebrated this wonderful event for me. And because you are the most wonderful, we have made this in your image." And it was a golden cake, that was round like the sun. And the sun looked down on it and said, "Well this is perfect, this is wonderful. Thank you for this gift." And so Changing Woman took the center, the heart of the cake, and gave it to the sun. And that is why we give the center of the cake to the medicine man and his wife, because that is the most wonderful part to get, because it is the heart of this cake. . . . So then the sun says, "For this . . ." He made the concession there, and said that umm, "From this day on nobody will have the right to yell at you, to think ill of you, to neglect you, and to hurt you. And should they do any of these things, I the sun personally will take their blessings from them. Slowly but surely they will end up a poor person." . . . I think that is the real essence of Kinaaldá, once you have become that, it is sort of like you're that for the rest of your life. . . . The moon took care of the cake while it was being baked, but it was not made in his image.

MS Well, what is that about the moon taking care of the cake?

SD The moonbeams, umm, while everybody was inside, you know, singing their songs, First Woman had a concern that the cake would burn [chuckles]. Because it was baking and the moon was the one that volunteered and said, "I'll take care of it." So, that is the only thing I've heard. Not that it was made in its [the moon's] image. (Sunny Dooley, Gallup, New Mexico, 8/19/92)

The batter for contemporary 'alkaan consists of ground roasted corn, ground sprouted wheat, raisins, and sugar or "natural sweetener" or both. Most families boil commercial sugar to form a syrup that is added to the batter. In some families, on the day before the cake will be made, prepubescent children who have no cavities are selected to make "natural sweetener." These children are supervised while they masticate corn, which is added to the cake batter as a sweetener after it has been allowed to ferment overnight. As Traci Michelle Begay recalls in the following narrative, the children who are chosen to perform this task are encouraged to act in a dignified manner because it is considered an honor.

TMB They use what they call "natural sweetener." Which is a group of younger adults who haven't had their menstrual, or and even boys can do this. They would take some of the already dried corn that was already ground, and they would put it in their mouths, and they would chew it in their mouths, and get their saliva and stuff and then they would spit it into a bowl. . . . The only ones that could do it were ones that didn't have cavities or braces, or anything in their mouths and their teeth were real straight. They were the ones that were chosen out of the group. . . . You couldn't do it yourself, but all the younger kids. And I remember how much fun they would have doing it. I mean they just thought it was really gross! And then they would get yelled at, because if they did think it was gross, or if they felt bad, then they would be scolded, because it was actually considered an honor, you know, a privilege to do that. You know, they were picked to do that.

MS Did anybody explain to you why they were doing this? Or why somebody had to have straight teeth, no cavities?

TMB Because you want a good healthy, clean mouth, you know, to do that. To do it for the people.

MS Oh, I see.

TMB And so, they would then be chosen and they would be doing this in the other hooghan. And they would get tired, but they couldn't eat anything, they had to just drink water. (Traci Michelle Begay, Many Farms, Arizona, 7/26/91)

On the day the cake will be made, the site of the Kinaaldá becomes a whirl of activity shortly after the kinaaldá's early morning run. Male relatives start two or three fires outdoors on which to boil the large quantities of water needed for the cake batter. Throughout this day, male relatives must continue to haul load after load of firewood, as they have already done for the preceding days of the ceremony. Large quantities of wood are needed to fuel the water-boiling fires and the numerous cooking fires, as well as the fire that will burn throughout the night on top of the cake. Women are busy in a summer shade or other structure designated for cooking, preparing food for the guests who will be arriving throughout the day and evening. Vast amounts of food are cooked, cleaned, and sliced—fry bread, melon, coffee, and mutton stew. This food, which is prepared as an act of generosity, has special significance to the kinaaldá's future. As Jean Jones explained, if family members supply the kinaaldá with abundant food at this critical time in her life, she will have abundant food always and will share it with them.

JJ When you're celebrating something like your daughter's [Kinaaldá], she would be celebrating. She would feel real good about herself and people are there to watch her and help her. So when she grows up she would be a real nice person. She will be nice to everybody. And then if you have a lot of food later on she'll have a lot of food to give away.

MS Oh, I see.

JJ You'll be coming to her for those things. (Jean Jones, north of Rock Point, Arizona, 7/15/92)

While several female relatives and friends continue to cook and prepare food, the Ideal Woman helps the kinaaldá sew two corn husk crosses from perfect specimens of white and yellow corn (Dooley, 8/19/92). These crosses will be placed at the center of the corn husks that will line the top and bottom of the cake while it cooks. About four hours before sunset, all the women in attendance bring their personal buckets and 'ádístiin (stirring sticks) to the hooghan in order to help mix and stir the batter. Like the Ideal Woman, these women have a profound effect on the success of the ceremony and the kinaaldá's future. Influence comes from all the men and women who help at the ceremony, and it is most immediately evident in the outcome of the cake.

> Some women who know how to weave rugs, baskets, or sash belts. Ones who are industrious and well informed are hoped to work at the Kinaaldá and help in all aspects of the ceremony, that's how it was and is done. Some are intelligent, those are the ones you seek and you would only want women of that caliber. You don't use just any women for your daughter's Kinaaldá. Kinaaldá is to take after these types of women, that's how it is done. . . . Those women who are known to have these traits are selected so they will pass on their trades and traits to the kinaaldá. That is what is hoped for at this ceremony. She will live her life similar, too. . . . I was instructed like that and by people like that. I am now able to weave rugs and baskets. I am able to be an industrious person. I am able to learn things fairly easily. Using that, I believe the teachings are true. I know it is true. My children participated in the ceremonies and are all like that, too. Now I have a granddaughter at that age. She is growing toward it. (The words of Mae Charley, north of Rock Point, Arizona, 7/15/92, translated by Wesley Thomas)

Once the women have gathered in the hooghan with their pails and stirring sticks, the woman in charge of the cake spreads a clean sheet or other cloth on the floor at the west side of the hooghan. With the assistance of the Ideal Woman, she empties the bags of cornmeal one by one onto the cloth. The cornmeal forms a large cone-shaped pile standing about three feet high on the exact spot where the kinaaldá stood to be adorned with jewelry on the first day of the ceremony. The kinaaldá is directed to grasp *hadahoniye'*, aragonite, in her right hand and to grind it against a small grinding stone that is held in her left hand. Once a small quantity is ground, she rubs the pulverized stone between her palms and then, starting in the east, bends over and scoops her hands through the pile of ground corn from bottom to top. She repeats this in each of the remaining cardinal directions—south, west, and north (Sadie Billie, 7/25/92; field notes, 7/16/93). Alternatively, the powdered stone can be placed underneath the ground corn, in which case the kinaaldá bends over, dips her hands into the pile, and draws the pulverized stone up through the pile of ground corn as she blesses the pile from each of the four directions (Kee, 8/3/92).

Once this blessing is completed, the kinaaldá uses a ceremonial basket to scoop cornmeal from the pile into the pail of a woman sitting on the eastern side of the hooghan. The woman in charge of the cake calls for a man to bring some boiling water. Men are virtually excluded from the hooghan while the mixing and stirring are in progress. They enter only when called upon to haul in buckets full of boiling water from the outdoor fires, which they pour into each container of batter as it is begun.

The boiling water is poured into each woman's pail while she stirs vigorously amid a torrent of hot steam. Not all women can or will participate in the batter mixing. Strict rules govern the behavior of all women wishing to participate. A woman who has danced at a Fire Dance cannot help with the mixing, and as I was told before my daughter's Kinaaldá, all women who wish to participate in this process must be sexually continent during the entire four days of the ceremony. Shortly before my daughter's ceremony, I asked Jean Jones and Mae Charley what would happen if I slept with my husband during the restricted period or if an incontinent women assisted with the mixing. They told me the cake would not cook properly.

> JJ It sort of like gets mushy. It won't cook right.
>
> MS The cake won't cook?
>
> JJ Yes.
>
> MS Now, who's restricted during that time, it is just me? Or are all the other women that are helping also restricted? Can they sleep with their husbands?
>
> JJ [To MC in Navajo] When you are participating in preparing the cake, one's told not to sleep with your husband it is said.
>
> MC [To JJ in Navajo] Yes [laughing].
>
> JJ [To MC in Navajo] She is asking about that. People told her about that. She is asking because of that.
>
> MC [To JJ in Navajo] Yes. It is right. It is powerful, and done according to the rules. It is the Blessing Way used. From the beginning of the Kinaaldá, it is considered sacred for the duration of the ceremony. Anytime during the event, you are not to touch your husband, at the site of the Kinaaldá or away from the Kinaaldá. During the preparation and the cornmeal mixing, you are to conduct yourselves accordingly because of the consequences. All things are taken into consideration including the conduct of the participants. The medicine man and his practice are considered very sacred. You are not to make fun of anything or anybody, you cannot joke or giggle. The taboo applies to the rest of the event, especially

at the time the cornmeal batter is poured into the pit. If any violation occurs the result is evident at the time when the cake is being
cut out. If a violation occurred, the cake will be watery, the cake
will never bake. It has been like that from the time it first started.
Sleeping with your husband is one of those violations. It will not
bake. (The words of Jean Jones and Mae Charley, north of Rock
Point, Arizona, 7/15/92, translated by Wesley Thomas)

Breach of continence rules on the part of any of the women who mix batter can
have long-term ramifications because, as Sadie Billie explained after consulting
with her father, such behavior will affect the kinaaldá's future behavior as well as
the outcome of the cake.

I guess the reason why they limit it for you to sleep with your
husband, or even just like maybe a single person that goes to do
that, when they mix the cake mush, goes back home and sleeps
with a guy, or something. In life, I guess it will affect the kinaaldá
in a way of like, lead her to like getting involved with different
men. . . . Committing adultery and stuff like, you know, she will
like, when there is marriage then, you know, she will still go off on
the side, and have a lot of affairs on the side. That is how it will
affect the individual, the kinaaldá. If the people that are involved
are, you know, sleeping with their husbands or going out and doing
different things. . . . Well he [Nakai Tso] said that, you know, when
it is done right, he said then it is done right. If everything fell in
place and, you know, everything turned out good everybody did
the right thing and she is going to have a good future. (The words
of Nakai Tso, Tsaile, Arizona, 8/8/92, paraphrased by Sadie Billie)

Moving sunwise, the kinaaldá takes a basketful of ground corn to the next
woman, a male relative pours boiling water into her bucket as she stirs, and the
process is repeated until each woman in attendance who has a pail and a set of
stirring sticks has a container of batter started. When an individual bucket of batter is close to the right consistency, a little boiled sugar syrup or natural sweetener
is added. While the other women are mixing batter, the woman in charge of the
cake carefully sorts through the corn husks that will be used to line the cake pit.
She flattens each one by carefully making half-inch tears along the butt end of the
husk. She then places all of them in a tub of warm water to soak and soften. The
hooghan is full of conversation and gentle laughter; this is a time for the women to
share in pleasant bantering about their batter mixing skills and to catch up on
family news.

We started to mix the cake batter. . . . We used those big steel tubs and then we used stirring sticks. . . . I was given my first set then by my mom. She was the one who gave me mine. And then everybody had their own. It is like they dusted it off, or took it from wherever they were at. . . . You have to use both hands, because it is just so hard to stir. And the men started the water boiling outside on a fire, it has to be boiling. Boiling hot water. And then they bring it in and, when they put the flour in the tubs and they pour in the water, you immediately start stirring. And it starts out real thick and you want to add more water into it, but what you actually have to do is break up the corn. And see, when it is boiling, it is cooking. So you have to stir it really fast and keep going. . . . All the women stir, everybody had their own tub and they stirred. They boil sugar until the point where it, it is not hard, but to the point where it is a liquid. And then they bring that in and they pour it into the batter, gradually. And then they use a natural sweetener. . . . And then they would start doing it again. . . . And, you would just keep stirring and stirring and this would happen all afternoon. And, like I was saying with the batter, you would keep wanting to add stuff to make it watery, because it would be hard to stir, but the more you stir, the finer it would get. And the more liquefied it would get. And so, that is what point you would get your batter. So everybody would be sitting around and the men would bring in the boiling water and they would add it in and then they would start going again. And it was funny because so many of my aunts had different ways, or consistencies and they would like, compete, or something. Real friendly like, but they would compete and talk about like, "Is your batter ready?" You know. There were specific things, consistency they would look for, and what not. And there would be like the older grandmothers who would go around and check to see how everybody was doing. And, I remember the young ones would say, "Well, add something to get it watery." "No, you keep stirring it!" And so everybody would just keep stirring it, and that is when there was a lot of socializing done with the aunts and the women that were there. Opportunities to talk. (Traci Michelle Begay, Many Farms, Arizona, 7/26/91)

Once the individual pails of batter reach the desired consistency, their contents are poured into several large steel tubs. Women take turns mixing the batter in the tubs with stirring sticks and then running their hands through it. Women visit with each other as they carefully massage the batter by rubbing handfuls of mush between their hands to break up any lumps and ensure an even consistency. This is a difficult task, because the batter is scalding hot, but women cheerfully dip their hands into the tubs. Soon they are literally up to their elbows in batter, and inevitably their turquoise bracelets and rings become covered with batter. When I commented on this at a Kinaaldá in July 1993, as we rubbed hot batter between our hands, a woman from Del Muerto, Arizona, told me cheerfully, "The batter likes to be caressed with turquoise" (field notes, 7/16/93). Through this process, the 'alkaan batter is molded by the kinaaldá's relatives into an ideal form, just as her body is molded in the image of Changing Woman. This arduous, exhausting process is repeated pail by pail, tub by tub, for two to three hours, until all the ground corn is mixed. Once mixed, the batter is allowed to rest in its tubs while the fire is removed from the pit outside.

When it is time to pour the batter, the kinaaldá carries the corn husk crosses out to the pit in a ceremonial basket. The women who mixed the batter sit on boards or carpet remnants along the edge of the scorching hot pit. The kinaaldá places the bottom cross, with the outside of the husk down, at the center of the bottom of the pit. The other women immediately begin placing additional corn husks around the center cross. These husks are laid sunwise, spiraling out from the center. Care is taken to maintain the trajectory of growth—each husk is laid butt to tip. Lining of the pit must proceed quickly to prevent the dampened husks from drying out or burning. Once the bottom is lined, a bowl is placed in the center and cake batter is carefully poured into it from the north side of the pit to avoid disturbing the husks. Additional husks are laid along the sides as the batter spreads from the middle of the pit outward.

When the batter pouring is complete, the kinaaldá takes her place on the eastern side of the pit with a basket containing either white cornmeal or pollen with which she will bless the cake. Using her right hand, she takes a handful of cornmeal or pollen and sprinkles it away from herself, from east to west. She sprinkles a second handful from south to north and finishes by sprinkling the substance used in blessing around the full circumference of the cake in a sunwise movement— east, south, west, north—being careful to leave an opening in the east. The cornmeal or pollen is sprinkled in this manner to form a "way out."

> Where the opening part of the basket is [east], that is where the beginning of the white corn is sprinkled, it is sprinkled in this direction [from east to west across the center of the cake] and from this direction [south] toward this way [north across the center of the cake], and finally sunwise, like on the rim of the basket. The point where the basket is started and where the sprinkling ends on the cake, they are considered openings in our world. Like the door to this house. It lets you into the house and once inside the house,

you are able to move around. By the same door, you can leave the house. In that same manner, you have to create these openings on the basket and the cake during the ceremony. That is how and why the blessing is done. (The words of an anonymous elder, Lukachukai, Arizona, 8/13/92, translated by Wesley Thomas)

Once the kinaaldá completes her blessing, others who wish to do so may make similar blessings with the remaining cornmeal or pollen.

Next, the kinaaldá lays the second cross on the center of the cake, taking care that the outsides of the husks are up. Her female relatives quickly place additional corn husks, butt to tip, around the husk cross in a sunwise spiral, until the top of the cake is covered. The women then spread newspapers over the cake and cover them with handfuls of fine dry dirt, followed by shovelfuls of hot ashes and coals to form an even layer. Gradually, the fire is rekindled on top of the cake. This fire is maintained throughout the night by a male relative. He must be someone who is deemed responsible and dependable, for his character and behavior influence the outcome of the cake.

The man who is the fire keeper should be the only one keeping the fire going for the duration of the baking. Sometimes, others can help, but only one person should be designated to be the overseer for the fire. He is responsible for the fire, the pit. His responsibility continues to the end, when the cake is cut. His participation is done wholeheartedly and he plays a major role in the final results of the cake. (The words of Mae Charley, north of Rock Point, Arizona, 7/15/92, translated by Wesley Thomas)

When I inquired what significance, if any, was associated with the baking of the cake in the ground, I was told that its placement there was a physical demonstration of the connection between the kinaaldá, who has just become a life giver, and Changing Woman, who is the inner form of the earth and, as such, the ultimate life giver. The young woman's reproductive energies and capacities are signified by the blood she sheds during her first and second menstrual periods. Oscar Tso told me that this blood is considered "very precious. It is looked upon as very sacred. This first blood from your period is considered 'life blood.' So you have a real special ceremony" (7/18/92). As Sunny Dooley points out in the following passage, placing the cake in the ground transfers some of the reproductive energy possessed by the kinaaldá back into the earth, the ultimate source of all reproductive energy.

MS What is the significance of the cake being buried in the ground? I mean other than the fact that it is a traditional cooking method.

SD It just means that once again you are going into the heart of your earth, the mother. . . . Your period, the fluid that comes out when you have your period is very sacred and in Navajo the word is chooyin, and it means that it has a, there is a sacred power about it. . . . I know that putting a lot of that back into the earth is sort of like this cycle. It is a real conservation of energy kind of thing. I don't know how you would say it but whatever comes out of you doesn't go anywhere but back into the earth. And this is your acknowledgment to the earth that we now have another human being who is capable of giving life. Just as Mother Earth gives us life. And it goes back to the heart. So that in our culture the women are the hearts of the families, not heart as an emotional, or that kind of thing, but just that they are like the rock, you know, they are the anchor to whatever is possible, whatever could happen. So I know that has something to do with that (Sunny Dooley, Gallup, New Mexico, 8/21/92).

The theme of recycling reproductive energy resurfaces later in the ceremony, during the kinaaldá's final run and after the cake is cut.

THE NO-SLEEP

As relatives, friends, and the ceremonial practitioner and his or her assistants arrive at the site of the Kinaaldá throughout the late afternoon and evening, they are served a meal of mutton stew, fry bread, melon, and coffee. Prior to the all-night sing, relatives and friends place property such as jewelry, rugs, saddles, bridles, and photos of absent relatives on a blanket spread on the west side of the hooghan. During the early evening, the kinaaldá returns to her place inside the hooghan, where she, the ceremonial practitioner, and other participants are allowed to rest in anticipation of the long night ahead. The Ideal Woman and other female elders complete the final preparations before resting. They dig up a four-inch section of yucca root that will be used to wash the kinaaldá's hair at dawn. Care is taken to note the direction of the root's growth. After its collection, the piece of root is set aside in a small bowl of warm water to soften. They secure the chííh, or red ochre, and dleesh, or rhyolite tuff, that will be used to paint the initiate at the close of the ceremony; these materials are brought to the Kinaaldá site by someone who was asked ahead of time to do so. In addition, a knife may be sharpened in preparation for cutting the cake.

At approximately 10:30 or 11:00 P.M., the ceremonial practitioner announces that the sing will begin. All relatives and friends who wish to participate in this portion of the ceremony enter and take seats on the appropriate side of the hooghan: females on the north, males on the south. Once all participants are seated, the singer or someone designated by him or her blesses the hooghan and its contents by first marking each of the cardinal directions with pollen or white cornmeal and then sprinkling this substance throughout the hooghan while saying a prayer asking for good thoughts and harmony.

After the hooghan is blessed, the kinaaldá is directed to rise, walk sunwise around the fire or stove, and sit down on the left of the ceremonial practitioner with her back straight, her feet outstretched in front of her body, and her arms resting on her legs with her palms up. The singer then blesses her in the following manner.

He takes a pinch of pollen from his tádídíín bijish and with it touches the sole of her right foot and then her left, her right knee and then her left, her right palm and then her left, the front of her chest, her back, and her right shoulder and then her left. He takes a second pinch and places it in her mouth and on the top of her head. Finally, he takes another pinch and sprinkles it forward (away from the kinaaldá), toward the east, while saying a clearly audible prayer (field notes, 7/25/92; see also Begay 1983:125).

After the kinaaldá is blessed, the singer passes his or her pouch of pollen among those assembled. Starting with the person closest to the doorway on the south side, all participants say a prayer with the pollen as they touch it to their tongues and the tops of their heads and then sprinkle it out in front of themselves before passing the tádídíín bijish sunwise. Once all in attendance have blessed themselves this way, the ceremonial practitioner blesses the personal possessions placed by relatives and friends on the blanket at the west side of the hooghan.

The singing begins with a set of Hooghan songs directed to Talking God, Changing Woman, and other Diyin Dine'é.

> Twenty-one songs are sung then the kinaaldá can go outside. . . . The first set of songs consists of twelve. That is sung first. . . . While these songs are being sung no one can leave the ceremonial hooghan. It is called 'atł'ááh [bottom]. The twelve songs in this set, each is represented by the twelve feathers, here [referring to the twelve tail feathers found on the mask of Haashch'ééłti'í, Talking God, who is said to have determined the number of songs]. Then the next set of songs is in a group of nine. So all together there are twenty-one songs. Then, the kinaaldá is permitted to leave the hooghan. For that matter, the rest of the people who are in the hooghan can venture outside the hooghan, also. Other people can go outside, too. (The words of an anonymous elder, Lukachukai, Arizona, 8/13/92, translated by Wesley Thomas)

Opinions vary regarding the exact number of songs, other than the prescribed twelve Hooghan songs (Begay 1983:131; field notes, 7/26/92; N. Tso, 8/8/92), required in this initial portion of the ceremony.[11] As Mae Bekis explains, according to some versions of the Kinaaldá there are a total of nineteen songs that must be sung in the first segment of the ceremony.

> When the medicine man is ready to sing, they usually start around about eleven or eleven-thirty, and the first seventeen songs he or she sings are about getting the hooghan ready, or the home for the young girl in the future. The songs they sing are about the hooghan. How it was made from the foundation up to the top. And then, there is some about the roads that you are going to take the rest of your life. And, uh, and then after that, after all the seventeen songs, and they have two closing songs there [for a total of nineteen], and then when they tell her to go out, and then she walks out towards the east and they tell her to have positive thoughts and turn clockwise outside, and then come back in. (Mae Bekis, Tó- 'tsoh, Arizona, 8/5/92)

When the first group of songs is complete, the ceremonial practitioner again blesses the kinaaldá from the soles of her feet to the top of her head, finishing with a sprinkle of pollen in front of her. He or she then passes the tádídíín bijish, or pollen pouch, sunwise among the participants. Starting with the person closest to the doorway on the south side, participants offer pollen to Mother Earth or other Diyin Dine'é, accompanying their offerings with quiet prayers. Once the last person on the north side of the hooghan has completed an offering or blessing, the kinaaldá is told to go óutside, take four deep breaths, each of which is followed by a full exhale, turn sunwise, and then return to her place within the hooghan. Following this, songs will continue until dawn, but participants are free to leave the hooghan at will for fresh air, coffee, or food.

When the singing resumes, men and women in attendance who have knowledge of appropriate songs may each sing a song or two dealing with livestock and other valuable possessions or skills. "And then, from there on different ones start singing. . . . Then they sing all night. . . . Some ladies that have songs about sheep, or about the horses, or about the jewelry, or about the weaving, or about the different weaving tools. And . . . then that is what they sing all night. Until way toward morning, about four-thirty or five, and then they tell her it is time to run" (Bekis, 8/5/92).

A wide variety of songs may be sung during this portion of the ceremony. In fact, nearly any song associated with or mentioning the east may be used. This group of songs focuses on the qualities, material possessions, and skills deemed necessary for the kinaaldá to attain a wholesome and rewarding life. "There are a lot of additional songs . . . too many to mention. . . . Any one of the songs which mentions the word east is applicable. . . . Some of the songs call for material goods for the kinaaldá, others request a good wholesome life. Then there are songs which are a combination of both" (anonymous elder, Lukachukai, Arizona, 8/13/92, translation by Wesley Thomas).

Near the break of dawn, the ceremonial practitioner notifies the Ideal Woman that it is time to uncover the cake and wash the kinaaldá's hair before her final run. While the last songs are sung by people in attendance other than the ceremonial practitioner, the Ideal Woman asks the kinaaldá's mother or another female relative to put some water on to heat and then to go outside and tell the man supervising the fire to begin uncovering the cake. Once the water is warm, the Ideal Woman begins to prepare the yucca suds needed for washing the kinaaldá's hair and jewelry, while the ceremonial practitioner begins the next series of songs, known as the Dawn songs. This group of special songs documents the events that took place from the time Changing Woman was found as an infant until her Kinaaldá: "They sing four, what we call basically about the growing of a child. The four songs that they sing, that is before the closing time. And the song it goes like about how you first heard the baby when you were at the hospital, the first sound of a baby, and then how it is talking to you and how you talk back, and how it answers you back, in crying. So those four songs are sung" (Bekis, 8/5/92).

As the singing progresses, the Ideal Woman quickly rubs the softened yucca root between her palms as a female assistant pours warm water over the yucca into the ceremonial basket. This process is continued until adequate suds are produced. Before shampooing the kinaaldá's hair, the Ideal Woman may apply a pinch of yucca suds to the kinaaldá's body, starting with the sole of her right foot and proceeding to the places where the ceremonial practitioner applied pollen earlier in the ceremony. With the assistance of the Ideal Woman, the kinaaldá washes the jewelry she is wearing and then her hair. The Ideal Woman places the washed jewelry on the kinaaldá while it is still wet. With her wet hair streaming down around her shoulders and back, the kinaaldá is directed to proceed sunwise around the fire and out the door to make her final run.

By now, the ceremonial practitioner and her or his assistants should have reached the Racing or Running song in the set of Dawn songs. The Running song is said to have been utilized by Changing Woman when she ran during her own Kinaaldá. The kinaaldá is directed to run sunwise around the edge of her recently uncovered cake and then eastward for as far as she is able. She is accompanied by several relatives and friends who yell to notify the Dawn People, Talking God, and other Diyin Dine'é of this important juncture in the ceremony. As Irene Kee explains in the following passage, at her own Kinaaldá she was told that the young woman must race the rising sun in order to win the material goods with which she is adorned and thereby ensure that she will possess such goods throughout her life. Unfortunately, despite all good intentions, such blessings are not always sustained, as Mrs. Kee laughingly notes:

> You are to run with the material goods you are dressed with, and run into the early morning, into good fortune. This happens immediately after the morning songs are completed inside the hooghan. The run indicates the material wealth you are dressed with, your intention is to run with it and beat the morning of its wealth. You will win the goods on you, they will all belong to you. But you are not to go to sleep until the daylight is completely gone, when it is dark move and engulf the environment. Yes, then you win and own all this stuff, here [touching her body in the places where she wore jewelry during her Kinaaldá]. Where are they [the goods with which she was adorned as a kinaaldá] now? They are not around here. There are none here [laughs]. (The words of Irene Kee, Crystal, New Mexico, 8/3/92), translated by Wesley Thomas)

After running as far as she possibly can, the kinaaldá stops, stretches out her arms, and takes four deep breaths, drawing in the dawn air with her arms each time. Next, she bends down, touches Mother Earth, and blesses herself by applying the moist soil to her body from her feet upward. Some of the reproductive power possessed by the kinaaldá during her first and second menstrual periods is transferred back to Mother Earth through this process, which rejuvenates Changing Woman.

> That is done when she runs and the cake has been finished, from the doorway of the hooghan, she runs a specified pattern. This pattern is called "encircling your food and all that nurtures you." Before turning back from the run, usually around a bush. You stop and embrace and inhale the dawn. You do this four times. Through this process you have internalized, inhaled, embraced, and conceptualized the force of the dawn and the entire Navajo universe. The internalization is externalized by transferring some of the power possessed by kinaaldá to the earth. This is accomplished when you touch the earth after you have embraced the dawn. This is so the earth will never grow old. The transfer is not complete—part of the power stays with the kinaaldá. After this procedure, she runs back. Before she has encircled the cake, she runs straight back. The reason for encircling or running around your cake is so, for the rest of her life the kinaaldá will always have food. It will always return

or recycle itself. (The words of an anonymous elder, Lukachukai, Arizona, 8/13/92, translated by Wesley Thomas) [12]

After the kinaaldá blesses herself with soil, thereby transferring reproductive power back to the earth, she turns sunwise and retraces her steps back to the hooghan. She speeds up when nearing the hooghan, stops at the door, walks sunwise around the fire back to her place, and sits. If her run was timed appropriately, her return and the completion of the last song in the Dawn song series will coincide with the break of dawn.

Her return is followed by a closing song. Upon the completion of this song, the ceremonial practitioner directs the kinaaldá to go out and greet the dawn with a pollen blessing if she has not done so at the end of her last run. As Mae Bekis explains, the purpose of this greeting is to internalize the powers of the Dawn People and the first and second Talking Gods.

> The one we call closing song ends in the morning. And after that the medicine man will tell the patient to go out and then use pollen. And then that is when you, from the stretch of your arm, he says to hold the tádídíín, pollen, and then he tells you to breathe that fresh air in four times, and then you put the tádídíín in your mouth, which is the pollen in your mouth, and then you put your hand back in there and take it out. And he says there is Haashch'éél'ti'í, which the First Talking God, that is watching you and you do the tádídíín toward the east. And then the next one you put your hand in there is for the Second Talking God [Haashch'éé'ooghaan], and you do the same thing, and then after that you put one on the top of your head, and then from there you do your own prayer [sprinkle pollen away from yourself in offering while saying a silent prayer]. Whatever way in Navajo if you know how to talk Navajo, but if you don't know how to talk Navajo you can say your prayer in English, of your future. (Mae Bekis, Tó'tsoh, Arizona, 8/5/92)

The tádídíín bijish is passed while the kinaaldá is outside greeting the dawn or immediately after the closing song if she has completed the greeting during her final run. In either case, the tádídíín is used in personal blessing by all in attendance.

The cake should finish cooking before the break of dawn is complete. The cake is fully uncovered and all dirt swept off of it. Once it has cooled sufficiently, the kinaaldá wraps her shawl around her shoulders and takes her basket out to cut and distribute the cake. She walks sunwise around the cake and takes her place at the east. She, her mother, the Ideal Woman, or the woman in charge of the cake cuts it, beginning in the east. Each piece of cake is placed in the basket as it is removed from the pit, and the Ideal Woman directs the kinaaldá to give it to a specific individual. Custom varies from family to family regarding who should cut the first piece—the kinaaldá, her mother, the woman in charge of the cake, or another woman—and to whom the first piece of cake and the center pieces should be given. But by most accounts a quadrant of the center, or the heart of the cake, should go to the ceremonial practitioner, and pieces of 'alkaan should be given to every participant for her or his efforts on behalf of the kinaaldá (Reichard 1928: 138; Frisbie 1993 [1967]:366, 412; field notes, 7/26/92, 7/17/93; Kee, 8/3/92; Bekis, 8/5/92; Dooley, 8/19/92). A giveaway bag containing fruit, candy, or other small gifts is often distributed to each participant with the requisite piece of cake. In addition, pinches from each quadrant of the center of the cake must be offered back to the earth (Frisbie 1993 [1967]: 25, 366; Begay 1983:147; field notes, 7/26/92, 7/17/93; Kee, 8/3/92; Bekis, 8/5/92), who, as Irene Kee points out, is a "demanding entity."

> The kinaaldá is the one who cuts the cake. The cake is like this, the first cutting is done from the east. That piece is removed, then another piece is cut out from the south. West and then the north sides are cut out. The cutting from the east is given to a male child. This one [from the south] is given to a female child. This one [from the west] is given to a male child, and this one [from the north] is given to a female child. . . . The center part, from here to here and from here to here are cut into quadrants. This is called the heart of the cake. It is moved to the side and a small amount of dirt is removed from the center of the fire pit. Pinches of the heart are removed from the four quadrants [which correlate with the four cardinal directions integral to Navajo cosmology] and they are inserted into the opening. Then the dirt is replaced over the pinches of cake pieces. These small pieces are an offering to the earth. You are to make an offering, it is returned to the originator. The earth is due an offering. It is required. The offering is returned in lieu of usage of the fire pit. From it you acquired a cake. The earth, which we are sitting on, is due an offering. It is necessary. It is a demanding entity [chuckles]. (The words of Irene Kee, Crystal, New Mexico, 8/3/92, translated by Wesley Thomas)

When I sought clarification from Mrs. Kee regarding why the cake is buried in the earth for baking and why an offering must be made to the earth, she explained that the original 'alkaan was made to signify that the kinaaldá had completed a transition from childhood to being a young woman with reproductive capacities.

The pieces of cake offered back to the earth signify the return to Mother Earth of some of the reproductive energy that empowers her.

> It is all because of First Woman's action, in the past. Where it all occurred first. I do not know what she did back then with this ceremony. I am sure she made a small one ['alkaan], now we measure it with the length of a long shovel. We have increased the size of the cake now. It is like that now. Then, it was made for a sign only, to indicate to others of a transition that has taken place. The four directions of the cake and the heart of the cake are offered back to the earth. This offering is the energy which empowers the earth. The other parts of the cake are distributed to the participants of the ceremony. The sanctification is always done. The procedure has taken place from time unknown to humans. Crossed corn husks are placed at the bottom of the cake and also on top, they are crossed, too. Then the corn husks are layered underneath, the sides, and finally on top. Corn husks are the only ones used and it has always been like that. Our ancestors made 'alkaan like that, our grandmothers established them, as such. (The words of Irene Kee, Crystal, New Mexico, 8/4/92, translated by Wesley Thomas)

Elders watch over the progress of the cake carefully through all stages of its production. They pay close attention to every detail, including the quality of the ingredients and the caliber of the people assisting with its production. Any unusual circumstances, such as inclement weather, can be cause for great concern. The cooked cake should have a smooth, firm texture. Distress ensues when a cake does not cook properly. Numerous factors are said to have the potential to cause the cake to come out "mushy." When a cake does not cook properly, explanations range from pragmatic statements such as "the fire was not hot enough" (Kee, 8/3/92) or "they didn't keep the fire up" (Bekis, 8/5/92) to more complex explanations such as a woman who has danced in the Fire Dance helped with the mixing of the batter (field notes, 7/16/93), the women who assisted told lewd jokes in the presence of the cake batter (N. Tso, 8/8/92), or "the girl has already fallen in love" (Dooley, 8/21/92). In addition, breach of continence rules on the part of participating women or, as Mae Bekis explains, on the part of the kinaaldá can ruin the cake.

> MS And what types of things would cause the cake to not come out right? Other than . . .
> MB Well having sex with your husband. Like the ladies, they are not supposed to make any jokes, you know, anything about a hus-

band or about their boyfriend or any jokes like that. That will ruin the cake. I was told. . . .

MS Is there anything else that would ruin the cake?

MB If a girl, the kinaaldá, the main one—if she has a boyfriend. If she had intercourse with a boy before the ceremony or in the long run. It will ruin the cake. . . . She is supposed to be a virgin all the way from, from birth to the Kinaaldá. Up to that stage, she is supposed to be a virgin. (Mae Bekis, Tó'tsoh, Arizona, 8/5/92)

In my experience, the most frequently given explanations for a ruined cake were breach of continence rules or jokes of a sexual nature having been told at the Kinaaldá (Charley, 7/15/92; Bekis, 8/5/92; Sadie Billie, 8/8/92; Dooley, 8/21/92; field notes, 7/18/93).

It rained throughout the night while my daughter's cake was in the ground. The soaked ground made it difficult for guests and the singer's assistants to travel to the site of the event. Mud made the roads so impassable that several relatives and friends were forced to turn back, and the singer's assistants were stranded and spent the night in their vehicle. The man in charge of the cake fire had an extremely difficult time sustaining the fire throughout the night. On her last run, Ragen and the people running with her slipped and slid in the mud. Despite all this, her cake was perfect. A week or so after her Kinaaldá, Oscar Tso and I discussed the significance of her cake's coming out satisfactorily despite the difficulties caused by the weather.

OT Something good is going to come out within her life. On the part of the people that participated there was a lot of sincerity put into the ceremony that was going on. And, uh, they are careful. These elders, you know, they try to create a situation, the environment, the atmosphere, that is really, I would say conducive to calmness, and cheerfulness, and those kinds of things, so that the life of this young person can be like that. . . . There must have been some sincerity on the part of the people that were there—the medicine man, people that gathered to help—for that cake to turn out the way it did. Because, I guess, that is kind of like a knowledge that these people possess that can come up with a perfect cake. And with the weather, and the situation as it was.

MS You mean all the rain?

OT Uh-huh. Sometimes it is pretty hard to come up with a perfect cake. You never know what is going to take place. Something might be missing, maybe the most important ingredient is not there. But somehow or other as you begin to put things together, things are going to fall in place for a person. So I guess it is like that with any ceremony. . . . Everything is going to be well with her. . . . The sincere thought that was put into whatever, like bringing the firewood, bringing water, you know, just the very thought of helping out. Just the very thought of maybe being there, as a support, you know. . . . All of that, in and of itself, like I was saying, has a lot to do with her future. Where people are helping out, they are having these nice thoughts as they are like you said "kneading the cake," getting the lumps out. So, that is what I was talking about, you know, the sincerity that people had in wanting to be there and wanting to help, and wanting things to turn out real good for her. . . . Even the rain itself, you know.

MS What did that mean?

OT Even when, to some extent it was, you know, it made it harder—

MS Much harder.

OT For her to run, and for people to, you know, there was that extra effort, you know, just to get firewood. Just to get that fire burning.

MS To keep it going!

OT Uh-huh, so even at that, you know, nature when it approves of something going on, it will rain, you know. A ceremony, especially a ceremony that is taking place. I guess as a sign to say that things are going to be well. So that is the only time when it will rain like that. (Oscar Tso, Many Farms, Arizona, 8/9/92)

Great emphasis is placed on the finished cake. As Sunny Dooley explains in the following narrative, when the cake "comes out right" it is said to signify many things. It demonstrates that the kinaaldá has been properly trained and prepared by her family and that as a result, her future will be good.

When the cake cooks properly it means that all the deities were there, and everybody was blessed. . . . Everything was done according to the original plan. And that all the people that were in attendance were also in a balanced state of mind. Nobody brought any kind of ill feelings to the ceremony and that kind of thing. And also I think the most significant thing is that the girl respects, how would you say it? The girl got a real sense of self respect. That is what the cake represents when it is all totally, completely wonderfully made, it means that the girl, at that point in time has been blessed with her full sense of respect. If it is a little mushy or if it is a little, you know, weird looking or something like that it means that you still have to, the relatives still have to somewhat form her. That she hasn't been completely formed, you know. I am not saying that the girl has reached her pinnacle in life, but that, you know she is still going to need a lot of help and assistance throughout her life. But if she, if her cake has been nicely made it means that she is going to be independent and wise and knowledgeable. (Sunny Dooley, Gallup, New Mexico, 8/21/92)

The outcome of the cake is viewed as an embodiment of the kinaaldá's abilities as a woman, as a reflection of the way her family raised her, and as a prediction of her future. The cake as a visible symbol does not simply represent the clan and family relations; rather, it embodies and presents them for all to see. The cutting and distributing of the cake are followed by a large communal meal served to the ceremonial practitioner and all guests and relatives in attendance. Following this meal, the kinaaldá and all other participants gather at the hooghan for the final steps in the public portion of the ceremony.

FINAL MOLDING, STRETCHING, AND PAINTING

The kinaaldá kneels facing east to have her hair brushed. The ceremonial practitioner or another elder sings one or two Combing songs while the Ideal Woman combs and reties the young woman's hair with the buckskin or mountain lion thong. Once her hair is securely tied and the singing complete, the Ideal Woman prepares the chííh, or dleesh with which the young woman will be painted. Depending on clan preference, the kinaaldá may be painted with chííh or dleesh or with both. If chííh is to be used, the Ideal Woman mixes a small portion of it with mutton fat between her fingers and sets the pigment aside in the ceremonial basket. Ground dleesh, which has been mixed ahead of time, is moistened with a small amount of warm water to form a slip.

Dleesh is used to symbolize she will grow old with "grace." Chííh is also used to "slow down" the process of aging. Her hair is brushed first. The chííh is applied and the dleesh, or white clay, is marked on her shoulders, on both sides of her cheeks, and on her forehead. When she becomes old these are markers which will indicate that she went through the Kinaaldá process. . . . The white clay markings are done in the morning of the final day. . . . It is done with a song. A song has to be used to apply the white clay. (The words of an anonymous elder, Lukachukai, Arizona, 8/13/92, translated by Wesley Thomas)

The kinaaldá is directed to sit with her legs outstretched in front of her, her arms resting on her legs, and her palms up. If it is to be used, the chííh is applied before the dleesh. As a Painting song is sung, a horizontal line of chííh is applied across the kinaaldá's cheeks from the right to the left cheek. Next, a small amount of chííh is dabbed first at the center of the young woman's forehead, then onto the right side of her forehead, and finally onto the left side.

The Ideal Woman pulls two or four straws from the kinaaldá's grass hairbrush. Remaining careful to follow the trajectory of growth, the Ideal Woman dips these straws into the dleesh and applies the substance with an upward motion at each of the following locations on the kinaaldá's body: "She painted her with dleesh on the sole of her right foot, the left sole, the right shin, the left shin, right knee, left knee, right palm, left palm. Sadie pushed her blouse aside to reach her breast bone and painted the center of her chest, right shoulder, left shoulder, ending with the center of the top of her head" (field notes, 7/17/93). Application "starts on the right, always on the right," beginning with the soles of the feet, and proceeds upward (Charley, 7/15/92; field notes, 7/26/92).

Once the painting of the kinaaldá is complete, the kinaaldá paints those in attendance who wish to share in the blessing. She dips the straws from her hairbrush into the dleesh and gently paints each individual's right and left cheek with one upward stroke as he or she stands before her. Alternatively, the people in attendance can file over to the basket one by one and apply the dleesh to themselves. "We were told that the women present could now bless themselves with the remaining dleesh. We went in clockwise order around the hooghan. The ceremonial practitioner's wife directed us to touch the dleesh with the fingers of our right hand and rub it up our bodies from our feet, legs, and torso to our shoulders, and then to brush it across the top of our heads" (field notes, 7/17/93).

The dleesh and chííh markings signify that the kinaaldá has ground corn, mixed batter, been dressed, sung, and prayed over to complete her initiation, and "outrun the clumsiness of her childhood" (Dooley, 8/19/92). Alone or in combination, the dleesh and chííh markings form a permanent layer on the outside of the kinaaldá's body. The Holy People recognize and identify her by these markings.

The white clay was touched to her. The white clay was touched here [touches his feet and legs] here [touches his palms], here [touches his chest and shoulders], and here [touches his cheeks]. She will be blessed with it. The Holy People will recognize her by that. Even if one does not know, the Holy People will recognize her from her white clay markings. According to touching the children [referring to the kinaaldá's painting of the cheeks of those present with dleesh], that is recognized by the Holy People since the kinaaldá is identified by her white clay markings. (The words of an anonymous elder, Lukachukai, Arizona, 8/13/92, translated by Wesley Thomas)

Once the painting is complete, the kinaaldá is again molded in the image of Changing Woman. Depending on family practice, this second molding may take place outside the hooghan (Frisbie 1993 [1967]:60–61, 70; Begay 1983:157; Ryan 1988:6; field notes, 7/26/92) or inside the hooghan (field notes, 7/17/93), where the kinaaldá lies down on a pile of blankets and other materials facing west. The Ideal Woman starts with the young woman's toes and moves upward to the tip of her head, giving careful attention to her torso and arms. After her molding, the kinaaldá stands and stretches people of all ages who come up one by one to stand in front of her facing west. Upon completion of the stretching, the kinaaldá carefully removes each item from the pile of materials and returns it to its owner, who thanks her profusely. The young woman is then directed to go back into the hooghan, where her hair will be brushed and tied into the traditional hair bun (Wyman and Bailey 1943:11; field notes, 7/26/92, 7/17/93). Next, she returns all borrowed items of jewelry to their owners.

At this point, a four-day period of quiet solitude begins, during which time the kinaaldá reflects on the ceremony, her family, and all that she has learned about her Navajo heritage. At dawn of the fourth day after the all-night sing, the girl must wash her hair, saving the shampoo rinse water in a pan or bucket. The female relative who is to assist her with this shampooing is given strict instructions regarding disposal of the rinse water.

> She should wash her hair after four days, it is said. The water is to be poured on the inside of the hooghan, by the doorway. That is how it is done. . . . Even if she is very busy, she can still observe the four holy days. She can wash her hair four days later, wherever she may live. You do not need to stay in one location to observe the holy days. The water from washing your hair is not thrown out but gently poured by the doorway, at whatever house you live. (The words of an anonymous elder, Lukachukai, Arizona, 8/13/92, translated by Wesley Thomas)

At the conclusion of the public portion of my daughter's Kinaaldá, Sadie Billie instructed me to pour the rinse water around the perimeter of our home so that my daughter would always be drawn home. The connection formed through disposal of the shampoo rinse water reinforces the kinaaldá's association with her home.

BEYOND THE KINAALDÁ

The puberty ceremony given for a boy when his voice changes or for a girl at the onset of menstruation signals the start of his or her path to manhood or woman-hood. The Kinaaldá ceremony is only the first step on the path to young adulthood, which will take several more years to complete. These young people, who are considered still malleable for some time to come, will be offered additional guidance by their elders on numerous occasions. Concerned relatives will carefully guide young men and women in matters of sexuality and in the roles and responsibilities of men and women. In addition, young adults will be initiated into gender-specific bodies of knowledge at the appropriate times in their lives. For example, male relatives will teach young men about hunting and warfare traditions, and female relatives will offer young women guidance on conception, pregnancy, child care, and other important topics when this information is needed.

CHAPTER VII

TALKING ABOUT
CONTEMPORARY
SYSTEMS OF
KNOWLEDGE
AND PRACTICE

Let's say this society or tribe, they all have one understanding in how they go about from day to day. What they follow and what are the necessary things to do, from day to day. Then, all these things were understood by all the people, and there is one way to understand or to see the world. And whatever practices [existed] were understood by all. . . . You don't talk about it, because you live it. You know? You don't need to talk about it. But when . . . another concept comes in . . . then you get mixed up within two different concepts. Then somewhere, you either get drawn into this new, in this really influential concept that came in, obviously that is what has happened to our people. So now even religion, we belong to different denominations and say we, you know, we belong to this and that. And even the life-style itself, we no longer practice, or we no longer live like the way we were supposed to be at one time. That is why there was, for long lengths of time we didn't know how to talk about these things because a lot of our elders still maintained, they still lived that life, they don't need to talk about it. . . . If you ask a really down-to-earth elder, they might say, if you ask what do you think about religion? Maybe the answer might be, "We don't think about it we live it." (Hanson Ashley, Shonto, Arizona. 7/27/93)

A special form of life exists within the area demarcated by the Navajo sacred mountains. Navajo people feel protected there, on the basis of their understanding of themselves as parts of a larger community of life sharing in a special form of existence established in the charter between the Nihookáá Dine'é and the Holy

People. As Hanson Ashley remarked, elderly Navajo in the past did not feel compelled to talk about the philosophical system that governed the construction and operation of this world; they simply "lived it."

Contemporary Navajo live in an increasingly complex world in which they must navigate between numerous powerful cultural systems, including the Navajo system or systems and the Euro-American system or systems. Changes in the modern world have altered the lived experience of Navajo people. In recent years, Navajo elders, intellectuals, tribal administrators, and educators have come to believe that they must talk about the Navajo philosophical system in order to educate contemporary Navajo people in how best to use it as a means for coping with contemporary problems. In an effort to understand who they are as a people, where they come from, how their world works, and where they are going as a nation, they have objectified, dissected, and analyzed that which was formerly only experienced. This "talking" has resulted in an opening up of communication among Navajo people from diverse backgrounds and persuasions—monolingual, bilingual, college educated, traditionally educated—as well as among Navajo people and outsiders. My research directly benefited from this trend, which, coupled with improvements in translation, has created new access to information, new perspectives, and, ultimately, new understandings.

My use of the role of effect as a framework within which to analyze Navajo notions of the human body, self, and personhood offers insight into Navajo views on these topics and sheds light on the complex ways in which system and practice interact in the modern Navajo world. Study of Navajo notions of effect as expressions of structural paradigms demonstrates that among the Navajo, as researchers have found among peoples throughout Melanesia, Southeast Asia, and Africa, philosophical constructs—not a universal human biology—govern understandings of the human body, self, and personhood. For this reason, information gleaned from the personal narratives contained in this book offers insights that might help extend disciplinary theory and practice through the application to native North America of lessons learned through analysis of societies elsewhere in the world. It might also expand anthropological theories of cross-cultural constructions of the human body, self, personhood, and systems of knowledge, contribute to more general understandings of Navajo views on these topics, and even help to further sensitize those charged with the delivery of health care and social services on the Navajo reservation.

The Navajo people with whom I consulted clearly consider their universe to be prior to humans, and humans to be made in the image of aspects of the universe that preceded them. They acknowledge that all members of this community of life are constructed of the same fundamental elements, share structure, and relate to each other as kin. Recognizing that diverse persons—baskets, looms, cradles, hooghan, masks, jish, or humans—may be constructed from a multitude of different components—pollen, rain, sound, turquoise, breath, sunray, jet, wind, lightning, abalone—they consider all these materials to be reducible to the primordial elements of the First World. As individual persons are formed, live a specified life cycle, and disintegrate, their compositional living elements—moisture, air, substance, heat, and vibration—are continuously formulated and reformulated to construct new entities whose structure, process, and use follow the paradigms established in the construction of the world at the place of emergence.

These paradigms, outlined in the origin and creation stories, established a world in which all life forms were constructed and interacted on the basis of three metaphorical principles—homology, complementarity, and synecdoche. At a fundamental level these constructs structure and define all aspects of life in the Navajo world, including the human body, self, personhood, and effect. This makes all persons in the Navajo world homologues. In the construction of basket, hooghan, cradle, and loom persons, directional orientation is maintained regarding sunwise movement, the trajectory of growth, and the need for a "way out." Wholes are made up of dual integrated components, as evidenced in the contrasting yet complementary nature of the left and right, male and female, and naayéé'jí and hózhóójí aspects of all entities. In thinking, planning, and doing, directional orientation is maintained through sunwise movement, adherence to the trajectory of growth, and close attention to the complementary sides or aspects of all Navajo persons. In addition, the principle of synecdoche dictates that every part is equivalent to the whole, so anything done to, or by means of, a part is held to take effect upon, or have the effect of, the whole.

Changing Woman constructed the first Nihookáá Dine'é from the primordial elements in accordance with these life-defining paradigms. As a result, the conception and subsequent development of contemporary Nihookáá Dine'é involve bodily fluids from the mother and father, powerful influences from the sacred mountains, and one type of blood from each clan with which the child is associated. Through this shared substance, each clan influences the development of the tenet of Navajo philosophy and the bodily system associated with its respective cardinal direction. In combination, these various elements, factors, and influences form a web of interconnection that anchors every Navajo person within the larger sphere of the Navajo universe.

The materials used in constructing the original Nihookáá Dine'é correlate directly with parts of the human body and other aspects of persons in the contemporary world. Air plays a pivotal role in the animation of every contemporary Navajo. Once an infant breathes and cries, the constitution of its body begins to change from soft to firm. The nature of the specific winds that enter a child after birth determine his or her personal characteristics. The air circulating in, through, and out of the body forms small winds over the entire surface of the body that make moving, talking, and thinking possible. The direction of Nihookáá Dine'é thought is sunwise, in accord with the plan for life embodied in the ceremonial basket. Hair is a physical embodiment of thought and lifelong knowledge. Because of this association, the Holy People gave the Nihookáá Dine'é strict rules for manipulation of the hair at specific stages in the life cycle and for careful everyday grooming. To enable Nihookáá Dine'é to think effectively, the Diyin Dine'é directed them to wear their hair in the traditional bun.

In addition to the sunwise wrapping of hair in the bun, structural homology among Nihookáá Dine'é and all other persons in the Navajo world entails the sunwise directionality found in the whorls at the back of the top of the head and on toes and fingertips; attention to the trajectory of growth in ceremonial contexts; the need for a "way out"; and duality. Navajo views on the cultural construction of the human body and personhood reveal that Nihookáá Dine'é embody the essence of duality—the pairing of contrasting but complementary components to make a whole.

The left-hand side of every individual is naayéé' k'ehjigo, the "warrior" or male side of the person, while the right-hand side is hózhǫ́ǫ́jigo, the "peaceful" or female side. According to the teachings of the Diyin Dine'é, the contrast between sides reflects dual facets of every trait or aspect of self-awareness and personhood, which has aggressive and passive as well as protecting and blessing facets. The hózhǫ́ǫ́jigo and naayéé' k'ehjigo aspects of the individual contribute to the development and maintenance of a physically, emotionally, mentally, and spiritually harmonious person. To be whole and remain harmonious, all Navajo must respect the maleness and the femaleness within themselves.

In recognition of these shared aspects of personhood and the complex network of effect that results from them, Navajo people acknowledge themselves as being fundamentally interconnected to every aspect of the world in which they carry out the activities of living. "You are a product of your whole environment. Now, it goes with you every place that you go. Your family, your household, and then like, you know, if I don't like you I can, I can go over there and do something to the ground that you walk on. You know, I find your footprint and bury something there, you know, because that is always a part of you, around your house" (Harry Walters, Tsaile, Arizona, 8/10/93).

The integration and interconnection fundamental to all life in the Navajo world is exquisitely demonstrated and reinforced in ceremonial contexts. When illness occurs because of imbalance, or when a new stage of life is broached, the structural aspects of the individual play important roles. The trajectory of growth and the distinction between the masculine and feminine sides of the human body are carefully observed in ceremonial manipulations of the body. In accord with the respective protecting and blessing aspects associated with the sides of the body, certain activities are exclusively done with, or to, the right or the left side of the body. Anything having to do with blessing and goodwill involves the right hand and side, while activities having to do with protecting are exclusively done with the left hand and side. Depending on the nature of the ceremony, the singer starts with either the right- or the left-hand side when applying blessing or protecting materials to individuals. Manipulations begin on the right and move to the left during ceremonies associated with blessing, and applications start on the left and move to the right in protection ceremonies. A variety of materials may be ceremonially applied to points on the patient's body, from the soles of the feet to the top of the head, as well as to the bodies of participating family members. Each application forms a permanent layer of protection on the surface of the body; as a result, people acquire multiple layers of protection during their lifetimes. In addition, a clear pathway or "way out" for expulsion of harmful phenomena is required.

Although Navajo healing ceremonies purport to focus on "the patient," the individual is not singled out for treatment. Instead, as Harry Walters notes, the "whole sphere" within which the patient is intimately connected on the personal, social, and cosmic realms is treated. "In the ceremony you don't just treat the physical being, you treat the mental, plus the spouse, the children, the household, the livestock, you know, the air that the patient is going to breathe, the earth that he is going to walk on, the water he is going to drink, the fire that he is going to use. Everything, you know, like you're, in this sphere you are one individual. So the treatment is to treat all of those, the whole sphere" (Walters, 8/10/93).

Understanding one's place in this sphere requires contextualization. Personal accounts document how individuals cope with dilemmas such as a child's having incessant nosebleeds or a child's being born with six fingers. Navajo people place problems like these within the context of their philosophical system. The Navajo cultural system governing the construction of fetuses dictates that fetuses are extremely malleable and susceptible to effect, and that the nature of an illness or problem contracted by a child in the womb is often patterned after the cause. Therefore, the nosebleed problem can be seen to have been caused by a father's inadvertent exposure to a fatal automobile accident. The deformity of the child's hands can be considered to have been caused by its mother's use of a six-prong weaving fork while pregnant. If the mother's behavior had been detected by an observant elder, the risk to the child could have been circumvented through timely performance of a Blessing Way, an effective means for correcting anticipated problems. Beyond relieving parental anxiety, answers such as these affirm the power of the cultural system.

Acknowledging that in order to acquire full Navajo personhood all new members of the family need guidance through the developmental stages of life, people use this system on a daily basis to fulfill personal wants and desires. For example, a woman who wants a son, a father who needs a good herder, an aunt who wants her nephew to be generous, a grandfather who wants his granddaughter to think properly, and a grandmother who wants her granddaughter to become a scholar all make conscious choices to manipulate the effects transferred to the body at critical points in the life cycle. Navajo people direct their efforts toward controlling and manipulating the potentially positive effects while limiting the negative effects of various substances, actions, and events on the development of children. Concerned elders seek to protect particular parts of the body, such as blood, hair, or umbilical cords, that are deemed more susceptible to effect than others, and to limit exposure of the human body to effect at critical times in the life cycle, such as in utero, at birth, and at puberty, when it is considered to be more open to effect.

The paradigms established by the Holy People governing the cultural construction of the body, self, and personhood offer guidance regarding how best to foster the development of persons through manipulation and treatments at critical points in the life cycle. Family members guide children through every step toward personhood in the Navajo world, beginning with the child's sex. Tradition provides a variety of means by which the sex of a child can be influenced before conception or during pregnancy, including the application of pollens or white shell directly to the mother's body, the wearing of white shell or turquoise, the ingestion of aragonite, white shell, or particular parts of sheep, and the power of prayer. The woman who wants a son may either eat the windpipe of a sheep or wear turquoise while pregnant to fulfill her desire.

Today, virtually all Navajo children are born in hospitals, but many traditional techniques for assisting births and caring for newborns and mothers are incorporated into the hospital birthing experience in modern facilities across the reservation. Families are allowed to have ceremonial practitioners come to the hospital to perform ceremonies for mother and child, and relatives are free to administer the child's first pollen blessing, mold the child, administer herbal medicines, bind the mother with a sash, or conduct whatever other practices they deem necessary. Staff at reservation hospitals are sensitive to family concerns over the care and disposal of the placenta, the water used in the child's first bath, the child's first stool, and the umbilical cord, because handling of these materials can have lifelong effects on mother or child. Placentas are taken home from the hospital to be buried, placed in a live bush or tree, or placed in another location of special significance to the family. Special care is taken with the umbilical cord after it dries and separates from the child. Cords, which may be placed in one of a variety of locations to influence the child's future occupation and personal proclivities, are most frequently buried to anchor the child to Mother Earth and establish a lifelong connection between an individual and a specific place. The father who wants or needs a competent herder may fulfill his need by placing a child's umbilical cord in a corral or on an animal, thereby assuring the development of herding skills.

Relatives again draw on the Navajo cultural system to guide young relations when, at the age of four to six months, the child laughs for the first time. This event is the occasion for the First Laugh ceremony, at which the child's initial expression of emotion is celebrated. Relatives take this occasion to anchor the child's emotional life firmly within his or her social landscape by initiating him or her into the complex network of communication and reciprocity that operates within extended families. The child gives a token amount of natural rock salt—and meat or other gifts if finances allow—to all relatives in attendance. The aunt who wants her nephew to be generous can attain her goal by insisting that he have a First Laugh ceremony, thereby encouraging his future generosity and ensuring that he will never be stingy.

Traditional wisdom dictates that Nihookáá Dine'é should never cut their hair. Adjustments to this belief have been forged through negotiation of multiple cultural systems. As a result, a child's hair may now be cut when it utters its first comprehensible words in a language of the Earth Surface People, or when its fontanel closes, or both. These developments are significant because they demonstrate simultaneously the child's developing control over voice and a weakening of the child's connection to the Holy People. In some families, male and female children are treated differently when they utter their first words. Many Navajo people believe that whereas it is appropriate for a boy to have his hair cut at this time, a girl's hair should not be cut until after her Kinaaldá. The grandfather who is concerned that his granddaughter maintain the ability to think properly could accomplish his goal by insisting that her hair not be cut and by encouraging her to wear her hair in a traditional bun.

The main themes established in the treatment of children at birth—bathing, molding, and blessing—continue at puberty. Pubescent boys and girls may be expected to run, grind corn, and be painted or dressed to ensure acquisition of lifelong characteristics deemed beneficial to success in the modern world. These ceremonies are used to instill desired skills and to guide contemporary Navajo young people into the earliest stages of adulthood. The grandmother who wants her granddaughter to become a scholar can ensure that the necessary qualities are transferred to the young woman by asking the Ideal Woman to mold her granddaughter with books or pencils during her Kinaaldá.

Personal narratives of efforts on the part of parents or other relatives to instill in their loved ones the skills and propensities deemed necessary for success in the modern world offer insights into how Navajo people manipulate and adjust the methods and theories inherited from the past to accommodate modern wants, needs, and desires. These narratives convey a powerful educational message to Navajo young people about the strength and efficacy of their cultural system.

APPLICATIONS IN THE HEALTH CARE
AND SOCIAL SERVICE REALMS

Beyond serving as an educational tool of potential use in Navajo and non-Navajo classrooms, information gleaned from personal accounts like those contained in this book has tremendous practical potential in the health care and social services realms. By offering a more comprehensive understanding of Navajo views on the human body, self, personhood, and effect than has previously been available, such information may yield valuable insights to biomedical health care providers and policymakers who are faced with introducing new methods of diagnosis, new technologies, or new therapy programs for chronic health and social problems on the Navajo reservation—diabetes, hypertension, obesity, teen pregnancy, and a spiraling population.

Under the guidance of Navajo experts, an educational program for the prevention of hypertension, diabetes, and obesity, or for the health maintenance of patients suffering from these conditions, could be developed that is based firmly on the Navajo system governing the cultural construction of health and illness. In an ideal world, such a program would call for a return to traditional foods—homegrown fruits, vegetables, and grains, wild plant foods, and meat from game as well as domestic animals. With land shortages, dependence on a cash economy, and, by extension, dependence on commercially processed foods, such a return simply is not feasible. An effective program, however, could be developed by incorporating biomedical views on nutrition into the Navajo theories of life.

For example, a direct correlation could be made between each of the four food groups of biomedical nutritional theory—meat, dairy products, grains, and fruits and vegetables—and a quadrant of the Navajo fourfold cosmology (see figs. 3 and 6). By extension, each food group could be linked to the cardinal point, sacred mountain, color, ntł'iz, time of day, time of year, phase of life, clan, bodily system, and tenet of Navajo education associated with that quadrant. Thus, an educational program emphasizing the attainment of harmony through a balanced diet could ground contemporary nutrition in the teachings of the Diyin Dine'é.

In regard to teen pregnancy and population concerns, I believe that teaching the roles of men and women in Navajo society as protectors and nurturers, respectively, is fundamental to educating Navajo youth. To be effective in the modern world, such a program must stress the powers possessed by traditional Navajo men and women who were armed with ancestral knowledge. For example, valuable lessons for young Navajo women lie in traditional knowledge about how to determine the sex of an unborn child and how to space pregnancies through breast-feeding and abstinence—knowledge that empowered their mothers and grandmothers. A similar program, emphasizing personal responsibility and abstinence, could be developed for the education of young Navajo men. An under-standing of traditional Navajo men and women as individuals with knowledge that equaled power and gave volition should strengthen self-esteem and instill a sense of self-determination in Navajo youth. The empowerment is traditional; contem-porary means can simply be synthesized into the Navajo model.

Whether programs are developed along these or other lines, the federal and state health care and social services systems serving Navajo people must become firmly grounded in Navajo understandings of the body, self, and personhood be-fore they can become fully effective. It is my hope, therefore, that this book will contribute to ongoing efforts by Navajo and non-Navajo experts alike to find new ways of incorporating Navajo theories into contemporary policies and practices.

CONTRIBUTIONS TO ANTHROPOLOGICAL UNDERSTANDINGS OF SELF AND PERSONHOOD

The structural principle of synecdoche informs Navajo notions of self and person, as well as human relationships. Both the awareness Navajo people have of them-selves as perceptible subjects—the self—and the social construct based on cultur-ally sanctioned rules governing rights, prerogatives, and agency embodied in the corporeal body—the person—are informed by the principle of synecdoche. This principle dictates that the boundaries of every individual extend around the full area in which parts of his or her body and thoughts exist. To maximize positive effect and minimize negative effect, Navajo people must demonstrate personal responsibility over parts and substances of their own bodies and those of children, because body parts and bodily substances can affect the health and welfare of the individual and, by extension, his or her kin, long past detachment or elimination. Without doubt, understanding of the potential consequences that may result from propitious or careless handling or disposal of detached body parts (hair and fin-gernails) and bodily secretions (saliva, blood, skin oil, and urine) influences Navajo perceptions of themselves as individuals with volition, as well as their perceptions of the web of interconnection that anchors them within the larger sphere.

The Navajo people with whom I consulted clearly have awareness of them-selves as individuals with volition (an independent and autonomous sense of iden-tity), yet they tend to highlight relations with other people and entities (an inter-dependent or relational sense of identity) over personal autonomy. The Navajo case, therefore, lends support to critiques of the position that an "interdependent or relational" sense of self is most frequently associated with non-Western soci-eties while an "independent or autonomous" sense of self is most frequently found in Western societies—critiques that clearly demonstrate how both forms of identification are experienced by Western and non-Western people in various contexts (Ewing 1990; Holland 1992).[1] The delicate balance negotiated between these two forms of identity is acutely demonstrated in the context of Naayéé'jí, or Protection Way, ceremonies, in which harmful factors directed at family members must be resolved through neutralization or return to their source.

> HW The Naayéé'jí ceremonies can also be used against people. . . . See what they are doing, they are protecting themselves from that [the harmful factors that have been directed against members of the family]. At the same time, you know, sometimes they would say, "Now that we have gotten all of this in order, what do you want to do with it?" Some say, "Send it back, we don't want it." . . . "Now that we have harnessed that, protected ourselves with that, what should we do with that?" And then sometimes they say, "We'll give it back to them. Since it came from them let them have it." And that is witchcraft. Other singers say, "No, I don't do that, I was taught never to say that. So therefore, we are just going to bury it right here. End it. Protect ourselves." . . . This is why we should always watch what we say. Especially [to] your children, your brothers and sisters. What you say to them, you know, they are a part of you, you know, you are saying [it] to yourself. This is why things like that, ceremonies like that, you know, you should never, if you say, if you have a real close relative and you say, "Hey, they are witching me. I want a protection ceremony." And you sent those things back, it's going to, you are a part of that family. This is what people don't realize. And they think they can turn and say, "You can work against that guy," you know, your uncle, or brother or someone and they never think that it is going to affect you [themselves]. . . . There is a fine line between protection and evil. And this is what people don't understand, see? If that man is your relative, you're also working against you [yourself].
>
> MS If you send evil towards a relative you're working against yourself because you're part of the relative?
>
> HW [Nods his head]. You're part of that. You're part of that. So this is why when you learn, when you learn the Protection Way ceremony, you know, you have to demonstrate responsibility. Otherwise you could do great damage. So, by knowing all of these and keeping that under control, and using that to the advantage of the good, is the ultimate goal, sǫ'ah naagháí bik'eh hózhǫ. Sǫ'ah naagháí is the negative side, [bik'eh] hózhǫ is, uh, uh, the hózhǫǫ-

jí [positive] side, but all together these are hózhǫ, is beauty. . . .
When they work [together] then you have balance. (Harry Walters, Tsaile, Arizona, 8/10/93)

The principle of synecdoche dictates that when a family chooses to direct the
harmful factors back to their source, the family ultimately threatens its own members. This principle operates within a relational framework that defines, codifies,
and delineates who or what can affect what or whom under specific circumstances.
This relational context shifts emphasis from the part (the individual) to the whole
(the social sphere) and, I contend, bridges the gap between the Navajo sense of
the self—perceptions of individuality and individual volition—and the Navajo person—the sum of the socially sanctioned rules governing rights, prerogatives, and
agency embodied in the corporeal body. That is, the complex network of effect
inherent in the Navajo world, a network that makes every human part of and dependent on the kinship group and the community of life, including plants, animals,
and aspects of the cosmos, also conflates the "self" into the "person."[2]

These findings contribute to the "critical anthropology of selfhood" current in
anthropological discourse (Battaglia 1995) by raising the following question: Does
the privileging of the interdependent or relational sense of self by individuals in
particular societies directly correlate with the presence or absence of the principle
of synecdoche? A reexamination of information available from societies worldwide—Western and non-Western alike—known to have magic, witchcraft, sorcery, or other methods intended to affect people through manipulation of detached parts of the body or bodily substances might shed light on cross-cultural
notions of selfhood and personhood. Systematic comparison of societies worldwide should be directed at discovering what correlation, if any, exists between the
principle of synecdoche and notions of self and person, as well as determining
whether beliefs about the extension of the boundaries of the body and personhood in these societies parallel those held by Navajo people. Further investigation
along these lines would, I am convinced, demonstrate that the principle of synecdoche bridges the gap between "self" and "person" in many societies, as it does in
the Navajo world.

CONTRIBUTION TO ANTHROPOLOGICAL MODELS
OF KNOWLEDGE

Navajo narratives about the variable effects particular events, substances, or behaviors can have on individuals and their kin reveal no uniform body of knowledge
that can comfortably be labeled as the Navajo theory of the human body, self, and

personhood, known and understood by all Navajo people. Instead, they reveal multiple levels of understanding based on age, gender, clan affiliations, and specialized knowledge, as well as multiple levels of philosophical abstraction that individuals can attain. Because of the individual nature of the transference of knowledge, parallel theories and bodies of knowledge coexist that can appear contradictory when compared by an outside observer unaware of factors such as gender and age restrictions or the twelve levels of abstraction fundamental to the Navajo cultural system of knowledge. These various bodies of knowledge present no conflict to Navajo people, for it is generally understood that personal access is limited by factors such as individual proclivities, one's stage of life, and one's reproductive capacity. It is widely acknowledged that only certain people know about menstrual restrictions, healing techniques, and other topics.

Individual explanations affirm that although homology, complementarity, and synecdoche are the structuring principles that frame relations among all persons in the Navajo world, a complex interplay exists between structure and agency. While it is true that the sum total of any person's knowledge is limited, insofar as he or she has access to, and understanding of, only some of the diverse methods and theories established by the Holy People, a range of possible solutions to specific problems exists. Performance of ceremonial activities is readily adjusted to fit the availability of materials and knowledge—if there is no white corn for sale locally, yellow corn will be substituted; if no singer of this ceremony lives in the area, another ceremony will be performed instead. When faced with day-to-day problems and concerns, Navajo people consider options, make choices, and negotiate solutions within the limitations of personal knowledge and access. They choose among the solutions at their disposal to maximize personal advantage and at the same time fit personal circumstances. These adjustments, within the broader context of the partial nature of all individual knowledge, constitute everyday life, which is the Navajo cultural system as it is lived, transferred, practiced, and experienced.

Following on the heels of more than a century of prior investigation into Navajo culture and society, the insights gained through understanding the twelve-level system of knowledge underlying personal and collective knowledge in the Navajo world raise a question of broader anthropological concern: To what extent have prior studies in other societies failed to reveal the full intricacy of knowledge systems? It has been long realized that multiple systems of knowledge exist within all societies—specialized occupational knowledge, for example, or knowledge limited by age or gender. The Navajo case, however, gives us cause to wonder to what extent other societies have overarching systems with inherent degrees of abstraction—layers or levels—that simultaneously integrate all bodies of specialized knowledge into the larger system while differentiating individual understandings of those same bodies of specialized knowledge.

These questions remain for future research endeavors. By offering a single example among many of the sophistication and eloquence of Native American philosophical systems, it is my hope that this partial explication of the complex beliefs structuring Navajo understandings of the human body, self, personhood, and effect will serve to increase respect for the native peoples of North America and encourage more scholars to investigate the intellectual systems of native peoples throughout the Americas with the powerful theoretical tools currently available.

NOTES

Introduction

1. It is beyond the scope of this work to summarize the voluminous literature extant on Navajo culture and society. Countless works have been published on the Navajo since their contact with Europeans and Euro-Americans; indeed, by some accounts, the Navajo are the most studied people in the world. Several bibliographies of publications on the Navajo are readily available (Kluckhohn 1940; Correll, Watson, and Brugge 1969, 1973; Iverson 1976). In addition, monographs on Navajo history and ethnography published prior to 1982, museum collections with substantial holdings of Navajo materials, and photographic records of Navajo life are summarized in Brugge (1983: 498–501). Concise overviews of the Navajo ceremonial system are available in Frisbie (1987: 1–10) and Griffin-Pierce (1992: 10–28).

2. This story fits well with master narratives documenting the migration of the first Americans across the Bering land bridge into what is today North America, and their dispersal through North, Middle, and South America between 15,000 and 35,000 years ago (Cavalli-Sforza 1991: 105). Linguistic and physical evidence supports the theory that the Americas were settled by at least three separate population movements. The three successful populations, in order of migration, are Amerind, Na-Dene, and Aleut-Eskimo (Greenberg, Turner, and Zegura 1986). The Navajo are members of the Athapaskan language family, deriving from the Na-Dene. At the time of European contact, Athapaskan-speaking groups inhabited a vast region that stretched from what is now the western interior of Alaska through the northern interior of Canada, and from the Yukon and British Columbia eastward to the western shores of Hudson Bay. Other regions inhabited by Athapaskan speakers are the Pacific coast states of Washington, Oregon, and California, and the southwestern United States. Linguistic diversification, which is used as a measure of the proximity of language groups to each other over time, indicates that "the diversity within Athapaskan as a whole is no greater than that within the northern group of Athapaskan languages and that the internal diversity of the Southern Athapaskan group is considerably less" (Hale and Harris 1979: 172).

These linguistic studies give rise to the view that the center of dispersal was in the north. Specialists agree that the Southern Athapaskan peoples came from the area of greatest population concentration in the Mackenzie Basin of Canada. Lexico-statistical data, which provide clues to the time of language-group separations, suggest that the Southern and Northern groups split well within the past 1,000 to 1,300 years (Gunnerson 1979: 162; Hale and Harris 1979: 172; Greenberg, Turner, and Zegura 1986: 479).

There is considerably less consensus regarding the length of time involved in the southerly movements, the route or routes taken by the early migrants, and whether more than one migration was involved (Opler 1983:381). An intermontane route through what is now Utah or Colorado and the Great Basin is supported by Julian Steward (1937, 1940), Betty and Harold Huscher (1942), and Morris Opler (1983). James Gunnerson (1956), James Hester (1962), and David Wilcox (n.d.) support a migration southwest through the northwestern and central plains close to the eastern edge of the Rocky Mountains. Estimates of the date of arrival of the Navajo in the Southwest range from A.D. 1000 to 1525. Whatever the migration route or routes may have been, the Querechos, as the Navajo were called by the Spanish explorers, were occupying Diné-tah when first contacted by the Spaniards in Antonio de Espejo's expedition in 1582 (Forbes 1960:57).

3. While readily acknowledging themselves as situated subjects who were in positions to "know" certain things but not to have access to other bodies of knowledge, the Navajo people with whom I consulted consistently referred to the "natural order"—the Navajo philosophical system that consists of the paradigms established by the Navajo Holy People during their construction of the Navajo universe—as if it were a cohesive whole. Hence, all totalizing statements found in the text, such as "the Navajo system" or "the Navajo view," are meant simply to refer to this philosophical system in the manner employed by the Navajo consultants with whom I conferred.

4. Oscar Tso, from White Valley, Arizona, is an educator and educational administrator who, at the time of this writing, teaches at Cottonwood Elementary School in Cottonwood, Arizona.

Chapter 1. Comparative Views on the Body, Personhood, and Effect

1. I use the term "effect" to refer to the power or ability one thing has to produce consequences or results on another thing.

2. To the best of my knowledge, this is the first such study in a contemporary native North American society. A solid core of prior works on related topics exists upon which to build: *Soul Concepts of the Navaho* (1943) and *Navaho Sacrificial Figurines* (1947) by Berard Haile; "Some Sex Beliefs and Practices in a Navaho Community" (1950) by Flora Bailey; "The Anatomical Atlas of the Navajo with Illustrations" (1971) by Martha Austin and colleagues; *Navajo Figurines Called Dolls* (1972) by Roger Kelly, R. W. Lang, and Harry Walters; *Holy Wind in Navajo Philosophy* (1981) by James McNeley; *Anthropology of Space: Explorations into the Natural Philosophy and Semantics of the Navajo* (1983) by Rik Pinxten, Ingrid van Dooren, and Frank Harvey; "The Sore That Does Not Heal: Cause and Concept in the Navajo Experience of Cancer" (1989) by Thomas Csordas; and, most recently, "Cultural Interpretations and Intracultural Variability in Navajo Beliefs about Breastfeeding" (1993) by Anne Wright and colleagues. Because these works are largely descriptive, I had to look elsewhere for theoretical insights.

3. Since the Victorian search for universal laws of human life, every generation of anthropologists has investigated such effects in specific cultures, and interest continues today (Nemeroff and Rozin 1994). Over the years, various terms have been used by anthropologists to refer to this type of influence, including "mana" (Mauss 1972 [1902]),

"pollution" (Douglas 1966), "taboo" (Leach 1964), "taint" (Jackson 1989), and "contagion" (Nemeroff and Rozin 1994). According to *Webster's Unabridged Dictionary,* "to pollute" is to make foul or unclean, or to defile. "Taint" refers to the action by which one thing physically infects, spoils, or injures another. "Contagions" contaminate and make impure or corrupt what they have contact with. I purposefully use "effect" in place of pollutant, taint, or contagion, owing to the predominantly negative connotations associated with these latter terms. It is crucial to use a neutral term, because in the Navajo world the influence one thing can have on another is inherently both positive and negative. That is, something can have either beneficial or harmful influence depending on the circumstances.

4. It is beyond the scope of this work to attempt to summarize the vast literature on the body that has developed over the last two decades. I refer the reader to John Blacking (1977), Margaret Lock (1993), Chris Shilling (1993), Anthony Synnott (1993, esp. pp. 228–64), and Brenda Farnell (1995:1–28).

5. In this work, the term "self" is used to refer to the awareness Navajo people have of themselves as perceptible subjects and and to the ways in which that awareness and that experience of themselves are culturally shaped. The term "person" refers to the social construct based on culturally sanctioned rules governing rights, prerogatives, and agency embodied in the corporeal body. As will be demonstrated through analysis of the rules governing association and effect, these constructs are inextricably linked in the Navajo world.

6. The theme of how the sharing, ingestion, or expulsion of gendered substances contributes to the development of the body and personhood was taken up by several researchers in Melanesia. This focus was central to Gillian Gillison's work among the Gimi (1980), to Gilbert Herdt's work among the Sambia (1981, 1982a, 1982b), to Fritz Poole's work among the Bimin-Kuskusmin (1981), and to Debbora Battaglia's work among the Sabarl (1990). For example, Gimi men induce vomiting by performing cane-swallowing to expel the effects of female substance, and Gimi women eat the bodies of deceased males to regain the male element lost through menstruation and childbirth (Gillison 1980:150, 157). Sambia youths undergo a six-stage initiation process of masculinization (Herdt 1981:203–54). Central to this initiation process is oral ingestion of semen, which is believed to be necessary for the development of secondary sex traits—a muscular body, pubescent glans penis, facial hair, voice change, and semen (Herdt 1981:218–19, 234–36). Ardent attention to systematic ingestion of male substance (semen), controlled expulsion of female substance (blood), and limited expulsion of male substance (semen) during heterosexual activities is needed to develop and subsequently maintain maleness in the Sambia world.

Ingestion of bodily substances other than semen and blood has been found to affect personhood in Africa and elsewhere. For example, in his study of child development in Fulani society, Paul Riesman learned that beyond its contribution to nutrition and development of the physical body, breast milk has lasting effect on the development of Fulani personhood. The moral qualities of the mother are passed to her children in breast milk (Riesman 1992:163). A parallel view about the transmission of personal characteristics through breast milk is found among the Navajo. In their study of Navajo beliefs about breast-feeding, Anne Wright and her colleagues (1993:786) learned that in the Navajo view a nursing mother is feeding the child "a part of herself," which marks the child both as her own and as human. Breast-feeding passes on traditional values (making the child better behaved) as well as some of a mother's own attributes (Wright et al. 1993:786–89). I have not personally investigated Navajo beliefs about breast milk. The findings of Wright et al. (1993), however, exemplify the Navajo beliefs about synecdoche and personhood discussed in this work.

7. Regina Hadley Lynch of Rough Rock, Arizona, is a member the Towering House Clan. She is a mother and grandmother who has been involved in the development of bilingual educational curricula for over two decades. She currently works for Northern Arizona University.

8. Orthography of Navajo terms in excerpts from interviews conducted by the author or in the text follows Austin and Lynch (1983) and Young and Morgan (1987, 1992). Orthography of Navajo terms in passages quoted from other publications are left as they appear in the original text.

9. For further information regarding the living nature of such entities, see Charlotte Frisbie (1987, esp. pp. 9, 118–19, 421–22) on *jish*, or medicine bundles; Trudy Griffin-Pierce (1992, esp. pp. 6, 55–62, 190–95) on sandpaintings; and Wesley Thomas (1996) on handwoven textiles and weaving tools.

10. Mae Bekis of Tó'tsoh, Arizona, is a singer of the Blessing Way ceremony. She is a mother and grandmother who actively campaigns for the rights of Navajo seniors.

11. Harry Walters is a husband, father, and grandfather from Cove, Arizona. Professor Walters demonstrates his profound commitment to the preservation of Navajo culture on a daily basis in his dual role as Chairman of Diné Studies and Director of the Ned Hatathli Cultural Center Museum at Navajo Community College in Tsaile, Arizona.

12. Anthropological interest in metaphoric structures such as homology and complementarity is not new. A substantial body of literature exists on homologous relationships, which are commonly constructed among physical topography, domestic architecture, social arrangements, and parts of the human body (see, for example, Griaule 1965; Reichel-Dolmatoff 1971; Turner 1980; Bastien 1985). Such homologies simultaneously create and reproduce the dominant social and moral order through time and space, constituting a culturally constructed landscape that is accepted as "natural" by the people living it (Lock 1993:135). Anthropologists have employed a wealth of theoretical approaches to understand the human predilection to organize the raw materials of experience and social life into binary contrastive domains or dualities. Claude Lévi-Strauss used such contrastive categories as a means for reducing the complexities of life to "hidden elementary structures" that he believed shed light on the universal aspects of the human mind. He concluded that it was a fundamental property of the human mind to think in opposites, and he posited that the most fundamental oppositions are self/other and nature/culture (Lévi-Strauss 1966 [1962]:191–216). Dualism in social life and symbolic classification has been taken up by numerous anthropologists as the means for understanding a variety of social phenomena, from dietary restrictions to maintenance of social distinctions. These works include the pioneering work of Robert Hertz on the preeminence of the right hand (1973 [1909]), the cross-cultural comparison of lateral contrasts (left and right) (Needham 1973), an analysis of dual organizations as mechanisms for attainment of harmony and order (Maybury-Lewis and

Almagor 1989), and, more recently, symbolic models of division (the world) and unity (the human body) in African cosmology and experience (Jacobson-Widding 1991).

13. In part as a response to the reductionism of structuralism, since the 1970s there has been a clear shift in cultural anthropological analysis from underlying structures to experience and the practices of ordinary life. In his influential *Outline of a Theory of Practice* (1977), Pierre Bourdieu detailed a method that transcended the subjective-objective opposition and got at the dialectical relationship between structure and agency. Continuing in the tradition of social theorists influenced by Max Weber's placement of the actor in the center of his model of social life, practice theorists emphasize the way cultural systems constrain action by controlling the definition of the world for actors, limiting their conceptual tools, and restricting their emotional repertoires (Ortner 1984: 153).

Following Bourdieu's lead, anthropologists began studying the social activities of daily life under the rubrics of praxis, action, and interaction to explain the complex relationships that exist between "human action" and some global entity referred to as "the system" (see, for example, Comaroff 1985; Ortner 1989; McCloskey 1993). Routines and daily scenarios are studied because they "are predicated upon, and embody within themselves, the fundamental notions of temporal, spatial, and social ordering that underlie and organize the system as a whole. In enacting these routines, actors not only continue to be shaped by the underlying organizational principles involved, but continually re-endorse those principles in the world of public observation and discourse" (Ortner 1984: 154). Practice theory was initially developed in opposition to classic structuralist analyses, but structure and practice are inextricably linked in daily life.

14. Prior studies of the metaphors of Navajo worldview (Witherspoon 1977; Farella 1984; Pinxten and Farrer 1990) serve as a foundation from which to extend understanding through application of new approaches to metaphor. These approaches focus on the "predictive and performative" aspects of metaphor that serve as a backdrop for understanding human experience, action, and interaction (Fernandez 1991: 7). In contrast to structuralist approaches, which saw metaphoric structures as static and elementary, an interactionist approach holds that metaphoric significance comes through the linking of domains of experience through action and interaction. Domains are reorganized as parts of a more powerfully integrated totality. This linking often results from ritual action in special circumstances such as healing or puberty ceremonies. See Turner 1991: 121–58 for an analysis of this point using Bororo, Kayapo, and Nuer data.

Chapter 2. Ancestral Knowledge in the Contemporary World

1. I interviewed Jennifer Jackson of Many Farms, Arizona, during her reign as Miss Navajo 1990–91.

2. No direct correlation exists between Euro-American notions of Navajo history and Navajo notions of their own history. A variety of different histories have been constructed about the Navajo since their initial contact with Europeans. David Brugge (1983) surveys the evidence on Navajo prehistory and history to 1850. Histories of the period of the "Long Walk" and Navajo internment at Hwéeldi (Fort Sumner, New Mex-

ico) have been based on Navajo remembrances (Roessel 1973; Bighorse 1990) as well as on military reports and other ethnohistorical documents (Correll 1979; Bailey 1988 [1964]). Robert Roessel (1980) supplies a pictorial history of the Navajo from 1860 to 1910 and a written history from 1850 to 1923 (1983). Peter Iverson (1981) presents a history of the development of the Navajo Nation, and Garrick and Roberta Bailey (1986) concentrate on the reservation years. Other histories focus on the rise of the Native American Church among the Navajo (Aberle 1982 [1966]), trading posts and traders (Gillmor and Wetherill 1953; McNitt 1962; Adams 1963; Moon 1992), individual crafts such as weaving (Amsden 1974 [1934]; Wheat 1977, 1979, 1988; Kent 1985) and sandpainting on boards (Parezo 1983), and the Navajo-Hopi land dispute (Kammer 1980; Feher-Elston 1988; Benedek 1993; Brugge 1994). Recent publications include an innovative and insightful historiography of the study of a single ceremony, the Night Way (Faris 1990). These histories constructed by Euro-Americans are each framed by a linear notion of time; therefore, historic events are objectified as "truth" and placed firmly in the past.

3. The account of the Navajo origin story given in this book is incomplete. More than four hundred individual accounts of the Navajo creation story have been transcribed to date; they vary widely in detail, but certain key elements are common to most recorded versions. Differences reflect personal factors such as the narrator's stage of life, clan affiliations, and ceremonial or other specialized knowledge acquired through occupational training. I rely largely on the versions documented by Goddard (1933), Haile (1981, and in Wyman 1970), Matthews (1994 [1897]), O'Bryan (1956), Yazzie (1971), and Zolbrod (1984), because they contain the most complete accounts of the events pertinent to my discussion. With the exception of Yazzie (1971), the accounts are limited by the fact that they were each collected from male consultants, the majority of whom had specialized training. In addition, many were heavily edited (see Zolbrod 1984:7–29 for an insightful and provocative discussion of the type of heavy editing done to make the stories conform to Victorian sensibilities). Only events critical to the central topics of this book are included in my summary, which serves as a general backdrop. Each of these events is analyzed in this or a subsequent chapter on the basis of information from contemporary sources, including the views of women and several Navajo people without specialized training.

4. Hanson Ashley of Shonto, Arizona, is employed as a mental health professional for the Indian Health Service. In addition, as a consultant to the Diné Philosophy of Learning program at Navajo Community College in Tsaile, Arizona, he specializes in translating ritual language for educators.

5. Sa'ah naagháí and bik'eh hózhǫ are ceremonial concepts relating, respectively, to "the essence of longevity (of the individual) and immortality (of the species)" and "the essence of harmony, peace, and order" (Young and Morgan 1992:1081). The terms are combined to form the ubiquitous phrase "sa'ah naagháí bik'eh hózhǫ," which can be glossed as "the essence of long life, harmony, and peace." This phrase is included in nearly every Navajo song and prayer. As noted by John Farella, for the last one hundred years outside researchers have attempted, with greater or lesser degrees of success, to define and codify these complex concepts by means of etymological analysis, abstrac-

tion, personification, or all three (1984:153–87). In Navajo oral history, Sạ'ah Naaghái and Bik'eh Hózhǫ́ are the forces fundamental to all life in the Navajo world (Witherspoon 1977:25–26). Contemporary Navajo philosophers consider Sạ'ah Naaghái (male) and Bik'eh Hózhǫ́ (female) to be separate but complementary beings who simultaneously embody and encapsulate the essence of the Navajo theory of life: duality. In this context, male and female refer to much more than mere biological sex. Navajo consultants use these terms to distinguish between the requisite complementary aspects of a whole; Sạ'ah Naaghái is the protecting component, and Bik'eh Hózhǫ́ is the blessing component.

6. Zolbrod refers to this as the fourth underworld and to these beings as First Man and First Woman (1984:50–51).

7. In Navajo philosophy, "Holy Wind gives life, thought, speech and the power of motion to all living things and serves as a means of communication between all elements of the living world" (McNeley 1981:1). For an analysis of the importance of wind to the Navajo, see James McNeley's Holy Wind in Navajo Philosophy (1981).

8. Nádleehé literally means "one who changes repeatedly." This term is currently used to refer to people of alternative genders in Navajo society.

9. Opinions vary regarding the physical appearance of the Navajo world as a whole. Some Navajo view this world as consisting of a slightly concave shallow disk covered by an inverted disk of similar form (Pinxten, van Dooren, and Harvey 1983:9, fig. 1). Other Navajo people conceive of the earth's surface as a flat circular form that is covered by an enormous transparent hooghan with the sacred mountains as its corner posts (Griffin-Pierce 1992:92, fig. 4.12). In either case, the boundaries of the Navajo universe are clearly delineated by the sacred mountains located in the east, south, west, and north. Hence, my use of the term "point(s)" rather than "direction(s)," which can imply the line in which a moving person or thing goes on to infinity. In light of the bounded nature of the Navajo world, when found throughout this work the term "direction(s)" should be understood as referring to the point(s) to which or from which a person or thing goes.

10. The relationship between "inner forms" and "Holy Winds" in Navajo philosophy is complex, and ethnographic interpretations of these concepts are fraught with ambiguity. Berard Haile equates "in-lying ones," or inner forms, with wind in the form of "wind souls" (Haile 1943). In his pioneering study Holy Wind in Navajo Philosophy (1981), McNeley distinguished between "inner forms" and "Holy Winds," noting that "important Holy Ones" were placed within the natural phenomena of the cardinal directions, whereas "Winds" were placed at the cardinal points (1981:22). In this work, McNeley associated a single, colored wind with each of the cardinal directions, stating that these winds influence individual humans on the earth's surface (McNeley 1981:32). More recently, during a discussion of the four foundational principles of Navajo education and philosophy at the Seventh Annual Navajo Studies Conference in Tsaile, Arizona, McNeley referred to a number of "Holy People" who are "natural teachers." He noted that a pair of such Holy People is identified with each of the cardinal directions (McNeley 1993). Avery Denny (8/11/93, 10/8/93) and Wilson Aronilth (1990:32) associate the following influential paired personages with the cardinal directions: Early

Dawn Boy and Early Dawn Girl (east), Blue Daylight Boy and Blue Daylight Girl (south), Yellow Evening Twilight Boy and Yellow Evening Twilight Girl (west), and Folding Darkness Boy and Folding Darkness Girl (north). Based on what I have learned to date, it remains unclear to me whether these personages are the inner forms of the sacred mountains at these cardinal points or another form of Holy People, and whether these personages reside *within* or *on* the sacred mountains or are instead associated *with* the cardinal directions.

11. Wilson Aronilth is a Navajo elder from Naschitti, New Mexico, who has taught a variety of courses at Navajo Community College since 1969, including Navajo philosophy and silversmithing.

12. These monsters played a vital role in Navajo explanations of the "mystery illness"—the hantavirus outbreak that claimed its first Navajo victim in May 1993 (Schwarz 1995).

13. I met Traci Michelle Begay, a mother from Ganado, Arizona, while she was a student at NCC in Tsaile, Arizona. She currently works in the health care industry.

14. Navajo views on the partial nature of individual knowledge coincide nicely with anthropological views on native consultants and ethnographers as situated subjects in positions to know certain things while being limited from knowing about other things (Clifford 1986:1–26; Clifford and Marcus 1986; Marcus and Fischer 1986; Rosaldo 1993:8).

Chapter 3. The Nature of Life in the Navajo World

1. Avery Denny of Low Mountain, Arizona, is a singer of the Hóchx̨ǫ́ǫ́'jí, or Evil Way, and the Tł'éé'jí, or Night Way, ceremonies. He currently teaches the foundations of Navajo philosophy at Navajo Community College in Chinle, Arizona.

2. Ursula Knoki-Wilson (M.S.N., University of Utah) works for the Fort Defiance Indian Hospital in Fort Defiance, Arizona, as a supervisory nurse-midwife. She is a leading authority on traditional Navajo concepts of prenatal health and childbirth. Her publications focus on traditional Native American child-bearing practices (Wilson 1980) and the challenge of multicultural health care (Wilson 1983).

3. Navajo people have made and used baskets since the first Nihookáá Dine'é were created by Changing Woman. The earliest ethnohistorical record of the Navajo notes that they were making fine baskets around 1700 (Hill 1940:400–1). Several different designs are found on Navajo ceremonial baskets dating from the nineteenth century (for a thorough account, see Whiteford 1988:36–37, figs. 26, 27, 28). The Navajo originally manufactured a variety of different styles of baskets for utilitarian and ritual uses (Franciscan Fathers 1910:293–94). Although most styles and designs became obsolete during the late nineteenth or early twentieth century as new forms of containers such as metal pots, buckets, cups, and plates were acquired though trade (Whiteford 1988:32), baskets continue to be made on a limited basis for use in ceremonies. The distinctive design illustrated in figure 2 has been made continually until the present and is the most pervasive of all designs found on Navajo baskets today. Baskets with this design are commonly referred to as "Navajo wedding baskets." This is a misnomer, for although they are an important element in wedding ceremonies, their ritual and

nonritual contexts are much broader. Baskets are inverted and used as drums in several ceremonies. They are used as portions of certain masks in the nine-night ceremonies (Tschopik 1940:447). As noted by Irene Kee, baskets serve as containers for the yucca suds used in ceremonial baths, as well as for religious paraphernalia, sacred cornmeal, and medicinal herbs. In addition, they are frequently used on a day-to-day basis as storage containers for jewelry (Wesley Thomas, 11/12/94).

4. The earliest account of the symbolism of the designs found on the basket was collected by the anthropologist Stanley Fishler in 1950 from a Navajo religious practitioner named Frank Goldtooth. Fishler credits Goldtooth with the following account.

> The center spot in the basket represents the beginning of this earth as the Navajo emerged from the cane. The white portion surrounding the center spot is the earth. The black represents the six or ten sacred mountains to the Navajo and forms a boundary-line of the early Navajo people. . . . Only six mountains are represented in some of the baskets, for that is the number of mountains brought up from below during the flood.
>
> Above the represented earth are clouds which have many colors represented within them, as do real clouds above the earth. . . . The white and black clouds are important. They represent the same thing—the making of rain. The rain represented in the basket is to bring comfort to the earth—to make plants and all things grow. . . . Next to the mountains is a red or brown section which represents the sun-rays. It also means the rainbow spectrum upon which the gods travel. The sun-ray is to make things on earth grow and to make things go the right way. This sun-ray in the basket is to bring comfort to the earth, to make plants and all things grow and to keep the earth and the people warm. The number of the clouds has no significance. The finish point of the basket always goes to the east. The path or opening always leads to the east. (Goldtooth, quoted in Fishler 1954: 208–9)

5. Irene Kee of Crystal, New Mexico, is a mother, grandmother, and great-grandmother who practices as an herbalist and diagnostician using the hand trembling method.

6. When the basket is inverted to be used as a drum in the nine-night ceremonies, the spiral expands outward from the center in a sunwise direction (Tschopik 1940:452).

7. All structures are female in their initial stages of construction because providing shelter is a female role in the Navajo world. Individual structures such as sweat houses or male hooghan do not take on their male attributes until the final phases of construction (Thomas, 11/12/94).

8. For a thorough discussion of this ceremony, see Frisbie (1970, 1980).

9. Such divisions are not rigorously maintained on a daily basis in the contemporary world. In fact, most Navajo people live in modern rectangular houses constructed of prefabricated building materials such as milled lumber or concrete block, or in mobile homes. They live in these dwellings to be close to their places of employment and to avail themselves of amenities such as running water, electricity, and indoor plumbing that often are unavailable in remote areas of the reservation.

10. Some ceremonies do not require the removal of cooking supplies and equipment. When the ceremony includes an indoor sweat, the stove pipe and stove must also be removed (Thomas, 11/12/94).

11. I have attended several ceremonies performed in rectangular houses. In each case the ceremonial practitioner and the patient occupied the areas that would correspond to the proper positions in a hooghan—the southwestern and northwestern quadrants, respectively. The dwelling was blessed before the ceremony commenced, and sunwise movement was rigidly adhered to. Adjustments were made to accommodate seating arrangements and movements to the shape of the dwelling and the positions of the doorway and firepit. For example, in one case a kinaaldá had to run sunwise around a wood-burning stove (in place of the firepit) that was north of center; in another instance, the singer's assistant had to adjust his movements in and out to accommodate a doorway on the south wall. Charlotte Frisbie told me that she has attended numerous ceremonies in modern dwellings where similar adjustments were made (Frisbie, personal communication 11/21/93).

12. Because the songs used to construct the loom are extremely precious and powerful, they cannot be reproduced or discussed further in this work.

13. For further information on the importance of the "way out" in Navajo philosophy, see Noel Bennett's *The Weaver's Pathway* (1974).

14. If a family member died inside a hooghan, the eastern doorway was blocked, a hole was cut through the north wall, and the dwelling was abandoned with the corpse and accouterments inside. For a full discussion of this practice specifically, and of Navajo burial practices in general, see the special issue of *American Indian Quarterly* dedicated to Navajo mortuary practices, edited by Charlotte Frisbie (vol. 4, no. 4, 1978), and Albert Ward's *Navajo Graves* (1980).

15. David Harrison of Wheatfields, Arizona, is a member of the Billie family, who sponsored my research. He assisted with collection of wood and water and supervised repairs to the family hooghan at Black Rock, Arizona, in preparation for my daughter's Kinaaldá in 1992.

16. In her plenary lecture delivered at the Ninth Annual Navajo Studies Conference in Durango, Colorado, in 1996, Jennie Joe, a medical anthropologist from the University of Arizona, mentioned that she had accompanied Navajo religious specialists to the Field Museum of Natural History in Chicago, Illinois, in September 1995 to assess the condition of and rebless these sacred beings (Joe 1996).

17. I accept at face value that things made for use in ceremonial contexts have more power and agency than things made or used in nonceremonial contexts. I did not attempt to elicit information on whether beings or entities could be ranked or ordered

hierarchically on the basis of relative power or agency. Several previous researchers have attempted to construct such hierarchies of beings and entities in the Navajo world on the basis of relative power or agency. Kenneth Hale (1973) considered possible rankings of nouns as a means for understanding rules governing subject-object inversion in Navajo sentences. Mary Helen Creamer used Navajo rules governing subject-object inversion to delineate eight ranked groups or categories into one of which all Navajo nouns fit (1974:33–37). Gary Witherspoon went a step further and devised a scheme to represent his understanding of the way Navajo people categorize the entire world (1977:75–81). Witherspoon's scheme is based on a distinction between "animate" and "inanimate" beings derived from his fundamental categories of "static" versus "active." He uses the term "animate" to refer specifically to the capacity for self-animation, that is, the capacity for self-propelled locomotion (1977:76). The Navajo experts with whom I consulted distinguished between entities with and without the means for self-propelled locomotion, but they did not use this capacity as the means for determining degree of relative power or agency. They used numerous examples, such as jish and masks, of beings with tremendous personal power and agency who did not have the capacity for self-propelled locomotion. These examples indicate that the Navajo experts with whom I consulted define animation as the capacity to think and acquire knowledge, which equals power and results in agency, rather than simply self-propelled locomotion.

18. The size of the requisite fee depends on the exact nature and extent of the information exchanged. Fees vary in size from a few dollars for a hand trembling diagnosis (Sadie Billie, 7/12/91) to several horses and concho belts for the songs and prayers associated with silversmithing (Flora Ashley, 7/29/91). For personal convenience I chose to use cash and groceries as the fee I offered to every consultant. For further information on the necessity of such fees, see Aberle (1967).

19. Nakai Tso was a Navajo elder who lived to the age of 104. Hastiin Tso consistently and patiently assisted the development of my understanding of Navajo culture. The heritage of his knowledge of, and appreciation for, the Navajo way of life will continue for years to come through the lives of his children, grandchildren, and great-grandchildren.

Chapter 4. The Cultural Construction of the Nihookáá Dine'é

1. Gary Witherspoon has argued that the Navajo reference to the earth as nihimá, "our mother," is based on more than simple metaphorical extension of Navajo concepts of kinship, as most prior researchers assumed. Through the process of emergence from the underworlds, the earth literally and figuratively gave birth to all living creatures. As a mother, the earth sustains the life of her children by providing them with sustenance and protection (Witherspoon 1975:20).

2. The clans most frequently mentioned as one of the four original clans are Honágháahnii, "One-Walks-Around Clan" (Matthews 1994 [1897]:148; Yazzie 1971: 74; Austin and Lynch 1983:3), Kinyaa'áanii, "Towering House Clan" (Matthews 1994 [1897]:148; Wyman 1970:458; Yazzie 1971:74; Austin and Lynch 1983:3; Aro-

nilth 1985:83), Tódích'íi'nii, "Bitter Water Clan" (Matthews 1994 [1897]:148; Wyman 1970:458, 634; Yazzie 1971:74; Austin and Lynch 1983:3; Aronilth 1985:83), Bit'ahnii, "Leaf Clan" (Matthews 1994 [1897]:148; Wyman 1970:634), Tó'áhaní, "Near The Water Clan" (Wyman 1970:458, 634; Aronilth 1985:83), and Hashtł'ishnii, "Mud Clan" (Matthews 1994 [1897]:148; Wyman 1970:458, 634; Yazzie 1971:74; Austin and Lynch 1983:3; Aronilth 1985:83).

3. This corroboration is not surprising, since Bailey participated in the influential Ramah project spearheaded by Kluckhohn, a collaborative project involving people from numerous disciplines. Fieldworkers on the project had their notes indexed and duplicated for use by other members of the research team, and they allowed each other to quote from their field notes.

4. Consider, for example, findings from the Bimin-Kuskusmin (Poole 1981) and Sabarl (Battaglia 1990). In the Bimin-Kuskusmin world, male and female substances contribute to complementary aspects of the child's anatomy. Semen builds strong, internal, and hard parts of the body such as teeth, nails, bones, liver, and lungs. Female fertile fluids build weak, external, and soft body parts such as feces, saliva, perspiration, flesh, stomach, and skin (Poole 1981:126). Poole's analysis reveals that the qualities associated with these parts of the body—soft, weak, and external versus hard, strong, and internal—correspond to base metaphors that permeate all aspects of Bimin-Kuskusmin society. Sabarl people believe that a child is conceived when "white blood" (father's blood) and "red blood" (mother's blood) mix in the mother's womb during sexual intercourse (Battaglia 1990:38). After conception, the white and red bloods separate and subsequently form the white parts of the child's body, such as the skeleton, and the red parts, such as the flesh and organs, respectively (Battaglia 1990:38–39). An elaborate system for classification of all foods and liquids derives from these colors in the Sabarl world. Red is associated with dry, lean, and cool; white is associated with greasy, sweet, and hot. A Sabarl body functions properly only when internal balance is maintained through controlled ingestion of these respective elements (Battaglia 1990:45–49).

5. This information does not account for the formation of a nádleehé. I have been given no understanding of how, or whether, a nádleehé is formed in the womb. The subject of nádleehé in the Navajo world was pursued by Carolyn Epple in her doctoral dissertation research (1994) and is currently under investigation from a Navajo point of view by Wesley Thomas.

6. Each of the consultants I asked about this indicated that attachment of the placenta to the right indicated female, and attachment to the left, male. Bailey noted, however, that although her consultants were unanimous that the location of the placenta was related to the sex of the child, she found them equally divided over which position, left or right, indicated male or female (1950:68).

7. These bodily fluids appear to have been the source of confusion on the part of prior researchers. These investigators failed to acknowledge that the Navajo model, unlike the Western biomedical model, holds that the act of conception is distinct from the development of the resulting fetus in the womb. Further, despite the fact that nearly all accounts in Navajo oral history refer specifically to the joining of male and female

"waters," previous researchers did not inquire into the nature of these "waters." Instead, they correlated them with the reproductive fluids with which they were most familiar—semen and menstrual blood. This clearly represents a case of superimposition of the Western biomedical theory of human conception onto the Navajo reality. Bailey explicitly stated that "accurate knowledge of the structure and function of the reproductive organs is not possessed by any of the Navahos interviewed for this study. Explanations given are vague and incomplete" (1950:18). Her choice of the terms "accurate," "vague," and "incomplete" suggests that she considered the Western biomedical model to be "accurate," "precise," and "complete"—in other words, universal. It appears that on the basis of this belief, she attempted to fit the information given by Navajo consultants into the biomedical model with which she was familiar, rather than attempting to elucidate the Navajo model of conception. Since the only fluids essential to conception in the biomedical model are semen and blood, she appears to have concluded that these were the fluids referred to by her Navajo consultants.

8. The wedding ceremony is well documented in the literature dating from the first decade of the twentieth century to the present. For accounts from the first half of the twentieth century, see Franciscan Fathers (1910:446–49), Fishler (1954:205–7), Reichard (1928:139–41), Stewart (1938:25), and Altman (1946:159–64). For information on a contemporary wedding ceremony, see Roessel (1993a:38–45).

9. In contrast to Denny (8/11/93, 10/8/93) and Aronilth (1990:32), who consider this guidance to come from the specific personages mentioned here, McNeley cited Holy Winds as the influencing forces (1981:32–35). He noted that wind from each cardinal point is believed to influence individual humans on the earth's surface. The White Wind in the east "directs our life," the Blue Wind in the south is "our power of movement," the Yellow Wind in the west is "our thinking," and the Black Wind in the north directs "our plans." Although these winds have individual dominions, all four are different aspects of "a single Wind that suffuses all living things" (McNeley 1981:32).

10. Further explication of the Navajo descent system can be found in Witherspoon (1975:37–48; 1983:524–35).

11. According to McNeley's consultants, these influences come through winds that combine with the male and female bodily fluids at conception. "From the man's bodily fluid is the Wind by which he lived and from the woman's is one Wind, too, by which she lived. So there are really two" ("CM," quoted in McNeley 1981:23). By this account, winds from each of the four directions must be placed within the fetus for proper growth and development to occur. Therefore, they come as pairs. One pair of winds is brought in the mother's fluids, and the other pair in the father's fluids (McNeley 1981:33).

12. McNeley attributes such guidance to Holy People rather than to clan "bloods." According to his account, a pair of teaching Holy People identified with each of the cardinal points is in charge of instructing Nihookáá Dine'é in the foundational principles of Navajo education and philosophy (McNeley 1993). McNeley, Walters, and Denny correlate identical principles with cardinal directions. The association is as follows: nitsáhákees (east), nahat'á (south), 'iiná (west), and sihasin (north) (McNeley 1993; Walters, 8/12/93; Denny, 10/8/93).

13. The constitution of specific parts of the human body is exemplified in the types

of ntł'iz inserted into figurines during the Remaking ceremony (Haile 1947; Kelly, Lang, and Walters 1972) and in the deer costume worn by hunters using the Stalking Way method (Hill 1938:123–24).

14. In the Navajo language, body parts and bodily substances fall into the Dependent class of nouns (Young and Morgan 1987:9). As a result, the terms used to refer to them must consist of a possessive pronominal prefix (such as 'a-) and a stem (such as -tsiighá, -tsoo', or -gáál). 'A-, which literally means "someone's" or "something's," is used when the person from whom the body part or bodily substance originated is unknown or unspecified. For ease of translation, this form of possessive pronominal prefix is glossed in English as "the."

15. Wesley Thomas of Mariano Lake, New Mexico, is, at the time of this writing, a graduate student in sociocultural anthropology at the University of Washington. His areas of interest are gender and sexuality, especially the special roles played by members of the alternative genders in traditional Navajo society.

16. Haile also notes that according to his consultant, 'agáál, "the moving power," found at each of the joints is constructed of white shell (1947:9).

17. This information is taken from an unpublished transcription of an interview Curly Mustache gave to Jones Van Winkle at Navajo Community College in 1970. During his life, Hastiin Mustache practiced as a singer and served as a tribal councilman. An edited version of his account is available in Roessel (1981:43–50).

18. A stillborn child does not require the same type of funeral or mourning behavior on the part of relatives as a child who dies after having breathed and cried. This practice is well documented in the literature (see, for example, Franciscan Fathers 1910:451; Wyman, Hill, and Osanai 1942:17; Brugge 1978:309–28; Shepardson 1978:385–86; Ward 1980:17–21).

19. For further information on the effects different types of winds can have on individual characteristics and habits, see McNeley (1981:32–49).

20. Flora Ashley of Shonto, Arizona, is a wife, mother, and grandmother who teaches Navajo language and culture at the boarding school in Shonto.

21. Sunny Dooley is a former Miss Navajo from Vanderwagen, New Mexico, who has retained the role of ambassador for Navajo culture to the non-Navajo world through storytelling. She performs traditional Navajo stories on and off the reservation, but her primary commitment is teaching traditional stories to Navajo children who have been raised without this important educational resource in their homes.

22. Ruth Roessel is a mother, grandmother, and educator from Round Rock, Arizona, who has taught at all grade levels, including at Navajo Community College in Tsaile, Arizona. She is best known for her edited collection of narratives on the Long Walk (1973) and her book *Women in Navajo Society* (1981).

23. Jean Jones of Rock Point, Arizona, is a mother and grandmother who teaches sash weaving at the Rock Point Community School in Rock Point, Arizona.

24. This holds true for male and female but not for nádleehé. Nádleehé have a unique capacity for simultaneously filling male and female roles.

25. Annie Kahn of Lukachukai, Arizona, is a Navajo elder and herbalist. For more information on her life and work, see Perrone, Stockel, and Krueger (1989:28–44).

26. Each of these terms consists of a possessive pronominal prefix (*bi-*) and a stem

(-ká' or -a'áád, respectively). Since Navajo pronouns are not gendered, this form of possessive pronominal prefix literally means "his, her, its, or theirs." The person to whom the possessive pronoun applies would be understood in context, but to avoid confusion, these terms are glossed in English as "its male or female sexual partner" rather than as "his, her, or their male or female sexual partner." Because of this choice of terminology, I initially wondered whether the Navajo people with whom I consulted were referring to a form of dual sexuality in the physical composition of the body. The characteristics and qualities associated with each side of the body make it clear, however, that this distinction does not refer to sexuality.

27. For example, Washington Matthews was the first anthropologist to note the Navajo distinction between that which is coarser, rougher, and more violent, called bika', or male, and that which is finer, weaker, and gentler, called ba'áád, or female (1902:60). Reichard observed that in ceremonial contexts these terms were employed to refer to the concepts of maleness, which included potency, mobility, bigness, energy, and dominance, and femaleness, which included generative capacity, passive power, endurance, smallness, and compliance (1950:176).

28. The complementary concepts są'ah naagháí and bik'eh hózhǫ permeate all levels of Navajo reality, structuring Navajo ideas of maleness and femaleness, the human body, reproduction, and personhood. The male and female components of the primordial complementary pair, Są'ah Naagháí and Bik'eh Hózhǫ, respectively, constitute the fundamental life-giving forces in the Navajo universe. Mother Earth and Father Sky, as male and female counterparts, form a homologue to this pair. A man and a woman, as husband and wife, form a homologue as well. As parts of a whole—a couple—the husband is są'ah naagháí and the wife is bik'eh hózhǫ. On another level, the human body, too, constitutes a homologue of this primordial pairing; the left side is są'ah naagháí and the right is bik'eh hózhǫ. The primordial pair also plays a critical role in heterosexual reproduction, the means by which contemporary Nihookáá Dine'é reproduce. The reproductive fluids needed for human conception form another homologue of this pair; semen is są'ah naagháí and, in combination, tó ał'tahnáschíín and tó biyáázh are bik'eh hózhǫ.

29. Photographs and clothing may be used in place of persons in a variety of other contexts as well. For example, when a family is holding a Blessing Way ceremony, photographs of family members who cannot attend are placed in the ceremonial basket with the jish (Thomas, 1/21/95). Photos are also frequently used for daily blessings. Mae Bekis told me that when her children are away from home, she and her husband use their photographs to include them in the benefits of the morning blessing (Bekis, 7/28/93). I was also told of an ill man's shoes being taken to a diagnostician by his mother when he was unable to visit the practitioner personally (Lynch, 7/31/92).

30. Lillie Tsosie is the eldest daughter of Irene Kee of Crystal, New Mexico. She is a mother and grandmother who works at the boarding school in Crystal, New Mexico.

Chapter 5. Becoming a Navajo

1. Elsewhere, the long-term influences that contact between detached parts of the body (hair, skin cells, nail clippings) or bodily substances (blood, urine, feces)

and nonhuman Navajo persons can have on Nihookáá Dine'é have been explored within the context of a series of snake sightings that occurred in July 1994 in a women's restroom in Administration Building Number 2 in Window Rock, Arizona (Schwarz 1997a).

2. Sadie Billie of White Valley, Arizona, is a wife, mother, and grandmother who coordinates a program for the March of Dimes Birth Defects Foundation in Tsaile, Arizona, where she resides. She has a profound commitment to the preservation of Navajo traditions. Mrs. Billie, who is frequently called upon to act as the Ideal Woman in Kinaaldá, served in this capacity at the puberty ceremony her family sponsored for my daughter, Ragen.

3. Louva Dahozy of Lupe, Arizona, is a mother and grandmother who was a 1994 recipient of a Lifetime Achievement Award from the University of Arizona in recognition of her commitment to education and the programs offered in the College of Agriculture. She lives in Fort Defiance, Arizona.

4. I helped butcher a sheep for my daughter's Kinaaldá, but I did not learn every part of the sheep's anatomy through this process. There are five parts to a sheep's stomach: the dorsal sac of rumen, the ventral sac of rumen, the abomasum, the omasum, and the reticulum. To the best of my knowledge, Mrs. Bekis was referring to the ventral sac of rumen, which is attached to the abomasum. Food moves on from there to the large and small intestines (Adair, Deuschle, and Barnett 1988:98, fig. 5).

5. Omentum is defined as the free fold of peritoneum connecting the stomach to the other visceral organs and supporting blood vessels, nerves, and lymphatics. Adipose tissue is defined as an aggregation of minute cells that draw fat from the blood, dispersed in the interstices of common areolar tissue.

6. The correlation between the serrated edges of *Cypraea* shell openings and female genitalia is taken a step further in stories told to children for disciplinary purposes. To control sexual experimentation, elders sometimes tell young boys that females have teeth on their vulvas that can be used to bite off the male's penis. Consider, for example, the following account given by Son of Old Man Hat:

> When I'd be out herding and the girls saw me they'd bring their herds close to mine, and we'd start playing. Sometimes my mother saw me. When I'd get back home she'd ask me if I'd been playing with the girls. I'd say right out, "Yes mother, I've been playing with the girls." . . . Every time she saw me playing with the girls she'd say, "You shouldn't bother the girls. It's bad for you. The girls will sometime take your c--- out and bite it off. It isn't only the girls that will do that to you, all the other women do just the same." As I was wondering if they'd do that to me with their teeth she said, "All the women have teeth where their c---s are." Then I wondered about the sheep, if the sheep were that way too. But every time a buck got on a sheep he would still have his c---. I thought, "Perhaps it's only women who have teeth." So, I began to be afraid and didn't dare go near them. But she didn't really

mean it, she only said this to me because she thought that I might
lose some sheep while playing with the girls. (Dyk 1966 [1938]:45)

7. Hand trembling is one of three diagnostic methods used by Navajo people: *ndishniih,* hand trembling, *'íísts'ą́ą́',* listening, and *déest'į́į́',* crystal gazing. A hand trembler washes his or her hands and forearms. Then, using one of a variety of designs and methods, pollen is sprinkled on the right forearm from the elbow along the radial margin, around the hypothenar eminence of the hand and along the palmar surface of the thumb to its tip, along each finger, and on the center of the palm. Then a prayer is said to Gila Monster asking for information concerning the specific problem at hand. Sitting with eyes closed, the diagnostician sings one or two songs, and during them his or her extended hand begins to shake. While the diagnostician's hand shakes, she or he thinks of various problems that might be the cause, and the hand stops when the mind focuses on the correct problem. For further information on Navajo methods for diagnosis, see Morgan (1931) and Wyman (1936a). For information on the oral histories associated with the origin of each method, see Wyman (1936b).

8. I did not conduct a systematic survey of the percentage of pregnant women in the Tsaile-Wheatfields area having Blessing Ways performed while pregnant. Each of the women with whom I consulted about this told me she had a Blessing Way ceremony sometime between the sixth and eighth months of her pregnancy. This does not seem to reflect the trend on other parts of the reservation. In her study of traditionality and nursing care, B. Carol Milligan noted that 58 percent of the pregnant women she interviewed in 1980 planned to have a Blessing Way (1984:94). In her study of the use of the Blessing Way ceremony for contemporary birth, Maureen Hartle-Schutte noted that only 14 percent of all the women in her sample had Blessing Way ceremonies during either pregnancy or childbirth (1988).

9. Agnes Begay was born in Many Farms, Arizona, in 1913. She was a mother, grandmother, and great-grandmother. In recognition of her special understanding of traditional Navajo values and skills, she was called upon to serve as a judge in the annual Miss Navajo pageants.

10. Since traditional methods for childbirth in Navajo society are well summarized in the literature, I include only a brief summary here. For additional information, see the following sources: Franciscan Fathers (1910:450), Reichard (1928:134–35), Kluckhohn and Leighton (1974 [1946]:207, 212), Leighton and Kluckhohn (1947:14–18), Stewart (1980:11–12), Begay (1985), and Waxman (1990:189–92).

11. Indian Health Service hospitals are located in Tuba City, Chinle, and Fort Defiance, Arizona, and in Gallup, Shiprock, and Crownpoint, New Mexico. Indian Health Service clinics are located in Winslow, Kayenta, and Tsaile, Arizona. In addition, mission-run hospitals are located in Monument Valley, Utah, and Ganado, Arizona (Waxman 1990:192–93).

12. This courtesy extends to all parts of the body that are removed during a patient's stay in hospital. For example, emergency-room technicians routinely offer toenail and hair clippings to Navajo patients so that they can dispose of them as they wish (Bell 1994:238).

13. Cords that are attached to livestock eventually disintegrate, and their parts fall off within the customary use area of the child's matrilineal clan. Thus, they simultaneously build a proclivity for animal husbandry and an attachment to a specific locale.

14. A system of generalized reciprocity is at the core of the Navajo way of life. For a full discussion of this important component of the social world, see *To Run After Them* by Louise Lamphere (1977, esp. pp. 35–65).

15. Wesley Thomas conveyed to me that he remembers his grandmother and aunts routinely wailing when reunited, until the early to mid-1960s (personal communication 3/6/94).

16. For additional information on Navajo humor, see *Navaho Humor* by W. W. Hill (1943), as well as Reichard (1928:72–73) and Kluckhohn and Leighton (1974 [1946]: 97–100, 260).

17. Reichard notes that this type of salt will give strength when added to food, and it can also serve as a weapon (1950:595). Specifically, salt was used as a weapon by the twins in their battle against the "monster which kills with his eyes" (Kee, 8/4/92).

18. Many contemporary people hold adamantly to this belief. Indeed, forced cutting of the hair of incarcerated adults is considered by some Navajo to be a form of "spiritual castration." In an article about support for the Native American Free Exercise of Religion Act of 1993 (NAFERA), Lenny Foster, director of the Navajo Corrections Project, was quoted as stating: "The discrimination and harassment of Native American prisoners at the institutions must stop. The cutting of long hair must stop. To cut a person's hair is a form of spiritual castration." Foster went on to explain that according to the traditional beliefs he was taught, cutting a person's hair affects his or her thinking and brings on depression (*Navajo Times*, March 17, 1993, p. A-6). Many contemporary people hold adamantly to this belief.

Chapter 6. Becoming a Young Man or Woman

1. I include here only the names of women who wrote specifically on the Kinaaldá. Women ethnographers who have worked on the Navajo reservation and could conceivably have learned of a male puberty ceremony are too numerous to list. For further information, see *Daughters of the Desert: Women Anthropologists and the Native American Southwest 1880–1980* (Babcock and Parezo 1988).

2. The male puberty ceremony is sometimes referred to as a Kinaaldá (Oscar Tso, 7/18/92; Mae Bekis, 7/28/93), and boys may be referred to as kinaaldá when their voices change (Elizabeth Yazzie, 12/5/93). The Navajo people with whom I consulted often qualified their accounts of such ceremonies with statements such as "it is not exactly a Kinaaldá" to make sure that I understood the differences between the male and female versions of this ceremony.

3. The female Kinaaldá is well documented in the literature. The most detailed account of it by any non-Navajo to date is Charlotte Frisbie's classic study *Kinaaldá* (1993 [1967]). Publications prior to this work that include information on the Kinaaldá are those of the Franciscan Fathers (1910:446), Reichard (1928:135–39), Wyman and Bailey (1943), Leighton and Kluckhohn (1947:76–77), and Keith (1964). Since the publication of Frisbie's influential book, several important works have become available

that offer a variety of perspectives, including a photo essay of a Kinaaldá (Roessel 1981:80–100), a detailed account written by a Navajo (Begay 1983), and accounts of contemporary ceremonies written for the popular audience (Ryan 1988; Roessel 1993b; Hazen-Hammond 1995).

4. Mae Charley is a mother and grandmother from north of Rock Point, Arizona, who teaches basket making at the Rock Point Community School.

5. According to an anonymous reviewer for the University of Arizona Press, in some areas of the reservation young women have the Kinaaldá performed for them four times, as was done for Changing Woman.

6. In the preface to the 1993 edition of *Kinaaldá,* Frisbie discusses these and other changes she has noted at Kinaaldá she has attended since the mid-1970s (Frisbie 1993 [1967]:xviii–xx).

7. A kinaaldá may be told to observe numerous other restrictions. See Frisbie (1993 [1967]:353–56) for a summary.

8. An account about the Kinaaldá cake recorded by Dorothea Leighton in 1940, reprinted in Frisbie (1993 [1967]:398), states that white corn should be used for the cake at a young woman's first Kinaaldá, and yellow corn for the cake at her second.

9. In an account collected by Berard Haile from Slim Curley, *'alkaan* are said to represent an offering made jointly to the sun and the moon at Changing Woman's first Kinaaldá. This offering was made to show appreciation to the sun and the moon, who cast their light upon all in attendance (Wyman 1970:174).

10. This reference is found in the following passage from an account collected by Stanley Fishler from Frank Goldtooth in 1950: "The grinding of the corn signified that the girl was now able to produce. The center of the corn bread meant that the girl actually gave that which came from within (the center of the corn bread). . . . The cake itself, which was round, represented the earth. The center of the cake represented the Sun" (Fishler 1953:40–41).

11. In addition, different songs are sung depending on whether the ceremony is a young woman's first or second Kinaaldá. Frisbie documents the singing of fourteen Hooghan songs in the initial portion of a first Kinaaldá (1993 [1967]:23, 25). For a second Kinaaldá, twelve (Nakai Tso, 8/8/92) or twenty-five (Frisbie 1993 [1967]:24–25) Haashch'ééʼooghaan (Second Talking God) songs are sung at this juncture in the ceremony. I refer readers interested in the songs and music to Frisbie's comprehensive documentation of Kinaaldá music (1993 [1967]:102–346).

12. This is similar to the belief that proper disposal of deer bones and entrails by hunters will ensure "luck" in future hunts, which will result in the ability to secure plentiful game (Steven Billie, 8/18/92; Harrison, 8/18/92; Bekis, 7/28/93; see also Hill 1938:96–176; Luckert 1975)

Chapter 7. Talking about Contemporary Systems of Knowledge and Practice

1. Many anthropologists maintain that the experience of "wholeness, continuity and autonomy" associated with the "self" in many Euro-American societies is a culture-bound notion that is not applicable to most cultures, in which the self is experienced

"contextually and relationally" (see Shweder and Bourne 1984). This type of self-representation has been referred to as "interdependent or relational" (Ewing 1990), as opposed to "independent and autonomous" (Spiro 1993). The former has generally been considered to be a non-Western construct and the latter a Western construct.

2. The notion that the constructs of "self" and "person" can be conflated is not a new idea. See, for example, Michelle Rosaldo's insightful critique of the conceptual opposition of self and person commonly found in anthropological discourse (1984: 145–50).

GLOSSARY

'a-. Possessive prefix for "someone's."

ááhdiłhił. Dark fog (female).

'abaní'. The unharmed hide of a deer.

'acázis. The pleurae.

'ach'íí'. Intestine(s).

'acho'. The male genitalia or penis.

'adátsoo'. The clitoris.

ádináályééł. Protective paraphernalia.

'ádístiin. A set of stirring sticks.

'agáál. The moving power.

ahéhee'. Thanks.

'ajéí. The heart and lungs.

'ajóózh. The vagina.

'akéshgaan. The toenails.

'aláshgaan. The fingernails.

'álííl. Supernatural or magical power.

'alizh. The urine.

'alkaan. The corn bread cake made during the Kinaaldá ceremony.

ałheesilá. A pair that functions by means of each other.

ałk'éí. Those considered to be kin.

Áłtsé Asdzáán. First Woman.

Áłtsé Hastiin. First Man.

Áłtsé Saad. First Language.

amá. Someone's mother.

'anáá'. The eyes.

Anaa' jí ndáá'. The Enemy Way ceremony.

anáályééł. Protective paraphernalia.

Asdzáá Nádleehé. Changing Woman.

asdzááango. The woman's side.

'atáá'ha'noots'eeí. The point at the top of the back of the head where the hair assumes a concentric spiral growth pattern.

'atá't'ah. The interior recesses, pockets, and folds of the body.

atiin. Road, pathway, or "way out."

'atł'ááh. Bottom.

atsąstíín. The embryo from conception to birth.

'atsiighá. The hair on the head.

'atsiighąą'. The brains.

'atsoo'. The tongue.

'Awéé' ch'ídaadlóóhgó bá na'a'n'ę́ę́'. The First Laugh ceremony.

'awééts'ááł. Traditional Navajo cradle(s).

'awoo'. Tooth or teeth.

'azid. The liver.

'azooł. The windpipe.

-baa'. To raid or make war; a stem used to construct female war names.

ba'áád. Its female sexual partner.

bé'ézhóó'. A grass hairbrush.

bi-. Possessive prefix for "his, hers, its, theirs."

Bį́įh. Deer (personified).

biil. Two-piece woven dress.

bijáád. His, her, or its leg.

biką'. Its male sexual partner.

bik'eh hózhǫ. The essence of peace, harmony, and order.

Bit'ahnii. The Leaf Clan.

chahałheeł. Night.

chahash'oh. A brush shelter.

chííh. Red ochre.

chííh dík'ǫ́ǫ́zh. A protective medicine.

Ch'óol'į́'į́. Gobernador Knob.

chooyin. Menstruation and menstrual fluids.

dah'iistł'ǫ́. Loom(s).

déest'į́į'. The crystal gazing method of diagnosis.

Dibé Nitsaa. La Plata Peak.

Diné. The contemporary Navajo people.

diné. Person.

Diné binííłch'ijí. The Small Wind Way ceremony.

dinego. The man's side.

Dinétah. The area demarcated by the sacred mountains that the Navajo consider their ancestral homeland.

Diyin Dine'é. Holy People.

diyin k'ehjí hane'. The second main level of knowledge in Navajo philosophy.

dleesh. Rhyolite tuff.

Dook'o'oosłííd. San Francisco Peak.

Dził Asdzáán. Mountain Woman.

Dziłná'ooditii. Huerfano Peak.

Haashch'ééłti'í. Talking God.

Haashch'éé'ooghaan. Growling God or Second Talking God.

haayoołkááł. Dawn.

hadahoniye'. Aragonite.

hajíínáí. The place of emergence.

Hashtł'ishnii. The Mud Clan.

hatááł k'ehjí hane'. The third main level of knowledge in Navajo philosophy.

hóchxǫ. Ugly, undesirable.

Hóchxǫǫ'jí. The Evil Way ceremony.

Honágháahnii. The One-Walks-Around Clan.

hooghan. Traditional Navajo home(s).

hooghan ba'ááad. Female hooghan.

hooghan bikạ'. Male hooghan.

Hooghan Da'ashdlishígíí. The House Blessing ceremony.

hózhǫ náshááadóó. To walk on the path of harmony, balance, and order.

Hózhǫǫjí. The Blessing Way ceremony.

hózhǫǫjí. Shortened version of hózhǫǫjigo.

hózhǫǫjigo. On the side of peace, harmony, and order.

hózhǫǫjí hane'. The first main level of knowledge in Navajo philosophy.

Hwéeldi. Fort Sumner, New Mexico.

'íígạsh. Sperm.

'ligeh. The Wedding ceremony.

'iiná. Living according to the Navajo way of life.

'íishghą́ą́ntsiighạạ'. The spinal cord.

'íists'ą́ą'. The listening method of diagnosis.

jaatł'óół. Earring(s).

jish. A medicine bundle or bundles.

Jóhonaa'éí. Sun (personified).

k'eet'oh. Bowguard.

kénitsaaí. Women's moccasins with leggings.

kétł'ááh. The attachment between a Navajo individual and the earth.

kéyah. Land or earth.

Kinaaldá. The puberty ceremony.

kinaaldá. The person for whom a puberty ceremony is performed; also, the first and second menstrual periods.

Kinyaa'áanii. The Towering House Clan.

K'os Diłhił. Dark Cloud (personified).

k'os diłhił. Dark cloud(s) (male).

łééchạạ' bik'ehgo. He or she is similar to a dog.

Naadą́ą́' Asdzáán. Corn Woman.

naat'áanii. A traditional leader, orator; a facilitator in the Navajo Peacemaker Court system.

Na'at'oyee. The Shooting or Lightning Way ceremony.

nááts'íílid. Rainbow.

nááts'íílid 'agod. Short rainbow.

nááts'íílid 'agod'i. Short rainbow being(s).

Nááts'íílid Dine'é. Rainbow People.

Naayéé'jí. The Protection Way ceremony.

naayéé'jí. Shortened version of naayéé' k'ehjigo.

naayéé'jí hane'. The fourth main level of knowledge in Navajo philosophy.

naayéé' k'ehjigo. On the side of protection.

Naayéé' Neezghání. Monster Slayer.

nádleehé. One who changes repeatedly. This term is currently used to refer to people of the third, or alternative, gender in Navajo society.

Nahasdzáán. Earth (personified), Mother Earth, Earth Woman.

nahat'á. Planning.

nahodeetł'iizh. Day.

nahootsoíí. Evening.

nanise' bikétł'óól. Vegetation roots.

ndishniih. The hand trembling method of diagnosis.

ni-. Possessive prefix for "your."

ni ałníí. The nadir of the earth.

Nihookáá Dine'é. Earth Surface People.

Níłch'i. Holy Wind.

níłch'i. Wind(s).

Níłch'ihjí. The Wind Way ceremony.

nitsáhákees. Thinking.

ntł'iz. "Hard goods," precious stones and shells.

są'ah naagháí. The essence of longevity and immortality.

Są'ah Naagháí and *Bik'eh Hózhǫ.* Together, the primordial life-giving forces of the Navajo cosmos.

shá bik'ehgo. Sunwise.

shawéé'. My child (term of endearment).

shi-. Possessive prefix for "my."

shimá. Mother(s).

shitah. Father(s).

shiyázhí. My little one (term of endearment).

sihasin. Confidence, assurance, and security.

sis łichí'í. Red sash.

Sisnaajiní. Blanca Peak.

tádídíín. Pollen.

tádídíín bijish. A pollen pouch.

Tł'ééhonaa'éí. Moon (personified).

Tł'éé'jí. The Night Way ceremony.

Tó'áhaní. The Near The Water Clan.

tó ał'tahnáschíín. All different kinds of waters come together.

Tó Asdzáán. Water Woman.

Tó Bájísh Chíní. Born For Water.

tó biyáázh. Child of water.

Tódích'íi'nii. The Bitter Water Clan.

ts'aa'. Ceremonial basket(s).

-ts'éé'. Stem for "umbilical cord."

tsiighá. The hair on the head.

tsiiyééł. The traditional hair bun.

Tsoodził. Mount Taylor.

yá ałníí. The zenith of the sky.

yá'át'ééh. It is good (traditional form of greeting).

Yádiłhił. Father Sky.

yé'ii. Deity or deities.

Yé'ii Bicheii. Grandfather(s) of the Holy People, including Talking God.

REFERENCES CITED

Aberle, David
    1967   The Navaho Singer's "Fee:" Payment or Prestation? *In* Studies in Southwestern Ethnolinguistics. Dell H. Hymes and William E. Bittle, eds. Studies in General Anthropology 3: 15 – 32. The Hague: Mouton and Company.
    1982 [1966]   The Peyote Religion among the Navaho. Norman: University of Oklahoma Press.

Adair, John, Kurt Deuschle, and Clifford Barnett
    1988   The People's Health: Anthropology and Medicine in a Navajo Community. Albuquerque: University of New Mexico Press.

Adams, William
    1963   Shonto: A Study of the Role of the Trader in a Modern Navajo Community. Bureau of American Ethnology Bulletin 188. Washington, D.C.: Smithsonian Institution Press.

Altman, G. A.
    1946   A Navaho Wedding. Masterkey 20: 159 – 64.

Amsden, Charles
    1974 [1934]   Navaho Weaving: Its Technic and History. Glorieta, N.M.: Rio Grande Press.

Aronilth, Wilson
    1985   Foundations of Navajo Culture. Unpublished manuscript on file at Navajo Community College Library, Tsaile, Arizona.
    1990   Foundation of Navajo Culture. Unpublished manuscript on file at Navajo Community College Library, Tsaile, Arizona.

Austin, Martha, Kenneth Begishe, Betty Manygoats, Oswald Werner, and June Werner
    1971   The Anatomical Atlas of the Navajo with Illustrations. Unpublished manuscript in the possession of Oswald Werner, Northwestern University.

Austin, Martha, and Regina Lynch
    1983   Saad Ahaah Sinil Dual Language: A Navajo-English Dictionary. Rough Rock, Ariz.: Rough Rock Demonstration School.

Babcock, Barbara, and Nancy Parezo
    1988   Daughters of the Desert: Women Anthropologists and the Native American Southwest 1880 – 1980. Albuquerque: University of New Mexico Press.

Bailey, Flora
    1950   Some Sex Beliefs and Practices in a Navajo Community: With Comparative Material from Other Navaho Areas. Reports of the Ramah Project. Papers

of the Peabody Museum of American Archaeology and Ethnology 40(2). Cambridge, Mass.: Peabody Museum.

Bailey, Garrick, and Roberta Bailey
 1986 A History of the Navajos: The Reservation Years. Santa Fe, N.M.: School of American Research Press.

Bailey, Lynn
 1988 [1964] The Long Walk: A History of the Navajo Wars, 1846–68. Tucson: Westernlore Press.

Bastien, Joseph
 1985 Qullahuaya-Andean Body Concepts: A Topographical-Hydraulic Model of Physiology. American Anthropologist 87(3):595–611.

Battaglia, Debbora
 1990 On the Bones of the Serpent: Person, Memory, and Mortality in Sabarl Island Society. Chicago: University of Chicago Press.

Battaglia, Debbora, ed.
 1995 Rhetorics of Self-Making. Berkeley: University of California Press.

Begay, Laura
 1974 Becoming a Navajo: The First Six Years of Life. Photocopy of unpublished manuscript in the author's possession.

Begay, Rita
 1985 Navajo Childbirth. Ph.D dissertation, Department of Public Health, University of California, Berkeley. Ann Arbor, Mich.: University Microfilms.

Begay, Shirley M.
 1983 Kinaaldá: A Navajo Puberty Ceremony. Rough Rock, Ariz.: Navajo Curriculum Center, Rough Rock Demonstration School.

Bell, Roxanne
 1994 Prominence of Women in Navajo Healing Beliefs and Values. Nursing and Health Care 15(5):232–40.

Benally, Herbert
 1994 Navajo Philosophy and Learning and Pedagogy. Journal of Navajo Education 12(1):23–31.

Benedek, Emily
 1993 The Wind Won't Know Me: A History of the Navajo-Hopi Land Dispute. New York: Vintage Books.

Bennett, Noël
 1974 The Weaver's Pathway: A Clarification of the "Spirit Trail" in Navajo Weaving. Flagstaff, Ariz.: Northland Press.

Bighorse, Tiana
 1990 Bighorse the Warrior. Noël Bennett, ed. Tucson: University of Arizona Press.

Blacking, John
 1977 The Anthropology of the Body. London: Academic Press.

Bourdieu, Pierre
 1977 Outline of a Theory of Practice. Cambridge: Cambridge University Press.

Boyce, W. T., C. Shaefer, H. R. Harrison, W. Haffner, M. Lewis, and A. L. Wright
  1986   Social and Cultural Factors in Pregnancy Complications among Navajo Women. American Journal of Epidemiology 124:242–53.
Brugge, David
  1978   A Comparative Study of Navajo Mortuary Practices. American Indian Quarterly 4(4):309–28.
  1983   Navajo Prehistory and History to 1850. In Handbook of North American Indians, vol. 10: Southwest, pp. 489–501. Alfonso Ortiz, ed. Washington, D.C.: Smithsonian Institution Press.
  1994   The Navajo-Hopi Land Dispute: An American Tragedy. Albuquerque: University of New Mexico Press.
Buckley, Thomas, and Alma Gottlieb
  1988   A Critical Appraisal of Theories of Menstrual Symbolism. In Blood Magic: The Anthropology of Menstruation, pp. 3–50. Thomas Buckley and Alma Gottlieb, eds. Berkeley: University of California Press.
Cavalli-Sforza, Luigi Luca
  1991   Genes, People, and Languages. Scientific American, November:104–10.
Clifford, James
  1986   Introduction: Partial Truths. In Writing Culture: The Poetics and Politics of Ethnography, pp. 1–26. James Clifford and George Marcus, eds. Berkeley: University of California Press.
Clifford, James, and George Marcus, eds.
  1986   Writing Culture: The Poetics and Politics of Ethnography. Berkeley: University of California Press.
Comaroff, Jean
  1985   Body of Power, Spirit of Resistance: The Culture and History of the South African People. Chicago: University of Chicago Press.
Correll, J. Lee
  1979   Through White Men's Eyes: A Contribution to Navajo History, vols. 1–6. Austin, Texas: Dissemination and Assessment Center for Bilingual Education.
Correll, J. Lee, Editha Watson, and David Brugge
  1969   Navajo Bibliography with Subject Index. Research Report 2. Window Rock, Ariz.: Navajo Tribe, Parks and Recreation Research Section.
  1973   Navajo Bibliography with Subject Index. Research Report 2, Supplement 1. Window Rock, Ariz.: Navajo Tribe, Parks and Recreation Research Section.
Creamer, Mary Helen
  1974   Ranking in Navajo Nouns. Diné Bizaad Náníl'įįh (Navajo Language Review) 1(1):29–38.
Csordas, Thomas
  1989   The Sore That Does Not Heal: Cause and Concept in the Navajo Experience of Cancer. Journal of Anthropological Research 45(4):457–85.
Daniel, E. Valentine
  1984   Fluid Signs: Being a Person the Tamil Way. Berkeley: University of California Press.

Douglas, Mary

1966   Purity and Danger: An Analysis of Concepts of Pollution and Taboo. London: Routledge and Kegan Paul.

1970   Natural Symbols. New York: Vintage Books.

Durkheim, Emile

1897   La Prohibition de l'inceste et ses origines. L'Année Sociologique 1 : 1 – 70.

Dyk, Walter

1966 [1938]   Son of Old Man Hat. Lincoln: University of Nebraska Press.

Emerson, Gloria

1983   Navajo Education. *In* Handbook of North American Indians, vol. 10: Southwest, pp. 659 – 71. Alfonso Ortiz, ed. Washington, D.C.: Smithsonian Institution Press.

Epple, Carolyn

1994   Inseparable and Distinct: An Understanding of Navajo Nádleehi in a Traditional Navajo Worldview. Ph.D. dissertation, Department of Anthropology, Northwestern University, Evanston, Illinois. Ann Arbor, Mich.: University Microfilms.

Evans-Pritchard, E. E.

1937   Witchcraft, Oracles, and Magic among the Azande. Oxford: Clarendon Press.

Ewing, Katherine

1990   The Illusion of Wholeness: Culture, Self, and the Experience of Inconsistency. Ethos 18(3):251 – 78.

Farella, John

1984   The Main Stalk: A Synthesis of Navajo Philosophy. Tucson: University of Arizona Press.

Faris, James

1990   The Nightway. Albuquerque: University of New Mexico Press.

Farnell, Brenda

1995   Introduction. *In* Human Action Signs in Cultural Context: The Visible and the Invisible in Movement and Dance. Brenda Farnell, ed. Metuchen, N.J.: Scarecrow Press.

Feher-Elston, Catherine

1988   Children of Sacred Ground. Flagstaff, Ariz.: Northland Publishing.

Fernandez, James, ed.

1991   Beyond Metaphor: The Theory of Tropes in Anthropology. Stanford, Calif.: Stanford University Press.

Fishler, Stanley

1953   In the Beginning: A Navaho Creation Myth. Anthropological Papers, 13. Salt Lake City: University of Utah.

1954   Symbolism of a Navajo "Wedding" Basket. Masterkey 33(6). Los Angeles: Southwest Museum.

Forbes, Jack

1960   Apache, Navaho, and Spaniard. Norman: University of Oklahoma Press.

Fortune, Reo

1932   Sorcerers of Dobu. New York: E. P. Dutton.

Foucault, Michel

    1973   The Birth of the Clinic: An Archaeology of Medical Perception. Translated from the French by A. M. Sheridan Smith. New York: Vintage Books.

    1978   The History of Sexuality. New York: Vintage Books.

Franciscan Fathers

    1910   An Ethnological Dictionary of the Navaho Language. Saint Michaels, Ariz.: Saint Michaels Press.

Frazer, James

    1959 [1890]   The Golden Bough. Theodor Gaster, ed. Garden City, N.Y.: Anchor Books.

Frisbie, Charlotte

    1970   The Navajo House Blessing Ceremonial: A Study of Cultural Change. Ph.D. dissertation, Department of Anthropology, University of New Mexico. Ann Arbor, Mich.: University Microfilms.

    1978   Introduction. American Indian Quarterly 4(4):303–8.

    1980   Ritual Drama in the Navajo House Blessing Ceremony. In Southwestern Indian Ritual Drama, pp. 161–98. Charlotte Frisbie, ed. Albuquerque: University of New Mexico Press.

    1987   Navajo Medicine Bundles or Jish. Albuquerque: University of New Mexico Press.

    1992   Temporal Change in Navajo Religion, 1868–1990. Journal of the Southwest 34(4):457–514.

    1993 [1967]   Kinaaldá: A Study of the Navaho Girl's Puberty Ceremony. Salt Lake City: University of Utah Press.

Frisbie, Charlotte, and Eddie Tso

    1993   The Navajo Ceremonial Practitioners Registry. Journal of the Southwest 35(1):53–92.

Gill, Sam

    1974   The Prayer of the Navajo Carved Figurine: An Interpretation of the Navajo Remaking Rite. Plateau 47(2):59–69.

    1981   Sacred Words. Contributions in International and Comparative Studies, 4. Westport, Conn.: Greenwood Press.

    1983   Navajo View of Their Origins. In Handbook of North American Indians, vol. 10: Southwest, pp. 502–5. Alfonso Ortiz, ed. Washington, D.C.: Smithsonian Institution Press.

Gillison, Gillian

    1980   Images of Nature in Gimi Thought. In Nature, Culture and Gender, pp. 143–73. Carol MacCormack and Marilyn Strathern, eds. New York: Cambridge University Press.

Gillmor, Frances, and Louisa Wade Wetherill

    1953   Traders to the Navajos. Albuquerque: University of New Mexico Press.

Goddard, Pliny

    1933   Navajo Texts. Anthropological Papers of the American Museum of Natural History 34(1):1–180. New York: American Museum of Natural History.

Gordon, Deborah

1988 Tenacious Assumptions in Western Medicine Examined. *In* Biomedicine Examined, pp. 19–56. Margaret Lock and Deborah Gordon, eds. Boston: Kluwer Academic Publishers.

Greenberg, Joseph, Christy Turner, and Stephen Zegura

1986 The Settlement of the Americas: A Comparison of the Linguistic, Dental, and Genetic Evidence. Current Anthropology 27(5):477–97.

Griaule, Marcel

1965 Conversations with Ogotemmêli: An Introduction to Dogon Religious Ideas. Oxford: Oxford University Press.

Griffin-Pierce, Trudy

1992 Earth Is My Mother, Sky Is My Father: Space, Time, and Astronomy in Navajo Sandpainting. Albuquerque: University of New Mexico Press.

Gunnerson, James

1956 Plains-Promotory Relationships. American Antiquity 22(1):69–72.

1979 Southern Athapaskan Archeology. *In* Handbook of North American Indians, vol. 9: Southwest, pp. 162–69. Alfonso Ortiz, ed. Washington, D.C.: Smithsonian Institution Press.

Haile, Father Berard

1938 Origin Legends of the Navajo Enemyway. Yale University Publications in Anthropology, 17. New Haven, Conn.: Yale University Press.

1942 Why the Navaho Hogan? Primitive Man 15(3–4):39–56.

1943 Soul Concepts of the Navaho. Annali Lateranensi, vol. 7. Citta del Vaticano.

1947 Navaho Sacrificial Figurines. Chicago: University of Chicago Press.

1981 Upward Moving and Emergence Way. American Tribal Religions, 7. Lincoln: University of Nebraska Press.

Hale, Kenneth

1973 A Note on Subject-Object Inversion in Navajo. *In* Issues in Linguistics: Papers in Honor of Henry and Renée Kahane, pp. 300–9. Braj B. Kachru et al., eds. Urbana: University of Illinois Press.

Hale, Kenneth, and David Harris

1979 Historical Linguistics and Archeology. *In* Handbook of North American Indians, vol. 9: Southwest, pp. 170–77. Alfonso Ortiz, ed. Washington, D.C.: Smithsonian Institution Press.

Hallowell, A. Irving

1955 Culture and Experience. Philadelphia: University of Pennsylvania Press.

Hardeen, George

1994 Hogans and Hospitals: Navajo Patients Want the Best of Both Worlds. Tribal College, Winter 1994:20–24.

Hartle-Schutte, Maureen

1988 Contemporary Usage of the Blessingway Ceremony for Navajo Births. Master's thesis. American Indian Studies, University of Arizona, Tucson, Arizona.

Hazen-Hammond, Susan

1995 Kinaaldá: Coming of Age in the Navajo Nation. Arizona Highways 71(3):14–19.

Herdt, Gilbert
  1981   Guardians of the Flutes. New York: McGraw-Hill.
  1982a   Sambia Nosebleeding Rites and Male Proximity to Women. Ethos 10(3):
          189–231.
  1982b   Rituals of Manhood. Berkeley: University of California Press.
Hertz, Robert
  1973 [1909]   The Pre-eminence of the Right Hand: A Study of Religious Polarity. In
          Right and Left: Essays on Dual Symbolic Classifications, pp. 3–31. Rodney
          Needham, ed., trans. Chicago: University of Chicago Press.
Hester, James
  1962   Early Navajo Migrations and Acculturation in the Southwest. Museum of
          New Mexico Papers in Anthropology, 6, Navajo Project Studies 5. Santa Fe:
          Museum of New Mexico Press.
Hill, W. W.
  1936   Navaho Warfare. Yale University Publications in Anthropology, 5. New Ha-
          ven, Conn.: Yale University Press.
  1938   The Agricultural and Hunting Methods of the Navaho Indians. Yale University
          Publications in Anthropology, 18. London: Oxford University Press.
  1940   Some Navaho Culture Changes during Two Centuries. In Essays in Honor of
          John R. Swanton, pp. 395–415. Smithsonian Miscellaneous Collections,
          100. Washington, D.C.: Smithsonian Insititution.
  1943   Navaho Humor. General Series in Anthropology, 9. Menasha, Wis.: George
          Banta Publishing Co.
Holland, Douglas
  1992   Cross-Cultural Differences in the Self. Journal of Anthropological Research
          48(4):283–300.
Huscher, Betty, and Harold Huscher
  1942   Athapaskan Migration via the Intermontane Region. American Antiquity
          8(1):80–88.
Iverson, Peter
  1976   The Navajos: A Critical Bibliography. Newberry Library Center for the History
          of the American Indian Bibliography Series. Bloomington: Indiana University
          Press.
  1981   The Navajo Nation. Albuquerque: University of New Mexico Press.
Jacka, Lois
  1994   From Lamb to Loom: This New Breed of Traditionalists Strives for Excellence.
          Arizona Highways 70(4):20–25.
Jackson, Michael
  1989   Paths toward a Clearing. Bloomington: Indiana University Press.
Jacobson-Widding, Anita, ed.
  1991   Body and Space: Symbolic Models of Unity and Division in African Cosmology
          and Experience. Acta Universitatis Upsaliensis, Uppsala Studies in Cultural
          Anthropology, 16. Stockholm: Almqvist & Wiksell International.

Jett, Stephen, and Virginia Spencer

1981   Navajo Architecture: Forms, History, and Distribution. Tucson: University of Arizona Press.

Joe, Jennie

1996   Looking for a Traditional Navajo in the Twentieth Century. Plenary lecture presented at the ninth annual Navajo Studies Conference, Durango, Colorado, April 12.

Kammer, Jerry

1980   The Second Long Walk: The Navajo-Hopi Land Dispute. Albuquerque: University of New Mexico Press.

Keith, Anne

1964   The Navajo Girl's Puberty Ceremony: Function and Meaning for the Adolescent. El Palacio 71(1):27–36.

Kelly, Roger, R. W. Lang, and Harry Walters

1972   Navaho Figurines Called Dolls. Santa Fe, N.M.: Museum of Navajo Ceremonial Art (Wheelwright Museum of the American Indian).

Kent, Kate Peck

1985   Navajo Weaving: Three Centuries of Change. Santa Fe, N.M.: School of American Research Press.

Kluckhohn, Clyde

1944   Navajo Witchcraft. Boston: Beacon Press.

Kluckhohn, Clyde, and Dorothea Leighton

1974 [1946]   The Navaho. Cambridge, Mass.: Harvard University Press.

Kluckhohn, Clyde, and Katherine Spencer

1940   A Bibliography of the Navaho Indians. New York: J. J. Augustin.

Kluckhohn, Clyde, and Leland Wyman

1940   An Introduction to Navaho Chant Practice. Memoirs of the American Anthropological Association, 53.

Lamphere, Louise

1969   Symbolic Aspects in Navajo Ritual. Southwestern Journal of Anthropology 25:279–305.

1977   To Run After Them: Cultural and Social Bases of Cooperation in a Navajo Community. Tucson: University of Arizona Press.

Lang, R. W., and Harry Walters

1972   The Remaking Rites of the Navaho: Causal Factors of Illness and Its Nature. In Navaho Figurines Called Dolls, pp. 47–75. Santa Fe, N.M.: Museum of Navaho Ceremonial Art (Wheelwright Museum of the American Indian).

Laqueur, Thomas

1987   Orgasm, Generation, and the Politics of Reproductive Biology. In The Making of the Modern Body, pp. 1–41. Catherine Gallagher and Thomas Laqueur, eds. Berkeley: University of California Press.

1990   Making Sex: Body and Gender from the Greeks to Freud. Cambridge, Mass.: Harvard University Press.

Leach, Edmund

1964   Anthropological Aspects of Language: Animal Categories and Verbal Abuse.

In New Directions in the Study of Language, pp. 23–64. E. H. Lennebuerg, ed. Cambridge, Mass.: MIT Press.

Leighton, Dorothea, and Clyde Kluckhohn

1947   Children of the People: The Navaho Individual and His Development. Cambridge: Harvard University Press.

Lévi-Strauss, Claude

1966 [1962]   The Savage Mind. Chicago: University of Chicago Press.

Lindenbaum, Shirley

1979   Kuru Sorcery: Disease and Danger in the New Guinea Highlands. Mountain View, Calif.: Mayfield Publishing Company.

Lock, Margaret

1986   The Anthropological Study of the American Medical System: Center and Periphery. Social Science and Medicine 22(9):931–32.

1993   Cultivating the Body: Anthropology and Epistemologies of Bodily Practice and Knowledge. Annual Review of Anthropology 22:133–55.

Lockett, Clay

1939   Midwives and Childbirth among the Navajo. Plateau 12(1):15–17.

Luckert, Karl

1975   The Navajo Hunter Tradition. Tucson: University of Arizona Press.

Luhrmann, Tanya M.

1989   Persuasions of the Witch's Craft. Cambridge, Mass.: Harvard University Press.

Marcus, George, and Michael Fischer

1986   Anthropology as Cultural Critique: An Experimental Moment in the Human Sciences. Chicago: University of Chicago Press.

Matthews, Washington

1894   The Basket Drum. American Anthropologist 7(2):202–8.

1902   The Night Chant: A Navaho Ceremony. Memoirs of the American Museum of Natural History, 6. New York: American Museum of Natural History.

1994 [1897]   Navaho Legends. Salt Lake City: University of Utah Press.

Mauss, Marcel

1972 [1902]   A General Theory of Magic. Robert Brain, trans. New York: W. W. Norton.

Maybury-Lewis, David, and Uri Almagor

1989   The Attraction of Opposites: Thought and Society in the Dualistic Mode. Ann Arbor: University of Michigan Press.

McCloskey, Joanne

1993   Changing Fertility Patterns of Three Generations of Navajo Women. Ph.D. dissertation, Department of Anthropology, University of New Mexico.

McNeley, James

1981   Holy Wind in Navajo Philosophy. Tucson: University of Arizona Press.

1993   The Pattern Which Connects Navajo and Western Learning. Paper presented at the seventh annual Navajo Studies Conference, Tsaile, Arizona, October 7.

McNitt, Frank
　1962　The Indian Traders. Norman: University of Oklahoma Press.
McPherson, Robert
　1992　Sacred Land, Sacred View: Navajo Perceptions of the Four Corners Region. Salt Lake City: Brigham Young University.
Meigs, Anna
　1976　Male Pregnancy and the Reduction of Sexual Opposition in a New Guinea Highlands Society. Ethnology 15(4):393–407.
　1984　Food, Sex, and Pollution. New Brunswick, N.J.: Rutgers University Press.
Middleton, John, and Edward Winter
　1963　Witchcraft and Sorcery in East Africa. London: Routledge and Kegan Paul.
Milligan; Carol
　1984　Nursing Care and Beliefs of Expectant Navajo Woman, Part 1. American Indian Quarterly 8(2):83–101.
Mindeleff, Cosmos
　1898　Navaho Houses. Seventeenth Annual Report of the Bureau of Ethnology for 1895–96. Washington, D.C.: Government Printing Office.
Mitchell, Frank
　1978　Navajo Blessingway Singer: The Autobiography of Frank Mitchell 1881–1967. Charlotte Frisbie and David McAllester, eds. Tucson: University of Arizona Press.
Moon, Samuel
　1992　Tall Sheep: Harry Goulding, Monument Valley Trader. Norman: University of Oklahoma Press.
Morgan, William
　1931　Navaho Treatment of Sickness: Diagnosticians. American Anthropologist (n.s.) 33:390–402.
　1936　Human-Wolves among the Navaho. Yale University Publications in Anthropology, 11. New Haven, Conn.: Yale University Press.
Mustache, Curly
　1970　Unpublished transcription of Mr. Mustache's interview with Jones Van Winkle, Tsaile, Arizona. Manuscript in the author's possession.
Nabokov, Peter, and Robert Easton
　1989　Native American Architecture. New York: Oxford University Press.
Needham, Rodney, ed.
　1973　Right and Left: Essays on Dual Symbolic Classifications. Chicago: University of Chicago Press.
Nemeroff, Carol, and Paul Rozin
　1994　The Contagion Concept in Adult Thinking in the United States: Transmission of Germs and of Interpersonal Influence. Ethos 22(2):158–86.
Newcomb, Franc Johnson
　1940　Navajo Omens and Taboos. Santa Fe, N.M.: Rydal Press.
Newcomb, Franc J., and Gladys A. Reichard
　1937　Sandpaintings of the Navajo Shooting Chant. New York: J. J. Augustin. Republished 1975, Dover Publications.

O'Bryan, Aileen

  1956   The Diné: Origin Myths of the Navaho Indians. Bureau of American Ethnology, Bulletin 163. Washington, D.C.: Government Printing Office.

O'Hanlon, Michael

  1992   Unstable Images and Second Skins: Artefacts, Exegesis and Assessments in the New Guinea Highlands. Man (n.s.) 27(3):587–608.

Opler, Morris

  1983   The Apachean Culture Pattern and Its Origin. In Handbook of North American Indians, vol. 10: Southwest, pp. 368–92. Alfonso Ortiz, ed. Washington, D.C.: Smithsonian Institution Press.

Ortner, Sherry

  1984   Theory in Anthropology since the Sixties. Comparative Studies in Society and History 26(1):126–66.

  1989   High Religion. Princeton, N.J.: Princeton University Press.

Parezo, Nancy

  1983   Navajo Sandpainting: From Religious Act to Commercial Art. Tucson: University of Arizona Press.

Perrone, Bobette, H. Henrietta Stockel, and Victoria Krueger

  1989   Medicine Women, Curanderas, and Women Doctors. Norman: University of Oklahoma Press.

Pinxten, Rik, and Claire Farrer

  1990   On Learning a Comparative View. Cultural Dynamics 3(3):233–51.

Pinxten, Rik, Ingrid van Dooren, and Frank Harvey

  1983   Anthropology of Space: Explorations into the Natural Philosophy and Semantics of the Navajo. Philadelphia: University of Pennsylvania Press.

Poole, Fritz

  1981   Transforming "Natural" Woman: Female Ritual Leaders and Gender Ideology among Bimin-Kuskusmin. In Sexual Meaning: The Cultural Construction of Gender and Sexuality, pp. 116–65. Sherry Ortner and Harriet Whitehead, eds. Cambridge: Cambridge University Press.

Reichard, Gladys

  1928   Social Life of the Navaho Indians. New York: Columbia University Press.

  1939   Navajo Medicine Man Sandpaintings. New York: J. J. Augustin. Republished 1977, Dover Publications.

  1950   Navaho Religion: A Study of Symbolism. New York: Pantheon.

  1968 [1934]   Spider Woman: A Story of Navajo Weavers and Chanters. Glorieta, N.M.: Rio Grande Press.

Reichel-Dolmatoff, Gerardo

  1971   Amazonian Cosmos: The Sexual and Religious Symbolism of the Tukano Indians. Chicago: University of Chicago Press.

Rhodes, Lorna

  1990   Studying Biomedicine as a Cultural System. In Medical Anthropology: Contemporary Theory and Method, pp. 159–73. Thomas Johnson and Carolyn Sargent, eds. New York: Praeger.

Riesman, Paul
    1992   First Find Your Child a Good Mother: The Construction of Self in Two African Communities. New Brunswick, N.J.: Rutgers University Press.
Roessel, Monty
    1993a   Navajo Wedding. New Mexico Magazine 71(6):38–45.
    1993b   Kinaaldá: A Navajo Girl Grows Up. Minneapolis: Lerner Publications.
Roessel, Robert
    1980   Pictorial History of the Navajo from 1860 to 1910. Rough Rock, Ariz.: Navajo Curriculum Center.
    1983   Navajo History, 1850–1923. In Handbook of North American Indians, vol. 10: Southwest, pp. 506–23. Alfonso Ortiz, ed. Washington, D.C.: Smithsonian Institution Press.
Roessel, Ruth
    1973   Navajo Stories of the Long Walk Period. Tsaile, Ariz.: Navajo Community College Press.
    1981   Women in Navajo Society. Rough Rock, Ariz.: Navajo Resource Center, Rough Rock Demonstration School.
Rosaldo, Michelle
    1984   Toward an Anthropology of Self and Feeling. In Culture Theory: Essays on Mind, Self, and Emotion, pp. 137–57. Richard Shweder and Robert LeVine, eds. Cambridge: Cambridge University Press.
Rosaldo, Renato
    1993   Culture and Truth: The Remaking of Social Analysis. Boston: Beacon Press.
Ryan, Danita
    1988   Kinaaldá: The Pathway to Navajo Womanhood. Native Peoples 1(2):2–6.
Schilling, Chris
    1993   The Body and Social Theory. Newbury Park, Calif.: Sage Publications.
Schwarz, Maureen Trudelle
    1993   Traditional Navajo Female Attire: Products and Processes of Navajo Aesthetic Artifice. In Proceedings of the Navajo Studies Conference, vol. 1, pp. 355–78.
    1994   The Biil: Navajo Female Attire as Metaphor of Navajo Aesthetic Organization. Dress 20:75–81.
    1995   The Explanatory and Predictive Power of History: Coping with the "Mystery Ilness," 1993. Ethnohistory 42(3):375–401.
    1997a   Snakes in the Ladies Room: Navajo Views on Personhood and Effect. American Ethnologist 24(3).
    1997b   Unraveling the Anchoring Cord: Navajo Relocation, 1974–1996. American Anthropologist 99(1).
Shepardson, Mary
    1978   Changes in Navajo Mortuary Practices and Beliefs. American Indian Quarterly 4(4):383–95.
Shepardson, Mary, and Blodwen Hammond
    1970   The Navajo Mountain Community. Berkeley: University of California Press.

Shweder, Richard, and Edmund Bourne
1984   Does the Concept of the Person Vary Cross-Culturally? *In* Culture Theory: Essays on Mind, Self, and Emotion, pp. 158–99. Richard Shweder and Robert LeVine, eds. Cambridge: Cambridge University Press.

Spencer, Katherine
1947   Reflection of Social Life in the Navajo Origin Myth. University of New Mexico Publications in Anthropology 3:1–140. Albuquerque: University of New Mexico Press.

Spiro, Melford
1993   Is the Western Conception of the Self "Peculiar" within the Context of the World's Cultures? Ethos 21(2):107–53.

Stephen, Alexander
1930   Navajo Origin Legend. Journal of American Folk-Lore 43(167):88–104.

Stephens, William
1962   The Oedipus Complex: Cross-Cultural Evidence. New York: Free Press.

Steward, Julian
1937   Ancient Caves of the Salt Lake Region. Bureau of American Ethnology Bulletin 116. Washington, D.C.: Government Printing Office.
1940   Native Cultures of the Intermontane (Great Basin) Area. *In* Essays in Historical Anthropology of North America, pp. 445–502. Smithsonian Miscellaneous Collections, 100. Washington, D.C.: Smithsonian Institution Press.

Stewart, Irene
1980   A Voice in Her Tribe: A Navajo Woman's Own Story. Socorro, N.M.: Ballena Press Anthropological Papers, 17.

Stewart, Omer
1938   The Navajo Wedding Basket—1938. Museum Notes 10(9):25–28. Flagstaff, Ariz.: Museum of Northern Arizona.

Strathern, Marilyn
1988   The Gender of the Gift. Berkeley: University of California Press.

Synnott, Anthony
1993   The Body Social: Symbolism, Self, and Society. New York: Routledge.

Tapahonso, Luci
1993   Sáanii Dahataał: The Women Are Singing. Tucson: University of Arizona Press.

Tedlock, Barbara
1991   From Participant Observation to Observation of Participation: The Emergence of Narrative Ethnography. Journal of Anthropological Research 47(1): 69–94.

Thomas, Wesley
1996   *Shił Yóółtʼoołʼ*: Personification of Navajo Weaving. *In* Woven by the Grandmothers: Nineteenth-Century Navajo Textiles. Eulalie Bonar, ed., pp. 33–42. Washington, D.C.: Smithsonian Institution Press.

Tschopik, Harry
1940   Navaho Basketry: A Study of Cultural Change. American Anthropologist 42(2):444–62.

Turner, Terence

1980 The Social Skin. *In* Not Work Alone, pp. 112–40. J. Cherfas and R. Lewin, eds. London: Temple Smith.

1991 "We Are Parrots," "Twins Are Birds": Play on Tropes as Operational Structure. *In* Beyond Metaphor, pp. 121–58. James Fernandez, ed. Stanford: Stanford University Press.

Turner, Victor

1967 The Forest of Symbols. Ithaca, N.Y.: Cornell University Press.

Tylor, Edward

1974 [1871] Primitive Culture. New York: Gordon Press.

Walker, Deward, ed.

1989 Witchcraft and Sorcery of the American Native People. Moscow: University of Idaho Press.

Ward, Albert

1980 Navajo Graves. Ethnohistorical Reports, Series 2. Albuquerque: Center for Anthropological Studies.

Waxman, Alan

1990 Navajo Childbirth in Transition. Medical Anthropology 12:187–206.

Weideger, Paula

1977 Menstruation and Menopause: The Physiology and Psychology, the Myth and the Reality. New York: Delta.

Wheat, Joe Ben

1977 Documentary Evidence for Material Changes and Designs in Navajo Blanket Weaving. *In* Ethnographic Textiles of the Western Hemisphere, pp. 420–40. Irene Emery and Patricia Fiske, eds. Irene Emery Roundtable on Museum Textiles, 1976 Proceedings. Washington, D.C.: Textile Museum.

1979 Rio Grande, Pueblo, and Navajo Weavers: Cross-Cultural Influence. *In* Spanish Textile Tradition of New Mexico and Colorado, pp. 29–36. Santa Fe: Museum of International Folk Art, Museum of New Mexico Press.

1988 Early Trade and Commerce in Southwestern Textiles before the Curio Shop. *In* Reflections: Papers on Southwestern Culture History in Honor of Charles H. Lange. Anne Poore, ed. Papers of the Archeological Society of New Mexico 14:57–72. Santa Fe, N.M.: Ancient City Press.

Wheelwright, Mary

1942 Navajo Creation Myth: The Story of the Emergence, by Hasteen Klah. Navajo Religion Series 1. Santa Fe, N.M.: Museum of Navaho Ceremonial Art (Wheelwright Museum of the American Indian).

Whiteford, Andrew Hunter

1988 Southwestern Indian Baskets: Their History and Their Makers. Santa Fe, N.M.: School of American Research Press.

Wilcox, David

n.d. Avonlea and Southern Athapaskan Migration. Unpublished manuscript. Flagstaff, Ariz.: Museum of Northern Arizona.

Williamson, Ray A.
　1984　Living the Sky: The Cosmos of the American Indian. Norman: University of Oklahoma Press.
Wilson, Ursula
　1980　Traditional Child-Bearing Practices among Indians. *In* Life Cycle of the American Indian Family, pp. 13–26. Janice Kekahbah and Rosemary Wood, eds. Norman: American Indian and Alaska Native Nurses Association Publishing Company.
　1983　Nursing Care of American Indian Patients. *In* Ethnic Nursing Care: A Multicultural Approach, pp. 272–95. Modesto Orque et al., eds. Saint Louis, Mo.: C. V. Mosby Company.
Witherspoon, Gary
　1975　Navajo Kinship and Marriage. Chicago: University of Chicago Press.
　1977　Language and Art in the Navajo Universe. Ann Arbor: University of Michigan Press.
　1983　Navajo Social Organization. *In* Handbook of North American Indians, vol. 10: Southwest, pp. 524–35. Alfonso Ortiz, ed. Washington, D.C.: Smithsonian Institution Press.
　1987　Navajo Weaving: Art in Its Cultural Context. Flagstaff, Ariz.: Museum of Northern Arizona.
Wright, Anne
　1982　Attitudes toward Childbearing and Menstruation among the Navajo. *In* Anthropology of Human Birth, pp. 377–94. Margarita Kay, ed. Philadelphia: F. A. Davis Company.
Wright, Anne, Mark Bauer, Clarina Clark, Frank Morgan, and Kenneth Begishe
　1993　Cultural Interpretations and Intracultural Variability in Navajo Beliefs about Breastfeeding. American Ethnologist 20(4):781–96.
Wyman, Leland
　1936a　Navaho Diagnosticians. American Anthropologist (n.s.) 38:236–46.
　1936b　Origin Legends of Navaho Divinatory Rites. Journal of American Folklore 49:134–42.
　1938　The Agricultural and Hunting Methods of the Navaho Indians. Yale University Publications in Anthropology, 18. New Haven, Conn.: Yale University Press.
　1965　The Red Antway of the Navajo. Navajo Religion Series 5. Santa Fe, N.M.: Museum of Navaho Ceremonial Art (Wheelwright Museum of the American Indian).
　1970　Blessingway. Tucson: University of Arizona Press.
Wyman, Leland, and Flora Bailey
　1943　Navaho Girl's Puberty Rite. New Mexico Anthropologist 15(1):3–12.
Wyman, Leland, and Stuart Harris
　1941　Navajo Indian Medical Ethnobotany. University of New Mexico Bulletin 3(5): 1–76.

Wyman, Leland, W. W. Hill, and Iva Osanai

    1942   Navajo Eschatology. University of New Mexico Bulletin 4(1):1−47.

Yazzie, Ethelou

    1971   Navajo History, vol. 1. Navajo Curriculum Center. Rough Rock, Ariz.: Rough Rock Demonstration School.

Yazzie, Robert

    1994   "Life Comes From I": Navajo Justice Concepts. New Mexico Law Review 24: 175−90.

Young, Frank, and Albert Bacdayan

    1965   Menstrual Taboos and Social Rigidity. Ethnology 4:225−40.

Young, Robert, and William Morgan, Sr.

    1987   The Navajo Language: A Grammar and Colloquial Dictionary. Albuquerque: University of New Mexico Press.

    1992   Analytical Lexicon of Navajo. Albuquerque: University of New Mexico Press.

Zolbrod, Paul

    1984   Diné Bahane': The Navajo Creation Story. Albuquerque: University of New Mexico Press.

INDEX

Slayer, 206; dressing, 164–67, 168, 170–71; in image of, 104; male puberty, 157–58; monsters, 28; naming, 170; quest, 23, 157–58; painting, 170; trials of, 164, 167

Bourdieu, Pierre, 249 n. 13

breath: of life, 51; of artifacts, 9, 43, 48, 185–86; of Nihookáá Dine'é, 36, 83–87

cardinal directions or points, 18, 20–21, 251 n. 9; 'alkaan, 221–22; associations with, 62, 67, 73–74, 233, 251 n. 10, 257 nn. 9, 12; in blessing, 210, 214, 217; in cosmology, 22 (fig.), 75 (fig.); in creation, 18, 20–21; hooghan, 42, 42 (fig.), 45; offering, 222–23

ceremonies: as ancestral knowledge, 24, 31; Navajo system of, xv; power acquired through, 53–55; use of space during, 42 (fig.), 44–45, 254 nn. 10, 11

Changing Woman (Asdzą́ą́ Nádleehé), 17; and childbirth, 128–29; cradle, 45; creation of Nihookáá Dine'é, 24, 56, 62–64, 65, 66, 233; dressing of, 26, 27, 173, 184–89; Dinétah, 17; emulation of, 196; finding of, 23, 25–28, 29, 49; as inner form of the earth, 24; Kinaaldá, 173; life cycle, 50; life giver, 215; matrimony, 70; as mother, 17, 23–24, 62; offering to, 43, 222–23; seasons, 24; and Sun, 23; teachings of, 30, 67, 96–97

Charley, Mae, 263 n. 4; on: 'alkaan, 202; baldness, 189–90; demeanor, 211–12; dressing, 181–82; fire keeper, 215; Kinaaldá, 175, 210; molding, 192; painting, 227; power, 175; running, 198–99

chííh dík'ǫ́ǫ́zh (protective medicine), 190–91

chííh (red ochre), 216; markings of, 227–28

clan, xiii; associations with, 74, 75 (fig.); bloods of, 73; influences of, 62, 72–73, 74, 233; original, 66–67, 255 n. 2; reckoning of, 73, 257 n. 10

clockwise. See Sunwise

complementarity, 4, 13; anthropological views on, 248 n. 12; Changing Woman, 28; pairings, 30, 93. See also naayéé' k'ehjigo and hózhǫ́ǫ́jigo

conception: biomedical model of, 69; cross-cultural pespectives on, 68; Navajo theory of, 67, 68–69, 256 n. 7

corn: in 'alkaan, 203–5, 263 n. 8; beetle, 23, 27, 28; to bless, 138, 204, 210, 214–15, 217; consumption of, 70, 71–72, 132, 200, 202; Corn Woman, 42, 42 (fig.), 44; in creation, 18, 19, 24, 49, 62, 63, 64, 80, 82; fertility symbol, 18; and human body, 49; husk crosses, 209, 212, 214–15; Kinaaldá, 175, 179; life cycle, 48–49, 67; male puberty, 169; as mother, 27

cosmology, 22 (fig.), 75 (fig.)

cradle ('awééts'áál): Changing Woman, 25; construction, 45–46, 46 (fig.), 47, 81; homologue, 45–47, 93; life cycle, 50

Creamer, Mary Helen, 255 n. 17

creativity: blockage, 110; and way out, 108

cultural constructionist perspectives, 8

Curley, Slim, 263 n. 9

Cypraea, 117, 121–22, 260 n. 6

Dahozy, Louva, 260 n. 3; statements on: First Laugh Ceremony, 145; sex of unborn, 118

Denny, Avery, 252 n. 1, 257 nn. 9, 12; statements on: bloods, 73; body,

prenatal period, 123; sexual maturity, 156; umbilical cord, 139–40

Knoki-Wilson, Ursula, 252 n. 2; statements on: Áłtsé Saad, 37; baskets, 38; bath water, 114–15; births, 133–34; complementary aspects, 96, 97, 101; conception, 67; detached parts of the body, 138; emotion, 142; hair, 147–49; knowledge, 156–57; male puberty, 163–64; malevolent factors, 107; molding, 135, 192; path of life, 133; prayers, 133; sex of unborn, 119–20; spouse, 94; unraveling, 134; way out, 109–10

knowledge: access to, 25, 31–32, 55, 156–57, 242; ancestral, 15; cardinal points, 71; as charter, 24, 30; as hair, 88, 147; influence on life cycle, 52; philosophical tenets of, 21, 22 (fig.), 32, 74–78, 75 (fig.), 257 n. 12; powers of, 31–32, 55–56; partial nature of, xvi, 31–32, 252 n. 14; restricted areas of, 32; sharing of, xxi, 31–32, 55; theoretical applications, 242; twelve levels of, xix–xx, 17, 24–31, 32, 35, 65–66, 96

K'os Diłhił (Dark Cloud): on basket, 70; in dressing of Changing Woman, 184, 188–89

language: as developmental step, 146–47; and hair, 147–53; primordial, 37

laws of sympathetic magic, 5

left hand and side: activities done exclusively with or to, 101–8, 235; at First Laugh, 144. See also naayéé' k'ehjigo; protection

Leighton, Dorothea, 261 n. 10, 262 nn. 3, 16, 263 n. 8; statements on: childbirth, 130; conception, 68; hair, 147; male sexual maturity, 156;

prenatal period, 123; umbilical cord, 139–40

Lévi-Strauss, Claude, 248 n. 12

life cycle: of artifacts, 49–51; Changing Woman, 50; individualized nature of, 36; Navajo views of, 15; of Nihookáá Dine'é, 68; and ritual purpose, 52; sacred mountains, 49; sandpaintings, 50; variations, 48

life: charter for, 16; cyclic nature of, 15, 35; theory of, 9–10, 35, 83, 255 n. 17

loom (dah'iistł'ǫ́): components, 47–48; as homologue, 48; orientation, 48; weapon, 47

Lynch, Regina, 248 nn. 7, 8; statements on: baskets, 9; breath of life, 84

malevolent factors, 23; entrance into body, 107; exit from, 108

marriage: establishment of, 66; need for, 19; as a union of clans, 72

mask: intiation with, 104; needs of, 52, 254 n. 16; power of, 54

massage: of elderly, 197; of newborn, 131; of parturient, 130. See also molding

Matthews, Washington, 259 n. 27

McNeley, James, 257 nn. 9, 11, 12; on Diyin Dine'é, 251 n. 10

medicine bag or pouch. See jish

metaphor: ancesteral knowledge as, 24; anthropological approaches to, 248 n. 12, 249 n. 14; relation to structure, 13

methodology, field, xv–xix; research sponsors, xvi–xviii

mind: basket, 38; cleansing of, 40, 159; as component of Navajo, 36, 80 (fig.); and designs, 111–12; directionality of, 88–89, 109; and hair, 87, 91, 147, 152; of hooghan, 43, 44; strength of, 200; susceptibility, 124; teachings, 75, 78, 159, 200; tobacco, 168; way out, 48, 110

and Born for Water, 165–66, 167–69; connection to mind, 168; smoking of, 64, 167, 168–69

trajectory of growth: adherence to, 9, 93, 233–35; in blessing of kinaaldá, 217–19; in ceremonial contexts, 103; in Changing Woman story, 28; in collection of yucca root, 216; in construction of artifacts, 39, 43, 46; in dressing and molding of kinaaldá, 180–82, 195, 228; in dressing and molding of Monster Slayer and Born for Water, 166–67; in First Laugh, 144; in Hóchx̨ǫ́ǫ́jí, 107; while painting, 226–28; in placement of husks, 214–15; reversal of during childbirth, 130; in stretching, 195

tsiiyééł (hair bun): direction of, 89; Diyin Dine'é directives on, 90; as identification, 91; illustration of, 90 (fig.); at Kinaaldá, 228; placement of, 151; purpose of, 90–92. *See also* hair

Tso, Nakai, xvii, 255 n. 19; creation of the Nihookáá Dine'é, 63–64; kinaaldá's body, 191; knowledge, 55; molding, 192; running, 199; singing at Kinaaldá, 180; statements on: 'alkaan, 223

Tso, Oscar, 246 n. 4; statements on: 'alkaan, 224–25; blood, 215; hair, 190; male puberty rites, 159–60; Monster Slayer and Born for Water, 165–66; naayéé'jí and hózhǫ́ǫ́ji, 92, 101; pedagodical method, xix–xx; pollen blessing, 101–2; running, 200; tobacco, 165–66

Tso, Rosie, xvii

Tso, Thomas, and loan of concho belt, 180

Tsosie, Lillie, 259 n. 30; on sex of unborn, 120–21, 122

Turner, Terence, 249 n. 14; on metaphor, 11

Turner, Victor, on the body, 6–7

umbilical cord (*-ts'éé'*): constant possessed state of, 115; cutting of, 131; influence of, 138–41; placement of, 138–39, 236, 262 n. 13. *See also* anchoring cord

universe, physical appearance of, 45, 251 n. 9

Unraveling ceremony, 130

voice: enhancement of, 164, 169, 172, 192; as marker of maturity, 155–69; of sex organs, 20

volition, influence of, on life cycle, 52

wailing, 262 n. 15; at reunions, 143

Walters, Harry, 248 n. 11, 257 n. 12; on: 'alkaan, 202–3, 204; anthropomorphism, 10–11, 12 (fig.); ceremonial treatment, 235; Changing Woman, 26, 27, 30; as colleague, xviii–xix, xxi; correlation between corn and the human body, 49; dressing, 104; garments as substitutes for persons, 105–6; hair, 147; kinaaldá, 196; life, 35, 53, 54–55; male puberty, 162–63; monsters as metaphors, 29, 30; naayéé' k'ehjigo and hózhǫ́ǫ́jigo, 93, 95, 96–97, 97–98, 102–3, 206–7; person, 61, 78–79, 80 (fig.); personal sphere, 234; primary elements, 37; running, 200; sex of unborn, 122–23; talents, 110–11; time, 40–41; tobacco, 168–69; twelve levels knowledge, 24–25, 27, 29, 30; wedding, 70, 71–72; world, 17

water: in conception, 68–69; of first bath, 114, 137; development, 69, 96; forms of, 122; as kin, 9; Hóchx̨ǫ́ǫ́'jí, 106; as reproductive fluids, 68–69, 96, 256 n. 7, 259 n. 28; sex of unborn, 117, 122–23; shampoo rinse, 3, 228–

29; in wedding, 71; Water Woman, 42, 42 (fig.), 44, 76

way out, 233, 254 n. 13; on 'alkaan, 214; basket, 39, 253 n. 4; cradle, 46 (fig.), 47; dangers of neglecting, 48, 108; forms of, 109; hooghan, 45; loom, 48; orientation of, 40; purpose of, 48, 93, 108–9, 234

weaving: histories of, 250 n. 2; origin of, 47; personification of tools and textiles, 248 n. 9; tools used to mold, 194

Weber, Max, 249 n. 13

Wedding ceremony ('ligeh), 67; description, 70–73; literature on, 257 n. 8

White Shell Girl or Woman: as Changing Woman, 26–28; and Nihookáá Dine'é, 63

Wilcox, David, 246 n. 2

Wind. *See* Níłch'i

witchcraft: anthropological perspectives on, 6; dangers of, 240–41; use of detached bodily parts and substances in, 6, 151

Witherspoon, Gary, on: conception, 68; kinship, 17, 257 n. 10; monsters, 28; Navajo concept of mother, 27, 255 n. 1; "static" vs. "active," 255 n. 17

women: as ethnographers, 156–57; influence of those assisting at Kinaaldá, 210, 212

Yádiłhił (Father Sky), 20; on cradle, 46 (fig.)

Yazzie, Alfred, on masks and jish, 52

Yazzie, Elizabeth, on molding, 191–92

Yazzie, Ethelou, 250 n. 3

yé'ii' (deity), 11, 12 (fig.)

ABOUT THE AUTHOR

Maureen Trudelle Schwarz is a professor of anthropology at Syracuse University, where she specializes in Native North America. Since 1991 her research, conducted on the Navajo reservation, has focused on the explanatory and predictive powers that native histories and philosophies offer to people coping with contemporary problems. Dr. Schwarz has published essays in *Ethnohistory, American Anthropologist,* and *American Ethnologist.* She is currently writing a book focusing on the life courses of Navajo women who are ceremonial practitioners.